A DEMOCRATIC ENLIGHTENMENT

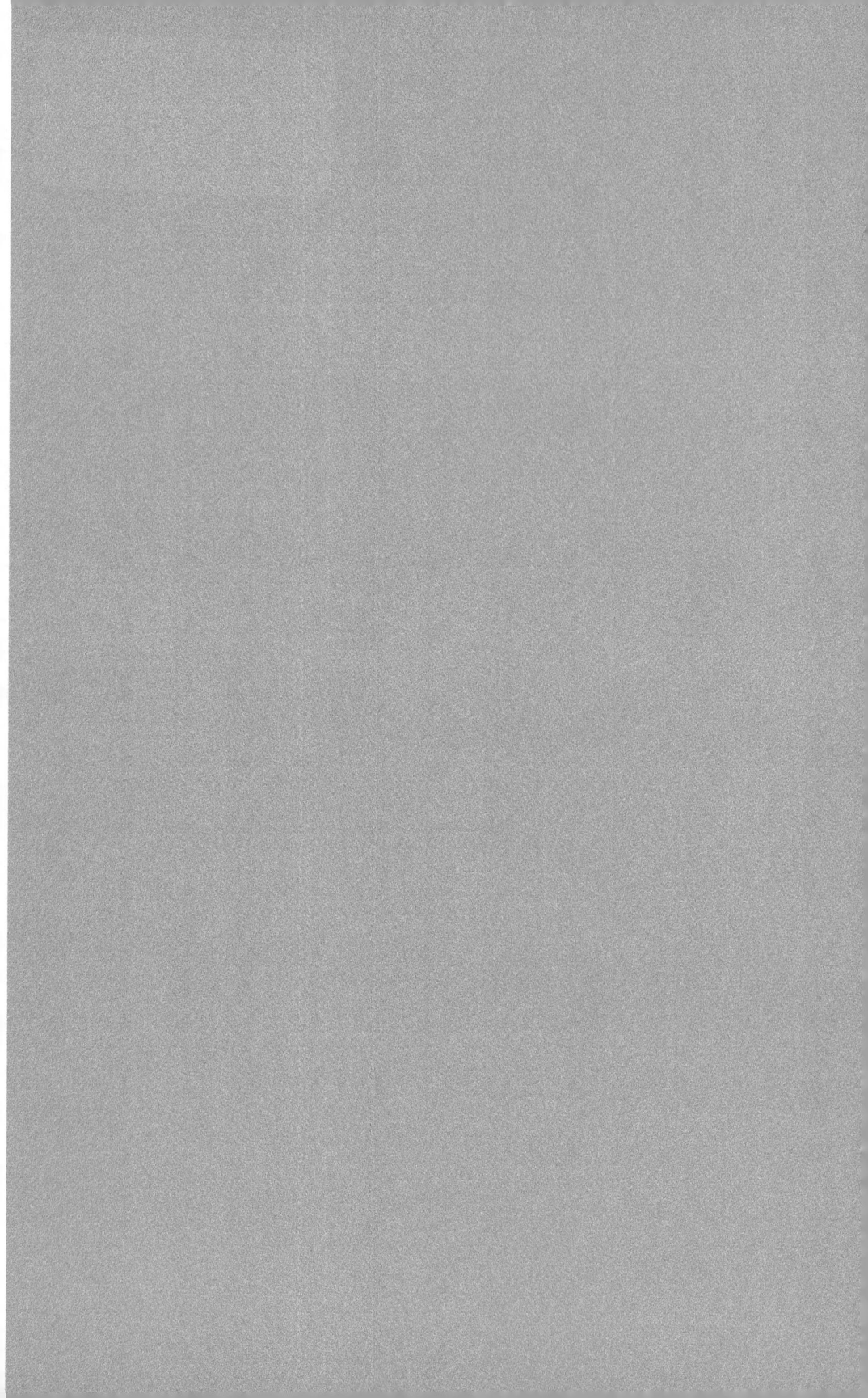

Morton Schoolman

A Democratic Enlightenment

THE RECONCILIATION IMAGE, AESTHETIC

EDUCATION, POSSIBLE POLITICS

DUKE UNIVERSITY PRESS DURHAM AND LONDON 2020

Designed by Amy Ruth Buchanan
Typeset in Arno Pro by Westchester Publishing Services

Library of Congress Cataloging-in-Publication Data Names:
Schoolman, Morton, [date] author.
Title: A democratic enlightenment : the reconciliation image,
aesthetic education, possible politics / Morton Schoolman.
Other titles: Reconciliation image, aesthetic education,
possible politics
Description: Durham : Duke University Press, 2020. |
Includes bibliographical references and index.
Identifiers: LCCN 2019033253 (print)
LCCN 2019033254 (ebook)
ISBN 9781478007654 (hardcover)
ISBN 9781478008033 (paperback)
ISBN 9781478009054 (ebook)
Subjects: LCSH: Whitman, Walt, 1819–1892—Aesthetics. |
Reconciliation in literature. | Adorno, Theodor W.,
1903–1969—Aesthetics. | Reconciliation in motion pictures. |
Toleration—Philosophy. | Visual learning.
Classification: LCC PS3242.A34 S36 2020 (print) |
LCC PS3242.A34 (ebook) | DDC 811/.3—dc23
LC record available at https://lccn.loc.gov/2019033253
LC ebook record available at https://lccn.loc.gov/2019033254

Cover art: Auguste Rodin, *Thought*. Alamy Stock Photo.

....

Long I was hugg'd close—long and long.
Immense have been the preparations for me,
Faithful and friendly the arms that have help'd me.
—Walt Whitman, *Song of Myself*

CONTENTS

....

ACKNOWLEDGMENTS

On this occasion I am in the enviable though also awkward position of belonging to a remarkable community of political theorists whose work has been so sustaining, instructive, and inspiring I can hardly begin to thank them all for their contributions to *A Democratic Enlightenment*. To recall Whitman, then, who in one of his most eloquent attempts to appreciate the democratic world that nurtured his great work, sang in "Salut Au Monde!" to "you each and everywhere whom I specify not, but include just the same!" I am indeed more grateful than I can say for your contributions and support.

Of those whom I can properly thank in the short space allotted for such acknowledgments, I want to begin with my editor at Duke University Press, Courtney Berger, whose involvement in this book and intellectual and professional guidance have been indispensable to enabling me to develop its potential. It has been a privilege as well as a pleasure to work with her, and I could not be more grateful for her time, energy, and patient support of my work. I am equally grateful to three theorists, all dear friends and colleagues, who in words both spoken and written generously provided invaluable commentary on nearly every thought in this work. My never-to-be-forgotten conversations with Jane Bennett, animated by our mutual love for the poetry and prose of Whitman and by our recognition of the political, philosophical, and aesthetic significance of his work for our time, the stunning insights into the complexities of identity and difference offered by Lori Marso's growing collection of influential studies of avant-garde films, and my discussions with Davide Panagia about theoretical issues multiplying with the steady growth of the field of politics and aesthetics to which he has made such original contributions, have been ever-present voices to which I have closely listened even when not in their presence. For more than four decades I have immensely enjoyed and immeasurably benefited from the friendship and intellectual companionship of Bill Connolly and George Kateb, whose thought has impressed itself irresistibly into the foreground of every project I have undertaken and, to my great good fortune, to an even greater extent in the present work.

For some time arguments throughout *A Democratic Enlightenment* have been aired and tested in more academic venues than I can list, though I especially benefited from speaking invitations at the University of Essex extended by Aletta Norval, the University of Southampton by David Owen, the Center for Cultural Analysis at Rutgers University by William Galperin, the University of Maryland by James Glass, Trent University by Davide Panagia, the University of Regina by Shadia Drury, a Fulbright Lectureship in St. Petersburg extended by Tatiana Venediktova of Moscow State University, and of course by our now decade-old Political Theory Workshop at the University at Albany.

A Democratic Enlightenment has been greatly improved by a large collection of anonymous reviewers, in particular by those solicited by Duke University Press for their critical commentary on the entirety of my manuscript, though also by reviewers solicited by *Polity*, the *Journal for Cultural Research*, and *Theory & Event*, where earlier versions of chapters of this book were published. And I am grateful to Ian Verstegen and Roger Rothman for including a selection from one of my chapters in their fascinating *The Art of the Real: Visual Studies and New Materialisms*, and to John Seery, whose inclusion of my work in his outstanding collection, *A Political Companion to Walt Whitman*, drew a review by Betsy Erkkila focusing my attention more intently on an important theoretical problem in Whitman's work to which I have responded in my introduction. And while each of the scholarly contributions to *A Political Companion to Walt Whitman* added to its distinction, the essays by Cristina Beltran, Jason Frank, Jack Turner, and of course Jane Bennett and George Kateb were indispensable to my efforts to think about Whitman in new ways.

I am also grateful to many friends, colleagues, and students who read and commented on chapters of *A Democratic Enlightenment* as its arguments were evolving. Elizabeth Anker, Emily Beausoleil, Stephanie Erev, James Glass, Sharon Krause, and Torrey Shanks were all extremely thoughtful in ways that pushed my work forward, and I am very grateful to Martin Jay for a challenging and important list of issues I addressed in the second part of the book. Several graduate students from the University at Albany political science and English departments, Sean McKeever, Nathaniel Williams, Aidan Thompson, and James Searle, have engaged issues in my work, teaching me as much as I hope to have taught them. Final preparation of my manuscript is indebted to Stephan Stohler's generous expressions of collegiality and computer expertise, which saved me considerable time. I am extremely grateful to Sandra Korn and Liz Smith of Duke University Press for their editorial care overseeing the production of *A Democratic Enlightenment*, and to William Hedberg, senior vice provost and associate vice president for academic affairs at the State University of New York at Albany, for approving sabbatical leaves without which this work would have taken considerably longer to complete.

Finally, my brother, Steve, was wonderfully generous with his time, video expertise, and intuitive grasp of how to convey the meaning of film, all of which were indispensable to his production of film clips from *The Help* and *Gentleman's Agreement* enabling me to study these two theoretically rich films far more closely than would otherwise have been possible. And to Maureen, also known as Na-Na, my dearest and best friend and heart of my heart for a half century, I am, as always, more grateful than I have been able to say in a lifetime for the love and support that has been forever unfailing, and I am as grateful to her for discussions of this work as thought provoking and helpful as any I have had.

Past as Prologue

Today's nationalist political climate, globally, though especially in America, is altogether at odds with the argument of *A Democratic Enlightenment: The Reconciliation Image, Aesthetic Education, Possible Politics.* So wholly at odds that my work's core ideas—all of which are included in its title—have gone unrecognized despite circulating in one of the most ubiquitous media of popular culture: film. Consequently, as I now introduce these ideas the danger exists they may be regarded as utopian even though they are in the process of taking shape in an advanced visual medium that is also our most advanced visual art form. For all the while they are beginning to crystallize in film, and in cinematic images announcing their cultural arrival and registering their political presence, they may appear chimerical in a political context hostile as well as deaf and blind to them.

In *A Democratic Enlightenment* I advance the possibility that a radically new type of enlightenment is emerging in our own dark democratic and most unlikely of political times. A "democratic" enlightenment is proceeding by way of an aesthetic education that in its earlier stages had relied on the "reconciliation image," as I call it, which had appeared in traditional art forms to teach an ideal of reconciliation ending identity's violence toward difference. At its present, more advanced stage, a democratic enlightenment relies on the pedagogy of the reconciliation image in film to teach that same political lesson.

The possibility of a democratic enlightenment thus emerges from a genea-logical history of visual images of reconciliation, from a past that is prologue to the reconciliation image in film, which envisions a possible politics of rec-onciliation transforming identity's relation to difference. This new type of en-lightenment derives its democratic character from the universality of cinema, which extends beyond the borders of modern democracies themselves, and from an ideal of reconciliation unequaled for including other core democratic values it also exceeds.

Before turning to my chapter descriptions, I propose to accomplish three things in this introduction. I want to first explain my reasons for writing this book, which are rooted in my deep ambivalence about the relationship be-tween liberal democratic politics and the liberal private sphere, where vio-lence toward difference is often bred, even though it may not be born there. While the private sphere is one of liberalism's greatest achievements, I also recognize it sets limits to liberal politics by erecting obstacles to political re-mediation that liberalism could only overcome through an antiliberal, Rous-seauian erasure of privacy. Teaching an ideal of the reconciliation of identity and difference through the reconciliation image, however, by means of aes-thetic education a democratic enlightenment could penetrate to the heart of the liberal private sphere to address a problem beyond the reach of liberal politics and its rule of law.

Second, I want to explain each of the core ideas of this work. Before I do, though, since *A Democratic Enlightenment* will no doubt appear as an overly ambitious if not presumptuous project for my interest in identifying an en-lightenment successor to its modern European predecessor, at the outset of this introduction I must add an important caveat. Even if a democratic en-lightenment is in the process of coming to pass, as I believe, I am not claiming the enlightenment project I theorize over the course of this book will shape the future of modernity as the European Enlightenment shaped its recent past. By the time this introduction concludes, though, it will be apparent I am claiming that however modest the impact of a democratic enlightenment on the liberal private sphere, it is not only as important as the European Enlight-enment. For those who above all value difference, the most human as well as most democratic of values, it is more so.

Finally, although I find a democratic enlightenment to be philosophically quite different from its European predecessor, I trace the development of the former in relation to the latter after explaining a democratic enlightenment's core theoretical terms. Here I want to establish the continuity as well as the differences between the emergence of a democratic enlightenment and its European forerunner by suggesting their historical relationship is genealogical in the antipositivistic, antiscientistic senses belonging to Nietzsche's, Bergson's, Foucault's, Deleuze's, Bennett's, and Connolly's thought. For each thinker, genealogy refers to a developmental path that is neither causal nor teleological but which becomes evident through a series of connections and resemblances between earlier and later events. While a democratic enlightenment emerges out of its relation to an earlier enlightenment, being "latent or potential," in Bergson's terms, it appears not as a determined, inevitable event but as a *possibility*.[1] If such a possibility does indeed appear chimerical today, that is a commentary on the times in which we live and not the possibility itself.

WHY A DEMOCRATIC ENLIGHTENMENT?

A Democratic Enlightenment originates in my abiding concern with the long-settled prejudice toward difference in Western democratic societies, difference's normalized construction as the racialized, gendered, sexualized, and Semitic "other." In whatever subtle or unsubtle forms of marginalization, exclusion, or discrimination this prejudice takes, for my purposes they are as much forms of violence toward difference as its extermination. Yet the normalized condition of otherness is only part of what I find distressing. Equally problematic is the way those who have struggled against violence toward difference in modern liberal democracies have formulated their opposition to it.

Juridical institutions have little by little enforced the rights of the other to make strides toward ending discrimination and to prevent the extermination of otherness. And even as nationalism today reaches near pathological extremes, on the one hand in reaction to waves of refugees and immigrants fleeing war, violence, and poverty fueled or caused by neoliberal and nationalist regimes, and on the other by revealing and emboldening inveterate, subterranean racism, anti-Semitism, misogyny, and homophobia its divisiveness then feeds off of, formal-legal systems and their political allies have pursued policies ameliorating the conditions of the other. Paradoxically, though, opponents of the cultural constructions of otherness have become their unwitting collaborators by framing debate about the relationship between democracy and difference in a way limiting ameliorative policies to "inclusiveness." Beyond this remedy for the violence toward difference defined by its liberal opposition, there is no recognition of possible reforms exceeding the narrow framework of this liberal political imaginary.

To be sure, I am not denying that juridical protections of constitutional rights furthering the inclusiveness of difference continue to steadily and successfully bring an end to much of the violence difference as otherness suffers in modern democracies. Surely this is proven in America and other democracies by the great achievements of the civil rights, feminist, and gay rights movements, and to an extent by the unfortunately too modest accomplishments of political struggles for the rights of immigrants who suffer so terribly today. But inclusiveness does not end, and can and does coexist alongside, the construction of difference as otherness in the liberal private sphere. It is the private sphere that is home to xenophobic communities of dominant genders, races, sexualities, religions, and ethnicities, to identities whose self-ascribed truths are constituted through constructions of otherness perpetuating violence toward difference.

Since it is in the liberal private sphere, beneath the threshold of the law and politics, where everyday violence toward difference flourishes unabated in ordinary social relations, it will not do to argue that so long as juridical institutions and their constitutional protections of difference are not violated, what goes on in the private sphere cannot be condemned. As Western democracies have discovered in the past and present, no sooner are they plagued by serious internal problems or external pressures than the violence toward difference confined to the private sphere is mobilized, intensified, and expanded by those eager to exploit its ethnocentrism to assign blame and capture political power. Festering in the private sphere, violence toward difference threatens infinitely greater political dangers than when openly in contempt of the law, where it can be confronted and contained. But this begs the question. How can the liberal political imaginary be expanded beyond inclusiveness to transform its private sphere?

If war is to be waged against violence toward difference where it thrives beneath the threshold of politics and the law, the liberal private sphere must become the domain of reconciling identity and difference, ground zero of a democratic enlightenment. Through aesthetic education the private sphere would become an *aesthetic* domain of ideas and ideals, senses and sensibilities, perceptions, dispositions, and orientations able to transform identity's relation to difference into an *aesthetic* relation. Though Alexis de Tocqueville found the private sphere to be apolitical if not antipolitical, as an aesthetic domain the private sphere would nurture a possible politics having the power to overcome the construction of difference as otherness and to remake the politics of civil society and its public sphere.[2] Neither utopian nor chimerical, the ideas I theorize in *A Democratic Enlightenment* are rooted in the work of two radically different thinkers. Both offer powerful theoretical support for how such a political transformation of the private sphere might occur by way of a democratic enlightenment aesthetic education can produce by teaching an ideal of reconciliation through the reconciliation image in film.

Beginning with Walt Whitman in part I, "The Reconciliation Image in Whitman," I find an ideal of reconciliation that takes its first visual form as the reconciliation image, whose evolution I then trace in part II, "The Reconciliation Image in Adorno," through its second and more advanced visual form in the aesthetic theory of Theodor Adorno. Its evolution still incomplete, in part III, "The Reconciliation Image in Film," I find Adorno's reconciliation image taking a third evolutionary form in film.

Throughout its evolutionary development the ideal of reconciliation that appears in the form of the reconciliation image is a democratic ideal. And the ideal of reconciliation the reconciliation image visualizes is the core idea of what I mean by a democratic enlightenment. Hence to recapitulate the principal terms of my argument, a democratic enlightenment, aesthetic education and its possible politics, and most centrally the reconciliation image around which all three revolve are all new terms for elaborating a political discourse of reconciliation through the thought of Whitman, Adorno, and the media of film.

NEW TERMS OF POLITICAL DISCOURSE

If we entertain the possibility of a democratic enlightenment, as I propose we do, Whitman's prose and poetry are thrilling to read in the twenty-first century. Writing at a time when America seemed fated to ever deepening divisions over the question of race, astonishingly Whitman proposes an ideal of reconciliation that is as alien to his own political times as it is to ours. Surely no ideal could be more out of sync with the settled prejudices of his day defined by the racial divide leading to, through, and beyond the Civil War, whose abolition of slavery and the mutual hatreds born in its wake greatly aggravated. Yet that very political condition seems to me to explain Whitman's interest, which was to create a model of aesthetic education whose reconciliation image taught the ideal of reconciliation when such an idea seemed incredible. Americans were to learn to overcome their violence toward difference, lessons mounting a democratic barrier to the evils of constructing difference as otherness. Through poetry, the reconciliation image would perform its pedagogical work in the private sphere, achieving beneath the threshold of the law and politics an ideal no politics and law had ever achieved, much less imagined, limited as they are to serving the political will of aesthetically unschooled majorities.

As I explain in part I, the ideal of reconciliation belonging to Whitman's poetry consists of three dimensions, which, as taught by the reconciliation image, are each one of its democratic effects or democratic lessons. The reconciliation image's first lesson, the all-inclusiveness of differences, imagines democracy immersing individuals in a world of differences, surrounding them with differences whose diversity, as Tzvétan Todorov reminds us and as Whitman agrees, is infinite.[3] Infinitely diverse, difference refers not only to those commonly constructed as other but to any ordinary and extraordinary way in which individuals appear to be different. And the ideal of reconciliation secondly teaches individuals to be receptive to differences around them, their receptivity taking forms not less infinite than the diversity of differences themselves. Finally, the reconciliation image teaches individuals to imitate differences to which they have learned to be receptive, thus through imitation becoming different themselves in the images of differences in which democracy immerses them.

So by means of the pedagogy of the reconciliation image it is not just democracy that becomes all-inclusive of differences. Through receptivity and imitation each *person* becomes, to recall Whitman's term of art, a "great composite *democratic individual*" of diverse differences.[4] Though, as Whitman adds, each one becomes only "more or less" like those one imitates, thus becoming different and discontinuous with one's self without sacrificing one's own identity.[5] Since the more all-inclusive democratic society aspires to be, the more differences there are to be imitated, through imitation individuals engage in "democratic becoming," as I call it, such that each comes to imitate a democratically all-inclusive form of life. In *Leaves of Grass* Whitman often represents himself as just such an image of democratic becoming to perfectly illustrate how his reconciliation image performs the work of aesthetic education. Modeling his receptivity to and imitation of all those personas his poetry's famous lists include, his verse models reconciliation as an aesthetic ideal and its relation between identity and difference as an aesthetic relation.

For Whitman, the ideal of reconciliation is thus expressed as an aesthetic ideal in a series of images, the all-inclusive, receptivity, and imitative images. Hence my term the "reconciliation image," which expresses the purpose or rationality of the series of images as a whole. What this means is that reconciliation is not only an aesthetic ideal *twice* over by virtue of its reconciliation image being created by verse to teach identity to create itself differently in the image of difference. Reconciliation is an aesthetic ideal in still a *third* sense, which brings me to the first of my three most controversial arguments.

Whitman writes poetry to create visual images. His reconciliation image is a verbal-visual semiotic hybrid whereby neither its verbal nor visual construction comes into existence without the other. He accomplishes this aesthetic transformation of the verbal into the visual by writing a poetry having a critically self-reflexive power to problematize language's capacity to express certain ideas, namely essences, realities, truths. Writing poetry to highlight its own incapacity to represent the essence of things, what lies below the surface of appearances, that is, Whitman confines poetry to appearances—and appearances find their natural, ideal aesthetic home in visual images. Several implications follow from his poetry's self-reflection.

Since appearances in their diversity are irreducible to essences, having nothing essentially in common all appearances the reconciliation image visually represents are different from each other, which explains why Whitman holds the diversity of differences to be infinite. And with the reconciliation image limited to representing appearances, at the level of essences differences are unknowable, mysterious, producing effects attracting our receptivity. Lastly, given its ontological primacy of appearances, the reconciliation image abstains from privileging any appearance of difference according to imperceptible qualities other differences can be said to lack, so that no difference can be constructed as an other according to some truth it allegedly fails to correspond to. Whitman's reconciliation image thus cultivates in each of us a democratic sensibility to difference, receptivity to the all-inclusiveness of differences through which they become eligible for our imitation. Involving us in a democratic becoming, he leads us to a possible politics of reconciliation beyond liberalism's tolerance of difference, which abides the everyday violence toward difference the private sphere nurtures beneath the threshold of the law.

Whitman's ideal and image of reconciliation are original discoveries for bearing no resemblance to the three best-known concepts of reconciliation: the Christian notion of reconciliation addressed by Paul and Jesus in the oft-cited "New Testament Letters," Hegel's concept in his *Phenomenology of Mind* and *Philosophy of Right,* and its recent codification by the South African Truth and Reconciliation Commission. While it is arguable that Whitman's ideal and image have counterparts in Friedrich Schiller's *On the Aesthetic Education of Humanity in a Series of Letters,* the latter more likely prefigures Whitman's discoveries, as I will make clear shortly. But in addition to their originality, Whitman's discoveries are also significant for their theoretical resemblances to Adorno's concept of reconciliation, which in view of those similarities I attempt to think anew.

As I reread Adorno's *Aesthetic Theory* in part II in light of Whitman's prose and poetry, I find it offers a second, more theorized version of Whitman's reconciliation image. And placed side by side, both their images appear as more and less theorized precursors of the reconciliation image I discover in film. So by studying the resemblances between Whitman's original form of the reconciliation image and Adorno's second form, I find Whitman has led us to Adorno's more highly developed theoretical form that, by circulating through the popular media of film, performs the work of a democratic enlightenment Whitman assigned to the visual image of reconciliation he created through poetry. Adorno thus becomes Whitman's and a democratic enlightenment's powerful theoretical ally. Yet when the theoretical resemblances between Whitman and Adorno are examined in the equally bright light of the profound differences between them, which cannot be ignored, how can such reconciliation between the two be imagined?

This brings me to the second of my three most controversial arguments. To begin with, at one level Whitman and Adorno have a fundamentally different relationship to enlightenment. Whitman thought America capable of reaching a stage of cultural development higher than the stage of material prosperity he believed to be its economic precondition. Taught by poetry, reconciliation would be the defining element of that higher stage of achievement, a democratic enlightenment by means of aesthetic education. Adorno rejects the concept of enlightenment, however, believing, as he and Max Horkheimer argue in *Dialectic of Enlightenment*, that enlightenment was driven by a faculty of reason by its very nature destructive of difference. For proof of reason's hostility to difference in the late modern world, they foreground the Holocaust's destruction of the Jews, though also the universality of the commodity form, whose economics impress patterns of sameness on all cultural forms of life. Most important for my purposes, no more than any other form of mass culture Adorno did not exempt cinema from commodification, which determined that only those films would be produced that reflected cultural values unreceptive to anything different.

But then there is a deeper level, where I take seriously Horkheimer and Adorno's overlooked allusion in *Dialectic of Enlightenment*'s original preface to a "positive concept of enlightenment," which, though their critique of the concept of enlightenment was intended to "prepare," they left untheorized.[6]

In that same work, I also find evidence for an *alternative* concept of reason *opposed* to the enlightenment concept of reason they indict for destroying difference. There is also the concept of aesthetic rationality Adorno began to theorize in *Aesthetic Theory*, which I believe was his attempt to construct the rational basis for the "positive concept of enlightenment" he and Horkheimer alluded to in their earlier work. As Adorno began to develop it in *Aesthetic Theory*, aesthetic reason was responsible for producing the reconciliation image in the modern artwork, where it served as the placeholder for a positive enlightenment's possibility. By sharing the reconciliation image, thus an aesthetic form of reason productive of the reconciliation image, and an enlightenment the reconciliation image could sustain, Adorno and Whitman become allies at this deeper level. Whitman's democratic enlightenment and Adorno's positive enlightenment become interchangeable terms.

For purposes of developing this deeper level of argument my approach is to read Adorno *against* himself, to find out whether he also made theoretical arguments opening up the possibility for a democratic or "positive" enlightenment that other of his well-known arguments, in particular with Horkheimer in *Dialectic of Enlightenment*, had foreclosed. My approach to Adorno has as its point of departure his and Horkheimer's allusion to a positive enlightenment in *Dialectic of Enlightenment* they had committed themselves to theorizing, or preparing, despite failing to do so in that work. It is the great significance of that allusion, together with the fragmentary evidence in that text for an alternative concept of reason to the idea of reason they indict for implicating us in the domination of difference, which led me to read Adorno against himself by fleshing out and further developing his central concept in *Aesthetic Theory*, his last work.

Now central to Adorno's *Aesthetic Theory* is art's "aesthetic rationality," which by means of its "elements" determines an artwork's aesthetic form whenever it becomes the focus of a unique aesthetic experience. When perceived in a certain way, an artwork can be imagined to begin to move as though under its own power, so it appears, *much like a film*, as an uninterrupted, continuously flowing moving image that changes as new images emerge to represent features of its aesthetic object not included in the artwork's original appearance. Since the differences between an artwork and its aesthetic object are inexhaustible, the movement of an artwork is endless, for aesthetic reason determines that aesthetic form is an *open whole*, open to *all differences* between the artwork and its object, all of which are representable in different images of an original artwork.

With every new image, through the aesthetic rationality of its aesthetic form an artwork achieves an instance of reconciliation between its original appearance, its identity, and differences belonging to its aesthetic object, while it also continues to form ever new images as it ceaselessly pursues reconciliation. By representing the achievement though also the continuous pursuit of reconciliation, Adorno's moving, changing reconciliation image represents reconciliation as a time arrived and a time yet to come, a dual temporality through its subordination of time to movement. It is thus what Gilles Deleuze calls a "movement-image," through which time itself is transformed from a chronological, quantitative to qualitative time as measured by the changing images of reconciliation between the artwork and its aesthetic object.

Adorno thus gives us an aesthetic theory of how artworks produce the reconciliation image. When I take up Whitman's reconciliation image in depth in part I, I stress those of its properties further anticipating Adorno's reconciliation image beyond what I earlier highlighted. For Whitman's reconciliation image also assumes the continuity of motion and dual temporality belonging to Adorno's. But all of that must be carefully assembled from Whitman's prose and poetry, for unlike Adorno he does not lay out an aesthetic theory of the reconciliation image. Despite the thoroughness of Adorno's theoretical explanation for the reconciliation image, though, a problem remains for him Whitman did not have. If Adorno's reconciliation image results from the transformation of an artwork set into *continuous* motion by aesthetic experience, should there not be images *in between* the artwork's original appearance and the reconciliation image its movement produces, intermediary images marking the artwork's progress *toward* the reconciliation of identity and difference? Whitman has such images, the all-inclusive, receptivity, and imitative images, each marking serial progress toward the reconciliation image. Adorno does not.

With this problem in mind I undertake a further development of Adorno's reconciliation image. To Adorno's elements of aesthetic rationality determining the artwork's aesthetic form as an open whole, I match Whitman's three images and their democratic lessons, which then precede the appearance of Adorno's reconciliation image as they do Whitman's. But Adorno's concept of aesthetic rationality invites further consideration of what additional intermediary images might correspond to its elements. Altogether I find Adorno's reconciliation image to consist of five corresponding images—the identity, difference, all-inclusive, receptivity, and imitative images, with distinct democratic lessons taught by each—that continuously unfold according to a durational concept of movement and time. This is the more highly theorized version of Whitman's reconciliation image I find in film in part III. As I describe there how Adorno's reconciliation image unfolds in film, my theoretical interest will also be to show that his image's meaning and politics are independent of the cinematic narrative to which it belongs. My third controversial argument, this breaks with the practice of those who confine the interpretation of the meaning and politics of film to its narrative structure.

VIRTUAL ENLIGHTENMENT

Everything I have said thus far has focused on the possibility of "the birth of the new image," as Deleuze puts it, and on a new form of enlightenment this new reconciliation image makes possible.[7] By theorizing both possibilities Whitman and Adorno then make it possible for me to discover the reconciliation image in film and to theorize the possibility it might serve as the vehicle of an aesthetic education having political implications for the liberal private and public spheres. But there is another set of possibilities I have yet to discuss. What prior historical developments may have contributed to the emergence of the reconciliation image and the forms of enlightenment, aesthetic education, and politics appearing in Whitman's and Adorno's work and in film?

Here Bergson is very helpful when he writes that "essentially virtual," the past "cannot be known as something past unless we follow and adopt the movement by which it expands into a present image."[8] Taking Bergson's recommendation seriously, I want to place myself in a more remote modern past to "follow and adopt the movement" out of which the reconciliation image expands into its three visual forms. As a result of doing so, it becomes clear to me that the reconciliation image did not inevitably and necessarily result from a teleological or causal path of linear historical development. Rather, the virtual often appears in the form of contingent resemblances and connections between various earlier and later developments, which, as they differently progress at various speeds, in different patterns, and according to different processes, unpredictably shape future events.

For my purposes the question thus becomes: Between what earlier thinkers and their ideas and Whitman's, Adorno's, and film's reconciliation images are there resemblances and connections from which the latter may have taken shape? One set stands out in particular, that of Voltaire's thought on enlightenment and language, Diderot's on enlightenment and the visual image, and especially Schiller's on democratic enlightenment, the visual image, aesthetic education, and reconciliation. Once the connections and resemblances between Voltaire, Diderot, and Schiller on the one hand and Whitman, Adorno, and film on the other are brought to light, we will have a solid grasp of how the past was prologue to the expansion of the reconciliation image into its several forms.

RESEMBLANCES AND CONNECTIONS:
VOLTAIRE, ENLIGHTENMENT, LANGUAGE

In his 1756 essay "Des Langues," appearing five years after the publication of Diderot and d'Alembert's *Encyclopédie*, the defining text of the European Enlightenment, Voltaire assigns languages the authority for the representation and production of all that is known and can be known—in a word, for *enlightenment*. Though he concedes languages' imperfections, when cultivated by "good" and "approved authors" of "sufficient number," they become "fixed," sovereign agencies to which we must "adhere absolutely" if "the books which provide the instruction and the pleasure of the nations" are not to be "soon render[ed] unintelligible."[9] Once fixed, a language would be made useless only if it were to be revised. By Voltaire's time certain languages had already achieved such an elevated status; he privileges Italian, Spanish, English, and French. And since Voltaire had not excluded the possibility other languages may in the future follow their example, I do not doubt his ambition is for languages to become the universal media of the Enlightenment and enlightenment.

For Voltaire, then, from its European inception enlightenment has a singular relationship to language. If we need additional proof for the powerful bond Voltaire forges between enlightenment and language, the first posthumous collection of his works provides it. Editors of the famous 1784 Kehl edition of his complete works added "Des Langues" as a final third section to a longer essay by Voltaire entitled "Langues," which had originally been included in his 1770–74 *Questions sur l'Encyclopédie*. By being arranged together with "Langues" in a text interrogating the *Encyclopédie*, "Des Langues'" further secures the connection between Voltaire's valorization of language and the astonishing enlightenment project launched by the *Encyclopédie*.[10] In the final analysis, of course, we need only recall Voltaire as the personification of the Enlightenment for the truest measure of the prerogative he accords language in the practice of enlightenment.[11]

Since Voltaire language has realized his aspiration by becoming the sovereign instrument he imagined would universally perform the work of enlightenment. This comes as no surprise given the civilizing force of language that for more than three centuries is owed to its ubiquitously dense modern cultural supports. Moreover the editors of the *Encyclopédie* to which Voltaire was a prolific contributor ratified his ambition. Any measure of the salience of language to the *Encyclopédie* must begin by considering the breadth, depth, and sheer magnitude of its collection of more than seventy thousand articles, which testifies to the unique burden Diderot and d'Alembert determined language would bear in their enlightenment project.

But then there are the *Encyclopédie*'s folios of more than three thousand engraved plates and drawings, visual images of the arts and trades whose publication was overseen by Diderot. Whereas from Diderot's account as reported in Arthur Wilson's study, they may have been introduced to compensate for the poverty of technical knowledge made available by craftsmen protective of their arts' and trades' secrets, or to correct misinformation craftsmen fed to *Encyclopédie* essayists suspected of being tax collectors in disguise, the images also were intended to accomplish what language could not. As Diderot wrote when he first described its engravings to his *Encyclopédie*'s subscribers, "everything in it [its collection of plates] is in action and alive."[12] Diderot should be distinguished from Voltaire by moving toward the visual image as a vehicle of enlightenment in its own right. The *Encyclopédie*'s images anticipate Diderot's later art criticism and preoccupation with the visual, where the meaning he attaches to visual images so often exceeds language's interpretive powers. Diderot's encyclopedic images, I am suggesting, signal not only a departure from but in addition a reaction to the privilege Voltaire accords language in the process of enlightenment.

RESEMBLANCES AND CONNECTIONS:
DIDEROT, ENLIGHTENMENT, THE VISUAL IMAGE

Since my interest is to record Diderot's *Encyclopédie*, as I shall now refer to it, as the first time in modernity when the discursive practice of enlightenment is uniquely connected to the visual image, it is instructive to distinguish him from Voltaire's linguistic bias. To learn why this connection is significant requires answering two questions: What is the concept of enlightenment at the heart of Diderot's *Encyclopédie*, and in what ways do his visual images contribute to its formulation? Answering these questions clarifies Diderot's connection between enlightenment and the visual image and also positions me to recognize the ways he may mark the beginning of a practice of enlightenment thought resembling and connected to Schiller's, Whitman's, Adorno's, and film.

Enlightenment scholarship has long been divided on the matter of the relationship between language and visual images in Diderot's *Encyclopédie*. In *The Discourse of Enlightenment in Eighteenth-Century France: Diderot and the Art of Philosophizing*, however, Daniel Brewer's interest in the "self-reflexive" work carried out by the encyclopedic form of Diderot's project seems to me on balance to help answer my two questions by equally weighting the *dominant* role the *Encyclopédie* assigns language and the *unique* role it accords visual images. Not only is the *Encyclopédie* distinguished by its Promethean efforts to represent all contemporaneous forms of knowledge; more important for Brewer, it is distinctive for its self-referential attention to its own mode of representing knowledge's extant forms. For by privileging its manner of representation—through meticulous display, classification, and interpretation—over the knowledge represented, the *Encyclopédie represents itself* as the order of knowledge best qualified to judge how all other forms of knowledge are to be ordered. At the same time, however, such a "critical relation to knowledge," in Brewer's words, also renders its privilege arbitrary for leaving its critical vantage point without justification beyond its brute self-reflexive construction of privilege itself.[13]

At the moment the critical vantage point of the *Encyclopédie* becomes arbitrary, its power to prevail over other forms of knowledge comes to rest on the power of the ideological values in which it is anchored, those that constitute the political order that underlies the privileged enlightened order of knowledge informing the *Encyclopédie*'s representations of knowledge. For Diderot the most powerful knowledge was the form valued for being most *useful*. Knowledge is therefore represented from the standpoint of the material interests and ends it serves. "The *Encyclopédie*," Brewer concludes, "is a manifesto of capitalist epistemology, a founding document of bourgeois ideology." So powerfully does the *Encyclopédie*'s own ideology of order emerge from its voluminous utilitarian exegeses of pragmatic knowledge it represents that it becomes an idealized exception to the arbitrary rule attached to the *Encyclopédie*'s representation of knowledge. But in the end Diderot's project becomes a casualty of its own success. Harnessing its critical relation to knowledge to the service of "practical ends," Brewer asserts, "Enlightenment begins to self-destruct. . . . Nature, as well as human subjects, become yet other objects of knowledge, possession, and domination."[14]

Now at this point Diderot's more specialized interest in the *Encyclopédie*'s engravings is of particular interest to me. Like the encyclopedic text they accompany, the visual images the plates portray affirm order, utility, possession, mastery—values instrumental to developing rationalized structures of production and consumption. Enlightenment is visually represented as *savoir faire*, as technical expertise able to "bridge the gap between theory and practice, between conceptual knowledge and its application in and on the material world," Brewer insists, and not as *savoir*, as knowledge for its own sake.[15] Once the privilege that images self-reflexively grant to technocapitalism becomes apparent, any challenge to its arbitrary status is overruled by the unique visionary power of the pragmatism of the approach to knowledge the *Encyclopédie*'s visual images help to enshrine. Yet, despite Brewer's argument that the *Encyclopédie* is the Enlightenment's anti-enlightenment text, I believe an alternative case for its visual images can be rooted in the theoretically more complex semiotic relation between language and visual image Diderot struggled with.

It is precisely this level of semiotic complexity Foucault invites us to consider in *The Order of Things* when he reflects on Velázquez's *Las Meninas*. With regard to how language might be used to coax Velázquez's image "little by little" to "release its illuminations," he writes, the "relation of language to painting is an infinite relation. . . . It is in vain that we say what we see; what we see never resides in what we say."[16] As we know from his *Salons*, Diderot does not lack Foucault's estimate of how the meaning of the image infinitely exceeds language's capacity to decipher it. And while the overlap of the *Salons'* composition (1759–81) and the publication of the *Encyclopédie*'s images suggests he thought of his engravings as possessing the same uncertainty of meaning as painting, Diderot had earlier been aware of an interpretive gulf between language and image informing his understanding of the relation between his *Encyclopédie*'s visual images and its texts. In his *Letter on the Deaf and Dumb* (1751), to cite one example, Diderot reveals "one of the points of view with which I always look at pictures." Namely, "everyone who walks through a picture gallery is really unconsciously acting the part of a deaf man who is amusing himself by examining the dumb who are conversing on subjects familiar to him."[17] Speaking in languages we neither hear nor speak, images convey meanings *exceeding* those the languages we do speak and hear have made sensible.

Here is where I locate the limits of Brewer's argument and possibilities for aligning Diderot's images with an order very different from the one Brewer alleges the encyclopedic images self-reflexively privilege. It is not that Brewer fails to recognize this chasm between language and image central to Diderot's thinking. Actually he highlights it, as when he recalls Diderot's comment in his *Prospectus* to the *Encyclopédie* that "a glance at the object or its representation says more than a page of language."[18] Or when discussing the *Salons* he problematizes "the ultimate incommensurability between word and image" troubling Diderot's art criticism. In fact, by speculating that the hermeneutic resistance Diderot attributes to the image "would thus make any truly critical vantage point inaccessible," Brewer questions whether the privileged critical standpoint he claimed was established by the self-reflexive performativity of Diderot's image is even intelligible. But regardless of this and other such evidence Brewer cites to point to the image's conflict with the *Encyclopédie*'s promotion of instrumental reason, he continues to press for the agreement between the two until concluding, "Perhaps no exclusively human values can be relied upon to judge this text's workings. The plates mark the beginnings of an uncannily familiar technologization of values, an epistemic shift towards a kind of techno-humanism that extends to the postindustrial, cybernetic age."[19]

Once the indeterminacy of the images' meanings is theorized, however, as Foucault allows me to do, I should ask why *exclusively* human values cease to be credible representations of the modernity visualized by Diderot's images. It is only when the *Encyclopédie*'s images are interpreted from the vantage point of what has become "uncannily familiar" to us in our *own time* that the human content they represent disappears behind their technohumanist dimensions. But rather than from the *retrospective* present point of view of the all-too-familiar, when I view Diderot's images from a location *immanent* to the *Encyclopédie* that becomes available to us when we place ourselves in the past, as Bergson directed, the images appear to represent other values and possibilities. Even a superficial study of Diderot's images, including those of the arts and crafts aligned with technocapitalist values, must also be impressed by their representations of the human imagination's creativity and play as offspring of an emancipated reason and by an aesthetic rationality whose relation to the world is expressed through his images' receptivity to the sheer diversity of different forms of life. This brief list of exclusively human values hardly begins to capture the extent of those that Diderot's images inscribe in their representation of enlightenment. So the connection forged by Diderot between enlightenment and the visual image is not reducible to the political economies of technohumanist, capitalist, and neoliberal cultures. Owing to the *Encyclopédie*'s images' excess of meaning beyond the text, unlike its text they represent human possibilities that have emerged from obscurity into the present alongside technocapitalism and should be recognized from a vantage point informed by the concept of the virtual.

RESEMBLANCES AND CONNECTIONS: SCHILLER, AESTHETIC EDUCATION, RECONCILIATION, THE VISUAL IMAGE, DEMOCRATIC ENLIGHTENMENT

Nearly a half century after the inauguration of the *Encyclopédie*, Schiller's *On the Aesthetic Education of Humanity in a Series of Letters* (hereafter *Letters*) revises and extends Diderot's connections between enlightenment and the visual image.[20] Rather than an enlightenment whose "great idol of our age" is "Utility," a complaint Schiller perhaps registers with Diderot's *Encyclopédie* in mind in the second of his twenty-seven letters, in various letters he imagines an enlightenment coauthored by cosmopolitan "liberal citizen[s]" committed to "liberal principles," "inalienable rights," and the "ideal of equality."[21] Far more than Diderot for his encyclopedic images' representations of exclusively human values, Schiller is the first to imagine the possibility of a *democratic* enlightenment. Also far more than Kant, as he conveys by indicting the "Enlightenment of the *understanding*" (*die Aufklärung des Verstandes*), which in his "Fifth Letter" he declares "has had on the whole so little of an ennobling influence . . . it has tended rather to bolster up depravity by providing it with the support of maxims [*Maximen*]," a critique of Kant's faculty of the understanding I shall return to shortly.[22] And the ideal a democratic enlightenment teaches is "reconciliation," which Schiller proposes is taught by the arts, especially by visual images, as he confirms in letter 26 by stressing that "appearance" (*Schein*) is "the very essence" of all the fine arts and "what we actually see with the eye."[23]

Hence Schiller's importance for his *resemblances* to Diderot by way of enlightenment's reliance on the pedagogy of the visual arts, and for *connections* he makes between the possibility of a democratic enlightenment, its ideal of reconciliation, and aesthetic education, notably by the visual arts. Schiller's connections create new values. Since art, which models a democratic enlightenment by teaching reconciliation, is the "daughter of Freedom," as he also declares in his "Second Letter," as the "construction of true political freedom" reconciliation is the "most perfect of all the works" of art, thus democracy's highest ideal.[24]

To show how Schiller's connections form the richest pool of possibilities from which the idea of a democratic enlightenment could evolve, my treatment of his *Letters* tries to answer four questions: What does Schiller mean by reconciliation? How is reconciliation taught by art? What is the relationship of reconciliation, art, and aesthetic education to *morality*, a question of special importance, as understanding democratic enlightenment as a possibility depends on its answer. Very often Schiller is thought to mean the aesthetic legislates morality as Kant thinks of moral laws, which would violate the boundaries Schiller drew between the aesthetic and the moral and nullify the ideal of reconciliation and the idea of democratic enlightenment as possibilities the work of art teaches. Finally, what is Schiller's relation to the European Enlightenment? The answer will help to explain the sense in which a democratic enlightenment is truly democratic.

Composed in the wake of the French Revolution's most violent period, Schiller's *Letters* are not less critical of the "crude, lawless instincts" of the "lower and more numerous classes" threatening to destroy the state than of "the cultivated classes" whose "depravation of character" defended a tyranny ensuring the mutual collapse of the classes, who together only maintained order as "an equilibrium of evils."[25] Though over the course of the Revolution Schiller found cause for optimism that a constitutional republic might emerge, his "Fifth Letter" admitted such a hope was in vain, and "a moment so prodigal of opportunity" was met by an "unresponsive [in the sense of callous human] race" (*ein unempfängliches Geschlecht*).[26] I want to pay special attention here to how he formulates the conclusion he draws from this state of affairs; the emergence of a moment of hope, "as if [humanity] were beginning anew" (*als ob er von vorn anfinge*), was met with absolute indifference by all warring sides.[27] Under conditions of such apathy Schiller declares, "The moral possibility is wanting [*fehlt*]."[28] I want to underscore that he writes of moral *possibility* to make it clear that the possibility for which he hoped in vain he does not also think of as a moral maxim or moral law but only as *the possibility* such a moral principle, that of a democratic republic, *might be conceived*. For it is against the backdrop of this clarification, which lays the basis for grasping the relation between the aesthetic and moral as Schiller intended it, thus of his relationship to Kant, that his concept of reconciliation and the pedagogical role art plays can be understood.

It is in the context of the French Revolution that Schiller's *Letters* lay the groundwork for his construction of a parallel between the political and philosophical dimensions of the conflict, which he believes to be internal to the individual as well as the state, and the pedagogical work of the fine arts. In his fourth through eleventh letters he frames the political condition of the state and the existential condition of the individual as each *divided and in internal conflict with itself*. Each is an identity opposed to an interiorized difference, a unity opposed to variety, permanence opposed to change. For Schiller this internal conflict between the immutable "I" and the continuously varying empirical forms of man, the unity of the state and diversity of those who compose it, admits of only two solutions. Identity is achieved by suppressing or by being reconciled with difference. Later, in his twelfth through fifteenth letters, he develops the aesthetic parallel to this opposition. As he introduces its central concepts, the sensuous, formal, and play impulses, he explains the work each performs separately and all perform together as he weaves them into a discussion of time, becoming, possibility, receptivity, life, humanity, and reconciliation.

Arguing in his "Eleventh Letter" from the premise that humans are involved in diverse conditions of willing, thinking, and feeling, all owed to a sensuous existence situating them in time and material processes of becoming, Schiller asks how identity (the "I," "person," "personality," the "self," "ego," or "rational nature") can persist unchanged in time through all such variations. Considered apart from its sensuous relation to what lies outside of it, unburdened by time, becoming, and sensuous existence itself, identity remains self-identical, an unsolicited potential for apprehending the infinitely diverse forms of life populating the world. Considered apart from identity and its untapped potential, sensuous existence constitutes us as "nothing but world," as the "formless content of time" and becoming until the mere matter we are and are indissolubly a part of becomes the object of identity's capacity for the sensuous perception of form. Then taking identity and sensuous existence together, as his concept of man requires, he implicates humans in the most fundamental of all human dilemmas, being internally divided within and against themselves. With the exception of the Hellenes, humanity has resolved this division in a historically one-sided way. Identity realizes itself through its sensuous perception of forms whose diversity it "subjugates . . . to the unity of [its] own Self."[29] At any particular moment in time, that is, humanity imposes its identity on difference, retaining its self-sameness by raising itself to the timeless level of universality.

Following his "Eleventh Letter" Schiller abruptly revises and refines the terms of this argument. Rather than speaking only generically of humanity as "something that endures and something that constantly changes," of the internal divide between "Person" and "Condition" or "the self and its determinations

[*Bestimmungen*]," and so forth, in his "Twelfth Letter" he speaks famously of the "formal" and "sensuous" impulses.[30] To the formal impulse Schiller assigns the powers of perception through which identity becomes implicated in time and becoming by giving form to the world. To the sensuous impulse he assigns the power of conveying impressions of that world responsible for the internal conditions of an I for whom life troubles its self-identity with its sensuous experience of diversity and relentlessly continuous change.

Yet why does Schiller make this terminological shift, which from this letter on will figure so prominently in his argument? I believe he wants to explain, in Kant's terms, his conception of humanity's internally conflicting ontological demands between identity and difference and their counterpart political form in the revolutionary struggles of his day. Schiller's purpose is to show the contradiction and its politics to be rooted in one of Kant's cognitive faculties: *the understanding*. Second, through its Kantian account he anticipates arriving at a solution to this contradiction and its political counterpart he will introduce in the aesthetic terms in which he will subsequently describe the artwork and its work of aesthetic education. By analyzing an all-important faculty Kant holds belongs to man, Schiller explains what it is in humanity that individually and collectively sustains internal divisions to oppose reconciliation, and what it is in art that models reconciliation as an ideal toward which individuals and the state, in a word, reason, can strive.

At the very outset of his *Letters* Schiller problematizes Kant's faculty of the understanding for producing concepts whose generalizations omit crucial particulars belonging to whoever or whatever they represent. He concludes his "First Letter," in fact, by alerting his readers to the shortcomings of his own arguments on the "appearance of beauty" (*Erscheinung der Schönheit*) and attributes their weaknesses to his need to refer an object of our sensuous existence to "the understanding," which by "dissolving the necessary combination" (*notwendigen Bund*) of beauty's elements "dissolved its very Being."[31] Powerfully launching this argument earlier in this letter in a reference to Kant's moral philosophy, he accuses the understanding of having to "first *destroy* the object of Inner Sense" before it can assist reason in forming moral judgments.[32] Moreover, he further takes the understanding to task for "*tear[ing]* the beautiful body [*schönen Körper*] [of nature] to pieces by reducing it to concepts."[33] While Schiller's aggressive critique of Kant's understanding lays the groundwork for his later claim in his "Fifth Letter" that it failed to advance the project of enlightenment, as I noted, his insight into the connection between Kant's faculty and a failed enlightenment is not fully clarified until his

"Sixth Letter," when for purposes of political critique he reenlists the philosophical terms with which he earlier indicted Kant's understanding. Schiller blames the state for employing a system of "classification" through which the "diversity [*die Mannigfaltigkeit*] of its citizens . . . the government [*der regierende Teil*] ends up losing sight of altogether [by] confusing their concrete reality with a mere construct of the intellect." He then censures the state's classificatory schemes for being productive of laws blind to the particulars of the lower classes, who cannot respond to such laws other than with a "primitive morality," annulling their bonds with the state.[34]

As Schiller thus argues, since Kant's faculty of the understanding is at fault for producing concepts omitting characteristics defining their objects, laws exemplifying the failings of such concepts are likewise at fault for failing to recognize differences among peoples that legislation must acknowledge to treat them justly. With this we grasp the meaning of perhaps Schiller's most significant claim in his "Sixth Letter"; namely, that "the all-dividing understanding bestowed its forms" (*der alles trennende Verstand seine Formen erteilten*) on we moderns.[35] Against this background, which anticipates his analogy between his *form*-giving, formal impulse and Kant's faculty of the understanding, beginning with his "Twelfth Letter" he will develop this analogy and its implications for surmounting the conflicts internally dividing the state and the individual at the forefront of his concerns in his "Eleventh Letter." His strategy is to show that Kant's faculty of reason bears the same relation to the formal impulse it does to the understanding. Just as for Kant reason works independently of the understanding while formulating principles that nevertheless must agree with the understanding's constitution of our experience of the world, Schiller similarly argues that reason's autonomous moral judgments are made in light of how the formal impulse shapes our sensuous experience. Ultimately his argument is that the formal impulse, like the understanding, limits reason, because its agreement with reason carries its constitutional biases into reason's domain. With this "Twelfth Letter" Schiller positions himself to mount an aesthetic theory of reconciliation.

Whereas Schiller concludes his "Twelfth Letter" by reiterating the problem he is concerned with upon concluding his "Eleventh Letter," the terminology he uses in his "Twelfth Letter" to newly conceptualize this problem paves the way to its solution. To recall, the "Eleventh Letter" ends with Schiller problematizing man's self-same identity, which persists without change only when he "*subjugates* the manifold diversity of the World to the unity of his own Self." Certainly Schiller intends to describe the self's unity as dependent on an act of violence that subdues but does not abolish the internal conflict between identity and difference. But here he does so after proposing that our impulse to subjugation originally lies not with our self, rather with the part of our nature that is "absolute" or "divine" and is expressed by our disposition to actualize our potential to give all possible forms to the world. For the "absolute manifestation of [man's] potential" possesses an "absolute unity of manifestation"; in other words, its *imposition* of forms is consistent with identity's unity.[36] While Schiller reminds us man's divine predisposition is awakened by his sensuous contact with the world, the reduction of the absolute to the self's formative *subjugation* of the world's diversity allows man's sensuous existence no claim to form beyond the self's all-too-human interest in form for identity's sake.

With his introduction of the formal and sensuous impulses in his "Twelfth Letter," however, Schiller can revise this argument, such that although the possibility of violence continues to shadow the self's relationship to its world, the language of subjugation drops out. Moreover, instead of continuing to speak of identity's divided interests between persisting self-same and continually becoming different through perception's prolific impositions of forms on a sensuously diverse world, he complicates this ontology of conflict between identity and difference by considering both in relation to reason. Distinguishing between the formal and sensuous impulses, on one side, and the rational nature of man, on the other, he describes the formal impulse as proceeding from the power of reason, which has "the freedom to bring harmony into the diversity of [man's] manifestations [of form], and to affirm his Person among all his changes of Condition."[37] Reason's autonomy, however, is limited by the very form impulse serving its ends. For the sensuous drive, which "embraces the *whole extent* of man's finite being," at every moment of time "presses for reality of [its] existence" against being "suppressed" by the formal impulse, whose work it is to impart form to the objects of the senses so that "knowledge have content and action [*Handelns*] purpose."[38] Reason's freedom, then, is limited to knowledge and purposes determined by the formal impulse's narrowed construction of sensuous experience, which despite encompassing man's phenomenal existence can, at any single sensible moment in time, deliver to reason only "individual cases" on which basis it judges (acts) and makes laws (content) for all time.

Tying together all these parts of Schiller's argument here is what I find. "Where, then, *the form impulse rules*" (*Wo also der Formtrieb die Herrschaft führt*) sensuous existence, which is to say where sensuous existence is ruled by Kant's understanding, reason's "freedom to bring harmony into the diversity of [man's] manifestations," to "affirm [man's] Person among all his changes of Condition" as "a unity of ideas embracing the whole realm of phenomena," means that "the judgement of *all* minds . . . expressed through *our* own, the choice of *all* hearts . . . represented by *our* action" *is no more than the universalization of the particular.*[39] What, then, is this particular that itself rules in the form of a universal law? It is the particular of *our* own minds and *our* own action, in Schiller's time the particularity of the reason of the European Enlightenment, which expressed as the *universal* judgment of *all minds* and the *universal* choice of *all hearts* he reveals to be the particularity of *our* reason *passed off* as the universality of the *all*. Put another way, Schiller shows the Enlightenment's interest in a unity of ideas and a unified, self-same identity, to be achieved at the cost of submitting to its "universal laws" the diversity of different interests of a plurality of identities within and beyond the European context. Here is an example of the failings of Enlightenment reason as Schiller grasps them. In *Between the World and Me* Ta-Nehisi Coates recalls Saul Bellow's question, "'Who is the Tolstoy of the Zulus?'"[40] As it was for Schiller, for us it is a simple matter to find such evidence of how the particularity of the Western mind, or in Coates's case the white Western mind, is universalized to sustain reason's "unity" against its divided recognition of nonwhite, non-Western difference.

What is then decisive in his next two letters is Schiller's preoccupation with the central problem of his "Twelfth Letter," where he worked out that for Kant, as for the Enlightenment, man's moral identity is achieved at the sacrifice of the world's moral diversity. As I earlier indicated, this was to be expected from Schiller's warning that the "forms" our world takes are given to us by Kant's "all-dividing understanding." Functioning like the faculty of understanding, a ruling formal impulse *excludes* forms of life from those eligible for universalization just as the concepts of the understanding exclude particulars from its generalizations. Consequently, when at the moment of the French Revolution Schiller declared, "The moral possibility is wanting," he was not referring to the want of political agreement among all warring parties about which of their conflicting moral solutions should be adopted, nor to a maxim reason could affirm as if it were a universal law. To the contrary, he meant a *possible* moral solution *had not yet been conceived.* Hence his critique of the state for its woefully narrow moral response to the plight of the underclasses, of "whole classes of men" who had used but "one part of their potentialities" for moral thought, and of all "the rest" whose moral positions proved how "stunted" their moral thought had also become.[41] So resolving the contradiction between the formal and sensuous impulses or between identity and difference in their political as well as ontological forms, turns on the possibility of reason first becoming aware of as diverse a representation of forms of life as possible. Only after such an awareness of diversity could reason formulate a universal accommodating all moral possibilities.

This is why in his "Thirteenth Letter" Schiller insists on permitting the sensuous impulse to become "receptive," open to the world, by being "labile," readily open to variation, on multiplying its "facets" to enlarge the "[receptive] surface it presents to phenomena" so humanity has "so much more world"—so many more possibilities—to "apprehend."[42] And so the formal impulse will not reprise its subjugation of the senses vastly expanding their domain, and the senses' work of reception not displace form's new work of representing possibility, he sets ground rules for their reciprocal relation. As he added in his "Fourteenth Letter," man "is not to strive for form at the cost of reality," which is to say he must not direct his reason, as all warring parties in the French Revolution sought to do, to universalizing a form of morality not first based on a prior apprehension of the world's diverse moral possibilities. And man must not strive "for reality at the cost of form," meaning he should not regard the world's unmediated diversity of moral possibilities as taking precedent over reason's finding a moral form of life inclusive of all differences. Can we not see why Schiller would conclude man's grasp of these rules would equal a "complete intuition of his human nature," for they amount to an intuition supposing two towering achievements.[43] As his "Thirteenth Letter" makes clear, first, by "procuring for the receptive faculty the most manifold contacts with the world" man will become aware of the widest diversity of moral forms of life possible at a moment in time, and, his receptivity excluding none, "all the more potentialities does he develop" for giving form to the world. Second, having such new formative powers at its disposal, reason would develop the "power and depth" to universalize out of all those possibilities it apprehends nothing less than a moral position encompassing such moral diversity.[44]

Clearly, Schiller unambiguously distances himself from the Enlightenment *and* Kant, whose moral imperatives, rather than oriented toward the universal reconciliation of identity and difference, achieve universality at the categorical expense of difference. While his relation to Kant has been a matter of controversy, Schiller appears to settle the matter for us in the astonishing second footnote of his "Thirteenth Letter." In Kant's "transcendental method of philosophizing," he explains, "where everything depends on clearing form of content . . . free of all admixture with the contingent, one easily falls into thinking of material things as nothing but an obstacle, and of imagining that our sensuous nature, just because it happens to be a hindrance in this operation, must of necessity be in conflict with reason. Such a way of thinking is, it is true, wholly alien to the spirit of the Kantian system, *but it may very well be found in the letter of it.*"[45]

As Schiller finally proposes, if there were historical "cases" of man's having such an intuition of his capacity to universalize moral principles from his apprehension of *all* contemporaneous moral possibilities, "this twofold experience" would "awaken in him a new impulse"—a "play-drive"—directed to "*reconciling* becoming with absolute being and change with identity."[46] Reconciliation and its moral possibility consequently emerge as the central political as well as philosophical problem of Schiller's *Letters,* which were to lead his readers, whoever they may be in particular at whatever particular time they may live, to the primary source of an aesthetic education igniting the intuition awakening humanity's play impulse. Oriented to the reconciliation of identity and difference, humanity's play impulse would "solve that problem of politics in practice" by approaching it "through the problem of the aesthetic, because it is only through Beauty," Schiller declares in his "Second Letter," "that [humanity] makes [its] way to Freedom."[47]

Hence art, which throughout the modern period Schiller's work stands at the end of proliferated new aesthetic forms he believed collectively modeled the play impulse's creative capacity to teach reconciliation. He makes this point precisely in his "Twenty-Second Letter" by referring to developments in music, poetry, and sculpture showing the arts developing "a more universal form" (*mehr allgemeinen Charakter*) through which they "tend to become ever more like each other in their effect upon the mind [*auf das Gemüt*]."[48] The arts' effect upon the mind, their sheer proliferation of aesthetic forms teaching humanity its potential for receptivity and perceiving diverse forms of life, model the fullest potential of humanity itself. But this aesthetic achievement, this art no matter how perfected by its proliferation of aesthetic forms collectively modeling reconciliation, "can of itself decide nothing as regards either our insights or our convictions, thus leaving both our intellectual and our moral worth as yet entirely problematic. . . . [Art] is nevertheless the necessary pre-condition of our attaining to any insight or conviction at all."[49] Aesthetic education only provides reason with a "moral possibility," the possibility of reconciliation, which had been "wanting." Art's pedagogical work consists in showing the "infinitude of phenomena" is "subject to the unity of reason," which for Schiller here means it falls within the "purview," as he says, of reason's interests and influence.[50] Modeling the reciprocally capacious sensuous apprehension and formal perception of possibility, art, through its proliferation of aesthetic forms, becomes the *precondition* for morality by teaching reason the possibility of reconciling identity and difference.[51]

THREE FORMS OF THE RECONCILIATION IMAGE AND ITS POSSIBLE POLITICS

As certain of its conceptual features have appeared in outline in Schiller's *Letters*, it becomes possible to begin to imagine what I have called a democratic enlightenment, which will assume ever more developed forms when I shortly trace its evolutionary movement from Whitman through Adorno to film.

First there is Schiller's concept of reconciliation, of identity relinquishing its certainty to become inclusive of and receptive to difference in all the world's forms and the moral possibilities they represent. In the concluding chapter of *A Democratic Enlightenment* I will have reason to take up Schiller's interest in the imitative (mimetic) aspect of reconciliation through which identity becomes different in the image of difference, a process of "democratic becoming" for which Whitman and Adorno will offer more developed formulations in my earlier chapters.

Then there is Schiller's concept of aesthetic education, of the pedagogy of artworks modeling reconciliation, especially images of reconciliation teaching receptivity and other democratic lessons, such as imitation, which both Whitman's and Adorno's reconciliation images offer mature versions of.

Finally, there is Schiller's concept of the reconciliation image appearing in a universal art form, which anticipates the centrality of film to democratic enlightenment in ways also to be taken up in my concluding chapter as I describe it at the close of this introduction.

While these three concepts I have found in Schiller's work place us on the threshold of imagining a democratic enlightenment as it takes shape in Whitman, Adorno, and film, as her work bears on this possibility I would get ahead of myself if I did not first engage Gayatri Spivak's *An Aesthetic Education in the Era of Globalization*. Not only is she committed to "productively undoing another legacy of the European Enlightenment—the aesthetic," which is also the defining legacy of a democratic enlightenment. Her project's critical point of departure is based on what she describes "as sabotaging Schiller," whose thought is clearly central to my work for its resemblances and connections to the event of a democratic enlightenment I believe took on its first well-articulated form with Whitman.[52]

Despite our different relations to Schiller, Spivak's efforts to revise the West's relationship to the European Enlightenment by productively undoing, not discarding, its aesthetic, and my interest in democratic enlightenment share strong commitments—first to aesthetic education, though by sabotaging Schiller she vetoes my claim to valuable pedagogical resources I want to preserve for the benefit of a democratic enlightenment, and second to overcoming identity's construction of difference as otherness. So I want to "productively undo" her argument to enlarge her already expansive view of enlightenment by defending Schiller's aesthetics as a decisive virtual moment of transition to the event of a democratic enlightenment. Here I take seriously her invitation that since "other imaginations of the Enlightenment will generate other narratives[,] I believe my argument can, *mutatis mutandis*, work with them."[53]

"Only an aesthetic education," Spivak declares, "can continue to prepare us" for the threats posed by globalization, for the imposition of a digital monoculture ruled by capital, that is, having the power to render us deaf to the voices and insensible to the desires of diverse subaltern populations in the Western and non-Western worlds, gendered voices and desires preeminent among them. With the marginalization of the humanities and the creative social sciences resulting from the alignment of the neoliberal university with globalizing forces, intellectual resistance "at the top" to globalization has been made "peripheral," she argues, intensifying her turn to "the subaltern end" for the oppositional means to disrupt and break through the uniformity of capital's cyberculture. Yet, as there can be "no global formula" for an aesthetic education, for that would only substitute one monoculture for another, "what," she asks, "is the nature of this aesthetic education?"[54]

At its core is her commitment to reforming the "culture of the citizen" through "deep language learning," whose effect on the "training of the imagination" would enable the West, as it enabled her, "to imagine the predicament of diaspora, exile, refuge." Hearing, speaking, and reading subaltern languages and literatures aesthetically educates the linguistically deaf and mute Western world to the plight of the subaltern other, which is not reducible to an awareness of unmet material wants and needs. When she pledges to "deny resolutely that the manifest destiny of the United States is (to appear) to give asylum to the world," it is not the physical absence of subaltern voices with which Spivak is preoccupied. Rather than whether America is a refuge, it is a matter of "remembering that in subalternity also reasonable and rational hang out as a difference." No matter how all-inclusive of the subaltern it may be, America's generosity toward the other turns on whether it *recognizes the rationality of difference*, which the Enlightenment's parliamentary model of democracy rejects through republican institutions substituting the reason of some for the reason of the rest for whom only some are elected to speak. In a phrase resonating with Adorno's negative dialectic, she defines imagination as "'thinking absent things,'" absent cultures or rationalities internal to different ways of life.[55]

According to such formulations, it is clear Spivak does not attribute the West's identitarian domination of subaltern worlds to globalization per se, which is only the latest stage of a process ideologically driven by Eurocentric reason originating with the Enlightenment. This is why she so often speaks of the need for "epistemological change" or "epistemological revolution" or specifically of aesthetic education as "epistemological preparation" for transforming the West's apodictic rationalist orientation to subaltern rationalities. Her stress on linguistic diversity does not entail disowning the ideas of the Enlightenment, however. As the pillar of aesthetic education's productive undoing, linguistic diversity enables the Enlightenment's other to "learn to use the European Enlightenment from below," to draw upon its own native historical and regional resources for the purpose of "cohabiting with, resisting, and accommodating what comes from the Enlightenment."[56]

Ultimately what is decisive for Spivak is why subaltern languages and their literatures possess the epistemological power to politically contest the transcendental status of Western reason and the globalizing authority of the nation-state buttressed by Western reason's claims to truth. Only those who hear, read, and speak subaltern languages can grasp how the West's insistence on its own languages as the world's lingua francas place subaltern populations in "double binds," which require they respond to contradictory demands forcing them to speak, think, and act in languages canceling out their own tongues' articulations of their own forms of life.

It is thus a very poignant moment in her book when an exasperated Spivak laments seeming "never to be heard"—as a member of a postcolonial majority—whenever she is constrained to respond in English to the same questions repeatedly asked of her. Here Spivak herself serves as an eloquent example of the way linguistic diversity illuminates the double bind in which Enlightenment rationality places subaltern populations. For by answering in English she loses contact with a world of vernacular meaning that would enable her to satisfactorily answer questions put to her, while to answer in her native tongue condemns her to remain the inscrutable other to Western audiences. Each such example of the double bind she analyzes differently illustrates what she understands to be aesthetic education's lesson. Namely, how linguistic diversity fosters "the work of displacing belief onto the terrain of the imagination," permitting the subaltern other to reimagine the rationality of its own form of life as it becomes aware of the linguistic constraint of tacitly affirming the transcendentalization of Western reason when speaking in a hegemonic tongue.[57]

Now for my purposes what is relevant is how Spivak's linguistic praxis leads through Kant to our conflicting estimates of Schiller's contribution to aesthetic education. As the double bind I cited shows, by highlighting the divided rationalities forming double binds, linguistic diversity incites the imagination to redistribute reason along a horizontal axis inclusive of subaltern rationalities *and* rationalities of hegemonic geographical contexts. With this move the imagination contests the transcendentalization of the latter to make it the epistemic equal of the former. This reterritorialization of reason, Spivak persuasively argues, is first suggested by Kant's "Toward a Perpetual Peace," which is "a source-narrative of 'European' access to a 'world'" revealing the double bind in which the world is placed by the European Enlightenment. Quoting Kant, "The spirit of commerce [*Handelsgeist*] sooner or later takes hold of every people, and it cannot exist side by side with war. And of all the powers (or means) at the disposal of the power of the states, financial power [*Geldmacht*] can probably be relied on most. Thus states find themselves compelled to promote the noble cause of peace, *though not exactly from the mainspring* [*Triebfeder*] *of morality*."[58]

Spivak goes on to argue that his "text signals its undoing and [geographical] re-location."[59] Kant, that is, intimates that perpetual peace rests on a moral position questioning its own rationality—the nonviolence of the peace secured by commerce falls short as an "ethical marker of a just society," such as economic equality.[60] Hence Kant recognizes that his claim, "reason has only a single united interest," implicates the world in the double bind of affirming commerce and peace at the cost of justice, or justice at the cost of commerce and nonviolence.[61] Yet, she adds, Kant does not try to evade the double bind "Perpetual Peace" illuminates. According to Spivak's argument, Kant acknowledges the divided interests of a divided reason entailed by the double bind, but he does so by placing under the category of an "intended mistake" or "as if" assumption his fundamental claim to the contrary that reason possesses a single united interest. What is decisive here is that, by acknowledging the double bind through a cautionary reflection on the interest of reason, in Spivak's view Kant emerges as "the best of the European Enlightenment, which recognizes the limits of its powers" of reason.[62]

Against the background of her framing of Kant, Spivak's Schiller emerges as a Kantian more loyal than Kant himself to reason having a single unified interest. While like Kant he thus becomes implicated in the double bind, unlike Kant his loyalty to an uncompromised unity of reason compels him to deny his implication. Bent on avoiding the unavoidable double bind of extending a unified Enlightenment reason to a plurality of rationalities, Schiller adopts "play" to achieve "a series of balances" between the single united interest of reason and the multiple interests of competing claims to reason. His unreflective allegiance to reason is embodied in the thought of the "Self as undivided, as something which can"—citing Schiller's "Eleventh Letter"—"'annul time,' or 'subjugate the manifold variety of the World to [its own] unity.'"[63] Spivak concludes that Kant and Schiller "show us two different ways of living in the double bind," with Kant forthcoming about the limits of Enlightenment waiting upon an objectively established single interest of reason, and Schiller seeking to defend such a unified interest by looking to the "'play drive'" and "art as a balancing act that will save society."

Siding with Kant of the "intended mistake" and the "as if" for broadening Enlightenment to include recognition of plural claims to reason, especially those of subaltern populations, Spivak's disavowal (or "sabotage") of Schiller for avoiding the unavoidable double bind in which she implicates him means he narrows Enlightenment to European reason. Schiller's aesthetics too are thus disavowed, as would be the possibility of a democratic enlightenment for its connections to his ideas of the artwork, aesthetic education, and reconciliation. If her critique of Schiller were correct, that is.

There is no doubt Spivak's conception of aesthetic education as linguistic diversity and deep language learning, the illumination of the otherness of subaltern rationalities through deconstructions of the double bind, and Kantian insight into the divided interests of an ungrounded unity of reason all add up to a singular aesthetic pedagogy. But there is also no doubt Schiller is innocent of the critique entailed by the invidious distinction she draws between him and Kant. I want to briefly summarize certain obvious conclusions from my discussion of Schiller's *Letters* to defend his theory of aesthetic education against Spivak's critique. I do this to secure the connection between Schiller's aesthetics and a democratic enlightenment, and to suggest how her concept of aesthetic education would derive strength from an *alliance* with his idea of aesthetic education and those influenced by it, such as my own. Is that not what Spivak means by "working with other imaginations of the Enlightenment and their narratives"?

To begin with, rather than affirming, in Spivak's words, "the Self as undivided," which is actually the concept of self Schiller *problematizes* in his "Eleventh Letter," as the eleventh and the letters following it I have also considered clearly show, Schiller's self is deeply divided within itself between the claims of reason and the claims of the senses. Moreover, it would again underappreciate his formulation of the self if its internal divisions were reduced to a mind-body dualism, as does Spivak at one point.[64] For in Schiller's view the senses do not merely convey impressions of the world, but by doing so are equal to nothing less than world itself and inclusive of all its variations in time. Hence, when in his "Fourth Letter" Schiller begins to frame his forthcoming thesis by arguing that in "the complete *anthropological* view . . . living feeling too has *a voice*," he is alluding to the diversity of peoples and their forms of rationality who speak to reason and to whom reason must listen and, upon hearing, must include. While Schiller *acknowledges* reason "does indeed *demand* unity," he insists to the contrary that to accede to its demand for law that "obtains unconditionally" is a "one-sided moral point of view" productive of a "defective education if the moral character is able to assert itself only by sacrificing the natural," only by sacrificing, repressing, subjugating the world of voices of reason held to lie outside of Reason, in other words. Regarding the self, then, he understands its faculty of reason to be divided between a loyalty to legislating unconditional universal laws *and* the "multiplicity" that "Nature demands" of reason because of its unavoidable implication in a sensuously inescapable world of becoming.[65]

If Schiller's formulation of a divided self were not evidence enough of his recognition of reason's divided interests, we can further recall his discussion of the state, which, being divided in a way precisely analogous to reason, highlights the latter's divided interests by arguing their parallel with the state's own. When he immediately follows his critique of the unity of reason by adding, "A political constitution will still be very imperfect if it is able to achieve *unity* only by suppressing *variety*," he impugns the reason of state through its analogy with reason itself.[66] Like reason itself the reason of state is divided between the interests of its own claims to moral law and the diverse and divergent moral claims of its own body—of its peoples. So prior to Spivak—perhaps even prior to Kant, as "Toward a Perpetual Peace" and Schiller's *Letters* were both published in 1795—Schiller brings reason's double bind into the open by giving it a body, a voice, and a face belonging to a diversity of different bodies, different voices, and different faces.

But for Schiller it is not enough to expose the double bind and its exclusions of subaltern rationalities, as is the purpose of aesthetic education for Spivak. Yet neither is he content to *balance* the divided interests of reason and state in order that the rationality of the politically powerful not always prevail over the rationality of its other. To Schiller aesthetic education has as its goal "reconciliation," which he thinks of as a special form of equality between unity and diversity, identity and difference, where the rationality of the powerful or of institutions representing the powerful is not privileged by constructing the rationalities of diverse differences as subaltern otherness. While Schiller's idea of aesthetic education privileged the arts as the vehicle best able to model and teach reconciliation, however, beyond theorizing the evolution of aesthetic form he failed to offer examples of artworks playing such a pedagogical role, a gap in his thought leaving this critical work to those who come after. With Schiller, we have the *concept* of reconciliation and of its visual image—but no reconciliation image itself.

FIRST FORM OF THE RECONCILIATION IMAGE: WHITMAN

With Schiller's theory of aesthetic education we are thus delivered to the moment a democratic enlightenment is revealed as a possibility in the long course of its development, when against the backdrop of a series of resemblances and connections to the work of Voltaire and especially Diderot and Schiller the reconciliation image appears in its first well-articulated form in the prose and poetry of Walt Whitman. Since this moment of historical possibility is the event *A Democratic Enlightenment* opens with, I can now turn to my chapter-by-chapter organization of its core ideas and arguments. To begin with, in my first two chapters I focus on how Whitman's poetry assembles the reconciliation image I subsequently take up again in Adorno's aesthetic theory, where it assumes the mature form that will eventually appear in film. As the vehicle of an aesthetic education visualizing a possible politics of reconciliation, the reconciliation image is the praxis of a democratic enlightenment, hence the best evidence for the emergence of its possibility. Whitman's great essay of 1871, *Democratic Vistas*, is the key text that launches my opening arguments.

While compared to the volume of scholarship on his poetry *Democratic Vistas* has earned less attention, among studies of special importance are two offering true measures of its indispensable contribution to understanding

Whitman. Betsy Erkkila's *Whitman: The Political Poet* and George Kateb's *The Inner Ocean: Individualism and Democratic Culture* are notable for approaches to Whitman's essay that in different ways are both groundbreaking. Erkkila finds Whitman's essay provided "his most sustained and eloquent meditation on the problems and contradictions of democracy in America," while Kateb estimates its greatness lies in providing the most powerful expression of the meaning of democratic culture, which he theorizes as "democratic individuality."[67]

My own interest in chapter 1, "*Democratic Vistas*: Democratic Enlightenment and Reconciliation," is to begin to flesh out in Whitman's prose and poetry the better articulated forms of the ideas their counterparts in Diderot's and Schiller's work have foregrounded. Namely, the purpose of a democratic enlightenment and the work accomplished through an aesthetic education whose vehicle, in the following chapter, will then become the reconciliation image, the visual image charged with teaching reconciliation as democracy's highest ideal. To accomplish all this in my first chapter I illuminate a map I believe Whitman sketched in *Democratic Vistas* instructing us on how to read his poetry. My opening chapter is thus divided between discussions of *Democratic Vistas* and *Leaves of Grass*.

Democratic Vistas is the site of Whitman's intellectual struggle with the issue of what America yet lacks following the prior achievements of its founding and economic development since. I identify the topics he examines and the questions he struggles with most and the unusual structural logic of his essay he crafts to discover their answers, and I explore how his questions and their answers relate democracy in America in the most radical way possible to the European past from which it emerged and with which, Whitman insists, it must decisively break. I also consider how his vision of what America lacks—a culture of democratic enlightenment revolving around an aesthetic education whose mission is to teach the ideal of reconciliation—situates its democracy in relation to future world history to become America's most important democratic vista.

Only aesthetic education's lesson of reconciliation can establish the democratic conditions for overcoming the construction of difference as otherness, which is to be democratic America's world-historical achievement. Thriving in the liberal private sphere beneath the threshold of politics and the law, violence toward difference lies beyond political remediation through formal equality and rights, which explains Whitman's preoccupation with a culture of democratic enlightenment and his relative inattention to democratic politics.

As politics' surrogate, though, art teaches democratic lessons, making art Whitman's politics by other means. America's democratic prospects rest on the creation of an indigenous art through which America would lead globally as the democratic lesson of reconciliation its art taught is replicated within and beyond American and Eurocentric contexts and wherever there are subaltern others. Such an art form would be a universal art form, its lesson of reconciliation the universal meaning of democracy itself.

By leading us to reconciliation as the ideal defining democracy, in *Democratic Vistas* Whitman thus guides us to the question he intends his poetry to answer: What is the ideal of the reconciliation of identity and difference? As my first chapter, halfway through, transitions from *Democratic Vistas* to Whitman's poetry, three dimensions of this ideal will begin to unfold through the medium of words. If it seems odd to make the point that his ideal of reconciliation takes shape through words as my interpretive work moves from *Democratic Vistas* to Whitman's verse, it is because it does so only in the first instance, as I explained and as I shall show when in my second chapter I document the transformation of this ideal as it appears in verse into the aesthetic form of visual images. In this first chapter my task is preparatory, to lay the groundwork for this transformation by showing how Whitman constructs his verse self-reflexively to call attention to certain limits of poetic language, though *also of language in general* since poetry in Whitman's view, regardless of its limitations, enjoys an epistemic privilege over all other forms of language. Various poems of his I examine establish these limits clearly, which are the epistemic premises for each of the three dimensions of his ideal of reconciliation I described in the first part of this introduction.

As I proposed there, poetic language's incapacity to fathom and formulate truth, essences, reality is paradoxically an epistemic limit of language empowering democratic society in several ways. Essences being inaccessible to poetry, poetry aligns democracy with appearances, though in actuality with differences, since in the absence of knowledge of essences all appearances lack commonalities and thus appear to be different. At the same time, unable to know and express truths, poetry offers democracy no apodictic basis on which it can construct difference as otherness in order to marginalize, discriminate against, exclude, or exterminate differences. Hence democratic society's "all-inclusiveness of differences," the first dimension of the ideal of reconciliation and the first democratic lesson poetry's aesthetic education teaches.

Yet in addition to mounting a barrier to violence toward difference, poetry's self-reflexive illumination of language's epistemic limits also creates the foundation for reconciliation's second dimension: democracy's "receptivity to differences." As long as differences, however they appear, are unfathomable, they are mysterious, and for Whitman mystery is one of the most inspiring and irresistible sources of our interest in, attraction, openness, responsiveness, in a word, *receptivity to* the world from which poetry's creativity flows. Hence democracy is not simply all-inclusive of differences for having no access to truths on the basis of which difference could be constructed as otherness. Rather, as Whitman's poetry also teaches, democratic peoples ought to find mystery to be a defining quality of differences, of persons, nature, and things, so that their fathomlessness beyond how they differently appear encourages our own receptivity toward them as it encourages poetry's. Which brings me to the final dimension of the ideal of reconciliation. Teaching the all-inclusiveness of and receptivity to differences, poetry then models the imitation of differences, so that through mimetic behavior the nation, its groups and individuals become different in the images of differences in which poetry's first two lessons immerse them. All three dimensions of the ideal of reconciliation, and the democratic lessons poetry teaches, model what I call "democratic becoming," which I believe sums up Whitman's conception of how aesthetic education is democratic education.

Before describing my second chapter, I want to note a possible critique of what I propose is Whitman's ideal of reconciliation I believe I am innocent of in this first chapter. As Erkkila correctly argues, when stressing both "'reconciliation'" and the "'achievement of reconciliation'" in Whitman's poetry, as I do, one should not give "insufficient attention to the fundamental *agon*—the dynamic tension between self and other, *I* and *you*—that shapes the drama of democratic identity in *Leaves of Grass*. . . . In the poems of *Leaves of Grass* as in *Democratic Vistas*, this drama of democratic identity remains more agonistic and open ended: a *democratic vista* that may—or may not—be achieved in history."[68] From the outset of my introduction I have been in agreement with Erkkila's warning on both counts. On the one hand, I have framed the ideal of reconciliation along with a democratic enlightenment as *possible* democratic achievements, though I also believe Whitman thought they might come to pass if certain cultural conditions were present, aesthetic education paramount among them. On the other hand, my theoretical interest is in Whitman's ideal of the reconciliation between identity and *difference*. In infinite ways different from how identities are socially constructed, differences are often at odds with identity, such that when identity imitates such differences it interiorizes its external agonistic struggles with difference to become different and discontinuous with itself. In these agonistic ways Whitman is reconciled with difference when he "*resist[s]* any thing better than [his] own diversity" or when he confesses to being at odds with himself by asking, "Do I contradict myself? Very well then I contradict myself, (I am large, I contain multitudes.)," which as I will show in my first chapter are produced by his imitative relationship to the world of differences that populate it—*even to the point of reconciling the agonistic struggle between his life and his death.*[69]

Earlier I engaged an argument we can now see resembles and has a connection to Whitman's. Schiller offers an agonistic image of a self internally divided between reason and sensuousness, the voice of the individual and the diversity of the world's voices, the timelessness of eternity and the temporalities of becoming, all contradictions finding reconciliation in the reconciliation of identity and difference.

In Jean-François Lyotard I find the ally the argument I next propose will need. What he centrally stresses in *Discourse, Figure* applies directly to my second chapter, "Whitman's Discovery: Aesthetic Education through the Visual Image." From the start of his work Lyotard goes on the offensive, knowing those who prize the word above all other aesthetic tools will find offensive his thought of their meaning ultimately being sublimated in the visual image lying "deep within discourse." As Lyotard declares, "This book protests: the given is not a text, it possesses an inherent thickness, or rather a difference, which is not to be read, but rather seen." To be sure, Lyotard does not mean that to grasp textual signification language must be left behind, for the word is where the visual, "the eye lodged at its core," is to be found. Since with Lyotard we must thus begin with language, I began with Whitman's prose and poetry in my first chapter, though their meanings, I argue, finally reside in how Whitman's verse, what he writes to be read, *becomes something to be seen.* What Whitman's words make seen is his ideal of reconciliation, and they do so in a visual form irreducible to language's pursuit of truth from which he wants to free it. To impute a double meaning to one of Lyotard's terms, it is through Whitman's creation of a "*screen* of appearances" that his verse's visual images of reconciliation will find a new form beyond poetry in film. The meaning of Whitman's words lie in their visuality.[70]

Having begun with Whitman's words, then, in chapter 2 I briefly recall my first chapter's discussion of his "Song of the Rolling Earth" to next show how his verse creates visual images of reconciliation to convey its complex meanings. Here my attention to his verse's interest in the epistemological limits of language moves beyond its work of narrowing his focus to appearances to showing how appearances find their natural and far more expansive home in his poetry's visual images. Whitman's verse abundantly parades visual images he creates in various poetic forms. He fashions self-standing visual images independent of the language from which they originated; he authors visual images that continue to rely for their meanings to some extent on language in order to teach us how to see; and finally he creates visual images that simply privilege vision outright, for the eye often appears to Whitman to be intrinsically democratic, taking in and attracted to more than its seer intended it to see, whose image the eye mimetically records on the interior of its lens.

Moreover, since language's inability to perceive essence, reality, and truth beyond what we can see not only shifts poetry's allegiance from essence to appearance, as I argued in my initial chapter, but from the invisible to the visible, his verse engenders multiple orientations to visual images of appearances. In the first instance an orientation to the opacity of the visible for offering no apodictic grounds for excluding the appearance of any, who in the absence of any perceived commonality must all visibly appear different. In the second instance an orientation to the unknown, to the mystery and enchantment the unseen attaches to the seen, which encourages receptivity to the fathomless visual appearance of difference. And finally the visible orients us to the imitation of differences to whose appearances we have become open and receptive.

Hence my first chapter's discussions of the three dimensions of reconciliation all give way in chapter 2 to new formulations of the all-inclusive, receptivity, and imitative *visual images*, each in this series a visual image of one of reconciliation's three democratic relations to the appearance of difference. All three visual images are moreover seen to produce visual effects, or more precisely "democratic effects" for teaching "democratic lessons" in a visual form, the lessons of all-inclusiveness, receptivity, and the imitation of differences. Together these effects are productive of a final visual image of reconciliation, a final democratic effect and democratic lesson expressing the rationality of the whole series of images tracing the process of becoming different in the image of difference and reconciliation as a time arrived and a time yet to come.

The reconciliation image is thus a visual image of democratic becoming whose democratic achievements are legion. All-inclusiveness and receptivity to difference supplant the mere tolerance of being indifferent to difference, which is a precarious political attitude of objectivity toward difference easily swayed toward intolerance. In addition, becoming, as Whitman puts it, "more or less" different in the image of difference through imitation, opposes the imitation of difference contributing to the formation of a mass. Whitman's becoming exemplifies what Deleuze means by "repetition as difference."[71] And the apotheosis of this series of visual images, identity becoming reconciled with difference through its all-inclusiveness, receptivity, and imitation of difference, overcomes the construction of difference as otherness. The reconciliation image thus visualizes the political possibility of democracy's barrier to evil, reconciliation as a democratic enlightenment's and democracy's possible politics.

When completed, this second chapter shows Whitman's poetry unfolding through an aesthetic form that is first and foremost political for its visual images' democratic pedagogy of reconciliation. But it is also the *future* aesthetic form the visual images of Whitman's verse anticipate that is among the most important and compelling aspects of the relation between his poetry's aesthetics and politics and certainly in my argument its most controversial. For as I show when I take up Whitman's poem "Eidolons," it is the *mobility* of his poetry's visual images that governs how their aesthetic form unfolds as continuously changing visual images of appearances and their differences. In a word, it is the "duration" of Whitman's visual images that prefigures the appearance of the reconciliation image in film. While I can make this argument through Whitman's work alone, I will also rely on a collection of theoretical voices to articulate it in more contemporary terms, notably Bergson and Deleuze, though also Barthes, Bazin, Foucault, Krog, Nietzsche, Plato, Schiller, and Lyotard to a further extent.

SECOND FORM OF THE RECONCILIATION IMAGE: ADORNO

Before going any further the question I should not postpone is whether Whitman's project of a democratic enlightenment can meet the objections raised by Horkheimer and Adorno's *Dialectic of Enlightenment*. There we find a critique of reason that, according to how this work has been interpreted by Jürgen Habermas, means there could be no form of reason able to provide the philosophical resources for the project of enlightenment I argue Whitman envisions. But such a critique of the totality of reason as Habermas attributes to Horkheimer and Adorno holds only if we allow ourselves to be overwhelmed by *Dialectic of Enlightenment*'s theoretical power, which was overdetermined by the historical context of the Holocaust at the time it was written. By pursuing a reading of this work sensitive to its contextual determinants, against Habermas I locate an alternative concept of reason stirring within the theoretical interstices of their critique of reason waiting to be discovered, one they abandoned and left in a fledgling state until years afterward Adorno again began to develop it in his final book, *Aesthetic Theory*. So forceful was their critique of reason in *Dialectic of Enlightenment*, in other words, I believe it all but buried an alternative concept of reason it continues to obscure if their critique's overdetermined theoretical power is permitted to conceal its possibility.

In "First Bridge: *Thinking with* Adorno *against* Adorno" my interest is thus straightforward, though as controversial as my argument that Whitman wrote poetry to create visual images. It is to open the way to a reinterpretation of the concept of reason in *Dialectic of Enlightenment* to which earlier interpretations of that work have not been sensitive, perhaps due to the historical-contextual explanation I have suggested, so that in the two chapters following my "First Bridge" I can then flesh out and develop that concept of reason's more expansive "aesthetic" form in *Aesthetic Theory*. The interpretive work I am proposing is therefore twofold. In *Dialectic of Enlightenment* there is an *alternative* concept of reason to the form of enlightenment rationality on which its critique is thought to be focused without qualification. After I first retrieve it, I then discover it has undergone a further, though as yet incompletely articulated development in *Aesthetic Theory* that I am able to flesh out and further develop. While I offer evidence for the first part of this argument in my "First Bridge," where I retrieve from *Dialectic of Enlightenment* theoretical resources for its authors' alternative concept of reason, later named "aesthetic rationality" by Adorno in *Aesthetic Theory*, the validity of this alternative concept depends upon the success of my efforts to then flesh out and further develop it beyond the form it takes in Adorno's final work. I carry out this second task in chapters 3, "Aesthetic Reason and Reflexivity, Twin Economies and Democratic Effects," and 4, "Aesthetic Analogues: Art and Film," to which my "First Bridge" leads.

Here is what turns on my approach in chapters 3 and 4 to the concept of aesthetic rationality in Adorno's last, great work. By fleshing out and further developing his concept of aesthetic reason in *Aesthetic Theory*, I secure the rational core of his concept of reconciliation that in several of its dimensions Whitman's own ideal of reconciliation resembles. So rather than allowing the historically overdetermined critique of reason in *Dialectic of Enlightenment* to deprive Whitman's project of democratic enlightenment of a philosophical basis in reason, after I show that work concealed an alternative concept of reason pointing toward an alliance with Whitman I turn to *Aesthetic Theory* to flesh out and further develop both that concept of reason and its counterpart concept of reconciliation. It is thus in this concept of aesthetic reason I find the theoretical resources for an image of reconciliation that emerges as Adorno's more evolved form of Whitman's reconciliation image. Whitman and Adorno's shared image of reconciliation thus solidifies their alliance supporting the former's project of democratic enlightenment—and also the "positive concept of enlightenment" Horkheimer and Adorno had alluded to but, along with aesthetic reason, abandoned and left undeveloped in *Dialectic of Enlightenment*. It will be Adorno's more evolved form of the reconciliation image, which in part he shares with Whitman, that I eventually find in film.

Finally, though, there is the question of Horkheimer and Adorno's critique of the culture industry and, for my purposes, especially Adorno's critique of film's contribution to the culture industry's creation of a society whose rationality is hostile to difference and to reconciliation as he and Whitman understand it. But if I can show Adorno's *Aesthetic Theory* is home to a concept of aesthetic reason that serves as the philosophical basis for a project of democratic enlightenment and its reconciliation image in film, Adorno is not only aligned with Whitman. I have also found evidence of theoretical resources in Adorno's later thought running in a direction *opposite* the line of critical thought dominating his thinking throughout his work on enlightenment, the culture industry, and film.

Hence "*Thinking with* Adorno *against* Adorno," the title of my "First Bridge." But a reading of Adorno such as I propose there is finally of a whole only if I then find evidence in his *Aesthetic Theory* that a reconciliation image he had confined to modern art can eventually be found in film. So before discovering the reconciliation image in film, fleshing out and developing the concept of aesthetic reason on which his reconciliation image rests must be my preliminary undertaking in my third and fourth chapters. Here, then, is the order of these arguments in all: "First Bridge," retrieval of an alternative, fledgling concept of aesthetic reason; chapters 3 and 4, fleshing out and developing that concept of aesthetic reason as the foundation for the reconciliation image; final chapters, discovering the reconciliation image in film. Given their controversial nature, a final interpretive note of explanation for this "First Bridge" and its two following chapters may be useful.

It is not uncommon for theorists and philosophers to read thinkers against themselves. One telling illustration of this intellectual strategy is included in my second chapter, where I briefly take up Deleuze's reading of Plato, through which he shows how Plato can be understood as having *supported* a position in the *Sophist, Theatetus,* and *Timaeus* productive of a "model of difference in itself" that is also *contrary* to arguments Plato made in his earlier dialogues.[72] The upshot of this is that Deleuze's juxtaposition of Plato's earlier opposition to and later support for his own concept of difference in itself in *Difference and Repetition* proves Plato to be a stronger ally than opponent of Deleuze, as Plato is shown as having created theoretical space in his work for a position Deleuze develops that other of Plato's works do not allow for. Such a radical approach to Horkheimer and Adorno as I have proposed, which parallels the strategy of Deleuze's reading of Plato against himself, is thus not without precedents. In my "First Bridge" and third and fourth chapters, I attempt to overcome Horkheimer and Adorno's stress on the catastrophic consequences of enlightenment reason in their work through my efforts to retrieve and develop other theoretical resources from both their earlier and later work in support of Whitman's and their own enlightenment ideal of reconciliation.

While there are many differences between our projects, a second example of this interpretive approach is Krzysztof Ziarek's *The Force of Art*. It begins, as do I, by recognizing that Adorno (and, for Ziarek, Heidegger) launched a revision of aesthetic categories that, since it was "only intimated and not carried through by these thinkers," failed to realize the "transformative potential for art." "Taking Heidegger's and Adorno's insights as [his] point of departure," Ziarek completes a revision of aesthetic categories leading to a reconceptualization of power as "power-free relationality." Importantly, his new concept of power *also runs contrary* to Adorno, whose claim "The violence and power in art . . . happen *for the sake of* nonviolence" Ziarek replaces with the idea of the artwork as a "forcework"—"a force that is *no longer violent* . . . but rather releas[es] forces into reciprocal shaping and becoming" that transform our ideas of "what it means to work and act."[73] A highly original argument, Ziarek reads Adorno against himself to propose a reconstruction of power other of Adorno's works would not support.

THIRD FORM OF THE RECONCILIATION IMAGE: FILM

When I conclude chapter 4 by completing my work of fleshing out and developing Adorno's concept of aesthetic reason begun in chapter 3, to which my "First Bridge" led, I have conceptualized a second evolutionary form of the reconciliation image for which I have found Adorno's aesthetic theory to be the philosophical basis. Before discovering the reconciliation image in film in the concluding chapters of part III, however, since my interest throughout has been to theorize the reconciliation image as the pedagogical vehicle of aesthetic education and a democratic enlightenment, there is a third and final controversial argument I must make. By focusing on theorizing the reconciliation *image*, I make implicit in my argument from its outset what I make explicit in my "Second Bridge: The Reconciliation Image versus the Narrative Structure of Film." With the reconciliation image I am proposing an alternative to the practice of understanding the politics of film through interpretations confined to films' narrative structures. Too often the politics of film narratives are interpretively privileged to the neglect of the politics of the images of which film narratives consist. Or the politics of images are reduced to the politics of film narratives.

Viewed apart from their narratives, images very often challenge meanings and politics attributed to the film narrative in which they appear, as does the reconciliation image in film, as I intend to show in my concluding chapters. Yet I also recognize the film image owes its very existence to the narrative structure of film. So after beginning my "Second Bridge" by summarizing the two forms of the reconciliation image I have theorized to that point, I then argue it is necessary to account for the aesthetic and political work the reconciliation image performs *independently* of its film's narrative, though *also for the collaborative work* between film narrative and its reconciliation image. Here I want to show the reconciliation image is at odds with the film narrative to which it belongs and, at the same time, is continuous with that narrative. This approach, I believe, is able to appreciate how the reconciliation image in film represents a possible politics of reconciliation opposed to the politics of a film's narrative structure.

Of the theoretical approaches to this problem, my preference is to base an understanding of film images on Bergson's model of perception, which I believe best allows film images to be thought about in ways I have just described. For theoretical support I turn to Brian Massumi's remarkable *Parables for the Virtual*, which develops Bergson's theory of perception in a way very useful to this project. As for the value of my argument on the politics of the image versus the politics of the narrative structure of film, if I am able to show that images possess possible meanings and possible politics exceeding those of the narratives to which they belong, I can speak of the reconciliation image in film as Schiller, Whitman, and Adorno (if he is read *against* himself) spoke of art: as a form of aesthetic education illuminating the political possibility of reconciliation.

With my "Second Bridge" behind me, in chapters 5, "*The Help*: Entangled in a Becoming," and 6, "*Gentleman's Agreement*: Beyond Tolerance," I bring all of the preceding chapters to bear on the task of discovering the reconciliation image and its possible politics in film. I analyze two films both concerned with the plight of difference constructed as the other, *The Help* and *Gentleman's Agreement*, whose interests are in racism and anti-Semitism, respectively. While neither film sets out to narrate a historical course toward reconciliation, in both films the reconciliation image is nevertheless there, aesthetically constructing and pointing to a possible politics of reconciliation to which the narrative gives birth even as it also explicitly and loudly opposes its possibility.

Following these analyses, in chapter 7, "The Reconciliation Image in Film as Universal Art Form," I explore the possibility that the reconciliation image in film approaches a universal art form as Schiller may have allowed us to imagine it. For if it were to model the reconciliation of identity and difference on a universal cultural scale, as the pedagogical vehicle of a democratic enlightenment the reconciliation image in film would encourage the thought that it represents an enlightenment oriented to difference beyond Western geopolitical borders, thus beyond the horizons of the European Enlightenment. It is in this context that Schiller's concept of imitation first comes into play as a determinant in the genealogical history of the reconciliation image in film imagined as a universal art form.

In dark democratic times such idealism as *A Democratic Enlightenment* represents hardly seems justified. So I look to those whose times were as dark as ours but who, despite their damaged worlds, miraculously imagined possible enlightenments. Hence I look to Schiller, and to Whitman and Adorno in particular, and to the latter especially when we ask him to think against himself. We can hardly ask less of ourselves.

Part I

THE RECONCILIATION IMAGE IN WHITMAN

The paths to the house I seek to make,
But leave to those to come the house itself.
—Walt Whitman, "Thou Mother with
Thy Equal Brood"

Democratic Vistas

DEMOCRATIC ENLIGHTENMENT AND RECONCILIATION

Let us follow Whitman's paths. At least twelve topics can be distinguished in his essay *Democratic Vistas*, all of which he brings to bear on three questions he struggles with most:[1] What constitutes the uniqueness of democracy in America? What is required for American democracy to develop its unique potential and break with all past societies, their cultures, and the principles on which they are based? How would global history be altered if America's unique democratic potential were to reach fruition? To appreciate how Whitman's discussion of these twelve topics answers these three questions, special attention should be paid to a structural feature belonging to the literary style of *Democratic Vistas*. As each is introduced none of the topics are discussed fully before he quickly moves on to the next. Each is examined only in part before summarily yielding to another, introduced for the first time or being taken up again. By the time his essay concludes, all topics have been returned to often, while certain have been treated more often and more completely.

Reading Whitman with the structural logic of *Democratic Vistas* in mind highlights the discrete topics around which it revolves, foregrounds any among them that play a more pivotal role in his argument, and focuses my analysis of his essay on its three central questions. Deleuze must have read Whitman in this way, as is suggested by his description of Whitman's style as spontaneously fragmentary, each fragment representing one of its "various immigrant peoples (minorities)," one of the plurality of differences of which

America consists.[2] I want to complement Deleuze's insight by adding that Whitman writes in his fragmentary way to then bind together the fragments of which *Democratic Vistas* as well as his poetry and prose throughout is composed. For the poet, as Whitman explains in "Song of the Answerer," "is the joiner, he sees how [the parts] join."[3] Reading Whitman as a writer and binder of fragments representing differences immerses us in the American project in which he is utterly absorbed. He writes to advance this project, which he will foreground in *Democratic Vistas* after having first named it in verse: "Reconciliation, Word over all."[4]

INDIVIDUAL, MASS, EQUALITY

Whitman writes more than four thousand of his nearly twenty-six-thousand-word essay before signaling his intention to "proceed with my speculations, Vistas."[5] In this "prologue," as I want to describe it, to *Democratic Vistas*, the structure of his argument unfolds as he introduces all but two of the topics he engages in his essay.

Whitman begins with brief observations on America's democratic ambitions with which he celebrates its "democratic republican principle" and "theory of development and perfection by voluntary standards, and self-reliance."[6] By the democratic republican principle, Whitman understands "political liberty [and] equality," or equal rights recognizing individuals universally to be the *same*, whereas "development and perfection by voluntary standards, and self-reliance" refer to the individual's right to self-determination, *the right to be and to become different*. Equal rights as sameness and individual rights as difference are suggested by the plurality of meanings he associates with equality and personal development in his essay as a whole. On the side of equality, equal rights, and sameness he speaks of the "People" (or the "people"), the "mass, or lump character," the "leveler, the unyielding principle of the average," while on the side of personal development, individual rights to be and become different, he refers to "lessons of variety and freedom," a "large variety of character," "personalism" or "varied personalism," "individualism" or "individuality."

Wherever Whitman discusses these and analogous terms, he is returning to his first and second topics, the individual and the mass, which he maintains stand in contradiction and must be reconciled. He has in mind this problem of contradiction and reconciliation when in short order he joins his opening observations to the promise not to "gloss over the appalling dangers of universal suffrage," specifically the "people's crudeness, vice, caprices," about which, he reports, "I mainly write this essay."[7] Untutored popular suffrage threatens a range of democratic convictions, individuality—or difference—the most important.

To balance the undemocratic sensibility expressed by such a blunt circumspection about the mass, Whitman attacks remnants of feudalism he insists America has to "surmount . . . or else prove the most tremendous failure of time." Feudalism, the caste-based enemy of equality, is "grown not for America." Whitman's concern with lingering feudal institutions extends to the influence of ecclesiastic practices on democracy's private sphere, where mores insinuated by religious teachings contribute to the perpetuation of inequality, religious and social inequality surely, and he may well have had gender inequality in mind as well. He objects to religion's sustained impact on "education . . . social standards and literature" *despite* "feudalism . . . palpably retreating from political institutions" in America.[8] His anxiety about feudal influences on moral education and manners not only illustrates his allegiance to equality. It reveals that for him the achievement of equality anticipates *the question of what form the civic education of the people in a democratic society ought to take.* Whitman will allow all "democratic vistas," America's future prospects, to rest on the answer to this question.

ARTWORK OF THE FUTURE, NATIVITY, CULTURAL REVOLUTION, HEGEMONY

Once his prologue begins to wind its way through the individual, the mass, and the affirmation of equality represented by the American imperative to surmount feudalism, Whitman has positioned himself to introduce the topic around which will revolve further considerations of the former three as well as all subsequent topics. Achieving all of America's democratic vistas depends, without exception, on the unique, native development of its art, specifically literature, the highest form of art for Whitman. From the opening to closing paragraphs of *Democratic Vistas* he is insistent: democracy in America needs "literatures . . . expressing . . . democracy and the modern," a "New World literature," and "democratic literature of the future," and it "can never prove itself beyond cavil, until it founds and luxuriantly grows its own . . . native literary and artistic" forms. A new class of literati must emerge univocally committed to "displacing all that exists, or that has been produced anywhere in the past, under opposite influences" of inequality and the absence of rights. To begin anew so comprehensively requires America to refuse the examples of "all the best experience of humanity." Remarkably, Whitman proposes that although the "Old and New Testament, Homer, Eschylus, Plato, Juvenal, &c," and "the likes" of these and "what belongs to" and "has grown of" these, all have arrived at America's shores as "little ships," which by "miracles . . . have [been] buoy'd [and] convey'd . . . over long wastes, darkness, lethargy, ignorance," America nevertheless must choose, "appaling as that would be, to lose all, actual ships, this day fasten'd by wharf, or floating on wave, and see them, with all their cargoes, scuttled and sent to the bottom."[9]

With one of the most startling recommendations in the history of Western literature, Whitman proposes that by means of the work of art America must break with all past cultures as the prerequisite for forging a new beginning. Indeed, although *Democratic Vistas* (1871) is published nearly a century after America's founding, Whitman believes democracy in America to be as yet in its "embryo condition." Despite its epic political revolution and economic achievements, which he designates the first and second stages of democracy for having ushered in the "American programme" of "universal man" and the "material prosperity" on which universal well-being rests, Whitman's claim is that America either is not quite born or yet remains in the circumstances of its birth. His thought is to join the fourth of his topics, the American artwork of the future, to the fifth of his topics, the nativity of American democracy, which lies in the "present . . . the legitimate birth of the past." American democracy will be born through the birth of an archetypal American art, a literature on which everything American will be patterned and that stands not in the least on the shoulders of the Western and non-Western cultural pasts. Through the work to be performed by such a "great original literature" America will have an art that is "the justification and reliance (in some respects the sole reliance,) of American democracy." An art of justification and reliance, Whitman means, is one from which democracy truly would develop. For Whitman the nativity of democracy in America is a "long-continued nebular state," a founding continuous with the evolution of an American literary culture that will sponsor the future formation of a fully developed democracy.[10] Why democratic development depends on art is Whitman's sixth topic.

Literature, the American artwork of the future and bridge to the democratic future of America, is assigned this weighty historical burden, ultimately a world-historical burden, as I shall make clear, to remedy the considerable deficiencies of the first two stages of American development. Each stage appears to have made as much progress on its own terms as to Whitman seemed necessary to have proven the nature and extent of its contributions to American democratic life. If Whitman estimates the accomplishment of the American Revolution, the "planning and putting on record the political foundation rights of immense masses of people," to be of an "amplitude rivaling the operations of the physical cosmos," he adjusts the value of this political stage of development by reminding us "that the people of our land may all read and write, and may all possess the right to vote—and yet the main things may be entirely lacking." And the requisites for democracy neglected by America's political revolution are multiplied by its second, economic stage of revolution. Notwithstanding the benefits of economic prosperity, "uplifting the masses out of their sloughs," through its "materialistic developments" democracy remains, "so far, an almost complete failure in its social aspects, and in really grand religious, moral, literary, and esthetic results."[11]

Here Whitman imagines what I call "a democratic enlightenment," a cultural revolution in its effects exceeding those of America's political and economic revolutions. His insight is greatly advanced. The enlightenment of modern times was not a womb from which democracy in America could be born, as it was limited to moral-ethical (political) and instrumental (economic) rationalities arresting its development after engendering its first two stages. Without a cultural revolution revolving around aesthetics, "our modern civilization," Whitman decides gravely, "with all its improvements, is in vain, and we are on the road to a destiny, a status, equivalent, in its real world, to that of the fabled damned." In his own time, Whitman concedes, America may "dominate the world" economically. Far more important will be America's world-cultural hegemony, his seventh topic, "a nationality superior to any hither known" able "to dominate," to the point of being able to "even destroy"—as in *Democratic Vistas* it is evident Whitman himself is bent on destroying—what antidemocratic institutions earlier cultures had bequeathed, those "little ships" bearing influential cultural traditions that yet continue in America. He foresees America setting the democratic example to be replicated globally, for only "Soul has ever really, gloriously led, or ever can lead." And "this Soul—its other name, in these Vistas, is LITERATURE."[12] Democratic enlightenment is to proceed by way of "aesthetic education," to recall Schiller's term of art.

Whitman's conception of democratic enlightenment by means of aesthetic education will not elaborate normative ideals comparable to democratic visions before, during, and after him. Although his work exhibits an abiding concern for the poor and suffering, and he finds extreme material inequalities to be obscene, he proposes no theories of classless society or formal-legal princi-ples of justice or of government maximizing the welfare of its citizens. As I shall show, his vision is designed to realize the ideal of reconciliation on which democratic societies, their political and legal systems and political economies, and their theories together all falter. Democratic enlightenment, proceeding by way of art, will teach us to overcome the evil of violence toward difference.

POETRY, RECONCILIATION, IDENTITY

Whitman's readers will go afield if they interpret his bold analogy between literature and the soul as implying an overly generous conception of what counts as literature. While he does not explicitly omit literary genres, through-out *Democratic Vistas* he accords only a few revolutionary merit. He admits to his specialized interest in the bearing on democratic vistas of "imaginative literature," and in this category to his still narrower interest in "poetry, the stock of all." "Perhaps a new metaphysics," though "certainly a new Poetry," Whitman reports, will be "the only sure and worthy supports and expressions of the American democracy." He is never equivocal about the privileged role poetry is to play, his eighth topic. Democracy can "prove itself" only by origi-nating poems. And he holds that "some two or three really original American poets . . . mounting the horizon like planets, stars of the first magnitude . . . would give more . . . than all [America's] Constitutions, legislative and judi-cial ties, and all its hitherto political, warlike, or materialistic experiences."[13]

Improving on the pedagogical work of existing institutions, poetry is charged with teaching America's citizenry lessons about democracy and the modern. Whitman's vehicle for democratic enlightenment, aesthetic educa-tion, cannot be a conventional education in the arts and sciences. If it were the latter, it would conscript the great books and authors, the miraculous "little ships" we saw him discard for their affirmations of an earlier cultural age. Surely equality is one of poetry's modern democratic lessons, as Whit-man conveys by inviting the poet to replace the priest—the "priest departs . . . the poet of the modern is wanted"—alluding to his demand to displace the remnants of feudalism in America as yet supporting systems of fixed caste and class relations. Equality is paired with another broad democratic objec-tive with regard to which he calculates the effect of poetry on democracy to be greater than "popular superficial suffrage." By "comprehending and effus-ing for the men and women of the States, what is universal, native, common to all," which is to compose works that absorb and express the "central spirit and the idiosyncrasies" of the people, poetry addresses the "whole mass of American mentality, taste, belief."[14]

Through generalities of this sort abounding in *Democratic Vistas*, Whitman stresses that a democratic ethos lying inchoate in America waits for its fullest expression and development upon poets, "races of orbic bards . . . sweet democratic despots of the west!" Yet, though painted with such broad-brush strokes as his essay develops it, his project of a democratic enlightenment comes to rest on poetry's capacity to articulate a cultural and political image for the People—a "single image-making work for them"—able to seep more deeply into hearts and minds to form democratic personalities and characters.[15] With this he arrives at the pedagogical mission to be carried out by poetry, reconciling the contradiction between the individual and the mass, his ninth topic. For future reference, what I now want to make special note of is Whitman's allusion to this "single image-making work" for the People. A great work of art, of poetry, that makes one single image only, specifically the image of reconciliation on behalf of which poetry will put Americans to work. Hence the work of poetry and the image of reconciliation to which my work on Whitman must eventually lead.

Reconciliation, which he makes a point of explaining is "our task," is implicit throughout Whitman's exhortations on the individual and the mass. "The two are contradictory, but our task is to reconcile them." If there are times he seems to favor one, either the individual or the mass, over the other, his reflections on balance neutralize the apparent prejudice to restore the image of reconciliation he is intent on maintaining. Nearing the halfway mark of *Democratic Vistas*, for example, he asks what it is that civilization, in the sense of a whole or society as a whole, both rests upon and has as its object, an object, he emphasizes, to which "all bends"? While seeming to privilege the individual, his reply, that civilization rests on "rich, luxuriant, varied personalism [individualism, individuality]," circles back to the sentiment expressed in the first line of his essay: "Nature through the universe" and "New World politics" together illustrate the "greatest lessons," those of "variety and freedom."[16]

Civilization, nature coextensive with the universe, and New World (democratic) politics, Whitman is arguing, all seamlessly incorporate parts moving independently and contingently in relation to their wholes. All are models of reconciliation, analogies to reconciled parts and wholes Whitman supports with a reference to John Stuart Mill, whose "profound essay on Liberty in the future" proved to Whitman's satisfaction that in modernity what ennobles the relations of peoples to their nations, what produces the whole of a "truly grand nationality," as he calls it, is individualism, "a large variety of character" and the "full play for human nature to expand itself in numberless and even conflicting directions." Still, though variety is given in nature and human nature, individualism in democratic society must be perfected—an individual's particular variety of excellence must be developed. And to the extent that what is unique to individuals does achieve perfection, which it is for "literature, songs [poetry], esthetics" to ensure, it is then that the "aggregate," the mass, will receive its "deepest tinges" and "character."[17] In all these and similar ways Whitman consistently reconciles the advancements he values for the one with the progress he secures for the many.

Of course, as much as an end in itself that also doubles as a means to the end of collective progress, individualism and its perfection are pursued by Whitman to internally differentiate and break up the mass, to weaken normalizing pressures constraining individual development or the proliferation of "variety." Precisely because he believes communities will "rule themselves" if political education, "beginning with individuals and ending there again," trains each in practice to be the "separate and complete subject for freedom" each is in principle, he worries about the individual's loss of self in "countless masses of adjustments."[18] Perhaps from such arguments it would be fair to conclude that Whitman does not equally weight the democratic salience of the mass with that of the individual, and that his valorization of variety, personalism, and individuality unevenly weights "difference," our late modern term of art favoring one of two values only *apparently* being reconciled for the future benefit of American democratic development.

For all the importance Whitman attaches to the individual, however, difference finally is neither more nor less important than the mass. He chastises literature for its past neglect of "the People," which he surmises issued from some basic hostility of the literati toward "the rude rank spirit of the democracies." To the contrary, Whitman imagines a "rare . . . artist-mind" able to dissolve this antipathy. An aesthetic sensibility of a "cosmical" breadth "lit with the Infinite" would discover its counterparts in the "manifold and oceanic qualities" spanned by the people and in *"their vast, artistic contrasts of lights and shades."* All such aesthetic qualities and contrasts illuminate a variegated, individuated, capacious mass ignored by a contemporaneous literature packaged for the "mean flat average."[19]

Focusing on the aesthetic differentiation of the mass, Whitman ingeniously revises our concept of the people. Rather than uniform throughout, the People are as internally differentiated as the individuals of which it is composed, the "particulars and details magnificently moving in vast masses."[20] Problematically, however, individual differences are suppressed or as yet remain undeveloped—the situation to be corrected by poetry. For this reason it makes sense when Whitman argues that the individual and the mass "are contradictory" and that "our task is to reconcile them," and in the same breath that "*only* [*from the mass*] . . . comes the other, comes the chance of individualism."[21] Whether aesthetic education perfects individuality or the mass, in other words, it has the same object of enlightenment. For in Whitman's aesthetic view, individuals as "variety" and the mass as "contrasts of lights and shades" *are one and the same*. Either art develops individual differences, "variety," or perfects differences within the mass, "contrasts." Actually two terms for difference, variety and contrasts indicate that the contradiction between the individual and the mass is only historical, not essential. At bottom, *essentially* one and the same, the individual as variety and the mass as contrasts of lights and shades are already reconciled, a virtual reconciliation—a "democratic vista" in Whitman's terms—that waits upon the poet and poetry to forge it into a reality justifying—developing or perfecting—democracy in the future.

Since reconciliation between the individual and the mass is a virtual reality, does Whitman at some point not also tell us what specific form reconciliation takes once developed in democratic America? At first the answer to this question seems beyond our interpretive reach because he conceptualizes reconciliation at a high level of generalization wherever he speaks directly either of an aesthetically enlightened people or individual. We hear of the people's "perfect beauty, tenderness and pluck," its "moral conscience" and "moral conscientiousness," and the strengthening of its belief in democracy and humanity and of the faith of men and women in each other. Regarding the individual, he refers to the perfection of character, "a main requirement," a "true personality, develop'd, exercised proportionately in body, mind, and spirit," and the fruition of "freely branching and blossoming" individuality, "bearing golden fruit," and the like.[22] Whitman regularly treats us to such vague normative aspirations for democracy, but whose poignancy is not diminished by their dream-like quality.

Perhaps to be impatient with Whitman is unfair. After all, can he say more than this since democratic vistas, including reconciliation, all are future achievements? At one point he pauses to frankly confess this handicap: "Thus we presume to write, as it were, upon things that exist not, and travel by maps yet unmade, and a blank." Yet at another moment he more confidently ventures to "formulate beyond this present vagueness" and succeeds in visualizing the future shape of certain democratic vistas. One such instance is his model of native personality, a vivid and detailed picture of a healthy, athletic, "well-begotten selfhood" belonging to future Americans.[23] Similarly, our inquiry into how Whitman understands reconciliation is not disappointed. To the extent it must if the meaning of his concept is to be fleshed out, Whitman's image of reconciliation comes into focus sharply in the context of his discussion of identity, the tenth topic he introduces in *Democratic Vistas*.

Whitman admits to being haunted continually by "the fear of conflicting and irreconcilable interiors and the lack of a common skeleton, knitting all close." Over the "long period to come," he worries, "nothing is plainer than the need . . . of a fusion of the States into the only reliable identity, the moral and artistic one." To be sure, at one level Whitman's concern with a shared identity is in reference to the Civil War and its divisive aftermath. America's problem was to secure a shared identity that had long been precarious. At another level, for Whitman this crisis represents only the latest, most egregious example of social differences in contradiction and need of reconciliation. For as *Democratic Vistas* progresses, Whitman evinces a broader sociological interest in society's exclusions of minorities: "Of all dangers to a nation, as things exist in our day, there can be no greater one than having certain portions of the people set off from the rest by a line drawn—they not privileged as others, but degraded, humiliated, made of no account." Approaching the conclusion of his essay, Whitman further broadens this sociological interest by thinking of the predicament of difference as a historical problem America could overcome. "Long enough," he writes, "have the People been listening to poems in which common humanity, deferential, bends low, humiliated, acknowledging superiors. But America listens to no such poems. Erect, inflated, and fully self-esteeming be the chant; and then America will listen with pleased ears."[24]

From our contemporary perspective it is impossible to read such thoughts as mere concerns with legal rights and formal equality. Certain of Whitman's terms have an even larger resonance; degradation, humiliation, bending low, and inferiority are symptomatic of the treatment of difference as otherness persisting beneath the threshold of politics and the law. Healing these injuries and ending the exclusions and other forms of violence toward difference they entail *require more than the tolerance of difference legal rights and formal equality bestow*, which is to become increasingly important when my argument focuses more directly on Whitman's ideal of reconciliation in *Leaves of Grass*. What he requires is that identity not simply include and tolerate but *mirror the differences* it had excluded, so that his "fusion of the States" would reconstitute America as a new, nonnationalist, shared national identity reflecting both northern and southern differences excluded by the way each side self-identified before and after the Civil War. And Whitman requires that the "People," whom he most often capitalizes to indicate it sets itself apart as a distinct identity, revise its identity to well articulate the individual differences he associates with the contrasts internally differentiating the mass of the common people.

So, as we shall learn when I turn to his poetry, Whitman's many examples of an all-inclusive American identity are actually parallel descriptions of reconciliation whereby identity, in addition, becomes different by reconstituting itself through its inclusion of difference. Inclusive of difference as the path to becoming different itself, identity no longer forces difference down or outside as the contradiction it required to affirm its own integrity whenever it believed difference threatening to that integrity. For Whitman the reconciliation of contradictions between social differences through aesthetic education will assume the form of an *aesthetic re-creation of identity*. Educated by the poetic image, identity's inclusion of difference to become different in the image of difference is an act of re-creation abolishing otherness. *Moving identity and difference beyond contradiction*, Whitman achieves reconciliation—between North and South, the People and the people, the individual and the mass.

Reconciliation between identity and difference is the democratic vista looming largest in Whitman's imagination. It is the answer to the three questions I proposed he struggles with most. First, it is the possibility of reconciliation that for Whitman makes democracy in America unique. Second, not just equality and rights or wealth, the first two, inadequate stages of democratic revolution, but poetry is required for American democracy to develop its unique potential for reconciliation through which it will break with all past societies, their cultures, and principles on which they are based. And, third, global history will be altered through America's record of reconciliation, a recorded history of proving democracy "alone can bind, and ever seeks to bind, all nations, all men, of however various and distant lands, into a brotherhood, a family . . . making the races comrades, and fraternizing all."[25]

THE UNKNOWN, DEATH

If Whitman's democratic ideal of reconciliation is to leave no one out of the ensemble of individualities composing the mass, how is such all-inclusive openness to difference to be accomplished and then sustained? Haunted by

the specter of divided identity, we saw, Whitman appears not entirely confident America can reconcile its social contradictions. To thus ensure America
creates itself as an open society Whitman builds two metaphysical safeguards
into democratic culture: the ideas of the "unknown" and of "death," the eleventh and twelfth topics he introduces relatively late in *Democratic Vistas*, although both fall within the province of poetry and aesthetic education.

Democracy's openness to difference appears tightly connected to the idea
of the unknown, for as Whitman says, "As we have shown the New World including . . . the all-leveling aggregate of democracy, we show it also including
the all-varied, all-permitting, all-free theorem of individuality, and erecting
therefor a lofty and hitherto unoccupied framework or platform, broad enough
for *all* . . . realizing . . . finally, the personality of mortal life is most important
with reference to the immortal, the unknown, the spiritual, the only perma-
nently real, which as the ocean waits for and receives the rivers, waits for us
each and all."[26]

To decipher the relation between democracy and the unknown, I draw
attention to Whitman's contention that those on the American platform—
which includes *all*—realize the unknown confers highest importance on mortal life. Although Whitman's claim is somewhat obscure, it is clarified where
he appears troubled such a realization is jeopardized the more democracy is
influenced one-sidedly by modernity through scientism and the alliance between scientific progress and material prosperity, or "realism." To "confront
the growing excess and arrogance of realism," Whitman advises, the idea of
the unknown "must be brought forward with authority."[27]

Whitman's contention is that the idea of the unknown marks the limits
of scientific understanding and by extension the limits of the civilized life
scientific progress makes possible. Establishing limits to what can be known,
the unknown shields the plausibility of metaphysical, spiritual, and religious
ideas (he does not distinguish one from the other) important to mortal life
if it is to graduate to a stage of existence higher than the second, materialistic stage it has reached. With this argument Whitman advances his project for a democratic enlightenment. By circumscribing the limits of science
the unknown protects poetry, for the metaphysical, spiritual, and religious
ideas shielded by the unknown are sources of Whitman's poetic inspiration
and sources he finds for great poetry generally. Just as Whitman had argued
democracy depends on poetry, he argues now that the possibility of poetry
depends on poeticizing the unknown so that it retains a prominent stature in
the popular imagination. Thus he so tightly weds democracy to the unknown.

How does poetry's work of aesthetic education, its pedagogy of democratic reconciliation through the all-inclusiveness of difference, rest on poeticizing the unknown? I will work this out shortly, when I discuss the first of reconciliation's three dimensions in *Leaves of Grass*. For the moment I can offer only a clue to the relation between poetry and the unknown since Whitman says little about it in *Democratic Vistas*. What little he does say nevertheless reflects profoundly on the enlightenment of a democratic society. Poets, he announces, must emerge who "make great poems of death." Such poems will not eulogize death or offer consoling images of the afterlife. Death, which Whitman understands philosophically in materialist terms, is not the end of life, rather its continuation in other and unknown and unknowable forms. "Nothing," he declares, "ever is or can be lost, nor ever die, nor soul, nor matter."[28]

If it were to incorporate this view of death, poetry would be consistent with the "rational physical being of man, with the ensembles of time and space, and with this vast and multiform show." By speaking of death as change of form and not life's end, poetry, Whitman is saying, would imitate nature, *to include, as nature includes, all things in their endlessly changing forms*, and thus all time and all space through which all things in nature pass as they assume eternally, infinitely changing forms. To certify nature as the standard for poetry, in fact, Whitman makes nature and poetry into interchangeable terms. Just as poetry, after nature's example, must include *all*, nature, containing all things in all their forms throughout all time and space in which their evolution continues interminably, is "the only complete, actual poem."[29] Here, then, we find the explanation for what is perhaps Whitman's most remarkable theoretical move, his claim that the American democracy of the future could have no finer teacher than poetry. Modeled on poetry as poetry is modeled on nature, democracy in America must not be less than all-inclusive of the infinite variations to be found in both.

FOLLOWING WHITMAN'S PATHS

> Whatever would put God in a poem or system of philosophy as contending against some being or influence is also of no account. —Walt Whitman, "Preface" (1855), *Leaves of Grass*

In these first arguments I have pursued an interpretation of *Democratic Vistas* informed by the structural logic of Whitman's composition. Throughout my discussion I have tacked back and forth between his "prologue," as I have called it, and the text following, to trace the twelve topics he introduces by way of a spontaneous and fragmentary style requiring he then weave them together into a whole by returning often to each to elaborate its meaning, significance, and connections to others. Reconciliation emerges as this whole—which in subsequent chapters I will redescribe and theorize as an "open whole"—an idea brilliantly illuminated by the braided, evolutionary helix of the fragmentary form of Whitman's essay perhaps even more than by its literal features. So densely packed with ideas is Whitman's essay, however, it could be argued to the contrary that his interest is in ideals other than reconciliation whose centrality I have here underscored. Hypothetically, it might be objected, in particular, that if Whitman's interest is in the twelve topics I contend he selected on the basis of his commitment to a project of aesthetic education dedicated to teaching the ideal of reconciliation, how am I to account for his glaring omission of both poets and poetry exemplifying, even to some small extent, the future aesthetic on which he argues the future of a democratic enlightenment depends? Should Whitman the destroyer of the cultural past not also have shown examples the literature of the future should resemble as it takes form with respect to the topics, the constellation of ideas, ultimately the ideal of reconciliation from which democracy is to be born?

To explain Whitman's alleged omissions, I could recall his self-conscious explanation of the necessary vagueness with which any future projections of democratic vistas must be surrounded. My preferred explanation, however, and my own response to our hypothetical objection, is that Whitman omits no such exemplars and there is one with us through all his formulations of the standards for a future poetry its poets must meet if they are to sponsor democratic growth. The poetry of the "future" Whitman describes in *Democratic Vistas* must be his own. After all, why would he recommend standards for an art he has not himself met? So I defend the topics I have found him preoccupied with in *Democratic Vistas* by proposing they are the *paths* to Whitman's own poetry, the key unlocking the deepest purpose and meaning of *Leaves of Grass*. That purpose is to offer an aesthetic ideal of reconciliation, ultimately a solution to the problem of reconciliation by means of a democratic enlightenment spread through a poetry equipped to educate or, recalling Whitman's oft-used term, "perfect" democracy by "erecting therefor a lofty and hitherto unoccupied framework or platform, broad enough for *all*."

Taking the paths to the poetry of *Leaves of Grass* to which Whitman leads us in *Democratic Vistas*, in the remainder of this opening chapter I will argue Whitman's ideal of reconciliation consists of three dimensions or principles. The first of these, the "all-inclusiveness of differences," *almost* seemed in *Democratic Vistas* to be the very meaning of reconciliation itself. If democratic society were taught to tolerate difference just as it appears, aesthetic education would foster an all-inclusiveness of differences that would become democracy's barrier to the evil of constructing, marginalizing, excluding, discriminating against, and exterminating an other. Reconciliation must be even more than all-inclusiveness for Whitman, however, if it is to deeply root democratic life. Once Whitman frames reconciliation as the all-inclusiveness of differences, he designs poetry to teach democratic peoples to become not merely tolerant of those who are different by extending constitutional protections and guarantees. They are, second, to become *receptive* to difference, welcoming of its inclusion in their own lives because difference represents an image of how their own lives could be different. Reconciliation would then entail a relation among individuals where they can, third and finally, actually become different themselves by *imitating* the differences around them through a mimetic relationship to difference.

ALL-INCLUSIVENESS OF DIFFERENCES: RECONCILIATION'S FIRST DIMENSION

> This is the meal equally set, this is the meat for natural hunger,
> It is for the wicked just the same as the righteous,
>   I make appointments with all,
> I will not have a single person slighted or left away.
>   —Walt Whitman, *Song of Myself*

If Whitman believed his own art discharged the cultural-political tasks of democratic enlightenment he assigned to poets, and that it met the standards to which he held poetry, he surely would have had confidence in the powers of language itself and in his ability to use language. Yet when he regards language, it may seem less than a potent media through which poetry can achieve his aesthetic ends. Of the verse contained in *Leaves of Grass* there is none that more precisely assesses the aesthetic resources language offers poetry than "A Song of the Rolling Earth."[30] From its first lines Whitman adopts a pedagogical strategy to correct a common misconception we have about language:

> A song of the rolling earth, and of words according,
> Were you thinking that those were the words, those upright lines?
>   those curves, angles, dots?

No, those are not the words, the substantial words are in the ground
   and sea,
They are in the air, they are in you.[31]

Whitman's purpose—poetry's purpose, that is to say—is not to imbue in us
a distrust of language and of poetry for its dependency on language, as these
lines may initially foretell. Rather, it is poetry's special capacity to highlight
the brute insufficiencies of language in order to insist on the ontological primacy of the world, of "the earth," "the ground and sea," "the air," "you," as a
"rolling"—changing and evolving—unfathomable habitat possessing an essential meaning inaccessible to language. Poetry identifies the absolute limits
of language, its impotence to express, in a word, truth.

By Whitman's design "A Song of the Rolling Earth" teaches us to appreciate
poetry for its "aesthetic reflexivity," let me call it, for being the form of language
uniquely qualified to grasp the constraints language imposes on our ability to
know. Through language poetry establishes the remoteness of the world, that
the world is unknowable or, as Whitman says, "inaudible." Empowering poets,
"masters," to speak the "inaudible words of the earth," Whitman commissions
poetry to apprize us of the boundaries dividing us from the world's fathomless
reality. Distinguishing between the audible and the inaudible, he is consistent
when he explains, "I speak not, yet if you hear me not of what avail am I to
you?" Poetry teaches us to hear the "eloquent *dumb* great mother" earth, to
hear the muteness of our reality, to hear the sound of the silence of the world
as the world is in itself.[32] Language clearly does not fail Whitman. Quite the
contrary, he evinces a robust confidence in poetic language springing from its
reflexive capacity to dissuade us of its romanticized potential to make extra-
linguistic realities, their truths and truth in general, known, and as it does so
to persuade us of the existence of such realities and truths. We have seen this
argument before. "A Song of the Rolling Earth" is poetry's self-reflection proceeding from the standpoint of the "unknown" to which Whitman assigned
such great importance in *Democratic Vistas*. In this poetic context the significance of the unknown receives a threefold clarification.

Proposing through its reflexive illumination of the unknown that truth is
wordless and reality inaudible, poetry shifts our regard for meaning away from
the elusive realm of essence to the realm of appearances. It is not that what is
real is meaningless. It is that the meaning truth confers on reality is no less
inaccessible than reality itself. Appearances become our domain and meaning
is conceivable for us only at the level of appearances. Any doubt regarding

Whitman's determination to render this position unassailable is dispelled in "Passage to India" by his move to redefine our relationship to the very idea of transcendence. Declaring his belief in God to be stronger "than any priest," he insists that God—"O Thou transcendent"—is "Nameless," as unavailable to us as any ultimate, essential reality he alludes to in "A Song of the Rolling Earth." If God is not permitted to secure our ideas of transcendence, regardless of any of their foundations such ideas can have no power or purchase over us. When Whitman instructs us in "Song of Myself"

> And I say to mankind, Be not curious about God,
> For I who am curious about each am not curious about God . . .
> Why should I wish to see God better than this day?

I understand him to be dramatizing his allegiance to the meaningfulness of appearances by this preference for the ordinary over the extraordinary, the immanent over the transcendent. For if God cannot lure us away from the day, surely nothing else purported to be beyond, or behind, or beneath appearances can do so either.[33]

At the same time, absent knowledge of anything essential, whatever appears then appears to be different, as it cannot be known at an *underlying, essential level of commonality* to be the same as anything else that appears. Everything that appears being irreducibly different from everything else that appears, the realm of appearances to which poetry orients us is actually a sheer diversity of differences.

Finally, lacking evidence of something belonging to appearances that transcends appearance, we have no recourse to a truth with which we can justify treating any form of difference as otherness. Embracing the unknown, disavowing truth, the poet and poetry model an aesthetic understanding of the world orienting us to appearances, all of which are different, none of which can be preferred or denied according to some claim to know the truth. Difference resists its construction as otherness, for no one or nothing different can be judged to be inferior on the basis of some presumed truth or denied as untrue or unfaithful to an unknowable truth. To paraphrase Whitman, we have appointments with all; not a single person can be slighted or left out. Poetry's reflexively driven pedagogy teaches us to *be all-inclusive of differences, the first principle of Whitman's ideal of reconciliation.*

A problem with Whitman's ideal of reconciliation arising at this point leads us directly to its second dimension, which is the problem's solution. Denying us knowledge of some essential reality underlying the diversity of differences surrounding us, Whitman seems to take us to be self-knowing and self-contained subjects disconnected from others and from the world. I find this problem confirmed by the one exception he offers to the inverted Platonism with which he valorizes appearances and their differences over unknowable truths and realities. While truths essential to differences are imperceptible, they do not elude those who themselves are different—as, in our own way, each of us is—and who alone have privileged insight into who they really are. As Whitman allows in "A Song of the Rolling Earth," "No man understands any greatness or goodness but his own, or the indication of his own."[34] Accessible only to those to whom they belong and to no others, our identities do not elude us as the identities of others do not elude them. Hence Whitman gives us "fair warning before [we] attempt [him] further": "I am not what you supposed, but far different," and he follows this warning with another on "the terrible doubt of appearances."[35] But how tragic it would be if Whitman's efforts to insulate differences from attributions of otherness finally insulated differences from each other, and if the inaccessibility of truths intrinsic to appearances establishing all-inclusiveness as the first defining principle of reconciliation introduced an unbridgeable divide between differences, ending the possibility of their reconciliation.

Here is how I believe Whitman solves this problem. Although unknowable, unfathomable truths embodied by all and by the world inhabited by all also resonate effects to which we would be receptive *if* we were to discontinue our exclusionary practices flowing from our will to truth. As Whitman adds in "A Song of the Rolling Earth," "underneath the ostensible sounds" our differences have identities in "possessing words that never fail," which, though themselves inaudible, "convey . . . a sentiment and an invitation," a "presentation of the unspoken meanings" toward which "all merges."[36] Whitman's view is that the unknowable truths belonging to appearances and their differences are productive of effects; differences convey sentiments, invitations, presentations, toward which everything and everyone then moves. Differences attract each other and us in plural ways, so that I would now suggest, anticipating my future discussion, that there is a cumulative effect of the unknown belonging to appearances. Differences that the unknown allows appearances to become attract each other as "a magnet to a field of iron filings," to introduce an idea of Adorno's of great importance in later chapters.[37] The effect of what is unknown and thus different about each of us is to make each of us attractive to all. Following Whitman's paths I thus come to "receptivity," the second principle of his ideal of reconciliation.

The young fellow drives the express-wagon, (I love him, though I do not
know him) —Whitman, *Song of Myself*

As the media of democratic enlightenment, poetry teaches that the all-inclusiveness of differences requires severing their connection to a presumptive truth determining their eligibility for inclusion. If reconciliation is to become the practice of a democratic society, however, poetry must do more educational work than problematize truths claimed as the grounds for the construction and exclusion of difference as otherness. Democratic enlightenment must surpass universal toleration, which abides the coexistence of all-inclusiveness and the proliferation of otherness until violations of formal-legal principles of equality provoke the state to intervene and correct discriminatory practices. But even then the construction of difference as otherness persists in the private sphere beneath the threshold of politics and the law. On its own or through state intervention, as an ideal the all-inclusiveness of differences is impotent to advance reconciliation without the cultivation of a sensibility to difference averse to social practices in the private sphere friendly to the construction of difference as otherness.

Whitman's poetry nurtures this very sensibility as our *receptivity* to differences. Here again he calls upon the unknown to serve as the metaphysical precondition for reconciliation. Unknown and unknowable, difference appears mysterious and its mystery becomes a source of wonder irresistibly attracting our reception. Poetic images model receptivity to difference as this sensuous response to mystery and wonder, defining it as the quality able to ensure that Whitman's *all* who have been included are differences to whom the rest are receptive and not forms of otherness victimized by the same. Appearances appear different, differences appear mysterious, mystery intimates wonder and kindles our receptivity. For Whitman the power of the unknown lies in its being productive of these multiple aesthetic effects.

Early in "Song of Myself" Whitman chastens science for its rationalization of the world, for the arrogant realism he complained in *Democratic Vistas* disenchanted nature at the cost of thwarting America's spiritual development. "I and this mystery here we stand," he declares, signaling that mystery and the unknown productive of mystery are to set parameters for his poetry, authoring his aesthetic relation to the world by shaping his poetry's aesthetic commitments. "Being" is that insoluble "puzzle of puzzles," a "life untold" of which the facts fetishized by science are no more than shallow "reminders." Poetry's unknowable world appears so mysterious it stimulates a radical sense of wonder, responses traversing the broadest range of expressions of receptivity from Whitman's more or less intellectualized reports of interest and curiosity and surprise to his uninhibited exclamations of awe and joy and its ecstasies. A mysterious world continuously offers the poet the promise of something unexpected and new, in a word, something *different* in every engagement with the world. Registering Whitman's sense of wonder in all these ways, poetry dramatizes the receptivity the unknown and its mysteries incite, which Whitman never more explicitly teaches than in "Salut Au Monde!" Here his receptivity places him on the threshold of experiencing the world in a new and different way, and as a new and different world: "O Take my hand, Walt Whitman! / Such gliding wonders! such sights and sounds!"[38]

By enclosing us in his responses to the wonders in which he immerses us—for is it not also us to whom he extends *his* hand so we are positioned to experience the world as he does—Whitman short-circuits any response on our part other than a receptivity equal to his own. In one verse alone duplicating the receptivity running through his every encounter, in "Song of Myself" he considers

> a curl of smoke or a hair on the back of my hand just as curious as any
> revelation . . .
> The bull and the bug never worshipp'd half enough,
> Dung and dirt more admirable than was dream'd.[39]

Curious, worshipp'd, admirable—modeling receptivity by way of such affections, poetry senses nothing without wonder or less filled with wonder and leaves no wonder out. Being democratic twice over—it is receptive to everything it includes, which is everything, the whole—poetry refines the sensibility it nurtures in us to the all-inclusiveness of differences. Because as the whole the world contains all, poetry's receptivity to a wonder-filled world immunizes us against acts of violence toward difference not incompatible with its all-inclusiveness.

Whitman's spectacular imaging of the mystery and wonder of an all-inclusive world therefore works to make receptivity a perfectly democratic sensibility. Still, his sensitivity to violence toward difference is even more acute. He also questions our deceptively harmless practices of assigning value, as they diminish meaning and worth the same as overt acts of constructions of difference as otherness. Adopting the Socratic style so often characterizing his verse, Whitman ties lessons about the significance of mystery and wonder to lessons about valuing. Asking rhetorically in "A Song for Occupations," "The wonder every one sees in everyone else he sees, and the wonders that fill each minute of time forever, / What have you reckon'd them for, camerado?," he means, in the first instance, to unburden us of believing our occupations, and thus each of us because of our occupations, are of unequal value. Ultimately, though, he wants to cure us of valuing what transcends value, namely the great diversity of achievements, experiences, and possibilities—the wonders—his poem recounts as included in the all-inclusive *gestalt* taken by modern democracy and that prove *all* to be invaluable. And he interrupts his soliloquy in "Song for Occupations" to remind us of the basis of this claim: "Objects gross and the unseen soul are one."[40] Objects in their entirety are unseen, unknown, and mysterious—the whole is wonder itself, which, fathomless, defies valuation. Difference poses no question of value.

Time and again Whitman returns us to the opacity of the world from which his poetry draws its spiritual power to resist calculations converting the world into means valued according to the ends it is required to serve. A sensibility to wonder is receptive to the world just as it appears as a diversity of differences all ends in themselves, which Whitman formulates categorically as a principle in his 1855 "Preface" when he declares, "Men and women and the earth and all upon it are simply to be taken as they are." It could not be otherwise, for despite how "great is the faith of the flush of knowledge and of the investigation of the depths of qualities and things," the "depths are fathomless." The world is unknown, mysterious, an object of wonder, unmeasurable by standards of equivalence translating it into a third term indifferent to difference. Receptivity to difference requires putting aside all such preconceptions so that "innocence and nakedness are resumed."[41] With receptivity Whitman returns us to our original encounters with the world, where naming everyone and everything recognized their differences, that there are "no two alike," as he wrote in *Song of Myself*.[42]

As Whitman's Edenic allusions suggest, he wants to remind us that the unknown is fundamental to human experience, an argument that works synergistically with his critique of modern science. This should not imply he is hostile to science, only that his strategy is to deeply inscribe the unknown into our lives by regularly stressing the limits of human understanding. What I have called his inverted Platonism is allied with this Kantian respect for things-in-themselves. Familiarity with his poetry and prose proves how often he also celebrates modernity and its achievements made possible by science, which finds its most unequivocal approval in "Passage to India." Our every experience with the world and with each other must, however, proceed from a sense that there is a congenital element of the unknown that ineliminably attaches to difference and by sustaining wonder sustains our receptivity.

So if the unknown circulates throughout Whitman's poetry to establish its ubiquity in and among us, it is because he believes modernity's process of disenchantment to have made the unknown precarious. In his *Calamus* poems he further opposes this development by reintroducing the unknown into everyday relations of intimacy, the area of life where it is most easily endangered by our modernist illusions of transparency. Here his approach is to insinuate something unknown about himself and hidden behind his appearance, making him different from what those with whom he is intimate take him to be, though what he hides is not so secret the idea of something unknown cannot come to mind. In "Earth, My Likeness" Whitman compares his appearance to the earth's impassive surface, which protects from view what he "dare not tell . . . in words, not even in these songs."[43] By deftly hinting at an unseen, unspoken sexuality, his unseen and unspoken reality, Whitman allows his appearance, like the earth—his "likeness"—to be filled with the mystery of the unknown. And bringing the unknown to mind to intimate he differs from how he may appear, Whitman leaves his difference unknown, an object of mystery and wonder attracting our curiosity and animating our receptivity, which are attracted to his *Calamus* poems for the questions about his identity their mysteries invite. Determined in *Calamus* to portray himself as inscrutable and thus different from how he appears even in his most intimate relations, Whitman pluralizes his identity in the extreme. Always different, his identity is always moving, unfixed and unfixable, surprising, new, discontinuous with itself, a source of wonderment, which exciting our receptivity to difference breaks us of our habit of constructing difference as otherness.

Yet among the diversity of differences that Whitman's democratic society includes, are there not those to whom we should be unreceptive? Are there no rules governing the extent of our openness to what departs from the norm? Unafraid of being implicated in a performative contradiction—for, as he boasts in "Song of Myself," self-contradiction is a condition of all-inclusiveness—Whitman's all-inclusiveness *excludes* those who would convert difference to otherness.[44] Beyond this minimalist formulation of a regulative principle, he has receptivity comply with only one other ethical criterion. "The earth, that is sufficient," Whitman declares in "Song of the Open Road," and in "One Hour to Madness and Joy" he wants only "to have the feeling to-day or any day I am sufficient as I am."[45] If all differences are sufficient as they appear, none is more or less sufficient, as either distinction implies that sufficiency must answer to a standard for judging differences that does not belong to the realm of appearances. Sufficiency justifies receptivity's openness to difference. By the force of sufficiency receptivity to difference transvalues moral distinctions and their exclusions to find all possible lives sufficient to earn our reception, save those who would demonize difference as otherness or who become the enemies of difference in less manifestly violent ways.

With my first two dimensions of Whitman's ideal of reconciliation I discover an image of democracy resistant to practices of treating difference as otherness insofar as democracy rests on our receptivity to differences of which it is all-inclusive. Receptivity supports all-inclusiveness through a sensibility hostile to all forms of violence toward difference, violence's construction of difference as otherness foremost among them. Reconciliation's first two dimensions begin to radically rework our image of democracy. Democratic society now swarms with differences surrounding us, each difference appearing equal to every other. Yet in the history of modern democratic theory Whitman's image of democracy is anomalous when compared with the standing of Tocqueville's opposite image of democracy in America. Democracy's core idea, and its most serious failing in Tocqueville's view, or the failing at the root of democracy's most serious failings, though one he also described as in other ways an accomplishment of world-historical proportions, was the principle of equality, or the "equality of condition," among other names by which he referred to it. He feared equality would produce sameness, eliminate difference, while Whitman, as I determined when considering *Democratic Vistas*, held that equality meant all-inclusiveness and the proliferation of difference, that the individual emerges from the mass, which is composed of contrasts of lights and shades, of differences. Why are two such remarkable theorists of democracy at odds on so basic an issue, and why is their disagreement of importance?

Tocqueville's prediction that equality in America would lead to sameness was rooted in his error of equating difference with class differences, which he argued equality would erase over time, except for extremes of wealth and poverty forming the boundaries of an ever-expanding middle class. In one of the many versions of this *embourgeoisement* thesis Tocqueville explains, "I seek to trace the novel features under which despotism may appear in the world. The first thing that strikes the observation is an innumerable multitude of men, *all equal and alike*, incessantly endeavoring to procure the petty and paltry pleasures with which they glut their lives."[46] Working out the political logic of this argument, we see that the "multitude's" shared middle-class identity not only supersedes the decline of class differences; it blinds Tocqueville to social differences other than class differences and implies the decline of difference as such. Tocqueville's "all equal and alike" was democratic capitalism's version of a classless, homogeneous culture, an image that has buttressed every critique of democratic mass culture since *Democracy in America*. Tocqueville can hardly be blamed for his error of equating the disappearance of classes with the disappearance of difference. In the aristocratic regimes whose passing he mourned class difference was the very definition of difference, encouraging his insensitivity to the plurality of other kinds of differences democracies would admit as democracy became increasingly inclusive and its equality of condition became universalized to lead class lines to become increasingly blurred. Receptive to this multiplicity of differences obscured by Tocqueville's analysis of equality, Whitman's image of America contradicted Tocqueville's.

Here is why this debate between Whitman and Tocqueville over the fertility or extinction of difference in democratic America is important for us. Among the several forces of equality driving democracy toward social homogeneity, there is arguably one of greatest critical interest to Tocqueville. In his words, "All classes . . . imitate and emulate one another."[47] Tocqueville reasoned that in a society propelled by the principle of equality, the most insignificant differences in fortunes become sources of envy and incitement for anyone to copy the circumstances of any other, dissolving differences between them. Now from Whitman's standpoint Tocqueville is partly correct. Americans do imitate and emulate one another, though for Whitman the democratic effect of their mimetic activity is not greater homogeneity but the contrary: the accumulation and intensification of individual and social differences.

With imitation I pass to democratic enlightenment's culminating stage of reconciliation. Americans imitating differences to which they are receptive allows each to become different in the image of differences surrounding them and thus each to become diversely different, intensely different as each becomes discontinuous with himself or herself. Whitman's *all* offer models of difference on which the identity of each can be created and re-created through imitation. Through receptivity and imitation I move beyond tolerance to complete the barrier to the evil of constructing difference as otherness that all-inclusiveness and universal toleration mark only the beginning of. As the motion of becoming different in the image of difference, reconciliation's imitative relation to difference turns otherness into democracy's other.

I reject none, accept all, then reproduce all in my own forms.
—Walt Whitman, "By Blue Ontario's Shore"

Imitation is a more problematic idea than even Tocqueville's indictment of democratic imitating and emulating would lead us to believe. Undoubtedly picking up on this thread of Tocqueville's critique of democracy in America, Emerson famously proposed in *Self-Reliance* that "imitation is suicide."[48] Emersonian suicide is committed by those who fail to develop the unique powers nature bestowed on every individual, and who instead are parasitic on the genius of those who do cultivate their natural gifts and who universalize their self-authored truths as truths for all. While Emerson is a philosopher of reconciliation in such essays as *Experience*, which introduces the concept of reception Whitman raises to the higher philosophical level I have uncovered in *Leaves of Grass*, there is no evidence for a concept of reconciliation in *Self-Reliance*. There Emerson's aggressive prose never allows our thinking to waver from the universalism he premises on the individual's self-conscious, egoistic indifference to the virtues of a democracy that thrives on the emulative and imitative sharing of individual differences, which only earns his contempt.

No less than Tocqueville and Emerson, Whitman holds individuality sacred, in *Democratic Vistas* referring to the "Miracle of miracles" of that "precious idiocracy and special nativity" defining every individual's personal identity, "yours for you, whoever you are, as mine for me."[49] On the matter of imitation it is thus ironic that Whitman, who must be tacitly responding to Tocqueville's and Emerson's attacks on democratic forms of copying and borrowing, is intent on proving in a demonstrably self-reliant way that imitation is neither suicide nor any form of self-sacrifice, not the death but in fact the very life of individuality as much as of democracy itself. For Whitman imitation is midwife to the birth of individuality and its apotheosis because he understands the extent to which even the most extreme, Cartesian versions of self-governance and self-creation rely not only on subjectivity but on intersubjectivity, of which imitation is a form. We can anticipate Whitman's insight into the value of imitation for individuality as well as for reconciliation in his verse from "By Blue Ontario's Shore": "I reject none, accept all, then reproduce all in my own forms." Reproducing—*imitating*—*all*, though in his *own* forms, Whitman reconciles individuality and imitation, a lesson he sets out to teach us.

How would Whitman have composed "Song of Myself," his greatest work, with thought of the mandate to which he will later give voice in *Democratic Vistas*, America's need to forge a literature that breaks with its cultural past and ushers in a revolutionary new epoch? I would first expect Whitman to write with an augural sense of the sheer originality of this work. And not to trust a culturally underdeveloped America to grasp the democratic lessons his poem sets out to teach, which requires that in the work itself he would assist readers with insight into its meaning, and perhaps subsequent to the work direct readers to his having done just that, as he did in *Democratic Vistas*. "Books are to be call'd for, and supplied, on the assumption that the process of reading is not a half sleep, but, in highest sense, an exercise, a gymnast's struggle; that the reader is to do something for himself, must be on the alert, must himself or herself construct indeed the poem, argument, history, metaphysical essay— the text furnishing the hints, the clue, the start or frame-work."[50]

If "Song of Myself" *furnishes the hints, the clue, the start, or framework* for its "construction," or interpretation, such assistance could only be the concluding line of verse 15 where Whitman explicitly ties the meaning of his text to his poem's very title: "And of these one and all I weave the song of myself."[51] With this line Whitman signals the creative act defining the work as a whole, actually plural acts of self-creation and self-invention through which he creates his identity from "these one and all" that are included in and also refer us back to what precedes it, verse 15's "list," an exemplar of Whitman's most used though most misunderstood stylistic device, often thought tedious and amateurish. From verse 15's list "of these one and all" he weaves his self from "the All, and the idea of All" he venerates in *Democratic Vistas*. There he proposes the *all* becomes the model for our concept of "Nature," which he thinks of as "the only complete, actual poem," hence the model on which he in turn bases his own poem, which, as does the exemplar of verse 15, then models his concept of democracy and identity. Whitman's concluding line of verse 15 is the clue to this great pyramid of imitations through which "Song of Myself" unfolds: the *all*, the idea of All, nature, poetry, democracy, identity, "yours for you, mine for me"—thus the clue to the significance of imitation itself.

The list of verse 15 assembles nearly a hundred personas: the prostitute and the President, the first child and the Patriarchs, the marksman and the flatboatmen, the contralto and the conductor, the lunatic and the opium-eater, young and old husbands and wives, the living and the dead, to name a few. Describing each matter-of-factly just as he or she appears—"the peddler sweats with his pack on his back," for example—Whitman obviously means to distinguish all those listed as a mere diversity of differences, one difference not more important than another to Whitman.[52] Each is listed without any necessary connection to others and one after the other is relentlessly added to the list to convey poetry's, democracy's, Whitman's own, continuous striving for all-inclusiveness as an unattainable ideal. As I try to grasp the significance of imitation I must foreground these several features of Whitman's lists. Lists are all-inclusive of differences; differences are included just as they appear; all-inclusiveness, the *all*, is the ideal after which Whitman continuously, endlessly strives. It is from a continuously and endlessly pursued all-inclusive diversity of different appearances that Whitman weaves his "song," his identity, through his identification *with* differences rather than *of* differences, for the identification of differences constructs difference in ways other than it appears, an argument also found in Adorno's *Aesthetic Theory* I take up in later chapters.

There can be no question Whitman's "weaving" is an act of self-creation through his imitation of those he lists "one and all." He reminds us of this often in "Song of Myself": "In all people I see myself, none more and not one a barley-corn less"; "Whatever interests the rest interests me." Pondering the fate of an escaped slave he tells us, "I am the hounded slave, I wince at the bite of the dogs." Of a soldier he says, "I do not ask the wounded person how he feels, I myself become the wounded person." "All these"—all those listed before and after, Whitman means, he not only feels but, as he reports— "I . . . am."[53] Throughout "Song of Myself" he strives through imitation to create that "great composite *democratic individual*, male or female," he revealed in the *Preface* of 1872 to "As a Strong Bird on Pinions Free" was one of the lyrical intentions of *Leaves of Grass*.[54]

But even if following *Leaves of Grass* Whitman had not so recalled his verses' intention, there is no difficulty in fleshing it out. As I have shown, in the spirit of aesthetic education outlined in *Democratic Vistas*, Whitman's poetry modeled this democratic individual and the imitative acts of self-creation productive of the continuous transformations his composite presupposes, and he offered us clues to make certain we did not fail to see this. Becoming different by imitating differences surrounding him, Whitman teaches that his composite individual is democratic in the extreme, imitating poetry that imitates nature inclusive of the *all* on which rests the idea of the All. What is more, to imitate those who are different is not pure becoming. Rather it is a determinant "democratic becoming" owed to a democratic society that, by continuously striving to be all-inclusive of differences, offers Whitman's composite individual limitless real possibilities for protean self-creation. And a self-creativity that is no less limitless than the democratic society on which it is modeled is, in the image of that democracy, similarly divided between its own identity and the differences it imitably includes and becomes. We can see why Whitman held identity to be miraculous. Woven just as fabrics are woven from threads at intersecting angles opposed to each other, the democratic individual is at odds with itself, large and containing multitudes of differences placing it in self-contradiction. There is no higher form of reconciliation than Whitman's ideal, an image of an imitative identity that does not abolish but continuously strives to include within it the *all* who are infinitely different, an identity that *sings in their voices* as it sings in its "own," as does Whitman by weaving the song of himself.

But on what does Whitman base his confidence that, once taught, there is also popular incitement to achieve reconciliation and it will not languish as a cultural ideal beyond the achievement of the equality of material interests belonging to the mass and the individual he hopes to reconcile? Whitman believes there are powerful encouragements to reconciliation already built into the fundamental structure of democracy itself, a "political economy of imitation," I would call it, which he candidly presupposes at the outset of "Song of Myself." In its opening lines he discloses an assumption that not only must underlie every verse of the whole of *Leaves of Grass* as it does his greatest poem; it must also underlie, as he claims it does here, democratic convictions held by every one of us. When Whitman announces,

> I celebrate myself, and sing myself,
> And what I assume you shall assume,
> For every atom belonging to me as good belongs to you,

he is proposing there is an idea of equality on which we equally, albeit tacitly, agree.[55] It is because we all share this assumption of equality that *all* can then claim, with Whitman, "In all people I see myself." For Whitman such remarks are declarations of the intent to imitate that follow from the principle of formal equality, the assumption at the core of democratic life he translates into relations of imitation, into a political economy of imitation whose actors commonly believe that, since we are all equal, what anyone says or believes or does or how anyone appears is eligible for imitation by everyone else. And our imitations of our equals, of the *all*, extend to our equality with Whitman. Each imitative act Whitman performs in *Leaves of Grass* is an act each of us can imitate to celebrate and sing our own self-weaving. As does Whitman, we too can say, "Whatever interests the rest interests me." What Whitman assumes we shall assume.

I believe we can now even more clearly understand where Tocqueville erred in his critique of imitation. Largely equating class inequalities with difference as such, Tocqueville concluded that by eradicating class inequalities the principle of equality and the increasing equality of material conditions it ushered in would eliminate difference—produce sameness—so that the imitation and emulation of sameness could produce only more of the same. Whitman, to the contrary, was alert to the panorama of differences that survive and multiply beyond materialism's mitigation of class differences, which he also included among differences to be imitated. For Whitman imitation would not produce sameness between equals. It would allow all those formally equal to each become different in each other's image, to each become different in the images of limitless differences, thus to each become the complexly composite democratic individual whose identity develops at odds with itself, as I have argued.

There is another formulation of this thesis that in two ways also clarifies Emerson's error. Whitman's composite democratic identity does not in any simple sense mirror differences about him. Differences he imitates become Whitman's means to further develop what he wishes himself to be: the means to his own self-reconstruction. Whitman could not be clearer on this matter or have made it more central to his thinking. As the penultimate line of verse 15 reads, "And such as it is to be of these *more or less* I am," which is the idea reiterated in "By Blue Ontario's Shore" when Whitman writes, "I reject none, accept all, then reproduce all in my *own* forms" (my italics). *Those who imitate become variations of themselves as well as variations of others whose images their imitations also re-create.* For Whitman, imitation is just such a doubling of creation: *the creator is re-created by becoming the re-creation of those who are different.* Originality does not flourish for Whitman by avoiding imitation, as it does for Emerson, but by practicing it. And if the creativity of life is measured by its diversity, then imitation is not suicide and the end of life, as Emerson foresees. *Imitation is life's determinant democratic becoming, life's creative evolution.* As Whitman in verse 16 of "Song of Myself" immediately confesses after weaving himself from his imitation of democracy's *all*, "I resist anything better than my own diversity."[56] Contrary to Tocqueville and Emerson, equality and imitation do not eradicate but proliferate difference in abundance and in ever-new forms. And what, must we not now ask, is life if not creation in continuously new forms?

Once Tocqueville's and Emerson's aristocratic reductions of imitation to mere copying no longer block the path to grasping Whitman's reinvention of mimesis, which ceases to be the enemy of individuality, of its becoming different, and becomes instead the means to radicalize its self-creativity and diversity, I also find us better positioned to appreciate how radical is Whitman's practice of receptivity. Whitman himself must have had such an appreciation. Framing his argument pedagogically, in "Song of the Open Road" he speaks of "the profound lesson of reception, nor preference nor denial . . . / None are but accepted, none but shall be dear to me." The profundity of his reception stems from the extent to which the composite democratic multiplicity of his identity is indebted to the imitable differences surrounding him. Including *all* as the precious wellspring of his becoming different, his receptivity highlights the dense intersubjectivity on which his individuality depends as it prepares the democratic soil for a true cosmopolitanism. Refusing to "deny" "the black with his *woolly* head," Whitman's receptivity works to reverse the otherness he names here and to restore and reclaim its difference in order to return it to the limitlessly diverse stock of differences he would imitate without "denial."[57]

To erase any remaining doubt about what he means by the profound lesson of reception, Whitman, ever the teacher of democratic lessons, explicitly couples receptivity to imitation in the defining verse 15 of "Song of Myself." Prefacing his intention to "weave the song of myself" from the "one and all" that "tend inward to me" as "I tend outward to them," he offers no more fertile source for the modern self than receptivity, which locates our self-creativity, our self-weaving, in either our receptively moving "outward" toward the world or being receptive to its movement "inward" toward us.[58] No other lesson could be more profound for the composite democratic individual than one ensuring the diversity of differences it requires to create itself in the image of a truly universalistic cosmopolitanism, the image of one who is composed of peoples who compose the world.

At an even deeper level than his cosmopolitan personality, perhaps, Whitman's receptivity and imitation may be so unthinkingly natural to him that the most radical evidence for his ideal of reconciliation is nearly swallowed up and lost within the imitated *all* of which it forms only one brief moment of his verse, whose unfolding tracks his own unfolding. As the original model for Whitman's *all*, nature qualifies for his receptivity and imitation no less than any form of difference in democratic society or of otherness whose form of difference his reception restores, as it did "the black with his woolly head." "I depart *as* air," Whitman reflects, as he concludes "Song of Myself," thus becoming—*more or less*—like one of nature's elements.[59] In this moment of reconciliation with nature air is no metaphor. It is the ether that enlivens Whitman's boundless and boundaryless receptive sensibility to the imitable means available for imagining the first of the many forms he will begin to assume with his life's "end."

Whitman finally anticipates the reconciliation of his life even with his death, the reconciliation of life and death. *Departing as air* he heralds his death as another form of his life, death as a different form taken by life, and reconciliation to be the philosophical venue for the "great poems of death" he proposed in *Democratic Vistas* must be written by poets who would create the American artwork of the future. There including death in life, we recall, Whitman explained, "I feel and know that death is not the ending, as was thought, but rather the real beginning—and that nothing ever is or can be lost, nor ever die, nor soul, nor matter."[60] Including death in life Whitman is as receptive to death as to anything of which the *all* is composed, as he affirms in "Song of Myself," singing, "And to die is different from what anyone supposed, and luckier."[61] Yet how does Whitman finally reconcile life and death? In "O Living Always, Always Dying" he argues:

> O living always, always dying!
> O the burials of me past and present,
> O me while I stride ahead, material, visible, imperious as ever;
> O me, what I was for years, now dead, (I lament not, I am content;)
> O to disengage myself from those corpses of me, which I turn and look
>   at where I cast them,
> To pass on, (O living, always living!) and leave the corpses behind.[62]

Becoming different, assuming those imitable forms from which he weaves the song of himself, his many "deaths" become his many more lives, he explains, so that his "death"—"To pass on"—becomes different by its imitation of life, by "living, always living!"

WHITMAN'S IDEAL OF RECONCILIATION: DEMOCRACY'S BARRIER TO EVIL

As the media of aesthetic education poetry bears the pedagogical burden of Whitman's democratic enlightenment. One of his poetry's paths to enlightenment is through language, though not without qualification. For there are occasions, such as the one marked by "A Song of the Rolling Earth," where his poetry stops along that path to reflect on the failure of language, including poetic language, to penetrate beyond or behind or beneath the world's appearances to its essences, where the reality of the world has been said to lie. Whitman's poetry emerges from these moments of aesthetic reflection transformed. Linguistic constraints paradoxically become the source of his aesthetic emancipation from truth and truth's sponsor of the construction of difference as otherness. Where language fails, Whitman finds his epistemic justification for an aesthetic allegiance to the overriding value of appearances and their differences from which he never wavers, as it then guides his verse down this path to democratic enlightenment, aesthetic education, and the ideal of reconciliation, democracy's barrier to the evil of violence toward difference.

However, there is far more to the transformation of Whitman's poetry than its orientation to appearances, which forms only the first stage of its metamorphosis. His reflections on the limits of language blaze yet another and radically new aesthetic path, which takes shape where the linguistic path his poetry travels finds its higher form in his use of poetic language to create visual images, as I will now try to show. At a later time, after Whitman has left us, his new path will lead us to film, which on the universal scale of democratic progress he imagined realizes his commitment to democratic enlightenment, aesthetic education, and reconciliation. Perhaps what Whitman meant to do all along was to give democratic enlightenment the aesthetic and educational media it requires, which he began to do by writing a poetry that imitated the visual arts without becoming a visual art, rather only "more or less."

As I have lived, as I have look'd through
my windows my eyes
—Walt Whitman, "Song at Sunset"

2
....

Whitman's Discovery

AESTHETIC EDUCATION THROUGH THE VISUAL IMAGE

A democratic enlightenment is achieved by means of an aesthetic education that teaches the ideal of reconciliation through the medium of poetry. Poetry's vehicle is language, its ideal formed through the word, yet while this is the case for Whitman's poetry it is so only instrumentally. In each of the three dimensions of our ideal of reconciliation Whitman uses language to create images that are *visual*. Poetry transforms the word from something written and read, spoken and heard, into something seen. It is through something seen that Whitman's poetry teaches reconciliation. Hence his discovery: democratic enlightenment by means of an aesthetic education through the visual image of the ideal of reconciliation.

Visual images of reconciliation created by poetry's transformation of the word have an ambiguous relationship to language, such that their visual effects originate in a linguistic context they stand more or less outside of. Often Whitman's visual images of reconciliation are *self-standing*, their meanings apparent. Once created in words, his visual images do the work of aesthetic education without further relying on language to elaborate their meaning, as do paintings or photographs displayed on a museum wall and accompanied by interpretive cards. In each of the three dimensions of reconciliation we find visual images that, rather than self-standing, teach us *how to see* to enable us to grasp the meaning of visual images with some assistance from language. Whitman offers us visual images that, with or without the support of the word, *privilege eyesight*. Then again, occasionally he adopts self-standing visual images, images that teach us how to see and that privilege vision all at once, not leaving it to chance we will see what he intends for us to see or grasp the purpose and power of seeing or simply not fail to look. Self-standing visual images along with images visually and verbally instructing eyesight and privileging vision are not only visual effects of Whitman's poetry. More to the point they are *democratic effects* because they are the *democratic lessons* taught by the visual images of each of reconciliation's three democratic dimensions, what I will call the all-inclusive, receptivity, and imitative visual images.

Importantly, whenever I speak of the democratic effects and democratic lessons of Whitman's images of reconciliation, their visual character is to be kept in mind, though in the special sense in which Lyotard speaks of the "figural" in *Discourse, Figure*. As the visual effects of Whitman's visual images, democratic effects, in Lyotard's terms, would always be "embedded" in language, so there would never be a question of the visual "leaving language behind." But at the same time, and even where they in part depend upon language for the lessons they teach, as the visual effects of visual images democratic effects transcend language as "sight on the edge of discourse," as a "difference" that is "visible." By thinking of democratic effects in Lyotard's terms I thus avoid reasserting their original associations with poetic verse in a way that reduces their figural visual meaning to the "logic of discourse, to its communicability and transparency," as Vlad Ionescu in his analysis of Lyotard puts it. Rather, the figural "breaks through language and reveals its purely visual forms" that keep open an interpretive range of meaning beyond what the logic of discourse allows, which is what occurs through the democratic effects of Whitman's poetry.[1] Nevertheless this argument installs the ineliminable paradox of our being in need of language to conceptualize Whitman's visual images of reconciliation and their democratic effects or lessons.

So I am arguing that Whitman's verse transforms the word into visual images of reconciliation that produce distinct democratic effects or democratic lessons. Visual images teaching the all-inclusiveness of differences will be known as all-inclusive images; those teaching receptivity to differences are images of receptivity; and those teaching the imitation of differences are imitative images. The all-inclusive, receptivity, and imitative images will teach their respective democratic lessons in visual forms that are self-standing or, depending in part on language, that teach us how to see or straightforwardly privilege vision. By teaching their democratic lessons in their various forms, visual images will together produce one final, cumulative democratic effect:

the visual image of reconciliation, the enlightenment ideal I have referred to as Whitman's discovery. As the expression of the rationality of a *whole series of prior images* that form it, the "reconciliation image," as I call it, is the democratic lesson envisioned from its antecedent all-inclusive, receptivity, and imitative images. From the standpoint of Deleuze's thesis that "the image . . . is legible as well as visible," the reconciliation image becomes legible and visible as the rationality of this whole.[2]

When I have traced this visual democratic landscape of reconciliation in Whitman's verse, I will have also begun to flesh out the politics of his aesthetics, which I will continue to pursue right through my final chapter's concluding thoughts on Schiller's idea of reconciliation as it is taught by means of a universal art form. For several reasons the politics of Whitman's aesthetics must not be treated as a matter of indifference to us. In the century following *Leaves of Grass* the visual image will increasingly become democracy's principal and universal medium of publicity. Visual images will be ubiquitous, unavoidable, and irresistible, eventually challenging the communicative public role of language, perhaps at times even seeming to threaten its eclipse. Whitman's reliance on the visual image anticipates democracy's visual culture if he does not already foresee it. What is more, because of the centrality of the visual image to his poetry, if the power of his images to enlighten politically proves to be drawn from their visual properties, his images attest to the possibility that a democratic culture revolving around the visual image is a culture of democratic enlightenment. Visual images may teach political lessons a democratic society would learn if it recognized the aesthetic pedagogy of the visual image. And by circulating through the medium of visual images, Whitman's project of democratic enlightenment would be realized in an era in which ever fewer read, especially poetry, and everyone increasingly looks. If we then discover Whitman's visual image of reconciliation to be a singular source of democratic enlightenment originating today in forms other than poetry, such as in film, Whitman the poet becomes more valuable than ever as a political theorist of democracy.

Let us suppose, then, that aesthetic education in the first instance is performed by Whitman's poetry, though his poetry's burden of enlightenment is not borne by its words or by its words only. Democratic enlightenment occurs through visual images of reconciliation created by Whitman's verse and that, when allied with the word, also teach us how to see the image and that vision ought to be privileged because, among the senses, eyesight is intrinsically democratic and enlightening. On this supposition I should return to the three dimensions of reconciliation I earlier found in his poetry to now find for each examples of the self-standing visual properties Whitman accords poetic images. And I must explicate Whitman's discourse, embedded in his poetry, along with visual images with which it is allied, instructing us how to see. In this schema of the part played by the visual image in his poetry I must ascertain the privilege Whitman extends to eyesight. If all this were carried out, it would be to have taken steps toward a theory of the visual image as an agency of democratic enlightenment or, more to the point, a theory of the visual image as the pedagogical tool of reconciliation.

THE ALL-INCLUSIVE IMAGE

> Sauntering the pavement thus, or crossing the ceaseless ferry,
>   faces and faces and faces,
> I see them and complain not, and am content with all.
> —Walt Whitman, "Faces"

When the all-inclusiveness of differences, my first dimension of reconciliation, was introduced in the last chapter, I found that one of Whitman's strategies for elaborating the aesthetic powers of poetry was to use poetic language paradoxically to illuminate the limits of language. In "A Song of the Rolling Earth" he defended the power of poetry to communicate the silence of an unknowable reality impenetrable to language. Poetic language vouchsafed the metaphysics of the unknown that Whitman, in *Democratic Vistas*, recommended as a topic for poets. Poets could hear the silence and use language to make it audible so that we too could hear the silence and learn of a mute, linguistically untellable and unknowable reality. In this way poetry reflexively taught the impotence of all language, including its own, to express essential meanings belonging to some world, whether to nature or to any or all of us in any of our individual or social forms. Whitman's poetry focuses our attention on appearances by pointing us away from language as the bearer of truth and as having the power to say what everything is at its depths. Once poetry's reflections on the relation of language to reality valorize appearances over reality and meaning at the level of appearances, appearances then become the natural home for perception. It is because *appearances are seen* that Whitman makes appearances and their meanings available to us in visual images. Confining perception to appearances, poetry bases perception on what we can see.

By recalling "A Song of the Rolling Earth" I am proposing that because Whitman's poetry is oriented to appearances it has a natural affinity for the visual image. Even though language is the means of constructing the visual image, with regard to the ideal of reconciliation Whitman assigns the responsibility for doing all or some of poetry's work to visual images and not to language at all or to language alone. What begins with Whitman's contesting the relation between language and truth ends with his disempowering language as the sole carrier of aesthetic discourse. Divided from the language that brought it into being, as the location of appearances the visual image is empowered to serve as the dominant location of perceptible meaning, to become what I have called the self-standing image. Redirecting knowing from reality to appearance and from the virtuosity of language to the percipience of seeing, poetry focuses attention not on what is beneath or beyond or behind appearances, on the supersensible, that is, but on what is immediately before us. Poetry thus teaches us what is and what is not visible, how we are to see, and that among our senses vision and the visual are to be privileged.

Produced by much of Whitman's poetry, these visual effects are exemplified in "A Song of the Rolling Earth" when his poem's titled figure, "mother" earth, assumes self-standing visual properties as she is emancipated from the poetic language to which she owes her genesis. Writing of mother earth's hand mimicking the "character of the mirror" as it receives her "glance," Whitman transforms earth's linguistically created image into the "character of the visual," I would say. Introducing this transformation by first describing her as "eloquent" though "dumb," in the sense of mute, he relies on verse to paradoxically reinforce the implications of the visual character of her image so the meanings collected around her throughout the poem are seen to be independent of the word that gave them birth. Whitman writes:

> With her ample back towards every beholder,
> With the fascinations of youth and the equal fascinations of age,
> Sits she whom I too love like the rest, sits undisturb'd,
> Holding up in her hand what has the character of a mirror, while her
>   eyes glance back from it,
> Glance as she sits, inviting none, denying none,
> Holding a mirror day and night tirelessly before her face.[3]

Whitman's self-standing visual image also privileges vision by leaving perception only one access route to earth, compelling us to *look* at her whom he loves like the rest of the "ceaseless cotillions of sisters" (the planets) with which she "dances."[4] With her back to us, with mother earth's image inaccessible unless we *look* at her reflection in the mirror she holds, her visual image becomes the only representation of earth available by night and day, which also works to further enforce the authority of appearances. Whitman's song produces visual effects that in whole or in part suspend the reliance of the poetic image on the word to create a visual image. His visual image also aspires to be self-standing where the character of the visual confines the reader's work to the "glance." And where vision is privileged and this privilege is to be exercised in the appreciation of appearances, the word must wait its turn to say what little the eyesight leaves it to say, such as expressions of Whitman's love for the earth and the many implied affections the beauty of its visual image arouses in him.

What is most important in "A Song of the Rolling Earth" now comes into view. The multiple visual effects produced by the aesthetic transformation of the word into the visual image create an image of a special kind, the all-inclusive image, a visual image modeling and teaching democracy's all-inclusiveness of differences, the first dimension of reconciliation. Because like nature, the universe, and democracy, mother earth is for Whitman one more embodiment of the all-inclusiveness of differences, as she gazes at herself in the mirror mother earth must see the *all* she contains at the very moment she sees her reflection, which offers a visual image of the *all* just as they appear on her surface. Why else would she invite none and deny none! Already including all, mother earth has no one left to invite. Nor can she deny anyone without losing her all-inclusive identity as earth. "A Song of the Rolling Earth" thus offers us a self-standing visual image of all-inclusiveness, and moreover an image teaching us how to see. For to focus our perception on appearances, without, that is, referring us to a supersensible reality, to a truth assigning unequal values to whatever we see, is to teach that seeing is democratic. And the visual image of all-inclusiveness and its lesson on how to see also privilege vision. As we look at mother earth looking, see her seeing, do we not imitate the poet as Whitman instructed in his 1855 "Preface" to *Leaves of Grass*, where he identifies the poet as the model of one who is inclusive of all just as they appear? "Now he has passed that way *see after him*! there is not left any vestige of despair or misanthropy or cunning or exclusiveness or the ignominy of a nativity or color or delusion of hell or the necessity of hell . . . and no man thenceforward shall be degraded for ignorance or weakness or sin."[5]

Late in "A Song of the Rolling Earth," while explaining that the shortcoming of words is that they are not themselves visual, Whitman again takes his discourse on the visual image to a didactic level of aesthetic instruction. By exploiting the figural power of the word "see" he disrupts a context in which its literal meaning is the convention—"I swear I begin to *see little or nothing in audible words*." His complaint is not that words convey little or nothing to us. Rather, what we hope audible words can decipher—the unspoken, inaudible meanings of the earth, the unknown and unknowable, reality, essences, truths—*are not what can be seen*. Whitman weans us away from the cognitive value of language as he simultaneously privileges vision and teaches us how to see by focusing perception on what we *can* see, visual images of appearances, which are made from "dictionaries of words that *print can not touch*," that make his "tongue . . . ineffectual" and render him "dumb."[6] Where poetry uses words, he is insisting, it does not speak. *Poetry sees*.

In this context such a palpable tension between the audible and the visible as Whitman dramatizes it has an instructive counterpart in the work tonality performs in music. Whereas Whitman's figural development of the visual dimensions of his poetic language opens to a realm of meaning beyond the constraints of language, opens to the realm of appearances, roughly about the time Arnold Schoenberg was trying to escape the constraints of tonality he also began his work as a painter. For both Whitman the poet and Schoenberg the musician-painter, in other words, "audible" meaning obeyed a logic whose constraints on expression were exceeded by visual appearances. This suggests that, just as in Whitman's case discursive limits were transcended by the visual, in Schoenberg's case the limits of tonality were exceeded by atonality for its own and by now well-established visual effects. Whitman and Schoenberg are thus allied in their struggle to overcome the limits of the audible through the visual.[7]

Ultimately, of course, Whitman's interest is not in appearances per se but in the appearances of differences, which is the emphatic first lesson taught by "A Song of the Rolling Earth." For want of some idea of a reality underlying appearances that language lacks the capacity to conceptualize, appearances become our reality. This lesson is not complete, however, until it is remembered that the unknown, the evidence for which largely rests on the incapacity of language, annuls every other term according to which appearances can be said to be essentially the same or similar. Appearances are thus different. Hence the *all*, those who later in Whitman's song are neither invited nor denied by the visual image of mother earth gazing at her reflection, hold nothing essentially in common and can be nothing other than the appearances of differences.

In other ways Whitman helps us to remember this lesson. Recall the lists in "Song of Myself" he conscripts for so many of his poems, which are matter-of-fact registers of the continually unfolding diversity of the *all* nature and democracy include, and are each also self-standing visual images distinguishing differences just as they appear.[8] That these matter-of-fact registers further serve as visual images that also teach us *how to see* differences among the *all* is itself reflexively taught by Whitman's poetry. "A Paumanok Picture," for example, bears a title alerting readers to a visual poem that will self-referentially explain that lists are visual representations meant to focus attention on the uniqueness of ordinary details as the correct way to "picture" the world:

> Two boats with nets lying off the sea-beach, quite still,
> Ten fishermen waiting—they discover a thick school of
>   mossbonkers—they drop the join'd seine-ends in the water,
> The boats separate and row off, each on its rounding course to the
>   beach, enclosing the mossbonkers,
> The net is drawn in by a windlass by those who stop ashore,
> Some of the fishermen lounge in their boats, others stand ankle-deep
>   in the water, pois'd on strong legs,
> The boats partly drawn up, the water slapping against them,
> Strew'd on the sand in heaps and windrows, well out from the water,
>   the green-back'd spotted mossbonkers.[9]

Two boats resting on quiet waters before moving in opposite directions until casually moored; ten fishermen who draw nets or lounge or stand in their own different locations; heaps and windrows of mossbonkers on the shore apart from the sea. Whitman's list encourages us to see differences among ordinary sights we ordinarily see as unremarkable. Visually remarking on differences between the "two" and the "ten," his increase in number challenges us to visualize the differences among the "school," among the multitude, that is, though surely not only among the multitude signified by the mossbonkers. The fishermen's catch piled high in long rows reminds us of the "particulars and details magnificently moving in vast masses" Whitman describes in *Democratic Vistas*, the democratic mass whose "contrasts of lights and shades" carry the promise of an incipient individualism articulating differences the mass already contains.

By illuminating appearances and their differences Whitman's visual images resist essentialist comparisons effacing differences. Again illustrated by his ubiquitous lists, the self-standing visual images his lists matter-of-factly serialize resist invidious distinctions leveraged through reference to some set of common endowments those held to be superior are alleged to possess and those constructed as forms of otherness lack. Hence the "pure contralto," the "duck-shooter," the "clean-hair'd Yankee girl," the "President," and the dozens of other personas depicted in verse 15 of "Song of Myself" are not merely different or mere differences. They are antiessentialist, nonfungible, incommensurable differences. Difference is qualitative. By teaching us that to see differences requires we resist essentialism, Whitman's visual lists sharpen our vision so it is drawn without hesitation to the differences between appearances, making appearances' differences—and thus difference itself—conspicuous. Fully occupying his reader's field of vision, visual images of differences block any thought of their possible commonality and commensurability. Fastened on visual images of difference, seeing is prevented from attaching an advantage or disadvantage to differences according to shared properties to which they can be reduced and said to conform. By *teaching* vision to differentiate, to tell apart, Whitman's visual images *teach* seeing not to discriminate, to set apart.

Here I cannot sufficiently stress how the authority of both of these democratic lessons depends on Whitman's thought of differences as qualitatively different, in other words on a concept of difference antecedent to its constructions. A comparison with Deleuze's formulation of difference in itself should offset any shortfall on my part to adequately stress how theoretically important for a democratic enlightenment is Whitman's idea of difference and how advanced it is for its time.

My point of departure is Foucault's "Theatrum Philosophicum," an essay on Deleuze's relation to Plato beginning its discussion with the issue of his "reverse Platonism" as it rests on his reading of the *Sophist* in *Difference and Repetition*, though in my reading of Deleuze he importantly involves other of Plato's dialogues in his reversal as well, notably the *Theaetetus* and *Timaeus*.[10] Turning directly, then, to *Difference and Repetition* to allow me to focus more expansively on the issue Foucault raises that bears on my discussion of Whitman, I find Deleuze dissatisfied with Plato's distinction between appearance and reality for its simplistic binary opposition between the ideal and its resemblances. Deleuze problematizes Plato's binary for limiting understanding of difference to the "terms of the comparative play of two similitudes: the exemplary similitude of an identical original and the imitative similitude of a more or less accurate copy."[11] Against this ontology Deleuze reads Plato *against* himself, countering it with Plato's *own* "more profound" and "true Platonic distinction," not that "between the original and the image but between two kinds of images [*idoles*], of which copies [*icones*] are only the first kind, the other being simulacra [*phantasmes*]." Deleuze complicates Plato's simpler "model-copy distinction," which now no longer functions "to oppose the world of images in its entirety" to the ideal model—"but to select the good images, the icons which resemble" the ideal and "eliminate the bad images or simulacra" not resembling it for being distortions of the truth. In light of this new formulation, through which simulacra become the equivalent of difference, Deleuze thus concludes that Plato subordinates "difference to the supposedly initial powers of the Same and the Similar, that of declaring difference unthinkable in itself and sending it, along with the simulacra, back to the bottomless ocean."

Now Deleuze's further development of this argument is of greatest importance to my discussion of Whitman. Calling on the *Theaetetus* and the *Timaeus*, he explicates their "anti-Platonism at the heart of Platonism" to argue that Plato further allows for the extraordinary possibility that "the different, the dissimilar, the unequal—in short, becoming—may well be not merely defects . . . *but rather models themselves*." Being such a "world of their own," standing completely apart from the original "model" to which they are opposed, as qualitatively distinct models themselves simulacra or differences must raise the question whether they "provide the means of challenging *both* the notion of the copy *and* that of the model?" With this Deleuze concludes that the very idea of "the model collapses into difference, while the copies disperse into the dissimilitude of the series . . . such that one can never say that the one is a copy and the other a model." Continuing to read Plato against himself, what Deleuze derives from Plato's anti-Platonism, in other words, is a concept of difference in itself whereby differences are no longer constructions formed in relation to an ideal on the basis of which they are judged.

Whitman's achievement is comparable, though his reversal of Plato is only implicit and he carries it out somewhat differently than Deleuze. For by declaring what is true and essential to be unknown and unknowable, Whitman *severs* the Platonic connection between appearance and reality, thus *emancipating differences (appearances; simulacra) from resemblances* to ideals. Even though the Platonic model is not dissolved and does not collapse into difference, Whitman, by utterly severing appearance from the ideal, as does Deleuze, reverses Plato so that every appearance becomes its own uniquely different model. Unlike Deleuze, however, Whitman *also* ironically *inverts* Plato so that difference is the image *imitated* by those who had originally declared themselves the ideal model of identities whose truth justified their conversion of difference to otherness. *For Whitman, the inversion of the Platonic "ideal," so that it now imitates the "copy," is the reconciliation of identity and difference.*

To further highlight what is at stake here between Plato on the one side and Whitman and Deleuze on the other, it is instructive that each of its three protagonists understood this debate in world-historical terms, namely, what is to be the political fate of difference? Surely Deleuze understands Plato in these terms when he describes Plato's position on simulacra in the *Sophist* as "in its purest state . . . a moral vision of the world. It is in the first instance for these moral reasons that simulacra must be exorcised and difference thereby subordinated to the same and the similar." By clarifying Plato's relation to difference in such terms, Deleuze helps us to realize that Plato was only erring on the side of caution when in the *Republic*, in obvious fear difference could enter the city by appearing in the guise of simulacra, he exiled all poets from the community once and for all to protect it from poetry's imitations of appearances. Hence Whitman, who must have been thinking of Plato in Deleuze's terms when he not only makes *poesis* the champion of difference and the democratic enemy of the republic Plato imagined it to be but also charges it with the responsibility for the *aesthetic* creation of an entirely new and different world. Indeed, Whitman's notion of a democratic vista hardly begins to capture the image of democratic life he envisions. Reconciliation is the ideal most suited to carry that burden, which is why Schiller's aesthetics of reconciliation, as I theorized it in my introduction, almost without a doubt inspired Whitman's political vision. For as Schiller puts it in his "Twenty-Sixth Letter," it is the "aesthetic mode of the psyche," the "indifference to reality and interest in appearance [*Schein*]" that "may be regarded as a genuine enlargement of humanity and a decisive step toward culture."[12]

Although Whitman's visual images teach sight to focus on appearances with regard to their differences, they also possess the power to make seeing *aware of* depths, which is not the same, however, as *revealing* what underlies appearances. In "Song of Myself" he writes, "Oxen that rattle the yoke and chain or halt in the leafy shade, what is that you express in your eyes? / It seems to me more than all the print I have read in my life."[13] Again privileging the eyes as portals of meaning, he invites us to consider the meaning of the visual. Being mute, the oxen cannot reply to the question Whitman puts to them, so he seeks his answer through the only means available: he *looks* into the oxen's eyes. And the answer is seen in the visual images of the oxen's expressions, which concentrate meaning at the level of appearances to convey an elusive deeper meaning underneath—mystery—belying the oxen's reputation for brute simplicity.

To truly appreciate the interpretive role Whitman's concept of mystery performs in his verse I call on Barthes's narratology in S/Z, which contributes to my argument that Whitman's attribution of an unfathomable, mysterious depth lying behind the oxen's eyes expresses a unique type of enigmatic element in "Song of Myself." In Barthes's terms, as an "enigma" of Whitman's text mystery has a "paradoxical" relationship to his verse by virtue of its having created a "dynamics" that is "static." Narrative must work to "*maintain* the enigma*," that is, "to keep it open" rather than resolve it, which manufactures "*delays*," slowing down a reader's sense of the text's narrative movement or progress. So long as it remains open enigma generates a sense of "expectation," which, as "narratives tell us," is the prerequisite for grasping their meaning "*at the end* of expectation."[14] To be sure, Whitman's poetry expends an abundance of just this sort of energy to abide by what Barthes refers to as the "hermeneutic code." When very early on in "Song of Myself" Whitman declares, "I and this mystery here we stand," he has announced at its outset that mystery is itself a defining element of his poem's narrative, which he "maintains" not only by discerning mystery behind his oxen's eyes but also by affirming mystery as the enduring enigmatic element throughout *Leaves of Grass* as a whole.

How very often we find Whitman relying on this hermeneutic code of mystery as a pedagogical strategy indispensable to explicating the power of visual images to privilege appearances and their differences. In "Song of the Open Road" he reports he "enter[s] upon and *look*[s] around" a road possessing "much *unseen*."[15] Visual images, such as of the road or the oxen at which Whitman looks, do not refute the existence of a mysterious, underlying reality belonging to appearances, only that it can be seen and known. By intimating an unseen depth to appearances, the visual image of the road frees Whitman to look around and see by not allowing him an interpretive access to reality limiting him to a deeper, mysterious, enigmatic essential meaning of all that is seen. Such deeper meanings in any event "are more than all the print" he has read in his life. Enabling sight to perceive, at most, a virtual depth belonging to appearances, visual images chasten knowing, limiting it to the perspective of appearance. By framing appearances to highlight their differences, visual images align seeing with a multiplicity of perspectives. Visual images secure a perspectivism teaching there is more to the world about which can be known only through what the visual image frames.

My examination of Whitman's poetry turns up three major theses shaping his verse. There is, first, his epistemological reflections on the limits of language opening up his art to a phenomenology of appearances and their differences.

These, second, establish the privileged role assumed by vision and the priority of visual images in his poetry, which in its entirety will come to rest on appearances being irreducible to essences. It is impossible to say whether it is Whitman's passion for seeing or his insistent positioning of absolutes—God, reality, essences, truth—beyond the reach of knowing, even to the extent of quieting our will to know truth, that is most responsible for his poetry's unflagging allegiance to the irreducibility of the visible. But recognizing his allegiance to appearances and the strength of its formulation in his poetry, what I should say is that through his uncompromising attachment to an "ontology of appearances" or an "ontology of the visible" Whitman erects a barrier to the construction of truths by those whose violence toward difference is rooted in their use of truth to construct difference as otherness. This connection between the irreducibility of appearances to essences and the all-inclusiveness of differences is Whitman's third thesis.

Moreover, by allowing an ontology of appearances to emerge from language's self-reflexive illumination of its epistemological limits, Whitman secures poetry's ties to language while at the same time he severs them, which is a philosophical move anticipating Nietzsche's position on the relation between language and the appearance-reality antinomy. When Nietzsche famously argues in "On Truth and Lying in an Extra-Moral Sense" that "the 'thing-in-itself' (which would be pure, disinterested truth) is also absolutely incomprehensible to the creator of language and not worth seeking," he expresses the epistemic position on truth, reality, and essence Whitman adopts as his rationale for wedding poetry to a language of visual images, appearances, and differences after abandoning language because it is unequipped for the pursuit of truth, which remains inaccessible to the word.[16] Hence Whitman's Nietzschean relationship to language is conveyed by such poesy as "Be not curious about God, For I who am curious about each am not curious about God . . . Why should I wish to see God better than this day," which is the precise sentiment Nietzsche expects of the creator of language Whitman surely qualifies as.[17] Nietzsche allows us to see that for Whitman poetry is allied with language for its ontologically correct visual orientation to appearances and for finding truth unintelligible, which also compels him to abandon language except insofar as poetry is to self-reflexively remind us of the futility of being curious about "God."

To say all this is to realize that the relationship of Whitman's poetry to visual images is even more remarkable than it appears to be thus far. For the ontological norms governing Whitman's relationship to language, which can also be thought of in Barthes's terms as a type of "cultural code" (or in Whit-man's case a "subaltern" cultural code) through which the voice of philosophy can be heard in Whitman's verse organizing and ordering society according to certain ideals, ensures that his visual images—which at the time he is writing do not yet have the photographic means of production and circulation he surely envisions—are to be the future media for which his prose and poetry's democratic vistas are the harbinger.[18]

After all, what is a vista if not a view, something seen, a visual image of the future seen by a seer? What are Whitman's "democratic vistas" if not visual images of the possible future of democracy in America? Yet if Whitman is to retain language as the midwife of visual images born to do the work of aesthetic education, he must secure visual images' ambiguous relationship to the word. For once the visual image is authored by poetry it consumes the word lest the word invade and reappropriate the territory of the unknown the visual image blocks access to—God's territory, the territory of essence and reality colonized by truth that Nietzsche also places beyond the limits of language. So as I have tried to show, to ambiguate poetry's relationship to the word Whitman cultivates three types of visual images. Sometimes his visual images break away from the language that gave them birth; at other times they partly rely on language to teach how they are to be seen; at still other times they simply privilege vision. In all their types, Whitman's visual images are aesthetic forms that teach us the Nietzschean lesson to abstain from every interest in truth to avoid all accounts of appearances that set apart some differences from others, marginalize, exclude, or punish difference by constructing it as forms of otherness. Whitman's visual images, to this point, are together productive of a democratic effect that teaches a democratic lesson, democracy's all-inclusiveness of differences, the first *visual* dimension of his ideal of reconciliation.

I want to further capture what may be most important about Whitman by paraphrasing another poet and democratic theorist of reconciliation. Antjie Krog has described reports presented during the trials conducted by the Truth and Reconciliation Commission, by black victims of crimes committed by whites under South African apartheid. "Now to seeing, speaking is added and the eye plunges into the mouth," she explains, referring to how the TRC finally provided black South Africans the opportunity to speak of what they saw when the horrors of their victimization under apartheid reduced them to silence.[19] For Whitman, I would say "the mouth plunges into the eye," for although his poetry is defined by his voice, it is defined far more by his vision. As he reveals in "Song at Sunset," "As I have lived, as I have look'd through my windows my eyes."

As the media of democratic enlightenment and aesthetic education, we begin to see, the visual image for Whitman constitutes knowledge—of the ideal of reconciliation, of democratic vistas. There appears to be no separation between his poetry and his political theory. Modeling the first dimension of reconciliation visual images begin to teach what it means to be democratic. Democracy is the image of each who appears—and the image of the *all* who appear—differently. Democracy is the image of the appearances of all differences, hence the image that includes all other images. Democracy is the image of images. As the all-inclusive image of images, democracy's potential for enlightenment is realized when the remaining two dimensions of reconciliation are formulated in light of poetry's full visual empowerment of the image. From my discussion of the visual image as the avatar of reconciliation, thus far, it is seen becoming the means of aesthetic education and the vehicle of democratic enlightenment.

THE RECEPTIVITY IMAGE

> And that the truth includes all, and is compact just as much as space
>   is compact,
> And that there is no flaw or vacuum in the amount of the truth—but that all
>   is truth without exception;
> And henceforth I will go celebrate any thing I see or am,
> And sing and laugh and deny nothing.
> —Walt Whitman, "All Is Truth"

Whitman had already grasped the power of the visual image though he wrote at the very inception of visual culture. Photography had just taken its first major technological strides at the time *Leaves of Grass* was published, and cinema was on the threshold of a leap forward that will correspond to the appearance of *Democratic Vistas*. Whitman must have sensed he was writing at an unprecedented moment of cultural transition. His project of aesthetic education by means of visual images suggests he interpreted such developments as heralding a visual culture.[20] Evidence I will cite when concluding this chapter's discussion further suggests as much. It will help us to be certain his aesthetic turn to the visual image indicates how he believes his aspirations for democratic enlightenment will be realized. At this point in our discussion here is what appears to be certain. Concerned with how aesthetic education can teach the ideal of reconciliation to perfect democracy in America, Whitman believes visual images offer thinking a higher order of reflection than language. To begin with, as we have seen, visual images model all-inclusiveness, and they do so in a way suppressing truth's enablement of moral imperatives threatening any of the all-included with the stigma of otherness. In the wake of cinema's later development such aesthetic pedagogy of visual images will be better understood and the foresight appreciated with which Whitman imagined their powers, which he does not exaggerate. To the contrary, he takes the measure of visual images through an argument that, as the leitmotif of his poetry, also prepares the transition from the all-inclusive image to a second image as powerful.

Affirming the unknown by rejecting the possibility that language possesses the capacity to know truth, I have shown, Whitman marries perception to appearances. This is his decisive first step and cannot be stressed too often, as appearances then appear in visual images. He entrusts appearances to visual images because they are the perfect instantiations of the pedagogical barrier appearances erect to truths allegedly anchored in essences belonging to peoples' and nature's infinite diversity of differences. Embodied in visual images, lacking such commonality, all appearances visually appear different, and not by degrees but in kind. By constituting a barrier to truth through visual images, appearances undermine grounds for excluding differences, which once visually insulated from judgments that they lack something essential shared by the rest (by the norm) must be accepted all-inclusively. This is why differences saturate the visual fields Whitman creates through verse, as his lists prove. And yet by their intimations of unknowable depths his visual images also transcend the mere all-inclusiveness of appearances to imply that appearances each possess unique if opaque multilayered lives, placing appearances in relief to force their differences to stand out further still.

But at the same time, Whitman well knows his readers are susceptible to believing truth claims underlying normativity and are prone to the violence toward difference such truths threaten. So while he entrusts appearances to visual images for their representations of the pedagogical barrier appearances erect to truth's violence toward difference, he does not entirely trust us to be open to reflection on these images so we may then learn that the absence of truth compels the all-inclusiveness of differences and the perception of appearances as qualitatively different. Since only visual images of appearances can be pedagogically all-inclusive, they must thus pique our interest and attract our attention. Otherwise we will ultimately fail to see the one all-inclusive aesthetic truth of reconciliation Whitman's idea of democratic enlightenment admits and that runs counter to every other and exclusive conception of truth. For "the truth includes all," he celebrates and sings and laughs and refuses to deny in "All Is Truth." Here, then, is where his receptivity image comes into play.

Regardless of their pedagogical powers Whitman's visual images are of no service to democratic enlightenment if, in the first place, his public is indifferent to their visual and democratic effects. How, then, does his poetry construct visual images able to attract us so they can perform the work of aesthetic education? To formulate this question in terms of his second dimension of reconciliation, how do the visual images to which Whitman's poetry is politically and aesthetically dedicated teach us to be *receptive* to the visual image that is all-inclusive of differences? For as I will make clear, there can be no reconciliation without receptivity.

Whitman's poetry offers us the means to answer this question if I continue to flesh out his aesthetic inventions and philosophical commitments to an unknown that is impenetrable by language, to an orientation to appearances, to the all-inclusiveness of differences, and to the necessity of visual images the unknown and the limits of language entail. Since his commitments to the unknown, appearances, differences, and the visual image are ontological, and his commitment to the limits of language is his ontology's epistemological condition, together they amount to a weak ontology as they collaborate to resist an essentialist commitment to truth.[21] Productively constrained by language's incapacity to know truth, Whitman knows he cannot just *say* "the truth includes all," so he invents an aesthetic alternative to language to show it. His project of democratic enlightenment and the poetry advancing it *require* the visual image, which cannot be one aesthetic technique of comparable importance among others in his poetry. For the aesthetic and philosophical work we have seen it perform, the visual image is Whitman's discovery—the discovery without which his project and his poetry are inconceivable.

This is the conclusion to be drawn from Whitman's philosophical commitments, and it can be framed precisely. Since appearances to which the unknown necessarily orients us can appear only in visual images, appearances and the visual image are inseparable, which answers my question how poetry teaches us to be receptive to the all-inclusive image. Because the visual image forms around what is seen, the unknown, which Whitman's poetry teaches is *the unseen*, renders visual images of appearances *mysterious*. Hence my earlier discussions of the importance Whitman attaches to mystery and his declaration in "Song of Myself," "I and this mystery here we stand."[22] Mysterious, the world *attracts* Whitman. He is *receptive* to it. *In the mystery only the visual image of unknowable appearances can do nothing else than convey is the source of his receptivity to visual images themselves.* Ineliminable mystery is the condition for our receptivity, ultimately for reconciliation.

With the unseen and mystery working together to form its backdrop, the visual image's other powers of attracting our receptivity can come into view. "Salut Au Monde!," to recall from chapter 1, opens with Whitman's enthusiastic expressions of wonder at the wonders the world contains. Each different wonder he then cites is a self-standing visual image, while all wonders together collectively parent the self-standing visual image of a mysterious, unknown world filled with wonder. Whitman is clear his perception of wonder is a visual response to mystery, as can be seen when he describes wonders as "masonries"—architectures—erected by the "unknown," which sends wonders as "venerable messages" he reports he is able to "see" and that will "remain after [him] *in sight* forever."[23] As we learn from the more than 120 lines he devotes to narrating what "I see" or "I behold," in comparison to the fewer than 20 lines he dedicates to what "I hear," the far smaller number highlights the far greater part played by seeing wonders. Whitman unselfconsciously models expressions of wonder in all their subtle and unsubtle voices; naïve and worldly interest, curiosity and fascination, surprise, amazement, and astonishment, marvel at the new and miraculous, love and lust, rare notes of incredulity, and myriad others. For the mystery and wonder it evokes, the unknown is the ubiquitous and tireless muse of Whitman's visual images as well as their metaphysical principle. It accounts for his depictions of wonder and his responses to wonder captured in visual images of diverse appearances, which in their self-standing vividness seem meant to imitate paintings or photographs. This is suggested by so many of his images, for example, "Earth of the vitreous pour of the full moon just tinged with blue!"[24]

Whitman's receptivity to visual images of wonder teaches us to see the world of appearances as mysterious so they encourage a similar receptivity to wonder in us. Thus "And to glance with an eye or show a bean in its pod confounds the learning of all times" pairs the *glance*, an ordinary act of seeing, with his intent to *show or teach* us how to see. Here Whitman's receptivity to one of a diversity of appearances—his expression of wonder at an object at which he need only glance for it to appear to him visually wondrous—along with his interest in stimulating *our* receptivity through his studied "show" of a bean in its pod, are connected conditionally to the unknown nature of appearances and their mysteries, to that which "confounds the learning of all times," as he says. And his receptivity and ours are abetted by how wonder, and the mystery and the unseen underlying it, accentuate the differences among appearances. Each appearance is able to attract us by appearing wondrous in its own striking way. When Whitman records his surprise in "Song of Myself" that "the press of my foot to the earth springs a hundred affections," he promptly reflects on his reception by adding, "They scorn the best I can do to relate them."[25] He means that none of the ways he is affected and responds— none of the ways he is receptive—to whatever appearances he senses can be known or understood by being related to his other responses to other things. He sees everything as being mysteriously different from everything else, thus everything to which he is differently receptive should be seen to affect him differently. Only appearances maintain such differences and their mysteries and wonders absolutely. And only the visual image maintains appearances.

Whitman frequently teaches by example in just these ways. He creates self-standing visual images of diverse appearances identifying the mystery of the unknown to be the origin of his visual responses to wonder. These images serve to teach the idea of the unknown and also to recommend the experience of wonder for its power to originate such visual responses to mystery by us. This pedagogical doubling of lessons often produces a third, where Whitman's best-articulated visual models of seeing appearances as mysterious and wonder-filled are supplemented by instructions on how to see. From this alliance between the visual image and words we are taught a democratic lesson: whatever appearances the visual image frames are all equally filled with mystery and are equally different sources of wonder.

In this light I should revisit an earlier considered example from chapter 1, "Not objecting to special revelations, considering a curl of smoke or a hair on the back of my hand just as curious as any revelation."[26] While visually modeling his receptivity to the mystery and wonder in the appearances of very ordinary though very different things, here Whitman also explains we would be similarly receptive if we were to abstain from objecting to everyday encounters with the likes of curls of smoke and hairs on the back of a hand because they do not appear to be the equal of "special" revelations. "Considering" and "curious" tell us the "curl of smoke" and "hair on the back of my hand" are being seen, which works to create self-standing visual images of their different appearances that frame the mysterious and wonder-filled revelatory quality of each. At the same time we are told revelatory experience must be our ordinary response of wonder to the ordinary, which is special for all of that. So Whitman's instruction on becoming receptive to mystery and wonder in everything ordinary, doubled with visual images of his own receptivity framing both, together teach that what is *seen* to be ordinary is no less worthy of *our* consideration and curiosity than of Whitman's. All people and things, excluding none, should be *seen* to be just as worthy of our receptivity as his own and equally able to attract it.

Whitman could not be clearer and more consistent on these points. Whatever he sees, whatever appearances he frames in a visual image, attract and strike him for their distinctiveness. Speaking in "Song of Myself" of a "negro" working outdoors, he creates a powerful self-standing visual image by observing the appearance of his body when lit by the sun. "*I behold* the *picturesque* giant and *love* him," Whitman exclaims, perfectly modeling and teaching by example the experience of how seeing or "beholding" the *visual* image—the "picturesque"—makes him receptive to the uniqueness of what he perceives, the "giant." When he immediately follows this visual image by proclaiming, "In me the caresser of life wherever moving . . . not a person or object missing . . . Absorbing all to myself," he is explaining to us it is the universe of appearances he *caresses*—to which he is *receptive*—as he *beholds* them, their mystery and wonder set off by the visual image of life's diversity of *moving*, that is changing and thus continuously novel and different, appearances that compel his receptivity.[27]

Whitman's intensive visual instruction is punctuated, of course, by occasions when he simply rests his eyes and allows us to rest ours too, and he falls back entirely on the word to explicate the connections between his lessons on the democratic nature of the visual image, how to see, and the privilege he accords vision. He is explicit about these connections, especially on those occasions his poetry offers guidelines for interpreting his verse, as in "Starting from Paumanok," the gateway poem to those forming the greater part of *Leaves of Grass* and standing as a portal between Whitman's "Inscriptions" and "Song of Myself." Writing, "And I will thread a thread through my poems that . . . all the things of the universe are perfect miracles, each as profound as any," Whitman next refers us to the source of his poetry's capacity to illuminate the equally miraculous character of all things the universe holds: "And I will not make a poem nor the least part of a poem but has reference to the soul, / *Because having look'd at* the objects of the universe, I find there is no one nor any particle of one but has reference to the soul."[28] "Having look'd at the objects of the universe," Whitman has determined the *all* consists of things that are to be *seen*. It is as *visual images of appearances*, then, that the *all* has "reference to the soul," to the unseen and unknown, in other words, which he thus names as the source of appearances' mystery and wonder. By being seen, he is arguing, appearances appear unknowable and mysterious and consequently must attract his reader's own interest in looking at the objects of the universe as they have attracted his. Here we must remind ourselves once more that the universe, as Whitman's counterpart term for nature, is along with nature and poetry one of his placeholders for democracy. When modeled on poetry that is patterned after nature and the universe, democracy will, as they do, include everything that appears. Through its imitation of the all-inclusive exemplars of the universe and poetry, democracy becomes the image that contains all other images. And as the image of images all the differences democracy includes are unknowable, mysterious, wonder-filled, and striking. As such they equally earn our reception. For to be included, objects need do nothing more than appear and be seen, and when seen have "reference to the soul," or the unknown, the source of their mystery, wonder, and our receptivity, thus the source that attracts our sense of sight.

From my analysis we see that Whitman's visual images include and teach us to be receptive to the differences belonging all-inclusively to the universe's diversity of appearances. If his poetry's visual lessons were well learned by Americans their democracy would be similarly all-inclusive and receptive. With the receptivity image he elaborates new ways of conceptualizing the visual image begun with the all-inclusive image. In particular, it is a remarkable aesthetic achievement that his visual images of receptivity exert their forces of attraction on us without favoring certain differences over the innumerable others his images capture. If Whitman's images are to avoid privileging some differences at the expense of others, which would then be less worthy of our reception, his images must be equally receptive to *all*. Whitman's *visual egalitarianism*, we might call it, is also explained by the actual though also virtual range of differences his visual images portray and by the technique of listing he adopts to display them. One of his most important aesthetic inventions, I have already considered Whitman's lists for how they orient us to appearances, record the continual unfolding of their differences, teach us how to distinguish among appearances, and construct visual images of differences. Now I want to take up his lists *to see* how they extend equality to all those differences included and yet to be included.

Whitman first introduces his technique of constructing lists in "Starting from Paumanok," where he uses it as he does so often throughout *Leaves of Grass* to model the all-inclusiveness of differences. With "exulting words, words to Democracy's Lands," in verse 14 he translates America by listing the different names of its states (for example, "Land of the Old Thirteen! Massachusetts land! land of Vermont and Connecticut!"); what America's lands differently produce or are distinguished by (such as "Land of coal and iron . . . Land of the pastoral plains"); the diverse locations of its lands (among others, the "land of the ocean shores! land of sierras and peaks!"); the diversity of experience each different land affords ("Splashing my bare feet in the edge of the summer ripples on Paumanok's sands, / Crossing the prairies"); and lands with regard to many other criteria according to which he can then include what he stresses amounts to "the diverse!" Whitman's ambition is twofold. It is to construct a list of "endless announcements," as he puts it, which by noting lands without further comment simply illustrates America's diversity by means of unembellished matter-of-fact visual images enabling us to grasp the all of what the *all* contains.[29] And it is to compose a list so densely packed with visual examples of America's diversity *our imaginations are led out of and beyond the descriptive limits of the visual gestalt mapped by his verse.* We are to visualize unnamed, undescribed, uncounted diverse other lands, possible democratic lands of democratic possibilities.

Beyond the diversity it *actually* records, Whitman's listing technique therefore works to visually forecast the *possible* all-inclusiveness of differences, a diversity also to be distinguished by its unique characteristics, meanings, and values. Visual images teach the *aspiration* to an all-inclusive democracy of differences all of which will be equally worth seeing, thus equally worth the receptivity seeing presupposes. When he then says of this diversity, "O all and each well-beloved by me! my intrepid nations! O I at any rate include you all with perfect love!" his immensely poignant "at any rate" projects an implicit "whatever happens or whatever may happen" in the future, which acknowledges the contingency of the possible democratic lands he plans to love equally despite their predictably unequal democratic accomplishments.[30] Whitman's loyalty to all-inclusiveness is uncompromising. It extends even to granting inclusion to those states who for a time themselves deny inclusiveness. Hence his rationale for democratic enlightenment. Overall the unbiased and unvarnished visual neutrality of the list indicates that, whether with love or with other affections, *all* are to be included equally and are of equal value to him. Visually establishing the equality of what they include, Whitman's lists do not endorse a value apart from their equality in light of which all they include are to be measured. All that democratic diversity now includes or in the future may include is equally valuable and thus equally sufficient to attract Americans' receptivity.

But most of what Whitman writes is not incorporated into lists. Does the disproportionate attention given to that not included in his lists imprint it with an aesthetic importance suggesting it has an unmatched value that voids the equality of value his lists assign to the *all*? Here we come to the two final and perhaps ultimate purposes of Whitman's lists. By visually establishing the equal value of *all*, lists define the normative background against which he then can take up anything else at all, dwell on it aesthetically, and remain unconcerned that he will be thought to favor it among the diversity of differences appearing as visual images in his poetry. And emphatically thematizing all-inclusiveness, his lists, which cannot but finally leave someone or something out, nevertheless impress us with a *ceaseless striving* to include all not yet included.

Throughout this section I have tried to show Whitman combating the possibility that the appearances of differences his all-inclusive visual images teach us to see could meet with the indifference and, intimately related, benign tolerance of the democratic audience they are intended for. His visual images encourage our receptivity on so many levels that we must plausibly conclude he may believe a poetry of visual images to be more powerful as a means of democratic enlightenment than a poetry only of words. Once he orients us to the appearance of differences on the grounds the world is unknowable, his words become visual images, which along with his outright privileging of vision and his instruction on seeing—compared to next to nothing he says about reading—imply he is convinced visual images are more percipient than words and that we are more perceptive when we see than when we read or write or speak.[31] Resting on the unknown, visual images of appearances are mysterious, wonder-filled. How could we fail to be receptive to such images, especially as they accentuate differences among appearances? Visually differences appear striking, highlighting the spectacle of their diversity. Displayed visually in lists, differences are valued equally. From their sheer numbers we must infer indeterminate other possible differences for which the word cannot make space but after which the visual image strives. Attracting us to difference and the all-inclusiveness of the diversity of actual and possible differences, Whitman's visual images attract us to a democracy striving to include them all. His images encourage our receptivity to the image of images, the visual image of democratic life.

Yet each individual's receptivity will be awakened in the first place only if he or she does not fail to look at the image of what a democracy includes. And only if we see what democracy's image *visibly* includes will it become legible to us. For only by being seen does Whitman's image of democracy have reference to the unseen and unknown and is revealed as mysterious and wonder-filled, a diversity of differences all valued equally and equally striking and containing "endless announcements" attracting our receptivity. Only as a *visual image* can the world be democratic in all the ways we have seen the image teaches. So engaging the paradox at the heart of his project of democratic enlightenment, Whitman *writes* the penultimate verse of "Starting from Paumanok," in which he offers final words of advice for understanding "Song of Myself," the poem following after, and the remaining poems of *Leaves of Grass*. He begins each of twelve consecutive lines of a thirteen-line stanza by instructing us to "See" in his poems America's native and immigrant peoples, occupations, natural wonders, landscapes, shores, cityscapes, and states, inventions connecting continents, ceaseless activity of the modern democratic.[32] *Seeing* is democratic, Whitman *writes*, as he must *for us to know to look and see*. So he writes to teach us to see as he sees, so we will learn to see democratically in all the ways we have now seen.

If this is correct, there is a connection between poetry and democracy, aesthetic education and democratic enlightenment still to be brought out. Since poetry is the "image-making faculty," as Whitman says in *Democratic Vistas*, then the image of images, democracy itself, is as indispensable to poetry as poetry is to democracy.[33] For more than any form of life, by Whitman's account it is democracy's all-inclusiveness—its *own* receptivity to difference—that provides poetry with the diversity of sensuous experience from which its "image-making faculty" becomes so visually creative. It would thus be one-sided to contend art is for democracy's sake. Democracy is also for art's sake, for the sake of the art of reconciliation.

THE IMITATIVE IMAGE

> I reject none, accept all, then reproduce all in my own forms.
> —Walt Whitman, "By Blue Ontario's Shore"

Since all visual images are based on the imitation of appearances, on mimesis, why must I distinguish an imitative image from the all-inclusive and receptivity images, which as visual imitations of appearances are themselves mimetic? After all, by picturing democratic all-inclusiveness and receptivity to difference in their plurality of forms, as in "Starting from Paumanok," the all-inclusive and receptivity images represent our actual and possible sensuous experience of democratic life. Unlike the latter two, however, the imitative image, as I call the third dimension of Whitman's ideal of reconciliation, has a unique relationship to imitation, earning it its nomenclature. As are the all-inclusive and receptivity images, the imitative image is formed by the conversion of democratic experience into visual images—formed by mimesis. But the imitative image also *teaches* the imitation of appearances as the means through which visual images are created, and not only visual images belonging to Whitman's poetry. The imitative image teaches imitation as *self-creativity* as well. If, like his poetry's visual images, the self is created through imitation, perhaps Whitman thinks of the self as resembling his poetry and possessing its creative possibilities. The unique relationship of the imitative image to imitation would thus lie in this. Whitman's imitative image teaches that poetry's imitation of appearances is to be imitated in the way the self is created as a visual image.

Nothing I have yet said about Whitman's ideal of reconciliation has prepared us for this. Up to now my discussion has revolved around ontological arguments embedded in Whitman's reflections on how language's epistemic limitations enable his poetry. At the forefront of these reflections was the idea of the unknown, which he could foreground due to the incapacity of language to penetrate appearances in the interest of discovering underlying truths about the nature of reality. Poetry's linguistic constraints were not in the least an aesthetic liability for Whitman, rather an aesthetic asset, as they afforded him the opportunity to take an aesthetic turn to the visual that with regard to his ideal of reconciliation and practice of aesthetic education becomes a defining element of his poetry.

With the supersensible beyond the linguistic reach of poetry, the unknown is ensconced and poetry is emancipated from its bondage to truth. Poetry is set free to relinquish its interest in reality and in all other philosophical proxies for truth and to focus all-inclusively on appearances and their differences, which in the absence of truth appear as mysteries piquing our receptivity to each and all. With appearances becoming its domain, poetry is wedded to what is seen, hence to the visual image, though this marriage of appearances and the visual does not replace one form of bondage with another. Fully opening poetry to the realm of appearances and the visual image, poetry's emancipation from its bondage to truth anticipates a perfect symmetry between poetry and life to which poetry's freedom from truth grants it nothing less than unrestricted access. Ultimately for Whitman, poetry is to be "done with reviews and criticisms of life, animating now to life itself."[34] *Animating now to life itself,* Whitman means for his verse to be alive, thus imitating life by becoming like life itself. Its visual images are to exceed even their all-inclusiveness of life's appearances and differences and their receptivity to the *all* life includes, thus exceed even the extent to which all-inclusiveness and receptivity have shaped his use of mimesis.

According to this formulation of the work of imitation in his verse, as the aesthetic object of poetry's imitation of or animation to life, life itself cannot be less appearance, thus less visual image and less composed of visual images than is Whitman's poetry. Whatever appears in his visual images must itself be a visual image. This is what my reading of Whitman's aesthetics has now to bring out and that I must find in his verse if the full contribution of imitation to realizing his ideal of reconciliation is to be appreciated. For with this it becomes possible to discover what lies at the heart of the unique relation of the imitative image to imitation, namely, the role of the self's imitation of appearances in its self-creation, which, as much appearance and visual image and imitative as Whitman's poetic images "animating now to life itself," *dissolves the difference between poetry and life.*

Twenty-four poems form the "Inscriptions" introducing *Leaves of Grass,* each announcing one or more of the principal ideas around which much of Whitman's collection will be developed. "Eidolons," the seventh inscription and by far the longest, is an explosive metaphysical prelude to *Leaves of Grass* for how it confirms and conceptualizes the visual character of Whitman's images. It must thus apply to his poetry as a whole. Regarding the meaning of the term "Eidolon," according to its Greek etymology it is commonly understood to be a visual image. "Eidolon" is a derivative of the Greek verb *eido,* "to see," though also of its offspring, including *Eidon,* which literally refers to perceiving by seeing. Composed of eighty-four lines broken naturally into twenty-one unnumbered verses, without exception all stanzas of "Eidolons" narrate what Whitman sets out to teach. Each either describes people, places, and objects as self-standing visual images or privileges seeing and elaborates on how to see the visual image itself. The thesis of "Eidolons": life itself is a visual image.

Whitman frames his poem as the report of his encounter with a "seer," with one who sees and as "prophet" sees the future. He describes his seer as an itinerant collector of "eidolons," of visual images that *are*—rather than of—the world's "hues and objects." His seer instructs him on what to include in his poetry; thus vision is Whitman's teacher, which privileges vision at his poem's very outset. Yet, as Whitman is their author, his seer's instructions mouth his own teachings about how to compose verse. He is to write of "eidolons":

> Put in thy chants said he,
> No more the puzzling hour nor day, nor segments, parts, put in,
> Put first before the rest as light for all and entrance-song of all,
>   That of eidolons.[35]

So Whitman announces the pedagogical work that visual images will consistently perform in his poetry. With the line "Put first before the rest as light for all and entrance-song of all," Whitman conveys his purpose in writing, the audience for whom he writes, and explains how he will achieve his purpose. "Light for all," democratic enlightenment, is poetry's reason for being; "for all" and "of all," democracy's all-inclusive receptivity, is the *all* and audience for whom and of whom "Eidolons" will be the "entrance-song" to *Leaves of Grass*; and Eidolons, visual images, being "put first before the rest," come before any other themes or aesthetic techniques are "put in." In a later verse Whitman returns to the theme of democratic enlightenment when we learn that, in addition to his earlier instructions, his poetry should "mediate" and "interpret . . . eidolons" to the "Modern" and to "Democracy."[36] With the assistance of language *Leaves of Grass* will rely on eidolons to instruct a modern, democratic society about the meaning of visual images. Finally, then, to "put first before the rest . . . / That of eidolons," first and foremost, Whitman is saying, he will use the visual image to educate the *all*, and language's function, which is to decipher the meaning and establish the superordination of visual images, will fit his art's hermeneutic needs. Yet what, specifically, does "Eidolons" teach?

"Eidolons" teaches that the *all*, everything the *all* consists of, life itself, as I have said, are eidolons, visual images. Democracy's *all*, itself modeled on life or nature in its entirety, consists of eidolons. Thus "Eidolons" measures the entire compass of *Leaves of Grass*. Since a poetry of the *all* thus could not take up anything at all without speaking through visual images, "Eidolons" proves the educational burden he intends the visual image to bear. Whitman conveys this by ending each of his twenty-one verses with the word "eidolon(s)." Three verses capture the breadth of what appear as visual images:

> Of every human life,
> (The units gather'd, posted, not a thought, emotion, deed, left out,)
> The whole or large or small summ'd, added up,

In its eidolon.

. . . .

    All space, all time,
(The stars, the terrible perturbations of the suns,
Swelling, collapsing, ending, serving their longer, shorter use,)
    Fill'd with eidolons only.

. . . .

    Not this the world,
Nor these the universes, they the universes,
Purport and end, ever the permanent life of life,
    Eidolons, eidolons.[37]

"Ever the permanent life of life"—the eidolon, the visual image—is what is living as life itself, and life excludes nothing. This is why, "animating now to life itself," Whitman's poetry is all-inclusively receptive, and by imitating life as a whole could not be more inclusive and receptive. Everything that is, has been, and will be is a visual image, the "visible" being the "womb of birth" for universal "tendencies," for that which at some point will visibly assume the form of something or other. Poetry's eidolons are thus the "true realities," which he insists are "like eyesight."[38] Reality can *appear* to us only as eidolons, as the visual, which privileges seeing while teaching us to see the real world as appearance.

Now all this begs the question: Why does Whitman think of everything included in the *all* as an eidolon? Everything is in continuous motion, he declares, changing continuously. Although it is perceived as "fix'd," it really is "unfix'd."[39] With nothing constant there are only appearances, and as long as there are only appearances we can have only visual images. Motion is Whitman's deep ontology, the ontological argument conditioned by his reflections on the epistemological limits of language and the ("weak," nonfoundationalist) ontology of appearances they support. It is what the poet is to mediate and interpret to modern democracy. Everything is in flux, and all that is known of this reality of continuous change are the different forms change takes, the moving fleeting images changing appearances make available to sight. Visual images. Eidolons.

A moment's reflection on Bergson is useful here, for it reveals just how Bergsonian is Whitman philosophically, especially with regard to the concept of duration, though at the time "Eidolons" was composed the publication of *Creative Evolution* was yet thirty-five years in the future. To be sure, what I have just referred to as Whitman's deep ontology more than resonates with Bergson's ideas of motion, continuity, flux, becoming, in other words with the continuous indivisible movement and qualitative change he theorized as duration. According to the terms of *Creative Evolution*, Bergson would say that "as one who installs himself in becoming" Whitman "sees in duration the very life of things, the fundamental reality," and is thus "prepared to discover real duration there where it is still more useful to find it, in the realm of life and of consciousness."[40] Further comparison between the two would show them to be of one mind on many other and related matters, even to the point of their common interests in reconciliation through imitation. And it is tempting to be playful and imagine that perhaps Whitman was Bergson's muse when he penned the second sentence of *Matter and Memory*, "Here I am in the presence of images," which powerfully resonates with Whitman's position in relation to images in "Eidolons."[41] For purposes of the argument remaining in this chapter, however, it will suffice to find Whitman such an explicit proponent of the duration of the image, for more than anything that will establish his connection to film.

Hence only visual images remain for Whitman, though he does not go as far as Nietzsche, who with his abolition of the real world abolished the apparent world as well.[42] However, Whitman's thesis is no less radical. While appearances continuously appear, their continuously changing forms mean they also continuously disappear. Hence the visual images of which life consists, and those of which poetry consists animating now to life itself through their imitation of life, equally express the impermanence of eidolons. But life and poetry are alike in another way. It is not just poetry that imitates life. To paraphrase Whitman, like poetry "*life* animates now to life itself," by which I mean that, like poetry, life also lives by imitating life and affirms its nature as visual image through such imitation. As strange as this sounds, it is an idea at the core of "Song of Myself" to which "Eidolons" prepares our return.

As "Eidolons" insists, as much as any form of life every aspect of personal identity is a visual image. How the self appears outwardly, "we seeming solid wealth, strength, beauty build," moreover identity as the inner self, in Whitman's words, "Thy body permanent, / The body lurking there within thy body ... the real I myself," are continuously changing visual images.[43] This can mean only one thing. All those personas Whitman distinguishes in his democratically modeled all-inclusive lists of "Song of Myself," the myriad identities—"the pure contralto ... spinning-girl ... lunatic ... connoisseur ... conductor ... opium-eater ... President ... prostitute ...

fare-collector . . . Coon-seekers . . . Patriarchs"—from whom he will "weave the song of [himself]," as he explains in the concluding lines of verse 15, are visual images he imitates to exemplify the ever-changing visual images of "Eidolons." Imitating what he sees, he is thus *life imitating life* to self-creatively weave from democratic life his own, ever changing self-image. And his poetry's visual images, *animating now to life itself,* likewise model his acts of seeing and imitating the seen. So as seer and imitator, and in the mimetic images through which his poetry represents and teaches seeing and imitating, both Whitman himself and his verse become continuously changing visual images of appearances and their differences. Life and poetry become indistinguishable, with Whitman and his verse becoming images in motion—*motion pictures*—which along with all other eidolons make up the "permanent life of life" in all its different forms: nature, poetry, democracy, and, finally, the self-creating self. For Whitman it is not only the "universe," as Deleuze says, that is "cinema in itself," but poetry as well as life.[44]

Finally, as forms of the imitative image Whitman's self-creativity and the creativity of his verse both have democratic roots. On the one hand, as an eidolon himself, Whitman becomes different through his imitation of differences with which democracy surrounds him. On the other hand, his poetry's visual images are imitations of those selfsame visual appearances. Through their joint creation of the imitative image, self-creativity, poetry, and democracy work together to justify Whitman's refusal to

> postpone [his] acceptation and realization and scream at [his] eyes,
> That they turn from gazing after and down the road,
> And forthwith cipher and show [him] to a cent,
> Exactly the value of one and exactly the value of two, and which
> is ahead.[45]

Democracy's all-inclusiveness of differences saturates Whitman's vision, kindles his receptivity, and sustains his self-creativity and verse with endless visual images to imitate. It is the fundamental source of his "acceptation" and "realization," of those receptions and imitations from which his self-creativity and poetry create that self-made "diversity" of self he confides in "Song of Myself" is the democratic incitement he is least able to "resist."[46] And here, it can be added, democracy is the source of Whitman's transvaluation of values. Opening his eyes and poetry to countless sensuous possibilities for becoming different, democracy's all-inclusive receptivity to differences immunizes his vision and his verse against habituation to a commodified existence. Surrounding him with difference, democracy does not coerce Whitman "to scream at"—to force—his eyes to converge myopically on what putatively has worth calculable by some measure of equivalency, some "cipher," like the "cent," determining "exactly the value of one and exactly the value of two" and which is better. To the contrary, denying Whitman equivalents on which value can be based, democracy's differences in kind, "no two alike and every one good," as he explains in "Song of Myself," transcend value.[47]

WHITMAN'S ALL-INCLUSIVE, RECEPTIVE, IMITATIVE (MIMETIC) EYE

Not only Whitman's self-creativity and poetry through their imitations of visual images, or eidolons, but vision itself must have democratic roots. Otherwise the eyes could learn neither to encompass nor to discern differences within the *all* able to stimulate our receptivity and represent differences in imitable forms. Whitman thinks of democracy as the habitus of the senses, especially the habitus of sight, thus shaping the ways democracy's own temporal and spatial features are to be visually experienced. By territorializing a visual space for differences, which it rescues from their constructions as otherness by enabling them to appear all-inclusively within this space as visual images to be viewed receptively and imitated, democracy forms our visual situation and doing so transforms our relationship to seeing. Its revolutionary accumulation and concentration of visual images of diverse differences produce a corresponding democratic visual sense, an all-inclusive eye, and in addition a receptive and imitative eye. All-inclusive, receptive, and imitative, vision, in turn, next plays its part in reproducing an all-inclusive, receptive, and imitable democratic space as its own political condition.[48]

Consider verse 33 of "Song of Myself," one of Whitman's longest poetic stanzas, where vision works in precisely this way. With seeming breathlessness— "Speeding . . . Speeding . . . Speeding . . . Storming, enjoying, planning, loving, cautioning, Backing and filling, appearing and disappearing"—he sets free an all-inclusive eye that steadily and radically decenters his subjectivity over the course of 160 lines.[49] Surely he means no subject to retain its self-same identity throughout the peripatetic flights through space and time his all-inclusive eye commands. Hence his peripatetic "eye" decenters his "I," for when Whitman declares "I am afoot with my vision" it is his vision that travels and not Whitman himself. It is his eye that defines and will redefine him as his world's itinerant viewer and reporter, fusing seeing and moving and matter-of-fact observations in just these sorts of visual images, which he may intend here to recall the visual plane of a painted canvas.

> Space and Time! now I see that it is true, what I guess'd at,
> What I guess'd when I loaf'd on the grass . . .
> My ties and ballasts leave me, my elbows rest in sea-gaps,
> I skirt sierras, my palms cover continents,
> I am afoot with my vision.
> By the city's quadrangular houses—in log huts, camping with
>   lumbermen . . .
> Over the sharp-peak'd farmhouse, with its scallop'd scum and slender
>   shoots from the gutters . . .
> Approaching Manhattan up by the long-stretching island . . .
> Under Niagara, the cataract falling like a veil over my countenance . . .
> At musters, beach-parties, friendly bees, huskings, house-raisings . . .
> I visit the orchards of spheres and look at the product . . .
> And look at quintillions ripen'd and look at quintillions green.[50]

We get the picture. Whitman's eye is all-inclusive. It is a democratic eye moving nimbly through space and time to capture visual images of diverse peoples and their occupations and conditions, places and histories, and of geological formations, nature's bounties and its insurmountable challenges, among infinite other things. Whitman lists too many to be cited here, though in any event he invests this list, his longest, with an inertia whose relentless and accelerating motion persuades us with a Dionysian urgency that its inclusiveness extends *beyond* everyone and everything actually listed.

Verse 33 is a democratic list of visual images, in other words, being all-inclusive not because it is actually all-inclusive, rather because its aesthetic form communicates the intention to *continually strive* to be all-inclusive of those "each and everywhere whom I specify not, but include just the same," as Whitman puts it democratically in "Salut Au Monde!"[51] As vision and movement collaborate to bring into view the widest panorama of differences, the all-inclusive eye merely records without elaboration all that it sees to confine our vision to appearances. It releases vision from any obligation to cease its movement, study, and penetrate visual images to discover an underlying, unmoving essential element belonging to appearances. The all-inclusive eye's creative interest is to see, observe, and move on to facilitate both. But as it moves and sees and simply observes it *constitutes the space in which it does so.*

An all-inclusive democratic eye, it erects a veritable barrier concealing the unseen beneath visual images of appearances, so that appearances remain unknown and inscrutable, in their opacity irreducible to some shared property effacing their differences and offering a criterion of value restricting the eyesight to certain similar differences and excluding others. The all-inclusive peripatetic eye is a democratic barrier to the construction of truth, a barrier to judgments forcing us to "postpone [our] acceptation and realization and scream at [our] eyes," to determine the value of some to exceed the value of others, who are excluded by that measure.

Whitman's all-inclusive eye thus constitutes the world it sees, or more precisely in the act of seeing it by erecting a barrier to truth ensuring everyone and everything are to be taken as they appear, thus seen as mysterious. For appearances are intrinsically mysterious and, immune to comparison with regard to some innermost commonality, appear incomparably different. In its necessary allegiance to appearances, to their mysteries and differences, the all-inclusive eye thus fashions a world solicitous of a receptive eye. Observing blacksmiths, for example, Whitman says, "I *follow* their movements"; imagining himself looking out over the prow of a ship he tells us, "My eyes *settle* the land"; in the midst of busy places, people, and things he reports, "Looking with *side-curved head curious* what will come next."[52] "Follow" suggests engaged, perhaps fascinated; "settle" implies focus, concentration; "side-curved head" conveys awareness, perhaps curiosity. All are movements of an eye receptive to a mysterious world, whose every impression of a different someone, someplace, or something awakens our responsiveness, affirming the belonging of difference.

And with a mysterious world in sight whose diverse democratic *gestalt* the habitus of his vision has partly configured, Whitman's all-inclusive and receptive eyes have placed his imitative eye on the sensorial threshold of further arranging its own unique experience of the world. When he proposes "In all people I see myself," he reveals what he has meant by his frequent claims to have become someone else: "I myself become the wounded person," "I am the mash'd fireman," "I am an old artillerist," and so on.[53] By re-creating himself in the image of each persona, which is to see himself in another, it is as though he is looking in a mirror at his reflection, though what he sees is not himself but someone else. Thus Whitman's eye mirroring his image as it appears in a different form is really an act of imitation performed by a mimetic eye that decenters his subjectivity the more he weaves himself from the visual images of differences about him. It is the action of an "I" becoming a "we" that pluralizes his democratic world by populating it with ever-new visual images of difference.

Imitation is so often confused with copying, I want to return to the problem I earlier visited in this and the preceding chapter on which a final comment is due before I summarize my findings on Whitman's aesthetics and politics of reconciliation. If Whitman's self-weavings are imitations, moreover pedagogical models for how the *all* included within a democratic society are to individualize themselves, is the outcome of each of us imitating others' differences not a democratic mass society of the sort feared by such democratic theorists as Emerson, Tocqueville, and Mill? One characterized by a suffocating homogeneity?

In reply to this concern I must stress the qualification Whitman attaches to the closing lines of verse 15 of "Song of Myself," where he recommends imitation as the democratic means of individualization. Immediately before he famously concludes, "And of these one and all I weave the song of myself," he first stipulates, "And such as it is to be of these *more or less* I am."[54] Whereas with his concluding line Whitman teaches by example that each of us is to imitate his practice of imitation as the vehicle for creating our own identities, by his penultimate line he means our imitations of differences are—by becoming more or less like others'—only approximations. Neither his self-weavings nor ours are mere copies. Differences represented by others are not *replicated* mimetically, but are diverse forms we imitate to develop ourselves in new and different forms.

Whitman is hardly alone in theorizing individualization as the act of self-transformation through imitation. Here, in fact, his idea of becoming "more or less" like another without becoming a mere copy may be motivated by his desire to avoid Emerson's indictment of imitation, in "Self-Reliance," for being the ruin of individuality. Ironically, though, it may also be inspired by Emerson's own contrary *defense* of imitation, in "Quotation and Originality," for contributing to an impure originality that throughout history nevertheless constitutes cultural progress. Among those whose great work is indebted to imitation, Emerson names Voltaire, Wordsworth, and Bacon for being "originals [who] are not original." Emerson does not mean to deprive such "imitators" of their reputation for originality. He wants only to make the point that all of us stand on the shoulders of those who come before us and that we are all, even in our best thoughts, to recall Whitman, thus "more or less" like them. Or, as Emerson makes the point in different words, "old and new make the warp and woof of every moment."[55]

Whitman and Emerson agree, in other words, that by imitating others we more or less re-form them and ourselves and our cultures in the process. To this I should add that imitation as cultural and self-transformation is at least as old as the Roman Seneca, and is perhaps responsible for every great cultural renewal since, which would be Emerson's view. Consider, for example, the transformation of Florence during its remarkable Enlightenment in the first half of the fifteenth century, when its politics, art, and language itself underwent a metamorphosis made possible by its imitation of Greek and Roman humanism, which Florentine culture could then be said to resemble *more or less.*[56]

For Whitman as for Emerson, then, imitation does not necessarily oppose originality and foster uniformity. Rather, we become different from ourselves and from others as we develop ourselves through imitations of others, through the forms, the images or eidolons, they present. Of obvious philosophical importance to Whitman, we find him again making this argument in "By Blue Ontario's Shore" when he explains, "I reject none, accept all, then reproduce all in *my own* forms."[57] In this context he is drawing attention to his tacit distinction between imitations as mere duplicates of the different forms offered by others and imitations reproducing differences in *our own forms.* We should further recall Whitman confirming this distinction with a caveat he adds in *Democratic Vistas.* When speaking to America's future poets about the "image-making faculty," which "alone," he believes, is the one aesthetic technique able to "breathe into [a specimen of literature or art] the breath of life," he cautions that it permits of no "exact likeness," no "daguerreotyping."[58]

Such regular instruction Whitman offers about its nature also confirms what I have all along argued he understands by the image. Images must be visual, which is to be inferred from his just noted insistence that poetic images are not of certain types, not daguerreotypes, exact likenesses, which confirms they are visual images not to be confused with photographs, the standard for visual realism when Whitman wrote. Here he is not tacitly answering the question whether images are visual to begin with, but what standards of mimetic accuracy visual images do, could, or should meet.

From this I further determine that because Whitman's imitative image is visual though not photographic, the visual images through which he models his imitations of differences as the vehicles for creating and re-creating his identity would only more or less resemble—would be different from—the forms he imitates. And they are different from our own imitations of those same imitable forms, while our imitations of the same forms would also be different from each other's. Put differently, if Whitman's imitations are more or less like those he imitates, our imitations of those same forms would be more or less like his and more or less like each other's. For, as his poetry visually teaches, each of us no less than Whitman could reproduce *all*—all differences—in *our* own forms. What is more, the imitative eye is no more photographic than the imitative image. As the eye does not see in the same way for one as for another—we might say our eyes more or less see the same—we all see differences differently. Thus the imitative eye introduces variation into imitation by seeing differences differently even before Whitman or we imitate differences in our own forms. And our different ways of seeing are in addition accentuated by the continuous movement of difference, for as eidolons the visual images of differences everyone sees are constantly changing. The creative work of the imitative eye, together with the continuously changing visual images of what it sees, preclude the possibility that the creative work of Whitman's imitative image would produce imitations that are exact likenesses of imitable forms.

Regarding the specter of mass society, then, I arrive at the counterintuitive notion that imitation does not produce sameness to create a homogeneous mass, Walter Benjamin's aestheticized masses. Imitation, on the contrary, is productive of difference in several ways. As Whitman understands it, through imitation each of us becomes more or less different from others as we become more or less different from ourselves. This dual pluralization of individual differences pluralizes democratic society as a whole. It is a democratic all-inclusiveness of pluralized differences produced by our imitations of those within, a continuously actual and possible mimetic practice made possible by the democratic all-inclusiveness of differences who, at one time or another, as forms of otherness had been kept outside—marginalized, excluded, discriminated against, exterminated. Imitation does not create a democratic mass; it breaks it up. To recall Whitman in *Democratic Vistas*, "only from it," the mass, "comes the other, comes the chance of individualism. The two are contradictory, but our task is to reconcile them."[59]

THE RECONCILIATION IMAGE: FIRST EVOLUTIONARY FORM

I can now summarize the main features of Whitman's reconciliation image and begin to project its importance beyond this first form that evolved out of his work.

Whitman's poetry creates visual images having an ambiguous relationship to the verse to which they owe their birth. They communicate their meanings more or less independently of their linguistic contexts, which issue self-standing visual images, though also visual images continuing to rely on language to teach us how to see and that privilege vision outright. Self-standing or semilinguistic, Whitman's visual images constitute an aesthetic-political pedagogy by teaching the ideal of reconciliation. Visual images take political forms—democratic all-inclusiveness, receptivity, and the imitation of differences—which I have named the all-inclusive, receptivity, and imitative images. Visual images are thus not only the figural, visual effects of the word but its democratic effects and democratic lessons. As a whole, the all-inclusive, receptivity, and imitative visual images enable us to visualize a final democratic image, a final democratic lesson and effect, the reconciliation image, which corresponds to a change in the identity of the whole series of images and expresses the rationality of the whole as the reconciliation of identity and difference.

For Whitman this whole can be a nation or community or group or individual who, through its identity's inclusion, reception, and imitation of difference, in a word, through its *reconciliation* with difference, becomes different in the image of difference, and becoming more or less like difference avoids the violence it would inflict on difference if it were to secure the truth of its identity by constructing such difference as otherness. Corresponding to how Whitman's "Eidolons" conceptualizes this whole as life itself formed of continuously moving, qualitatively changing images, or life as *duration*, in Bergson's terms, the images of which the reconciliation image is composed, thus the reconciliation image itself, are always in motion. Continuously in motion, the reconciliation image not only records continuous real instances of reconciliation; it reflects a continuous process of identity striving to be ever more inclusive, receptive, and imitative of differences. Already in Whitman's aesthetics we find the paradoxical political character of the ideal of reconciliation and its reconciliation image that will dominate its aesthetics from here on. At one and the same time the ideal and image of reconciliation envision both the real achievement of reconciliation and a continuous—endless—striving for its achievement, what I referred to earlier as the dual temporality of a time arrived and a time yet to come.

Visual images of reconciliation are ubiquitous in Whitman's poetry, which finds in the rationality of the reconciliation image the rationality of democratic society, the image of images, and the rationality of the democratic nation, community, group, and individual. Thus the reconciliation image is the rationality of his poetry, an *aesthetic rationality* that is its aesthetic reason for being, which by sometimes erasing and at other times blurring the boundaries between the art of the word and the art of the visual image has created a new type of political concept. Whitman's image of reconciliation is not a creation of politics that reproduce social structures and relations as the repetition of the same, but of democratic politics whose repetitions—inclusions, receptions, and imitations—continuously change the identity of the part and the whole *as difference*.

There is another way to put this. Since Whitman's ideal of reconciliation is also a type of visual image and in all its dimensions I have laid out corresponds to this type, if "Eidolons" is correct and everything is a visual image owing to its continuously changing, durational nature, then as a concept Whitman's reconciliation image is the continuous movement of reconciliation itself, the continuous movement of identity becoming different in the image of difference. His poetry thus anticipates if it does not already foresee the future of the reconciliation image as it will appear in film, which by performing the work of aesthetic education as he understood it would constitute a democratic enlightenment through the visual image as he envisioned it. While this concept of the reconciliation image will be further fleshed out in future chapters, there is additional evidence I earlier promised encouraging us to appreciate Whitman's discovery in these terms.

In 1927 a poem by Whitman, long buried in one of his early notebooks belonging to a private collector and waiting to be discovered, was first published in its entirety as a barely thirty-page book that included a very brief introduction by Emory Holloway, its editor. Composing it five years more or less before the publication of the 1855 edition of *Leaves of Grass*, Whitman entitled his poem *Pictures*, devoting more than a hundred lines to accounts of events, figures, and scenes spanning recorded history and the history of life, from Adam and Eve through ancient Egypt, Greece, and Rome to the birth of modernity and its founding of the democratic republics, including America.[60] Whitman describes each account as a "picture."

Pictures included both the embryonic form of ideas Whitman later developed into poems and lines he distributed throughout poems in editions of *Leaves of Grass*. In addition to *Pictures*, Holloway had access to Whitman's accompanying notes and to miscellaneous relevant notes on manuscript scraps of the same period that Whitman bequeathed to a friend. Holloway cites Whitman's plans for the future of *Pictures*:

Break all this into several Pictures.
Poem of Pictures. Each verse presenting a picture of some characteristic scene, event, group or personage.

O Walt Whitman, show us some pictures;
America always Pictorial! And you Walt Whitman to name them
Yes—in a little house I keep suspended many pictures—it is not a
    fixed house,
It is round—Behold! it has room for America, north and south,
    seaboard and inland, persons.[61]

So in 1850 Whitman conceptualizes the type of image he will develop in *Leaves of Grass*, the visual image of democratic life, which formulates in words what will find its proper form as a "picture." In these notes I find an early, first iteration of Whitman's reconciliation image: America is "not a fixed" but an *all-inclusive* house, *receptive* to "all the varieties," as he then adds in line 5 of *Pictures* itself, which as a "Poem of Pictures" foregrounds imitation for the mimetic work performed by his visual images.

Holloway restricts the value of such poems as *Pictures* to their "biographical significance rather than in their poetic effect."[62] Against Holloway, among the great values of Whitman's poetry, beginning with *Pictures*, is his discovery of how the visual image can become the medium of democratic enlightenment. Hence we should say Whitman's visual images possess poetic effects that reside in the reconciliation image's democratic effects, its democratic lessons. Insofar as we are concerned with the enlightenment of democratic societies, Whitman's discovery thus brings us to the question we must ask in our time and that I will attempt to answer before *A Democratic Enlightenment* is completed: What is the most ubiquitous visual medium in which the reconciliation image could circulate in our own democratic world? Or, to get right to the point, are there reconciliation images in film?

If, in light of the infancy of cinema at the time he was writing, it seems improbable Whitman is the seer I make him out to be, his relationship to the future might be further estimated if I place his work in a broader theoretical context. To Deleuze's conception of film as composed of images whose movement reproduces the continuous movement, the duration or "becoming," of their aesthetic objects, can be added André Bazin's durational theory of cinema, which supports Deleuze's claim. Cinema, Bazin argues, "is objectivity in time. . . . Now, for the first time, the image of things is likewise the image of their duration."[63] With Deleuze and Bazin in the background, Whitman's reconciliation image, his poetry's creation of the visual image of "democratic becoming," as we have repeatedly seen, corresponds to their ontological conceptions of cinematic moving images as images of duration.

Yet there is something more. For Deleuze and Bazin, as for many theorists of duration (excluding Bergson), cinema is a critical practice opening up cultural possibilities associated with duration that emerge from historical relationships far more complex than those captured by teleological or linear or comparable causal models of development. While this would be true for Whitman, he would have also understood cinema, as he understood the visual dimensions of his poetry, to constitute a critical *political* practice for its reconciliation image being a durational image of "democratic becoming." Indeed we find Bazin offering an even more radical formulation of cinema than Deleuze that captures the political character of Whitman's reconciliation image. Cinema, Bazin further theorizes, possesses a photographic quality of *resemblance* to the object it represents that determines it to be "the being of the model of which it is the reproduction; it *is* the model."[64] Not only cinema, however. Recalling the argument of "Eidolons," for its dissolution of the difference between poetry and life, by sharing the being of the *all* it imitates, which is appearance and visual image, the visual image belonging to Whitman's poetry is likewise the being of the model it imitates; it *is* the model. It is "image." It is for this reason and this reason principally that the reconciliation *image* is the *model* of reconciliation.

At the ontopolitical level, this means the critical political practice of Whitman's visual image of reconciliation appearing in his poetry also appears in film. Put another way, what is decisive about the duration of the reconciliation image is not that one of its forms is poetry and the other film, which is a distinction without a difference according to the argument of "Eidolons" that being itself is image. As aesthetic models of a process of duration, of reconciliation, in both poetry and cinema the reconciliation image is the political being of the image (model) of reconciliation it reproduces. This is finally what is entailed by Whitman's ontological erasure of the difference between poetry and life.

How nice it would be if, under the present circumstances, one could claim that the less films appear to be works of art, the more they would be just that.

—Theodor W. Adorno, "Transparencies on Film"

Thinking with Adorno *against* Adorno

What are the challenges to Whitman's project of democratic enlightenment, to his conviction that modern democratic society can achieve reconciliation and that reconciliation can be taught through the visual image, the pedagogical vehicle of an aesthetic education? Surely no challenge calls Whitman's project into question more fundamentally than Horkheimer and Adorno's *Dialectic of Enlightenment* and their related works on art and mass culture. For no other critique of enlightenment offers a more sweeping rebuttal of the possibility Whitman envisioned for an enlightened democratic culture able to enlighten democratic America. Not only do Horkheimer and Adorno appear to refute our belief in reason itself as a force able to originate and then continuously author enlightenment, so that they seem to completely redefine enlightenment as a catastrophic human history for which they hold a congenitally toxic reason responsible. Since modern democracy owes its birth to the European Enlightenment, they also insist democratic culture reproduces, albeit in less toxic forms, the injurious features of enlightenment reason they identify. A democratic enlightenment consequently requires its possibility be defended against the critique of enlightenment posed by their work.

The difficulty of defending democratic enlightenment against a critique that could not be more damaging is mitigated by an unlikely alliance between Whitman and Horkheimer and Adorno running far deeper than their differences. At the heart of Horkheimer and Adorno's critique of enlightenment, and anchoring their challenge to Whitman's project, is an understanding of reason also offering resources for a defense and even an elaboration of the ideas of enlightenment and of democratic enlightenment. Of course, they anticipated no such contributions made by their critique to a project such as Whitman's. After all, the principal motif of their critique of enlightenment is an innately diseased reason, making their thesis equally deadly to ideas and ideals of modernity conceived as legacies of enlightenment reason, democratic ideas and ideals foremost among them. To rescue reason, the possibility of enlightenment and of an enlightened modernity from their critique of enlightenment, Horkheimer and Adorno's most damning critic, Jürgen Habermas, contends they wrongly equate the totality of reason with instrumental rationality. By implicating the entirety of reason in a history of violence, they are left without a normative concept of reason on which to base their own critique of enlightenment, which implicates them in a contradiction refuting the rationality of their own claims.[1]

When we consider Habermas's position, however, we find it mistaken in a way that contributes importantly to the formulation of the next part of my argument about the possibility of Horkheimer and Adorno's tacit alliance with Whitman, and how this alliance erects both a defense and an elaboration of a democratic enlightenment through its relation to their critique of reason. Briefly put, Habermas errs by taking Horkheimer and Adorno's principal motif at its face value, which is to misunderstand the critique of reason at the core of *Dialectic of Enlightenment*. Contrary to Habermas, they do not equate reason in its totality with instrumental reason. Rather, throughout *Dialectic of Enlightenment* we can discern analyses that intimate an *alternative* notion of reason to the concept of instrumental reason, the critical focus of their study.[2] This alternative concept of reason is the defining normative standpoint of Horkheimer and Adorno's critique of enlightenment rationality. But at the same time, their alternative concept is almost completely obscured, in part due to its fledgling nature, though in greater part by the sheer theoretical power of their critique of instrumental reason, precisely the thesis Habermas mistakenly insists dominates *Dialectic of Enlightenment* to the omission of any other conception of reason.

What, then, is this alternative concept of reason awaiting its retrieval from the most damaging critique of reason produced in twentieth-century political thought? And how does it create an alliance between Whitman and Horkheimer and Adorno able to offset the critique of the project of a democratic enlightenment the latter theorists' work at first appeared to entail? To answer these two questions I must get somewhat ahead of myself.

In this "First Bridge" and the two chapters that follow, I will trace the emergence of this alternative concept of reason as it gradually crystalizes. We will learn how it initially assumes an underdeveloped form in *Dialectic of Enlightenment* its authors importantly, though very generally, alluded to as their "positive concept" of enlightenment. And we will see how, a quarter of a century later, it achieves a far more developed though still not yet fully articulated conceptual form with the publication of Adorno's *Aesthetic Theory*. It is in this later work, Adorno's last, where he assigns this alternative concept its proper name: "aesthetic rationality" (or aesthetic reason, a usage *Aesthetic Theory* allows).[3] As I trace its crystallization in *Dialectic of Enlightenment* through *Aesthetic Theory*, I will also focus on the parallel development of Adorno's concept of reconciliation, for which aesthetic rationality is the philosophical foundation, and on the idea that for Adorno an image of reconciliation is modeled and taught by the modern artwork, which is the very avatar of aesthetic reason. In *Aesthetic Theory*, I shall thus show, Adorno proposes an alternative concept of reason, whose theoretical elements he assembles to then discover in the modern artwork an image of reconciliation from which a new form of enlightenment could be imagined, the rational alternative to the dominant catastrophic process of enlightenment theorized in *Dialectic of Enlightenment*.

To answer my second question, Adorno's aesthetic concept of reason is not only the normative standpoint of his and Horkheimer's critique of reason and enlightenment. It is likewise the deeply embedded philosophical basis of Whitman's project of democratic enlightenment that is revealed when, in the course of fleshing out Adorno's alternative concept of reason from *Aesthetic Theory*, I find the image of reconciliation for which it is the foundation to be a more evolved form of Whitman's own image of reconciliation. So it is not simply a matter of meeting Horkheimer and Adorno's objections to a democratic enlightenment with the arguments made in my previous chapters. When Whitman's and Adorno's two forms of the reconciliation image are placed side by side, all of those arguments—for Whitman's ideal of reconciliation; for his idea of an aesthetic education through a poetry that creates visual images that model and teach reconciliation; and for reconciliation, aesthetic education, and the visual image forming a project of democratic enlightenment—make it clear Whitman shares Adorno's concept of aesthetic reason. It is this shared philosophical concept of aesthetic reason on which their common ideas and ideals rest, the concept in which their tacit philosophical alliance is rooted, and the concept that insulates Whitman's project of democratic enlightenment against Horkheimer and Adorno's critique of enlightenment.

For there to be a true philosophical alliance, though, both sides must have benefited from their shared concept of aesthetic reason, which should not one-sidedly favor the defense of a democratic enlightenment. Here what becomes of interest is the contribution Whitman's project of a democratic enlightenment makes to what Horkheimer and Adorno hoped to achieve through an aesthetic conceptualization of reason. If a democratic enlightenment is eventually seen to rest on what Adorno conceptualized as aesthetic reason, which after a long interval of time appears in *Aesthetic Theory* to be the basis for the "positive concept" of enlightenment he and Horkheimer earlier alluded to in *Dialectic of Enlightenment*, could Whitman's project also qualify as this "positive concept" his unwitting allies had hoped to produce, though left underdeveloped? As I work this problem out, what is especially important is the depth of their alliance based on their shared concept of aesthetic reason, which includes the ideal of reconciliation and the idea it can be modeled and taught through visual images. Ultimately this means that Whitman's concept of a democratic enlightenment may correspond to Horkheimer and Adorno's concept of a "positive enlightenment" to which *Aesthetic Theory* paved the theoretical way.

Insofar as these are the essential terms of their alliance, Whitman's project cannot double as their positive concept of enlightenment, however, if Horkheimer and Adorno preclude the form of aesthetic education democratic enlightenment requires. Whitman looked to poetry in the first instance, though finally to the visual images poetry created for the democratic medium able to model and teach the ideal of reconciliation to democratic America. Horkheimer and Adorno's visual images of reconciliation are limited to modernist artworks, though, and in comparison to poetry are a more rarified form of aesthetic education inaccessible to a democratic majority. Yet as their reliance on modern art points up, it must also be admitted that poetry has not become the "New World Literature" that in *Democratic Vistas* Whitman proposed could become the popular artwork of the future, equipped to bear the educational burden of democratic enlightenment. No less than Horkheimer and Adorno, Whitman appears to finally lack a cultural medium to perform the pedagogical role of teaching the ideal of reconciliation.

It is at this point that the philosophical alliance between Whitman and his two would-be critics becomes fascinating. At the conclusion of chapter 2 I raised the possibility that through his use of words to create visual images Whitman brought his poetry to the threshold of the transition from the cultural period in which he lived to our own, a culture increasingly less defined by the word and ever more dominated by visual images in motion. Whitman's verse thus prefigures a popular culture in which not poetry but film would teach the ideal of reconciliation to become his vehicle of aesthetic education through the visual image. Against such a possibility, we shall see, Horkheimer and Adorno held that film, like popular culture in general, is governed by enlightenment reason hostile to difference and reconciliation and incapable of the aesthetic education Whitman's project anticipates. To the contrary, however, here is what I propose to show.

The aesthetic form of reason Adorno conceptualized in *Aesthetic Theory* may not be confined to the modern artwork, as he insisted. Rather, in light of the close examination of Adorno's *Aesthetic Theory* I intend to carry out in my following two chapters, specifically of its elements of aesthetic reason and how they create the reconciliation image, I will position us to consider whether the reconciliation image aesthetic reason produces in the modernist artwork is discoverable in an entirely different aesthetic form: *film*. If this proves to be the case, Whitman and Horkheimer and Adorno would share not only a concept of aesthetic reason and its ideal of reconciliation but the idea to which Whitman's project pointed: that reconciliation can be taught through special types of visual images, by images in motion, by film. And if it were on the basis of this revised relationship between reconciliation and film that Horkheimer and Adorno benefited from the concept of aesthetic reason they shared with Whitman, his contribution to their alliance would be significant. It would mean Whitman's idea of a popular culture of democratic enlightenment would thus double as their positive concept of enlightenment.

So here we come to a radical theoretical turn of events. A critique of enlightenment reason threatening to revoke Whitman's greatest democratic vista potentially proves to be its great ally. In the course of formulating their critique, Horkheimer and Adorno begin to conceptualize an alternative, aesthetic form of reason on which Whitman's idea of a democratic enlightenment, married to an ideal of reconciliation and a practice of aesthetic education through which it is taught, can also be seen to rest. At the same time, this alliance promises to further develop aspects of Horkheimer and Adorno's critique of enlightenment, specifically a possibility that can be raised in light of the concept of aesthetic reason forming the basis of their "positive concept" of enlightenment. The possibility to be investigated is whether the visual image of reconciliation animated by aesthetic reason, which Adorno believed was limited to modern art, can also be found in film. Such a possibility first emerged from my construction of Whitman's project of democratic enlightenment, which, by relying on words to create the visual image of reconciliation, pointed toward film as the democratic vehicle of aesthetic education. It is therefore a possibility that serves to elaborate Whitman's project while it develops Horkheimer and Adorno's attempts to think positively about enlightenment. Hence I develop the implication of this possibility that through film Whitman's democratic enlightenment fulfills Horkheimer and Adorno's theoretical ambitions for a positive concept of enlightenment.

To be sure, in the final analysis this possibility will come to rest on my analysis of Adorno's *Aesthetic Theory*. There I work hard to flesh out and further develop the concept of aesthetic reason from its elements he had assembled in his last work, so that we might then understand clearly how it produces the image of reconciliation. For if we were to systematically break down the reconciliation image into the elements that compose and produce it, as I intend, we would finally be in a position to entertain the possibility of whether those same elements, thus the possibility of the reconciliation image itself and the event of a positive *and* democratic enlightenment it fosters, can be found in film. If it can be discovered in film, this image of reconciliation rooted in Adorno's aesthetic theory would then certainly be a second and more evolved form of the reconciliation image I originally found in Whitman's poetry.

It cannot be stressed too greatly, of course, that for Adorno film and popular culture more generally were hardly cultural media for images of reconciliation, but on the contrary were governed by enlightenment rationality's opposing urge to eliminate difference, as I also intend to show. So if such an analysis as I am proposing allows us to discover the reconciliation image in film from the elements in *Aesthetic Theory* he argues form it in modern artworks, I will have *thought with* Adorno *against* Adorno.

Here is how I will proceed. In the remaining pages of this "First Bridge" I will reconstruct Horkheimer and Adorno's *Dialectic of Enlightenment* with an eye to ultimately retrieving their orphaned concept of aesthetic reason, while all along focusing my analysis on their critique of enlightenment and then extending that analysis to Adorno's subsequent critiques of the culture industry and especially of film, which among all products of the culture industry in his view falls victim to enlightenment rationality. Once the embryonic, incipient form of aesthetic reason is retrieved, to learn how it produces Adorno's image of reconciliation in the modern artwork, in the two chapters following I will then flesh out and further develop aesthetic reason in a more fully articulated conceptual form than Adorno left it in *Aesthetic Theory*. With this I will be able to eventually pursue Adorno's image of reconciliation in film to determine if film offers democratic society visual images of the ideal of reconciliation, which as Adorno theorizes the reconciliation image are a more highly evolved form of the image Whitman first imagined could be modeled and taught by means of an aesthetic education through poetry. Completing that task will eventually allow me to say whether Whitman's democratic enlightenment provides the missing terms for Horkheimer and Adorno's positive concept of enlightenment.

TWO CONCEPTS OF REASON

Dialectic of Enlightenment assumes the commonplace understanding of enlightenment as the ascendancy of reason, though Horkheimer and Adorno do not confine reason's ascendancy to the European Enlightenment. They understand enlightenment to be a historical *process* originating millennia before what they and others commonly recognize to be "the Enlightenment of modern times [*der neueren Zeit*]" dating in Europe from the seventeenth through the eighteenth centuries.[4] They also reject the concept of enlightenment as it has been formulated narrowly to sum up its modern history, the belief that reason is responsible for ushering in human progress. Against this they argue the enlightenment process charted an unrelenting course of violence of a very special sort. From its most primitive beginnings and according to its nature, reason principally exhibited the defining quality of enlightenment, a type of violence unable to do otherwise than inflict violence on difference in all its diversity of forms. This is the central thesis of *Dialectic of Enlightenment*, which further maintains the process of enlightenment achieves its apotheosis during the Enlightenment of modern times, when reason and violence are fused from that time forward. For Horkheimer and Adorno anti-Semitism's extermination of the Jews during the twentieth century offers recent evidence for the modern perfection of reason's capacity for the onslaught of violence toward difference enlightenment has waged unabated throughout its history.

Dialectic of Enlightenment's final chapter, "Elements of Antisemitism: Limits of Enlightenment," summarizes a complex logic of analysis of reason's violence toward difference as its authors trace it from its origins to the extermination of the Jews. If elements of anti-Semitism set limits to enlightenment, and enlightenment is an immemorial historical process, then these elements have been at work in reason from the very birth of thinking onward, throughout thought's entire history of enlightenment up to the very moment anti-Semitism threatens "the Jews are to be wiped from the face of the earth." Horkheimer and Adorno's thesis is catastrophic. Anti-Semitism and enlightenment share essential elements, and those elements common to both are common to the genesis and evolution of reason, the process of enlightenment itself. Since genocide and holocaust are the culminations of a process of enlightenment fueled by elements of anti-Semitism present when thought began, when they begin *Dialectic of Enlightenment* they must be centrally concerned with the nature of reason from its origins. Enlightenment's defining element is "the urge . . . *to make everyone the same*," by which they mean *the urge to eliminate difference.*[5] Moreover the urge to eliminate difference is the defining element of anti-Semitism's destruction of the Jews. Hence it is the element to be looked for when *Dialectic of Enlightenment* opens, and which must guide any reading of their text from that point through its final chapter.

Before turning to their argument, however, we must also recognize its logic is more complex than I have acknowledged thus far. "Elements of Antisemitism" ends on a note of optimism utterly at odds with the dire pessimism of *Dialectic of Enlightenment*'s five preceding chapters and the "Notes and Sketches" forming its afterword. "Enlightenment itself, having mastered itself and assumed its own power, could break through the limits of enlightenment."[6] Here Horkheimer and Adorno have returned to the promissory statement of their original preface, where they explained that from their first chapter they "intended to prepare a *positive concept* of enlightenment." The implication is clear. In the first chapter and those following they will conceptualize an idea of enlightenment that is an *alternative* to the enlightenment thwarted by elements of reason belonging to anti-Semitism—thwarted by the urge to eliminate difference—through which enlightenment becomes "entangle[d] in blind domination."[7]

In the pages between their preface's declaration of intent and their closing statement of optimism, then, along with the elements of anti-Semitism sabotaging enlightenment we must also search for evidence of a positive concept of enlightenment, or for properties of reason from which one could be conceptualized. On the one hand, we see Horkheimer and Adorno historically unmasking reason to show throughout its history that its relation to difference is essentially and predominantly violent. On the other, their history of reason shows reason to be in conflict with itself. Within reason there is a struggle between a "formalistic" and "aesthetic" side determining whether reason's relation to difference will be violent or oriented toward reconciliation. In their broad historical narrative, formalistic reason's violence dominates and its reconciliatory aesthetic orientation has but a fleeting presence. Nevertheless aesthetic reason's profile can be made out distinctly in exceptional episodes where it stands its ground in its epic struggle with formalistic reason. It is through *Dialectic of Enlightenment*'s history of reason that their positive concept of enlightenment, or aesthetic reason's power to effect reconciliation with difference, begins to take shape.

Taking up "the concept of enlightenment" at the outset of *Dialectic of Enlightenment*, Horkheimer and Adorno immediately locate enlightenment's key element in reason's earliest, "preanimistic" stage. It is the element they trace forward to anti-Semitism, which in that form allows them to realize it sets limits to enlightenment. To the primitive mind the unknown is terrifying, and its enlightenment coincides with its urge to abolish the unknown to be rid of the fear it inspires. Nietzsche's influence resonates here: "Danger, disquiet, anxiety attend the unknown—the first instinct is to *eliminate* these distressing states."[8] Reason's orientation to the unknown is born from its aboriginal, instinctual responses to nature's incomprehensible power, in the face of which reason habitually transcribes the unknown. Whatever appears unfamiliar, whatever, in a word, appears *different* from what reason knows, to an unreflective reason assumes the image of the unknown with its deep historical registers of terror. Reason eradicates fear of the unknown by compulsively eradicating what or who everywhere appears different.

Horkheimer and Adorno discover reason's compulsive behavior throughout the history of thought. At every stage enlightenment's advancing efforts to abolish the unknown put difference perennially at risk. Reason's compulsion, its terrible modus operandi unvarying in time or place, is driven to make everyone and everything "known" through recognition of their commonalities. All that is unknown and threatening becomes known and unthreatening if it resembles something familiar and already "known." Identity thus becomes the formalistic expression of reason's urge to eliminate difference. Everyone and everything becomes known with regard to how they share an identity, with regard to *how they are the same*. Reason is hostile toward those falling outside the norms defining shared identities. Whoever or whatever differs from the norm risks being constructed as the other, whose fate is to suffer assimilation, marginalization, exclusion, discrimination, or, at the extreme, extermination. Reason's compulsion to eliminate difference through identity's normative allegiance to sameness is the violence in reason. This is why Horkheimer and Adorno consider it the most basic element of anti-Semitism and the limit of enlightenment beyond which it cannot progress.

From its inception, however, reason has a more complex makeup than is evinced by its habitual predisposition to be frightened of the unknown and violent toward difference. Making nature *known* according to the universal property of being *unknown*, primordial thought catches itself in an inconsistency. Known everywhere as the unknown, nature's identity is familiar *and* mysterious at the same time, a paradox Horkheimer and Adorno root in reason itself. If nature is understood to be the known and the unknown, then "language expresses the contradiction that [nature] is at the same time itself and something different [*anderes*] than itself, identical and not identical."[9] *Reason is divided against itself.* Set on the mastery of knowing nature to dispel the fear of the unknown, thinking is also open to the possibility nature may be *different* from how reason knows it, and universally different from how it is universally known.

Now if we are sensitive to the nuances of this argument we have an indication Horkheimer and Adorno do not absolutely equate reason with violence toward difference. And if we do not miss it here, then reason's antiformalistic power can subsequently be seen to surface episodically in *Dialectic of Enlightenment.* While Horkheimer and Adorno leave it unnamed in that work, I believe it is the original formulation of what Adorno in *Aesthetic Theory* will later call "aesthetic rationality." Hence it is a power laying the basis for a second and alternative concept of reason to formalistic rationality. But since reason's second and alternative concept is prefigured anonymously in *Dialectic of Enlightenment,* from here on I will refer to it as "aesthetic reason" in preparation for fleshing it out and further developing it in Adorno's later work in my following two chapters.

In anticipation of that discussion I now note its significance. Whereas violence characterizes the dominant identity-imposing power of formalistic reason, aesthetic reason is unafraid of the unknown, subdues violence by being *receptive* to difference. Reason's *receptivity* augurs the reconciliation of identity and difference, which allows us to project a novel, future configuration of reason and to envision Horkheimer and Adorno's ultimate goal, a positive enlightenment where reason's formalistic side relinquishes its sovereignty over its aesthetic, receptive side. If we continue to recover the aesthetic side of reason from *Dialectic of Enlightenment* we first see glimmering in preanimism, it becomes possible to project reason's evolution beyond its late stages, where it is dominated by its urge for sameness.

To that end Horkheimer and Adorno's analysis of myth, the second stage they distinguish in reason's evolution, is decisive. With its pantheon of deities populating the world with mysterious powers, Greek myth honors the unknown by acknowledging that the world exceeds our understanding. However, the explanations myth offers for human and natural events, and the hope to influence those events through entreaty to the gods, also records the ancients' fear of the unknown and their need to dispel it. Hence the formalistic *and* aesthetic sides of reason can both be seen playing formative roles in shaping human relationships to mythical forces. Although Horkheimer and Adorno underscore the dominance of formalistic reason in myth by concluding that Homeric epics prove mythology "set in motion the endless process of enlightenment," each of the *Odyssey*'s episodes they analyze show in its early history that reason traced out a path challenging its dominant tendency.[10]

Of these episodes I will limit myself to a brief discussion of Horkheimer and Adorno's treatment of the Sirens (*Odyssey*, book 12), as it is especially significant for offering potent evidence for reason's aesthetic dimension. For by revealing the defining connection between reason and art it provides strong justification for referring to formalistic reason's opponent as "aesthetic rationality," the name it assumes in *Aesthetic Theory*. Thus by studying this episode we firm up this connection between art and reason as prelude to my next two chapters, where it becomes the focal point of my analysis, which fleshes out Adorno's concept of aesthetic reason forecast in *Dialectic of Enlightenment* from the elements of it he assembled in *Aesthetic Theory*.

In their reading of Homer's famous Sirens episode, Horkheimer and Adorno explain how formalistic rationality guides the ingenious plan Odysseus devises to experience the Sirens' song while protecting his life and the lives of his shipmates from its dangers. Having his crew bind him to the mast of his ship and plug their ears with wax so that deaf to the Sirens' lure they can row safely past, Odysseus also deafens his men to his plea to be released from his bonds as he listens to the Sirens' beckoning call. Horkheimer and Adorno accentuate the work of formalistic reason in the prototypically bourgeois figure cut by Odysseus. By means of mental labor anticipating the calculating enlightenment rationality on which capitalism thrives, Odysseus enjoys the Sirens' song while avoiding the mortal threat it poses. His self-preservation is ensured and the terror of the unknown is mastered through elements of reason featured in myth through which reason progresses toward the enlightenment of modern times. Yet what "difference" the Sirens represent, the utter fulfillment of desire, which threatens the freedom from mortal danger reason secures only by resisting such unconditional pleasures, is not completely mastered. Able to indulge in their music as he sails past the Sirens, Odysseus bound experiences a compromised pleasure, a pleasure experienced not in an immediate but in a sublimated way—*rather like the pleasure taken in an artwork.* "The bonds by which [Odysseus] has irrevocably fettered himself to praxis at the same time keep the Sirens at a distance from praxis: their lure is neutralized as a mere object of contemplation, as art."[11]

While formalistic reason dominates the Sirens episode, a form of aesthetic reason persists in a subordinate role that—analogous to the pleasures of art in the modern world—foreshadows Adorno's concept of aesthetic rationality in *Aesthetic Theory*. In *Dialectic of Enlightenment* we have just seen Horkheimer and Adorno make this analogy explicit. When in the next two chapters we look closely at the relation between art and aesthetic reason, we will better appreciate how the Sirens episode offered us precious clues into the nature of aesthetic reason pointing us to its more evolved concept in Adorno's *Aesthetic Theory*. And when we focus on the concept of aesthetic reason in *Aesthetic Theory*, we will know for certain that in *Dialectic of Enlightenment* the Sirens myth tied the aesthetic rationality of the artwork to a positive concept of enlightenment, which is based on reason's receptivity to difference represented by its pleasures taken in art.

Beginning with Greek philosophy, however, reason enters a new stage. Whereas reason in myth had not been obedient to one principle but internally divided, granting difference representation against reason's far stronger compulsion to construct difference as otherness, from Greek philosophy through the European Enlightenment and the development of modern science demythologization advances rapidly. Reason finally expels mythical powers, gods, cosmic and spiritual forces from its conceptions of the universe, leaving nothing in nature or the world mysterious and unknown or unknowable. Since reason's aim is to ensure nothing *different* from what it renders familiar will threaten self-preservation, from Plato's mathematical models through Bacon's experimental methods, Sade's manipulations of body and mind to the culture industry's rationalizations of consumption, reason's erstwhile alliance with difference is rescinded in the interest of quieting reason's fears of the unknown. For Horkheimer and Adorno reason's demythologization is coextensive with the enlightenment of modern times.

ENLIGHTENMENT AS DE-AESTHETICIZED REASON,
FILM AS DE-AESTHETICIZED ART

With their analysis of the culture industry Horkheimer and Adorno approach an event horizon marking the extreme point of their critique of enlightenment. "Culture today," they declare, "strikes [*schlägt*] everything with sameness," which proves reason's evolution had been propelled by the urge to make everyone and everything the same.[12] Or, because the process of enlightenment inevitably culminates in fascism, by the urge to exterminate difference. Fascism's destruction of the Jews for believing in an unknowable God casts them as the very embodiment of *difference*, as the "negative principle as such," which establishes the Holocaust as reason's highest stage of enlightenment.[13] Throughout human history formalistic reason's violence toward difference proves to be reason's governing drive, the fundamental element of anti-Semitism constituting the absolute limit of enlightenment, the black hole from which the light of aesthetic reason cannot escape.

There can be no more extreme position than this *too* extreme position, and though Horkheimer and Adorno lead us there they too must believe it is too extreme. For as we learned at the outset of our discussion, their intent was to elaborate *two* concepts of reason: a critique of enlightenment that in the course of analysis would also "prepare a positive concept" of enlightenment. Yet that second project, stirring in the attention they paid to the aesthetic properties of reason at its two earliest stages of enlightenment, was checked by the increasing force of their analysis of formalistic reason's evolution. Enlightenment *de-aestheticized* reason, neutralizing its receptive orientation to difference in favor of satisfying reason's urge to make everything the same. Do the extremes of their theoretical position reflect Horkheimer and Adorno's loss of control of their argument due to their historical situation? How could it have been otherwise? They wrote from the standpoint of the Holocaust, which by threatening the annihilation of the Jews—the "negative principle as such," we recall—threatened the ultimate annihilation of difference. Reason bent on the extermination of difference overwhelmed and obscured any counterevidence their work turned up potentially forming the basis on which they could develop a positive concept of enlightenment.

Decades after *Dialectic of Enlightenment* the Holocaust continued to haunt Adorno's essays on the culture industry, which in the intervening years seems to him to have further perfected its power to stamp everything with sameness, especially film, as is evident when we compare his earlier essays on the culture industry to those published much later. As in "The Schema of Mass Culture," in 1942, and his coauthored chapter with Horkheimer in *Dialectic of Enlightenment*, "The Culture Industry: Enlightenment as Mass Deception," in 1944, for which the former essay was the rough theoretical template, in his later essays on the culture industry, notably "Transparencies on Film" in 1966 and "The Culture Industry Reconsidered" in 1967, Adorno concentrates his energies on the critique of film.[14] Of the reasons for this, two are particularly important.

Film carries the brunt of the ideological burden of the culture industry. It is the increasingly ubiquitous medium of formalistic reason, as Adorno had argued early on in "The Schema of Mass Culture" when referring to our age as "an age of film."[15] In addition, although as an art form film was (and is) often considered to be the continuation of modern art in another form, it was not by Adorno. Rather, in relation to culture at large, Adorno considered film to be the medium of formalistic rationality continuing enlightenment's de-aestheticization of reason. And in relation to modernism in particular he considered film the de-aestheticization of art, specifically of the modernist artwork in which aesthetic reason had been the factor determining aesthetic form's creation of images of reconciliation. If we compare Adorno's early critique of the culture industry, including his collaboration with Horkheimer, with its subsequent versions, we find three themes remaining constant in his critique of film.

There is, first, the problem of "sameness" we have seen to be the defining feature of the long historical process of enlightenment. It is no less defining of film. Sameness is the commodity form of film itself, and thus its value rests on the degree to which films are equivalents of one another. Hence Horkheimer and Adorno regard cinema as a branch of culture managed as an industry producing essentially interchangeable films. Precisely because Hollywood studios market variations of films already proven to be "successful prototype[s]," the film industry is "unanimous within itself," an integrated "system" obedient to the principle of equivalency, as Adorno argues in "The Schema of Mass Culture" and with Horkheimer in "The Culture Industry: Enlightenment as Mass Deception."[16] Horkheimer and Adorno proliferate a constellation of concepts that capture the multidimensionality of filmic sameness, of film's "reproduction of sameness" and "unending sameness."[17] Stressing in "The

Schema of Mass Culture" that authentic and inauthentic film images alike appear "so frequently that they are no longer perceived in their own right but only as repetitions whose perpetual sameness always expresses an identical meaning," in "The Culture Industry Reconsidered" Adorno ironically concludes, "No homeland can survive being processed by the films which celebrate it, and which thereby turn the unique character on which it thrives into an interchangeable sameness."[18]

Second, all other aspects of film follow from its commodity form or sameness, which as argued by Horkheimer and Adorno in "The Culture Industry: Enlightenment as Mass Deception" and by Adorno in "The Culture Industry Reconsidered" recapitulates thematic elements of Adorno's earlier "The Schema of Mass Culture." Taking the arguments of all three essays together, by determining the types of films produced the principle of equivalency works to construct viewing experiences as ideologically interchangeable as film itself. Hence a key concern is the perceptual erasure of differences between film and the everyday world by the "sound film." Held hostage technologically to the "unbroken surface of existence" beneath which the origins of conflict are hidden, sound perpetuates an ideological image of an undisturbed world where "there are no longer any real conflicts to be seen."[19] Sound is thus a means of mechanical duplication that "trains those exposed to it to identify film directly with reality."[20] Or conflicts are resolved through "predetermination," referring to the ways film inevitably resolves conflicts to suppress awareness of possibilities for social change the development of conflict would have encouraged. Time, emptied of transformative possibilities stemming from contradiction and conflict, is emptied of meaning. Time is overcome.[21] Technology and techniques, such as predetermination, guarantee viewers will make uniformly seamless transitions from a film experience where conflict is only an uncomfortable but soon to be resolved momentary disruption of the status quo ante to a world outside the theater mirroring such illusions. All such properties of film determined by the commodity form are presupposed in "The Culture Industry Reconsidered," when Adorno later stresses the culture industry's products "are no longer *also* commodities, they are commodities through and through."[22]

"Predetermination" leads us to a third element of Horkheimer and Adorno's critique of film. Since film narrative artificially resolves conflicts that if made visible would reveal contradictions beneath the surface of society and call its normative and structural legitimacy into question, then film's narrative structure is important in relation to film's aesthetic details, which have a potential for critique over and against the film plot. Sufficiently numerous, multidimensional, often accidental and unscripted, aesthetic details can escape the organizational mastery of the film industry's technical apparatus. Film characters, for instance, are sufficiently complex to qualify as aesthetic details possessing a life potentially independent of the film plot. Once set into motion by a film's narrative structure, its characters could possibly evolve in multiple ways, some of which could communicate deeper, structural understandings of the contexts of characters' predicaments than their plots are scripted to offer. But plots, Horkheimer and Adorno complain, are "willfully denied the development called for by characters." So the potential for critique attached to aesthetic details as central to film as its characters is short-circuited by the typical underdevelopment of film narratives.[23]

As are the potentials for critique associated with a film's more subtle myriad aesthetic details. Right down to the level of "the raised hem of the leading lady's dress," an "explicit and implicit, exoteric and esoteric catalog of what is forbidden and what is tolerated" shapes film, such that "even the most minor details are modeled according to this lexicon."[24] The aesthetic autonomy of each image of an aesthetic detail is canceled as film's narrative structure brings it into harmony with a script's affirmative ideological identity as a whole. Narratives may require images to repeat themselves with a regularity ensuring their connotations are lost to the prepared literal meaning their repetitions are meant to convey. Or their repetitions may betray such a fixed denotative meaning that images act as commands to viewers "to translate the images back into writing," which identifies the image with a literal narrative meaning ideologically subservient to the established society. Once its meaning is captured by a film's ideologically infused narrative, the image "turns into immediate reality" and film and society mirror each other.[25] Such formulations of the technical mastery of the aesthetic detail as film commands highlight the extent to which Horkheimer and Adorno believe the process of enlightenment manufactures a self-enclosed societal whole whose ideological identity includes no parts—a film industry, a film, an aesthetic detail—different from what contributes to its perpetuation in its given form.

"Sameness," the manipulation of viewers' cognitive experiences of film through such techniques as "predetermination," and the administration of the aesthetic detail—in a phrase, the tyranny of the commodity form—all de-aestheticize the rationality of film. De-aestheticization deprives film of the aesthetic autonomy belonging to aesthetic rationality responsible for creating an image of reconciliation between identity and difference, which in modern art illuminated society's violence toward difference as it modeled the possibility for overcoming that violence. What this means is that any aesthetic theory of the reconciliation image in film must show that, like forms of modern art before it, film resists de-aestheticization to become the avatar of aesthetic reason and the aesthetic representation of Horkheimer and Adorno's positive concept of enlightenment.

THE RECONCILIATION IMAGE IN ART AND FILM

If Horkheimer and Adorno's critique of enlightenment as the de-aestheticization of reason, and of film as the de-aestheticization of art, continue to register the impact of the Holocaust on their work, there is something else we must consider. Should the extremity of their theoretical position not be reassessed in a historical context removed from the crisis that shaped their thinking? Surely our own present historical standpoint is improved over Horkheimer and Adorno's. Although the world has not rid itself of genocide, the current historical situation made possible by the social evolution of Western democracy after the Holocaust is more favorable to difference. Our own historical standpoint thus encourages us to return to Horkheimer and Adorno's *Dialectic of Enlightenment* to cultivate what fledgling resources it prepared to help us to imagine how to break through the limits of enlightenment so we can reconsider the possibility of reconciliation.

To be sure, I have tried to make progress toward this reassessment by being sensitive to and retrieving the divergent properties of reason that surfaced in my reconstruction of *Dialectic of Enlightenment*'s genealogy of reason, properties suggesting there is a form of reason not fearful of but receptive to difference. Alert to the connection between these properties of reason and art, I found evidence in that work proving Horkheimer and Adorno were developing not one but two concepts of reason. Formalistic (instrumental) reason is violent toward difference. Aesthetic reason is oriented to the reconciliation of identity and difference. With a narrative of reason now more complicated than one confining its interest, in Horkheimer and Adorno's own words, to the "tireless self-destruction of enlightenment," it becomes possible to anticipate the development of a more fully fledged concept of aesthetic reason in *Aesthetic Theory* from which, most importantly, an alternative, positive concept of enlightenment can be envisioned.[26]

Since we now know this concept of aesthetic reason first appeared in an embryonic form in Adorno's coauthored work with Horkheimer, we should begin again where they left off. With the powerful advantage *Aesthetic Theory* offers of a far more developed concept of aesthetic reason than the one they prematurely abandoned in *Dialectic of Enlightenment*, I believe Adorno's later concept can be fleshed out and even further developed to allow us to reassess their critiques of film in light of the possibility that aesthetic reason plays a far more prominent role in film than they were able to understand in the light of their work's earlier incipient forms of aesthetic rationality. Such a reassessment has important implications for the possibility of Whitman's democratic enlightenment and Horkheimer and Adorno's positive concept of enlightenment, which both had reconciliation as their enlightenment's animating ideal, whose visual images we will discover in my final chapters circulating through film.

So against the critique of the culture industry in *Dialectic of Enlightenment* and its reprise in Adorno's later essays, let us suppose film does not de-aestheticize art. As a cultural expression of aesthetic reason film may be an aesthetic vehicle for the image of reconciliation. If this supposition proves correct, insofar as the rationality of film is aesthetic, enlightenment would not have completely de-aestheticized reason either.

But what genres of film could provide grounds for this supposition? When answering this question I will have more in mind than those "liberal deviations of the kind the film industry can still permit itself in its own preserve," by which Horkheimer and Adorno meant films whose criticisms are tolerated and even encouraged and demanded by a culture unafraid of such occasional challenges to its sovereignty.[27] More in mind, in other words, than the independent films conventional studios sometimes risk and those exceptional films once produced by film studios that were independent of the major film studio system.[28] And I will have more in mind than films whose critical disposition is the outcome of temporary immaturities in technical mastery, to which Adorno in "Transparencies on Film" attaches a "liberating quality" resulting from what yet remains technologically "uncontrolled and accidental." Finally, I will have more in mind than cinematic attempts to counter the false everydayness of film realism with narratives that cannot avoid sounding "pompous and inauthentic" in relation to the illusory images of harmony such attempts try to shatter.[29] I will look elsewhere than for all such cinematic anomalies, which Horkheimer and Adorno discount as meager sources of positive enlightenment for failing to produce images of reconciliation.

Even if they had not discounted such cinematic anomalies, however, and we could look to the anomalous film for an image of reconciliation, this would not satisfy the most important criterion in my search for films that become means of enlightenment by modeling images of reconciliation. Film must be a medium, not only of enlightenment but of *a democratic enlightenment*. Genres of *popular films*, I will show in my final three chapters, satisfy that criterion, though Horkheimer and Adorno's critique of the culture industry rules out such films as aesthetic vehicles of the reconciliation image.[30]

Furthermore, Adorno's late 1966 essay, "Transparencies on Film," not only recapitulates his earlier critique of the culture industry with Horkheimer. It aggressively draws an invidious comparison between the modern artwork and film by arguing that film can transcend its commodity form only by emulating the *motionlessness* of the modern artwork, which in the two chapters that follow I will argue contradicts his aesthetic theory of the modernist artwork in *Aesthetic Theory*. Praising films that are "uncinematic," for example, in "Transparencies" Adorno recommends that the film industry adopt technology favoring natural perception, which would enable viewers to experience images as though they were projected on a wall, "much like the magic lantern slides of our childhood." No doubt Adorno preferred these mechanical precursors of the cinematograph because they projected images that could *move slowly enough* or whose motion could be *stopped* to allow viewers time to reflect on a single image's meaning in relation to images preceding and following it. Similarly Adorno insists the "obvious answer today, as forty years ago, is that of montage which does not interfere with things but rather arranges them in a constellation akin to writing."[31] Here he must have in mind early montage techniques using multiple images in one shot by way of split screens or the layering of multiple images. Both techniques prompt viewers to reflect on any particular image in the montage from the perspective of any of its other images, as though both were *still shots* mimicking writing's capacity for formulating independent thoughts reflecting upon one another. Finally, praising Chaplin's acting for performances "reminiscent of old-fashioned photographs," Adorno again seems to recommend that films incorporate *still shot techniques to interrupt the flow of moving images* to offer viewers time to decipher the meaning of distinct images.[32]

While there are many other such examples throughout Adorno's "Transparencies" essay, they always appear to entail the same claim. It is only the fixed image of the modern artwork that models images of reconciliation, which film's moving images are by their nature unable to produce. Consequently, when in my next two chapters I turn to his *Aesthetic Theory* for a concept of aesthetic reason allowing us to see that in *both* the modern artwork *and* in film it is actually images in motion that produce images of reconciliation,

I will be theorizing his concept of aesthetic reason beyond the form Adorno left it in his final work.

Before concluding my discussion of Adorno's "Transparencies on Film," I want to briefly comment on Miriam Hansen's account of this essay in which she had a very special interest. For while there are similarities in our interpretations, we have certain fundamental differences that should be highlighted for how they bear on my attempt to construct an alliance between Adorno and Whitman through which the possibility of a democratic enlightenment revolving around the ideal of reconciliation can be theorized.

In her posthumously published work, *Cinema and Experience*, Hansen offers a bold reading of "Transparencies" in an effort to discover theoretical resources for developing film aesthetics.[33] To be sure, such an aesthetics as Hansen intended would be of great theoretical value for its power to illuminate ways that film also opposes and is not simply complicit in the culture industry's commodification of human experience. As readers can quickly determine from my own discussion of Adorno's essay, however, I do not believe it offers the resources Hansen finds, but is on the contrary consistent with Adorno's critique of film throughout his essays on the culture industry. In light of my own reading of Adorno's "Transparencies" I believe Hansen's interpretation to be problematic in the following way.

At the outset of her analysis of "Transparencies" Hansen holds Adorno's aesthetic theory of modern art and critique of film to be dichotomous, thus rendering his aesthetic theory of no use to film aesthetics. Hence at first considering it apart from his aesthetic theory, Hansen then proceeds to base Adorno's contribution to an aesthetics of film on his discussions of cinematic technologies and techniques. Among those technologies and techniques Adorno included in "Transparencies" Hansen finds theoretically promising—each of which I took up in my own discussion of Adorno's essay—she mentions the magic lantern projector in use between the early seventeenth and early twentieth centuries, early montage techniques of the 1920s, and Chaplin's filmic abilities to resemble earlier photographic images through his indifference to cinematographic techniques of his own time.[34] But as all of these were common decades *before* the film industry Adorno critically examines, I believe we are hard-pressed to imagine how such early aesthetic resources as these Hansen believes to be of theoretical value would contribute to an aesthetics of film either contemporaneous with Adorno or with Hansen's and our time.

Ultimately, though, Hansen concedes that what "Transparencies" contributes to Adorno's film aesthetics "does not amount to a coherent theory" or even "constitute a larger set of interconnected propositions." Thus in place of her opening argument, when concluding she makes a recommendation she herself had already begun to follow in the second half of her essay in the aftermath of her analysis, one that in the context of my own approach to Adorno's aesthetics of film I find unimpeachable. "For Adorno," she finally determines, "the aesthetic possibilities of and for film have to be gleaned from elsewhere, from his writings on art in general and music in particular."[35] Now this not only reverses her claim about the dichotomous relationship between Adorno's aesthetic theory and theory of film. It is to adopt precisely the approach to Adorno I have pursued here. For to glean aesthetic possibilities from elsewhere, namely from his aesthetic theory for his aesthetics of film, would be to discover and then develop theoretical resources from his aesthetic theory to carry out a sweeping revision of his critique of film and of the role film plays in the construction of mass culture.[36] Nevertheless, despite our agreement on the contributions of Adorno's aesthetic theory to the aesthetics of film, for extremely good cause Hansen and I are not then theoretical allies in our approaches to an aesthetics of film rooted in Adorno's thought. Here is why.

For argument's sake, let us assume Hansen's own turn to Adorno's aesthetic theory would discover theoretical resources leading to the formulation of a film aesthetics alternative to the critical theory of film at the core of his critique of the culture industry. For one decisive reason such an aesthetics of film would be for naught. As she makes perfectly clear in her text and endnotes, Hansen disavows what she refers to as Adorno's "metaphysical promise" or "paradigm" or "philosophy of reconciliation."[37] This is, I believe, a tragic mistake, since it divides Adorno's aesthetic theory, if not his critical theory as a whole, from the ideal they both consistently and absolutely served—*the possibility of reconciliation*—without which the entirety of his thought may have neither meaning nor reason for being.

Moreover, Hansen's disavowal of Adorno's philosophy of reconciliation seems to have followed Albrecht Wellmer's earlier move to the same effect, when he harnessed Adorno's concept of reconciliation to a theory of communicative action whose pragmatism was designed to overcome its metaphysical character.[38] Regarding its metaphysical status, however, certainly to the contrary Adorno's ideal of reconciliation does not transcend our social and political experience. Succinctly put, and I cannot stress this too greatly, we should not conclude, as do Hansen and Wellmer, that Adorno's ideal of reconciliation has a metaphysical form and formulation apart from the *immanent form* its image and politics take in modern art and, as we shall see, in film.

Such a conclusion is to misunderstand Adorno's ideal as a "dream of ultimate reconciliations" that never come to pass, rather than as a time that can always arrive no less than a time that is always yet to come.[39]

So against all such accounts as Hansen's and Wellmer's of Adorno's aesthetics of reconciliation, and against all refusals to find in Adorno's work theoretical possibilities for discovering such an aesthetics of reconciliation in media he also thought inimical to reconciliation, it is now time for *thinking with* Adorno *against* Adorno. Yet this does not mean, as Fredric Jameson has argued in his remarkable study of Adorno's thought, that "much of Adorno's philosophical work turns precisely on this question of how we are to engage a living thought that is no longer historically current."[40] Rather, the question is how to engage a living thought whose aesthetic theory is *even more* historically current today than ever for its bearing on the possibility of discovering the reconciliation image in film and for the implications of that discovery for rethinking his critique of mass culture in modern democratic societies.

Keeping in mind Whitman's project of democratic enlightenment, its ideal of reconciliation and idea of aesthetic education teaching this ideal through the visual image, while also keeping in the foreground the critique of democratic enlightenment we saw take shape through Horkheimer and Adorno's critique of enlightenment and film, the tacit alliance I have worked out between these two opposing positions is the point of departure for my argument in the following two chapters. Examining Adorno's *Aesthetic Theory*, I will flesh out its concept of aesthetic rationality from its elements he had assembled in that work to determine how the modern artwork produces images of reconciliation. It is on that basis that I will then more fully theorize an account of how the reconciliation image is created *from a series of moving images* that unfold according to what I find to be the logic of aesthetic reason. *Rather than a motionless image*, I will argue *Adorno's modern artwork is actually an image in motion*, and by virtue of being in motion produces and models the reconciliation image.

I can put this differently: according to Adorno's aesthetic theory, the modern artwork is already a kind of *film*. By my account, in this respect Adorno has a predecessor in Whitman, in whose "Eidolons" the motion of images had already been figured and whose reconciliation image, by reason of its visuality and duration, anticipates such a moving image being found in film. So much of Whitman's own reconciliation image is included in Adorno's, I will eventually describe Adorno's reconciliation image as its second evolutionary form.

If this is correct and the modern artwork is not a motionless image but an image in motion, a kind of film, then we can understand what Adorno meant when he said, "How nice it would be if, under the present circumstances, one could claim that the less films appear to be works of art the more they would be just that." The less we judge films in comparison with works of art understood as fixed images, in other words, the more films become works of art when artworks are viewed as images in motion.

As we will next learn from Adorno, as we already have found in Whitman, the reconciliation image progresses from the modern artwork to film because from its birth in modern poetry and painting it had from the start been a visual image in motion. Put another way, as we at last learn, beyond Whitman and Adorno film becomes to date the most evolved form of the reconciliation image produced by aesthetic reason. It is in this evolutionary sense that films appear to be works of art.

Part II

THE RECONCILIATION IMAGE IN ADORNO

> Paradoxically, art must testify to the un-
> reconciled and at the same time envision
> its reconciliation.
>
> —Theodor W. Adorno, *Aesthetic Theory*

Aesthetic Reason and Reflexivity,
Twin Economies and Democratic Effects

Adorno wrote *Aesthetic Theory*, his final work, against the background of crises he and Horkheimer had diagnosed in *Dialectic of Enlightenment*. An ongoing crisis in reason as ancient as thinking itself, a crisis no less defining of the
Enlightenment of modern times than of the much longer process of human
enlightenment before and after, had produced a crisis in history. In the preface to the new edition (1969) of *Dialectic of Enlightenment* they recalled the
"National Socialist terror," the historical crisis in response to which the work
was first born, while also calling attention to crises that followed steadily in its
wake. A totally "administered world," the world's "political division into immense blocs," "conflicts in the third world and the renewed growth of totali-
tarianism," proved that the National Socialist "horror has been prolonged."[1]
Neither fascism nor the other crises to which they referred were simply historical interludes disturbing an otherwise rational course of civilized development. All were modern infections of a chronic, congenital disease of reason,
the crisis in reason at the root of each. When *Aesthetic Theory* appeared the
year after the new edition of *Dialectic of Enlightenment*, Adorno's preoccupation with crisis resonated palpably on nearly every page. Before completing its
first paragraph he proposed that the autonomy of art, which had been "nour-
ished by the idea of humanity," was shattered when through enlightenment's
pandemic spread of formalistic or instrumental reason "society became ever
less a human one."[2]

It is clear from his comment that the crisis in art holds a special significance for Adorno. Art's loss of autonomy, evident to him from modernism's new directions in the decades immediately preceding National Socialism, meant modern art would cease to offer the critical cultural refuge he believed it alone had provided for aesthetic powers of reason capable of opposing the violence toward difference inherent in instrumental reason's diseased rationalization of society. With this last sphere of cultural resistance to such violence fallen under the spell of formalistic reason, critical theory could only cling to modern art as a historical artifact of a truly enlightened aesthetic rationality whose time had since passed. It was not that Adorno trapped critical theory in the aporia of leaving critique without a basis in reason, as Habermas and others have insisted is entailed in *Dialectic of Enlightenment* by Horkheimer and Adorno's alleged "totalizing critique" of reason.[3] Rather than the totality of reason, their critique focused on enlightenment's failure to reflect on its own thought processes, a capacity for reflection they rescued by locating it in the aesthetic elements of reason that enlightenment's instrumental rationality excludes. Nevertheless, when later in *Aesthetic Theory* Adorno narrowly rests his concept of aesthetic rationality on a modernist art he argued modernism retired within its first half century, he did trap critical theory in the past and, along with it, the possibility of a positive enlightenment that depended on the aesthetic form of reason he concluded enlightenment had made anachronistic.

As Adorno writes *Aesthetic Theory*, we see he feels deluged by historical and cultural crises he attributes to a crisis in reason. Under these circumstances, we could hardly expect that in light of the theoretical advances he would begin to make in his final work, notably with his concept of aesthetic rationality, he would revise his critique of film. If, in *Aesthetic Theory*, he had found aesthetic reason circulating through film as he had found it circulating through modern art, instead of finding that it disappeared with an expired modernist aesthetic, film would have afforded Adorno the opportunity to resurrect the concept of a positive enlightenment resting on an aesthetic form of rationality. But as we saw in my First Bridge, the unrevised critique of film he formulated in essays since the original publication of *Dialectic of Enlightenment* was no more than an elaboration of the latter's indictment of the culture industry. With little qualification, film seemed to Adorno to reproduce the commodity form's logic of equivalence by which the culture industry produced its goods. Films contributed to the uncritical reproduction of the existing society by duplicating its dominant ideology, which implicated film in the shattered autonomy of art, the loss of modernism's aesthetic claim to reason, and the crises Adorno sensed closing in.

Yet Adorno's concept of aesthetic rationality possesses an unappreciated richness we can capture and bring to bear on film if we first bracket his inability to do so in the context of his sense of crises. Then we can take up where he left off in *Aesthetic Theory* with the concepts of aesthetic reason and reconciliation to recover the philosophical resources of both concepts beyond the modernist artworks to which they were confined. Though Adorno did not hold that aesthetic reason originally belonged any less to human rationality in general than to modern art, he (and Horkheimer) believed that from the very beginning of thought aesthetic reason had been increasingly eclipsed by the historical ascendancy of enlightenment rationality. Absent from cultural spheres beyond art, aesthetic reason had been modeled by certain modernist artworks. In *Aesthetic Theory* Adorno assembled the elements of aesthetic reason in order to show how, within the artwork, they work together— "communicate with one another," as he put it—to oppose the violence to difference defining enlightenment rationality.[4] Modern artworks become images of this opposition when they are reinscribed as *images of reconciliation* through the logic of aesthetic reason. So that we may also discover the reconciliation image in film, the eventual aim of my investigation is to flesh out and further develop *Aesthetic Theory*'s aesthetic form of reason productive of this image of reconciliation Adorno believed could be found only in the modern artwork.

To locate the reconciliation image in film, then, I must flesh out Adorno's concept of aesthetic reason by reassembling its elements in the modern artwork, determine how they communicate with one another and how they produce the image of reconciliation, which is one purpose of my analysis in this and the following chapter. We will find many such elements—"art's elements," in Adorno's words, "heterogeneous elements," the "reflexive" and "processual" elements, the elements of "continuity" and "receptivity," of "motion," and the "elements of equilibrium," the "constructive" and "mimetic" elements, among others. Images of reconciliation issue from what Adorno refers to as "the *economy of the elements* out of which the artwork is composed."[5] As I analyze the modern artwork to flesh out the concept of aesthetic reason, I will find that the elements forming this aesthetic economy work together as a whole, while each element also performs its work as a discrete functional part of an aesthetic economy's organized relations internal to the artwork. So we shall see that aesthetic reason in the modern artwork is productive of an image of reconciliation emerging not only as a consequence of its economy of elements as a whole. In addition, I will propose that as aesthetic reason's elements independently unfold, they *also* produce other images along the way from which the image of reconciliation is ultimately born. Here I argue there is an *economy of images* in the modernist artwork, a *twin economy*, let us say, corresponding to Adorno's economy of elements.

Although the images forming this twin economy are not Adorno's aesthetic inventions, in this chapter and the next I introduce the identity image, difference image, all-inclusive image, and the receptivity and imitative images as an additional layer of conceptualization that Adorno's aesthetic theory allows for, though also requires for the further development of its concept of aesthetic reason. I argue that by thinking of the modern artwork as productive of an image of reconciliation, Adorno not only imagines it changing from artwork to image but, by becoming image, to have also become *a continuously changing appearance*. This must mean that aesthetic reason not only pictures an artwork's metamorphoses in one final, dramatic image of reconciliation; to do so, its elements first produce continuous changes in the artwork's appearance whose representations require the economy of images—a plurality of images communicating with one another—that corresponds to the economy of elements with which they together produce the final image of reconciliation. The great advantage of this twin economy of images I further theorize on the basis of Adorno's aesthetic theory is that it will enable us to see that the artwork, as he understood it, and film, *contrary to how he misunderstood it*, are what I will later call *aesthetic analogues* because *both art and film* produce images of reconciliation from continuously changing images—in other words, *from images in motion*. Through my further development of the theoretical resources offered by Adorno's aesthetic theory, modern artworks and film will increasingly appear to be two forms of motion pictures that model aesthetic reason and reconciliation.

After the modernist artwork, I am proposing, film inherits the powers of aesthetic reason to hold an even greater promise for the emergence of a positive, aesthetic form of enlightenment Adorno narrowly confined to a fleeting period of modernism. If I am able to discover aesthetic reason and its reconciliation image circulating in film, Adorno's positive concept of enlightenment would prove to be the counterpart to what I have called, in light of my reading of Whitman, "a democratic enlightenment." Not "enlightenment as mass deception," as Horkheimer and Adorno wrote mournfully in *Dialectic of Enlightenment.* Rather enlightenment as the reconciliation image in film, the democratic ideal of reconciling identity and difference taught through the democratic media of popular culture.

To flesh out Adorno's concept of aesthetic reason by focusing on its economy of elements is to engage his theory of the modern artwork in *Aesthetic Theory.* As I move along, to provide needed theoretical clarifications I will consider examples of modernist works absent from Adorno's philosophical arguments though comparable to those he simply alludes to with little or no elaboration. My examples of modernist artworks will be decisive for our eventual turn to film, as they will enable us to discover the extensive parallels I am seeking between his theory of the artwork, for Adorno the very avatar of aesthetic reason, and film, in which I will find aesthetic reason working in remarkably similar ways. If film and the artwork prove to be aesthetic analogues, in essence I revise his critique of film. And by adopting his theory of the artwork as the basis for revising his critique of film I in essence think with Adorno against Adorno, an approach that imitates the aesthetic image of reflexive reason his theory of the modern artwork conceptualizes, which pictures thinking set into motion and reaching beyond its settled representations to include differences belonging to its object it had left out. *Thinking with* Adorno *against* Adorno, I will find that film replicates the modern artwork as a model of aesthetic reason, reconciliation, and positive enlightenment, and that it is, in its democratic effects, the aesthetic vehicle for democratic enlightenment's own ideal of reconciliation envisioned by Whitman.

Before proceeding, however, I must make brief note of the uniqueness of Adorno's aesthetic theory so we will not confuse it with the more familiar theories of aesthetic judgment concerned with the subjectivity of taste and the role of community in resolving conflicts in taste, such as Kant's, Arendt's, or Habermas's. Adorno's aesthetic theory is a theory of the artwork in music, literature, poetry, painting, and sculpture, though for the purposes of my interest in film I focus on artwork belonging to the fine arts of the visual image, specifically painting and sculpture.[6] Of greatest consequence for Adorno is what goes on *within* the artwork quite apart from subjectivity's aesthetic judgment, which for Adorno the artwork independently models. As I flesh out and further develop his argument, to ensure I remain faithful to his theoretical interests I introduce the distinction between the *artwork*, which models an image of aesthetic reason and reconciliation, and the *work of art*, which refers to the work of aesthetic reason the artwork *internally* performs to create the artwork's image of reconciliation.

AESTHETIC REASON

Throughout *Aesthetic Theory* Adorno makes the artwork intelligible in terms typically reserved for descriptions of thinking. For Adorno the artwork *is* thinking, so to consider the artwork in his terms is to speak of a reasoning process that takes the artwork as one of its possible forms. The *work of art* is this *reasoning process* belonging to the *artwork*. Hence "aesthetic rationality," Adorno's most often used term to refer to the work of art, although *aesthetic reason* (my term), which I use interchangeably with aesthetic rationality, is also implied by his practice of speaking of "art's own reason," "reason immanent to artworks themselves," the "aesthetic *ratio*," and so on.[7] As the reasoning process internal to the artwork, aesthetic rationality or aesthetic reason is the *reflexive* engagement with a second type of thinking—instrumental or formalistic reason, often referred to by Adorno simply as "rationality"—that the artwork also incorporates within it. Aesthetic reason's reflexive relation to instrumental reason is synergistic in the sense of producing an aesthetic outcome that neither aesthetic nor instrumental reason can achieve without the contribution of the other. Aesthetic and instrumental reason are qualitatively different precisely because the latter lacks the reflexive capacity, the "reflexive element," in Adorno's terms, belonging to the former, although without the role played by instrumental reason aesthetic reason would have nothing to reflect on and we could not speak of aesthetic rationality.

Several questions about the work of art can now be taken up. Within the artwork, what is the role of instrumental reason, and why is it subject to the reflexive work of aesthetic rationality? What is the purpose of *aesthetic reflexivity*, as we can also refer to the work of art when stressing the transitive action of aesthetic reason in relation to instrumental reason, and how does it work? What image of reconciliation does aesthetic reason engender? What image of enlightenment?

In part the work of art is the work of instrumental reason, which as the "identity-positing reason" within the artwork, Adorno explains, works to create the identity of an object by which the artwork is known. Identity, the artwork's *aesthetic identity*, is *semblance*, water lilies' *appearance* in Monet's painting by that name, for example. Aesthetic identity is the creation of instrumental rationality insofar, and *only* insofar, as the artwork's aesthetic object, the actual water lilies themselves, are to serve as the *means* to construct their semblance. *Means* already implies *that the instrumental work of the artwork attaches some meaning or end or purpose to its object,* that aesthetic identity does not necessarily belong to the object prior to the artwork, and that a purely identifying, instrumental rationality would be *blind* to aesthetic identity's foreignness to its object. For prior to the artwork its object is the particular, the "nonidentical, heterogeneous, and not already formed," just as water lilies are without an aesthetic form, an aesthetic identity, are not yet an aesthetic object, in advance of becoming the aesthetic semblance of Monet's *Water Lilies.*[8]

Coupled to the artwork's instrumental power to form its object into semblance, the reflexive rationality of the artwork works to challenge the correspondence of an object's semblance to the object itself. In artworks where the aesthetic power of reflexivity is at work, as it is in many modernist works, the aesthetic identity for which instrumental reason is responsible is revealed to inadequately correspond to the object itself whose semblance it portrays. For Adorno, aesthetic rationality thus consists of the artwork's instrumental power to construct aesthetic identities by capturing something of an object in its visual semblance *and* in the artwork's aesthetic power to be self-referential and self-critical by reflexively drawing attention to the inadequacy of the object's aesthetic appearance. What is this inadequacy of aesthetic identity, this lack of correspondence between an artwork's semblance and its object? It is here that *difference* enters into the picture.

AESTHETIC REASON, INSTRUMENTAL REASON, AND DIFFERENCE

Taken *together,* the instrumental and reflexive work of art, or *aesthetic reason,* is reasoning of a very special kind. Aesthetic rationality is a twofold reasoning process working through the artwork's aesthetic form to create a semblance or appearance or an identity for the purpose of illuminating a gap—or *difference*—between the artwork's semblance of its object and the object itself, between identity and nonidentity, identity and difference. Aesthetic reason's entire purpose, if not the entire purpose of the artwork itself, Adorno appears to say, is to aesthetically form an image that reflexively refers to the unformed, unidentified, and heterogeneous aspects of its object that aesthetic identity has not yet given form, has not yet included but left out.

Whether or not aesthetic reason is at work in the artwork, *there is always a difference between a semblance and its object,* between the aesthetic identity of the object and the object itself. But where aesthetic reason is at work, the artwork recognizes and brings this difference to light. Aesthetic rationality allies itself with difference against identity, with the integrity of the object prior to its appearance in the artwork, by canceling the impression conveyed by aesthetic identity that there is nothing more to the object than what its semblance captures. Aesthetic reason nullifies instrumental reason's equivalency between semblance and object. While there can be no doubt that Adorno valorizes modernism for its great artworks, the highest value he accords modernism lies in the rational capacity of modern art to reflexively reveal the artwork's failure to be inclusive of difference, which is where aesthetic identity's inadequacy and semblance's lack of correspondence with its object lies. Artworks are rational not because they create aesthetic identity *by identifying difference*, which is the work of instrumental reason, but because art "identifies *with* it," with difference, which is the work of aesthetic reason.[9]

Adorno's insight into the rationality of the work of art begins to explain why he privileges the artwork as a model of thinking, ultimately as a model of reconciliation and positive enlightenment. Aesthetic reason is thinking correcting the deficiencies of instrumental reason through reflexive activity that formalistic reason is unable to perform on its own. If the artwork is thinking, by reflexively problematizing formalistic reason's relation to difference the thinking it performs is *thinking difference*, where *difference* is the aspect of an object that the artwork's work of art, aesthetic rationality, reflexively reveals instrumental reason not to have included in the artwork's appearance. As a model of aesthetic reason, the artwork becomes a model of reconciliation and enlightenment precisely because its reflexive disclosure of instrumental reason's exclusions motions, in the first instance, toward the democratic *all-inclusiveness of difference*, ultimately toward enlightenment as the reconciliation of identity and difference.

Far more often than reflexively disclosing their relation to difference, however, under the disproportionate influence of the identifying, instrumental rationality peculiar to some modernist and perhaps most premodernist aesthetic forms, artworks are compelled to disavow aesthetic reflexivity and to appear under the pretense there remains no difference between their semblances of objects and the objects themselves. Its reflexivity paralyzed, the artwork manufactures the *illusion* that aesthetic identity and difference have been reconciled—the illusion the image has omitted nothing belonging to its object, that it has included its object in all its heterogeneity and multiplicity. Art's *illusion of reconciliation* conceals the aesthetic object under a *false* image, forcing it to suffer the imposition of appearing *other* than it is in its plurality. With this illusory, false image of reconciliation, difference, the object as it is distinguished from any and all aesthetic semblances, *is subjected to the violence of being constructed as otherness.*

By reflexively disclosing the artwork's exclusion of difference, then, aesthetic reason's orientation toward the inclusiveness of difference is at the same time an acute sensitivity to the violence in illusory images of reconciliation, the violence the artwork inflicts on its object by its feigned equivalency between a semblance and its object. Adorno is quite clear on this when discussing "the *closure* of artworks," which he associates with classicism's paralysis of the reflexive work of aesthetic reason by means of highly formalistic techniques used to construct images of their objects' diversity of different features. Classicist artworks exemplify those in which instrumental reason prevails over its aesthetic counterpart rationality to construct semblances that appear as closures—as perfectly finished "unities" of heterogeneous differences, as Adorno also puts it—which by conveying the false impression that nothing of their objects has failed to be included in artworks are "inescapably the *violence* done to multiplicity." Adorno implicates classicism's aesthetic ideals in such aesthetic violence for their reliance on formalistic techniques that create the illusion of reconciliation, the illusion that semblance has rendered the object just as it actually is.[10]

To illustrate Adorno's claim, we can visit the representations of nature in the classically inspired idyllic landscapes of Poussin (*Ideal Landscape*, 1650) and Lorrain (*Ideal View of Tivoli*, 1644), whose aesthetic formalism suppresses the extent to which nature differs from such idealizations and thus the idea of a different nature itself. To the contrary, Adorno argues, artworks are faithful to the idea of reconciliation only if they "become conscious of the nonidentical," of difference, meaning the artwork must perform the work of art by becoming reflexively aware that an image of reconciliation is one that is cognizant of *never* including everything or everyone—belonging to nature, a landscape, a city—its object entails. Identifying with difference, true images of reconciliation convey the awareness that—*in art and thus in life*—there are *always* persons and things, ideas and ideals not yet and still to be included, not yet and still to be reconciled. There is *always a yet to be* realized democratic all-inclusiveness to which the work of art must ceaselessly point. Otherwise, as in classicism, art feigns reconciliation as it subjects difference to the "manipulative, 'composed' violence of [art's] exemplary works," where "reconciliation as an act of violence, aesthetic formalism, and unreconciled life forms a triad."[11]

Aesthetic identity's illusory unity of diverse differences is not an act of violence originating with the artwork, however. Rather, the violence the artwork inflicts on its objects "derives from the violence that *reason* does to things," reason originally outside the artwork, that is, human reason in general as it is shaped by the process of enlightenment in all its historical forms. Artworks reproduce the violence toward their "objects"—nature, the world, individuals in all their forms of life—that was first inflicted by instrumental reason throughout its own history of enlightenment. Artworks reproduce formal reason's violence in every semblance closed to the reflexive critique that its object does not correspond to the objectivity the artwork depicts. But when the work of art reflexively discloses the difference between the artwork's identity and its object, "the domination of nature" is "neutralized aesthetically" and "renounces its violence."[12] As a model of thinking, the artwork models an enlightened, aesthetic rationality able to relate nonviolently to nature, to the world, and to everything and everyone in it by recognizing the difference between what they are and how they are constructed by thought. "Positive enlightenment" appears as "aesthetic reason," I should now say. While instrumental reason has no more thought of the world than is captured by the unreflected finished thought and by the closures of aesthetic identity, aesthetic reason knows aesthetic identity excludes difference and through its reflexive orientation to all-inclusiveness prevents the violence done to difference in every false appearance difference is forced to bear.

AESTHETIC REFLEXIVITY

Although other elements are to become as important, aesthetic reflexivity, our first element of aesthetic reason's economy of elements, has moved into the foreground as the feature of aesthetic reason on which much of what I initially say about Adorno's theory of the artwork will depend. For to this point my analysis of aesthetic reflexivity has led us to our first, preliminary images of reconciliation and positive enlightenment. As it is reflexively visualized by the work of art, reconciliation appears to be an orientation to the all-inclusiveness of difference as an ideal that remains forever unrealized. And it is this reflexive image of difference's excluded, ineliminable outside that would constitute an *enlightened* awareness of the violent character of illusory images purporting to be inclusive of their objects as they are, as though all-inclusiveness has been achieved and artworks never omit anything of the world. For its democratic value and sensibility to violence, every such reflexively produced image of difference's excluded, ineliminable outside, every such image of reconciliation, would be such an image of enlightenment.

Moving beyond this point is somewhat problematic, however, because these first provisional images of reconciliation and enlightenment can be fully developed only in light of Adorno's theoretical clarifications of aesthetic reflexivity, which want for examples. Of the few examples he provides, the one most instructive, in his terms the "unity of the history of art," illuminates the reflexive work of aesthetic reason by illustrating a unique critical relationship between and among artworks in their history as a whole. Such a strategy, though, overshadows decisive aspects of aesthetic reason in the *individual* artwork Adorno's example was also meant to convey by showing that, through the reflexive work of art, artworks steadily advance toward the image of reconciliation. Consequently, to help us flesh out the ensemble of aesthetic reason's elements and the properties of each, the "unity of the history of art" will be useful primarily for offering guidelines for arriving at supplementary examples of artworks that will move us forward. We should consider it to that end.

By proposing that the "truth content of artworks is fused with their critical content," Adorno offers us a formulation of his basic insight into how the reflexive capacity of the artwork (its "critical content") produces images of reconciliation and enlightenment (its "truth content"). His formulation is especially useful for the example of aesthetic reflexivity to which it is tied. What defines the "unity of the history of art," by which he means a property common to all artworks throughout their history, is the "dialectical figure of determinate negation" whereby "each artwork is the mortal enemy of the other."[13] To this dramatic statement Adorno adds that it is only as determinate negation that art is able to "serve its idea of reconciliation."[14] Here Adorno means that over the long history in which artworks exhibit their sheer variety of aesthetic forms and objects, every artwork is a critical commentary on all those before and after it with regard to a particular truth. Namely, how artworks, if they were compared side by side with one another, are more or less inclusive of their objects. Every artwork being such an aesthetically reflexive critique, or determinate negation, or enemy of every other by illuminating the representational limits of other artworks' aesthetic forms, in their history as a whole artworks reflexively disclose their *truth*: that there is a *difference* between their semblances of aesthetic objects and the objects themselves artworks omit, an excluded difference that comes into view by its inclusion in one artwork and its omission in others.

I can illustrate Adorno's example in this way. Compare Degas's *The Mad-am's Name Day* (1876–77), Picasso's *The Name Day of the Madam, Flowers and Kisses, Degas Enjoying Himself* (1971), Delacroix's *The Women of Algiers in Their Apartment* (1834), and Picasso's *The Women of Algiers, after Delacroix* (fifteen versions, 1954–55).[15] What would define, in Adorno's sense, this collection's historical unity is not its common interest in prostitutes and odalisques but the greatly varying ways a common subject matter is portrayed. While Degas's prostitutes are playfully sweet, Picasso's share Degas's semidetached voyeuristic attitude toward the playfully perverse. Delacroix's odalisques are reduced to simple idlers resembling prostitutes, whereas Picasso's multiple versions of Delacroix's odalisques highlight their differences, which range from the playful to the godlike. Not only are prostitutes different according to these representations, but their differences are accentuated by their resemblances to odalisques, who are themselves different. Each artwork includes something different belonging to its object that it reveals the aesthetic forms of the other artworks have left out. Taken together, their critical content is this image of limit or determinate negation they collectively produce to unify their history between 1834 and 1971—images of inclusions of differences reflexively disclosing other artworks have excluded. As a whole, these aesthetic images determining limits serve the idea of reconciliation, the truth content—the artwork's orientation to the all-inclusiveness of differences—with which the images' critical content is fused.

With the assistance of these artworks, Adorno's example of the "unity of the history of art" begins to clarify the element of aesthetic reflexivity. It is a democratic process whereby certain artworks include differences belonging to aesthetic objects excluded by other artworks. To put all of this in a sentence: reflexivity's work of inclusiveness, the work of art's "critical" content, tacitly recognizes the limit of the artwork, its exclusions of difference, which creates the artwork's "truth" content, its service to reconciliation, the work of art's striving for the all-inclusiveness of difference.

But there is a further clarification of aesthetic reflexivity to be had from Adorno's example, as it offers evidence that the reflexive process by which artworks form images of reconciliation unfolds *seamlessly* through three distinctly identifiable constituent moments of which aesthetic reflexivity must therefore consist. To recall Delacroix, Degas, and Picasso, I illustrated Adorno's example by supposing the simplest side-by-side comparison of multiple artworks in the history of art to allow each one to set off the limits of the others with regard to their representations of aesthetic objects. By way of such a comparison, *at one and the same moment* aesthetic reflexivity distinguishes each artwork's aesthetic identity, its semblance of an aesthetic object, in relation to the aesthetic identities of the other artworks; which is to recognize each artwork's capture of something different belonging to its object omitted by the others; thus giving prominence to the work of art's striving for the all-inclusiveness of difference. With these three almost perfectly overlapping moments of aesthetic reason clarifying the artwork's work of art, my provisional image of reconciliation and enlightenment is also clarified. Every image of the artwork's striving for all-inclusiveness grasps the violence done in the history of art by artworks parading the illusion denied by the image of reconciliation, the illusion that nothing belonging to art's object has been omitted by the artwork, the illusion that the all-inclusiveness of difference has been achieved.

Through my illustrations of Adorno's example of the "unity of the history of art" we have entered more deeply into the interior of the artwork. What I have called the artwork's "work of art," aesthetic reason, now has greater visibility as a reflexive process that is a principal element of an emerging economy of elements whose moments are so tightly interrelated as to overlap almost indistinguishably. Another way to express this is to say that this economy unfolds continuously, *without any break or gap* in its process of aesthetic reflexivity. This is what is entailed by arguing that in relation to other artworks, every artwork at one and the same time exhibits an aesthetic identity constructed from its aesthetic object's diversity of features, identifies with a difference in its object omitted from other artworks, and in league with other artworks strives toward aesthetic reason's all-inclusiveness of difference. So Adorno must have selected the "unity of the history of art" to argue not only that aesthetic reason is a reflexive process formed through an economy of elements but also that the critical work of art performed by this economy is *continuous*. Adorno thus adds *continuity* to the reflexive artwork's aesthetic economy, a second element to become increasingly important as we go on. As we shall see, only as a continuous, unbroken or uninterrupted, process of reflexivity does aesthetic reason resist becoming a degraded, instrumental form of rationality through which the artwork's aesthetic identity avoids negation by other artworks and creates the impression it omits nothing of its object. This "illusion of reconciliation" terminates the artwork's reflexive *striving* for all-inclusiveness, represents all-inclusiveness as aesthetic reality, and forces the aesthetic object to suffer the violence of imposed, false images of otherness instrumental to political and social ends reifying identities whose truth depends upon their exclusions of difference.

Here I should recall the classicist aesthetic forms of Poussin and Lorrain, which create aesthetic closures to persuade us of the illusion that nature conforms to its aesthetic idealizations portraying a pristine natural world unsullied by human interaction. Or let us imagine Degas's images of prostitutes and Picasso's re-presentation of prostitutes in his version of Degas's painting. Viewing one independently of the other immunizes each against the continuous reflexive disclosure of its limits by the second artwork. Each free of reflexive critical comparison with the other, Degas's image sanitizes the condition of women by making it appear familial and cheerful, while Picasso's sanitizes it by depicting it as an artist's aesthetic ideal. Each alone imposes aesthetic closure by creating an illusory equivalency between women and prostitutes or prostitution and the playfully erotic or prostitution and the aesthetic ideal. But as examples of the continuity of aesthetic reflexivity working through the "unity of the history of art," side by side they highlight comparisons inviting thought about how much more different their objects—women and their conditions—remain actually and potentially from each artwork's aesthetic identity. And, of course, we can extend the logic of aesthetic reflexivity still further to highlight the excluded differences of Degas's and Picasso's works when we take them together in relation to other artworks. In relation to Manet's *Olympia*, for example, their images appear reducible to male fantasies of prostitutes, as we might conclude from Germaine Greer's claim that while "artists have always glamorized prostitution ... Manet['s *Olympia*] savaged all their delusions."[16] Manet's painting traces the boundaries of male fantasy within which Degas and Picasso enclose the female image to deny it the continuity of reflexive critique that it could appear differently.

When I later elaborate on aesthetic reflexivity as a continuous process, I will not only explain more adequately aesthetic reason's resistance to the degradation and violence toward difference of aesthetic closures and their illusory images of reconciliation manufactured by instrumental reason. "Continuity" also inscribes a temporal signature in artworks qualitatively different from that inscribed by instrumental rationality. Before I can take up this relationship between images of reconciliation, enlightenment, and time, however, I must focus on examples of aesthetic reason that distinguish its elements more sharply than Adorno's construction of the "unity of the history of art." By so precisely overlapping aesthetic reason's moments to illuminate the element of continuity, Adorno's example obscures the distinctive contribution of other elements to the reflexive process forming images of reconciliation in modern art that would allow us to discover their counterparts in film. It also leaves unanswered the question of how the work of art unfolds in such a seamless way, an answer without which we cannot explain why aesthetic reason in modernist artworks resists their degradation to illusory images of reconciliation.

What is more, remembering that Adorno adopted the "unity of the history of art" as a whole to illustrate the work of aesthetic rationality, we must keep in mind that his example of multiple artworks was also intended to demonstrate how aesthetic reason works within the *individual* modernist artwork. If I am to further clarify aesthetic reflexivity with respect to these three issues— developing the cinematic counterparts for aesthetic reflexivity's economy of elements, what I earlier called an economy of images; uncovering properties of the image accounting for the continuity of aesthetic reflexivity and its resistance to a degraded form of reason engendering illusions of reconciliation; and looking to the individual artwork for evidence that every aesthetic identity constructed according to the logic of aesthetic reason necessarily moves toward reconciliation—I must provide additional examples consistent with Adorno's own in order to flesh out aesthetic reason and the additional elements of which it is composed. This means his example should largely guide my selection in the following way.

At the same time as Adorno's example of the "unity of the history of art" begins to clarify the process of aesthetic reflexivity and the way it forms images of reconciliation and enlightenment, it also offers an ingenious clue to the discovery of other examples that will continue to clarify how aesthetic reflexivity is at work in the artwork. According to the logic of Adorno's example, it appears that, in order to gauge the limits of the artwork, aesthetic reason's reflexive illumination of its exclusion of difference does not require that there is actually an object present (water lilies, for instance) with which to compare the artwork (Monet's *Water Lilies*). Rather, since Adorno interprets the "unity of the history of art" as a series of images that critically reflect on each other, artworks must perform the reflexive work of illuminating the differences between their semblances of objects and the objects themselves through their proliferation of images.

Following the logic of Adorno's example, two additional examples can then be recommended with which to further understand the reflexive process of aesthetic reason. The first, by Monet, will more sharply differentiate Adorno's overlapping, continuous moments of aesthetic reflexivity and begin to clarify the basis for the twin economy of images I am seeking in the modern artwork and film. The example from Monet's work is theoretically preliminary to the second, by Rodin, which I will take up in my next chapter to explain why the artwork's economy of elements seamlessly unfolds and how the elements of aesthetic reason in Adorno's example of *multiple* artworks are also at work in the *individual* modernist artwork. Together the examples by Monet and Rodin will enable me to complete the work of fleshing out and further developing aesthetic reason and the images of reconciliation and enlightenment in modern art for which it is responsible.

MONET: TWIN ECONOMIES AND DEMOCRATIC EFFECTS

Between 1890 and 1895 Monet produced three famous collections of paintings that each represented a single object in a series—haystacks, poplars, and the Rouen Cathedral—during various seasons and times of the day, under varying ambient conditions. Although Monet's paintings were to instruct us about the situated, embodied, and relative nature of perception, there is much more at work in each series. As Monet paints one, ten, twenty, eventually more than thirty paintings of the west façade of the Rouen Cathedral, for example, even more than how the Cathedral itself actually appears his artworks *also* convey its elusiveness, so that the series not only reflects the Cathedral being represented; it reflects upon what it means to represent the Cathedral.

With Monet's Rouen paintings instructively complicating the meaning of representation, let us consider his series *retrospectively*, as it were, by imagining it in its entirety on display before us, so that for purposes of fleshing out aesthetic reason we can trace its work of art after the fact of its already having completely unfolded with the completion of his series. Through this series and his others, painting's claim to representational truth is reflexively called into question. Each serial artwork in comparison with others shows an earlier or later representation of the Cathedral having left a deficit, an excluded difference it makes up until another artwork shows it, in turn, to have left its own deficit, and so on. Since each artwork belonging to the series includes something different about the Cathedral omitted by the others, Monet might be misconstrued to wish his series to represent all differences left out. But a series inclusive of all differences between its artworks and their object, especially as differences multiply with continually changing ambient and temporal conditions, would require an infinite set of artworks, and it would soon be apparent the series *ceaselessly strives* to be all-inclusive of difference while never achieving all-inclusiveness.

Striving for—and not simply the achievement of—the all-inclusiveness of differences between the artworks and the Cathedral itself would be the series' reflexively driven representational interests. When the series of artworks concluded, differences not yet included would be tacitly recognized as still missing, because the more than thirty serial representations of excluded differences would have reflexively inscribed *the presence of the absence of difference,* a *virtual image* of difference. From the standpoint of the work of art, of the work of aesthetic reason, aesthetic reflexivity would have taught us that art is not *only* about what it represents but *also* about what it does not represent. Studying Monet's series teaches us the Cathedral is and will remain *actually and virtually* different from any and all artworks the series could include, no matter how representative each artwork on its own or all together considered as an artwork itself appears to be.

Considering his completed series retrospectively, then, allows us to see that a productive tension surfaces between two contradictory loyalties generated by aesthetic reason's work of art, each struggling against the other while they also work together to bring about two very different results. Under the pretense it can exhaustively represent its object, each individual painting's aesthetic identity or the aesthetic identity of the series as a whole implicitly seeks to terminate its reflexive relation to the Rouen Cathedral, to divide its semblance of its object from the object once and for all to establish the truth of its own representation. Yet it is this very truth the series also denies by continuing to reflexively identify with the Cathedral to force every semblance to abandon itself to a new aesthetic identity (a new artwork), which will then aggregate representational truth to itself, in turn, to ceaselessly propel an endless series of such affirmations and denials of an artwork's truth of its aesthetic identity. It is precisely this contradiction that defines reconciliation, as Adorno makes clear when he declares, "Art must testify to the unreconciled and at the same time envision its reconciliation."

By reconciliation Adorno thus paradoxically means, on the one hand, aesthetic reason's *allegiance to identity* through which its instrumental powers "envision reconciliation" by forming all that belongs to the aesthetic object, the unreconciled or not yet identified, in a word, *difference,* into an artwork appearing under the pretense it represents its object without remainder and loss of any of its features. On the other hand, there is the artwork's *allegiance to the unreconciled* in its reflexive capacity to remain aware the object is forever different from its representations. For Adorno, reconciliation is *always* this *dual allegiance,* this twofold endless striving to realize, once and for all, the achievement of the all-inclusiveness of difference, while reflexively recognizing there always remain differences belonging to the object to be included.

The reconciliation image envisions the achievement of all-inclusiveness as it also and always reflexively testifies to its not yet having arrived. So as my retrospective analysis of my imagined display of Monet's completed Rouen artworks shows, the struggle between identity and nonidentity, semblance and difference is at work in Monet's series to throw into sharp relief the element of aesthetic reflexivity Adorno associates with aesthetic reason.

Moreover, by pursuing such a retrospective analysis after the fact of Monet's series having been completed, I interrupt the otherwise continuous motion of the reflexive work of aesthetic reason to distinguish each of its moments and its contributions to forming the Rouen series into images of reconciliation and enlightenment. Aesthetic reflexivity's first moment is perfectly articulated in Monet's construction of the Cathedral's aesthetic identity, which is sustained by its more than thirty different aesthetic incarnations as the Cathedrale Notre-Dame de Rouen, erected in the twelfth century, exhibiting a long history of architectural styles until becoming Monet's aesthetic object. Each artwork mounting its own pretense to truth, to representing the Cathedral just as it actually is, each of Monet's serial representations envisions its aesthetic identity's final, all-encompassing reconciliation with all possible ways the Cathedral could remain different from its artworks. Aesthetic reflexivity's second moment is articulated as the work of art, by compelling the artwork to continuously assume ever-mutable serial images, seems animated by a consciousness of unreconciled differences belonging to the Rouen Cathedral its aesthetic identity has still to include. And there is aesthetic reflexivity's third moment, its development of an irresolvable tension through which aesthetic reason affirms aesthetic identity while also compelling it to perpetually vary with difference, to continuously become different itself by continuing to assimilate to ever new images features of the Cathedral that the series's work of art reveals to be inexhaustibly different. Precisely agreeing with Adorno's concept of reconciliation, here aesthetic reflexivity's moments vouchsafe aesthetic identity and envision reconciliation while *also* testifying to the unreconciled by ceaselessly striving for the all-inclusiveness of that diversity of differences belonging to the object aesthetic reason finds to be an eternally unfinished project.

By distinguishing each of the three moments of the work of art's reflexive element, retrospective analysis of Monet's Rouen artworks improves on Adorno's example of the "unity of the history of art" as a model of aesthetic reason while being consistent with the strategy of negation it entailed. And by clarifying aesthetic reflexivity, retrospection allows us to see that as the distinct moments producing the Cathedral's images unfolded, they reflexively produced three clearly defined *democratic effects*: the effect of the artwork having constituted an aesthetic identity through its construction of its object; the effect, as the series progresses, of an awareness of differences aesthetic identity ought next to include; and the effect, as the series concluded, of an aesthetic identity identifying with and striving endlessly for an inclusiveness of differences that would finally leave no difference out.

It seems clear that each democratic effect produced by the three moments of aesthetic reflexivity corresponds to a qualitatively different Rouen image, with the first moment constituting and the second moment reconstituting the aesthetic identity of the Cathedral through plural identifications with difference, and the third moment creating an identity that also, paradoxically, finally appears to lie perpetually outside of it. With the third moment of aesthetic reflexivity crystallizing in this last image as the Rouen series concluded, however, aesthetic reason's serial articulations of *all* three moments now *all* work together reflexively to create one final image productive of one final democratic effect. This image is the image of the Rouen series as a whole, an image so qualitatively different from any and all of the images preceding it that the democratic effect it produces can only be described as a qualitative leap. As the image of the Rouen series as a whole, this final image must express the aesthetic rationality of the whole. It can be none other than the image of reconciliation, whose democratic effect is to "testify to the unreconciled and at the same time envision its reconciliation," to recall how Adorno defines the reconciliation of identity and difference. Only a degraded, nonaesthetic, nonreflexive rationality creates the *illusory image* of reconciliation, the illusion there are no longer differences to be included.

But our richer description of aesthetic reflexivity invites an even further elaboration of aesthetic reason that moves us much closer to its complete formulation. If aesthetic reason produces a democratic effect that, by virtue of being a qualitative leap, corresponds to a distinct type of image, the reconciliation image, which expresses the rationality of the series of images as a whole, then the serial images forming the whole with their own qualitatively distinct democratic effects must be distinct types of images as well. They must form an *economy of images corresponding to the economy of elements* from which they are produced, which to this point largely corresponds to the element of reflexivity that has been our focus. So it is not simply, as it has to this point seemed with the element of reflexivity in Monet's series, that an economy of elements produces serial images, which despite their conveying distinctly identifiable democratic effects are themselves without any distinction beyond being designated mere serial images of the Cathedral that are qualitatively different from one another. Much to the contrary, we should align a *distinct* type of qualitatively different image with the *distinct* type of democratic effect it conveys with the economy of elements that produces both. Since there are three democratic effects forming the rationality of the whole expressed by the reconciliation image, which is distinguished by its own democratic effect of reconciliation, we can distinguish the following distinct types of qualitatively different images corresponding to their own distinct democratic effects.

There is first the "identity image," whose democratic effect is the artwork's creative act of self-identification (i.e., *La Cathédrale de Rouen, Le portail, soleil matinal; harmonie bleue*, 1892–93), its self-presentation appearing as a distinct true-to-life semblance through its construction of its aesthetic object (the Rouen Cathedral); second, there is the "difference image," whose democratic effect is to register awareness of differences between the artwork's aesthetic identity and its aesthetic object to be identified with and included in identity's semblance; and, third, there is the "all-inclusive image," whose democratic effect is of the artwork's interminable striving for the further inclusions of differences between its aesthetic identities and its aesthetic object. These images and their democratic effects align with the element of aesthetic reflexivity we first clearly observed at work in Monet's series. Monet's Rouen artworks, each an "identity image" of the Cathedral, are each also "difference images," subsequent artworks reflexively produced by an awareness of differences between the Cathedral itself and its image (or images), which are succeeded by the "all-inclusive image," where the work of art has reflexively identified with difference to foster the perpetual attempt to create images of all possible ways the Cathedral remains different from its every other image. All three types of images, and the types of democratic effects they produce, together create the *reconciliation image*, which paradoxically expresses the democratic effect of the whole series of images of the Cathedral by testifying to its unreconciled, yet to be included features, while also envisioning the final reconciliation of its image with the Rouen Cathedral itself just as it actually is.

When completely fleshed out in the following chapter, our twin economies of elements and images and their democratic effects will enable us to relate Adorno's theory of the modern artwork to film in a way that shows art and film are far less different than Adorno had argued. Modernist artworks and film, two media Adorno considered to be essentially different, with film failing to rise to the level of the aesthetic rationality of the artwork, will in fact prove to be essentially the same with respect to the aesthetic form of reason on which art is based, the economy of images aesthetic reason's economy of elements creates, the types of democratic effects these images produce, and the contribution of these twin aesthetic economies to the production of the reconciliation image. Supposing these elements and images and their effects do circulate in film, they would lay the foundation for new concepts transcending Horkheimer and Adorno's invidious distinction between art and mass (or popular) culture by allowing us to refer, instead, to two visual forms in which these aesthetic economies commonly appear. Art and mass culture, the former held by Horkheimer and Adorno to be the parent of the aesthetic type of rationality orphaned by the latter, would be conceptually displaced by the "reconciliation image in art" and the "reconciliation image in film." Art and film would be aesthetic analogues.

Before I can discover in film the same twin economies of elements and images and their effects I have begun to find in the modern artwork, however, I must turn to our second modernist example. For although I have made progress in fleshing out and further developing Adorno's concept of aesthetic reason, I have yet to adequately explain why this aesthetic process unfolds in the way I have described. To do this requires I complete my analysis of aesthetic reason through an example of the individual modernist artwork—Rodin's *Thought*. Fully disclosing aesthetic reason's remaining properties, Rodin's artwork will explain why it follows a developmental logic on its way to its creation of the reconciliation image, whose economy of images and democratic effects will also be found to consist of images and effects in addition to those I have already identified through my analysis of Monet's series. This explanation will further clarify the element of continuity and why the reconciliation image unfolds seamlessly to form a qualitative image of time. With Rodin I will thus complete the task of fleshing out and further developing Adorno's concept of aesthetic reason, which possesses additional resources even beyond those I have so far introduced for discovering parallels between the modern artwork and film that will prove the reconciliation image circulates in both.

Adorno describes nonidentity as a presence
that acts upon us: we knowers are haunted,
he says, by a painful, nagging feeling that
something's being forgotten or left out.
—Jane Bennett, *Vibrant Matter*

4

Aesthetic Analogues

ART AND FILM

With Monet's serial paintings of the Rouen Cathedral I have begun to flesh
out and further develop Adorno's concept of aesthetic reason. By differentiating aesthetic reason's interrelated moments of aesthetic reflexivity, I have
clarified the logic of the work of art belonging to the modernist artwork as
that which creates the identity, difference, and all-inclusive images and their
democratic effects, and how this economy of images and its effects together
with Adorno's economy of elements to which it corresponds contribute to
the formation of the reconciliation image. Before this chapter concludes I will
have found aesthetic reason consisting of additional elements, images, and
democratic effects from which the reconciliation image is produced in both
modern artworks and film.

Although at first it will seem counterintuitive, Rodin's *Thought*, a sculpture
he completed circa 1895, exemplifies as much as Monet's Rouen paintings how
the process of aesthetic reflexivity works through serial images. This means
that where aesthetic reason is at work in modern art, the artwork—even the
individual artwork—is never a single image but always a series of images, an
economy of images unfolding from the one. As models of aesthetic reason,
Rodin's sculpture and Monet's paintings, the individual artwork and the series, both exemplify how the very same process of aesthetic reason is at work
through its proliferation of images, although as we shall see there also will
be important differences between these examples revealing things previously

unknown. Before I turn to my Rodin example some preliminary remarks will clarify these differences and the significant contribution they will make to my efforts to flesh out and further develop the concept of aesthetic reason.

THE ELEMENT OF MOTION, COMPLEXITIES OF ITS ANALYSIS

As Rodin's *Thought* will show, though almost any of his sculptures would as well, the serial images of which the modern artwork is composed continuously unfold from the single image the individual artwork presents at the outset. Through this continuous unfolding of the economy of images from the one, *motion*, a new though also decisive element of aesthetic reason Monet's series did not illuminate, comes to the surface along with other new elements of aesthetic reason the element of motion brings to light. This is not to say motion was absent from Monet's collection. While his series, complete and on display before us, did not illuminate the element of motion in the artwork, it did record motion after the fact when we studied it retrospectively. For as we saw, his series displayed images that had *already unfolded* to reveal the reflexive logic of aesthetic reason. Nevertheless Rodin's *Thought* illustrates what a series of images already unfolded and viewed retrospectively cannot. Aesthetic rationality endows the modern artwork with the capacity to *initiate* the motion that originates a continuously unfolding series of different images. In continuous motion the modern artwork's *fixed identity* is converted to the *ever-changing image*. Artwork continuously becomes image. Aesthetic identity continuously becomes different.

What my Rodin example will thus newly bring to light—the image's capacity to initiate motion, the image in continuous motion, the fixed artwork as a continuously moving and changing image and aesthetic identity—are key differences from the Rouen artworks that will allow me to further elaborate on aesthetic reason beyond what we learned from Monet's series. What I found through Monet to be aesthetic reason will now be revised to account for the element of motion introduced by Rodin. For as *Thought* will show, motion, the capacity for which I will later find is owed to the mimetic powers of the artwork, is the element responsible for the continuously unfolding, unbroken economy of images, the *open whole* of images forming the reconciliation image. *Thought* shows that by expressing the rationality of the economy of the whole series of images of which the artwork consists, the reconciliation image is the image of aesthetic reason in motion, the motion of images continuously becoming different.

The significance of this move for my argument cannot be overstated. Only as such an image of the movement of aesthetic identity continuously becoming different can the reconciliation image not only envision the *achievement* of reconciliation, but the reconciliation image becomes the open whole able to testify to differences the image *has yet to include*. Only as such an image in motion can the reconciliation image avoid the temporal illusion represented by an artwork's fixed aesthetic identity—the illusion that with the artwork's continuous motion arrested, time, as the motion of continuous change, has been arrested as well. It is an illusion of time emptied of change, an empty time. But as the image of the continuous movement of becoming different, the reconciliation image bears a different relation to time. As the unfolding of qualitatively different images through the continuous movement of an open whole, the reconciliation image becomes a *qualitative image* of time and an image of time as qualitative change.

With Rodin's *Thought*, consequently, I want to further show that where it is created by the modern artwork the reconciliation image is in continuous motion in three determinant senses. It is the movement of aesthetic reason as an open whole's ceaseless unfolding of an economy of images and effects; it is movement forever striving toward the all-inclusiveness of difference through the continuous appearance of new differences in qualitatively different serial images; and it is movement through which time itself unfolds in continuously changing, qualitatively different images, time as the creation of the image of identity continuously becoming different and new, a form of what should be called *democratic time*. As with the *effects* of images, the *time* of images is democratic by virtue of its contribution to achieving the ideal of reconciliation.

By contributing in these ways to my efforts to flesh out the concept of aesthetic reason, my Rodin example will differ from the Rouen artworks in the important respect just introduced. Because Rodin's *Thought* illuminates motion, it will also offer a reconciliation image that improves on the one offered by Monet's series, whose image of reconciliation is essentially ambiguous in relation to motion and could appear to be either real or illusory. As we shall see, *Thought* produces the reconciliation image through a continuous motion from one image and one effect to another. Without cessation, its motion proliferates serial images continuously inclusive of something qualitatively different about the aesthetic object of the artwork, whose unfolding images of differences are continuously unfolding qualitative images of time, time understood as qualitative change. In contrast to *Thought*, however, with his final Rouen artwork Monet's completed collection of serial images could appear to be of a cathedral ceasing to appear different from its images having been frozen in time, rather than a series remaining in motion according to the logic of aesthetic reason. Its motion appearing to be arrested, Monet's series would appear to be an *illusory* image of reconciliation. Motion would have ceased to continually run the endless gamut of serial images and effects that produce a true image of reconciliation testifying to differences belonging to an object yet to be included. Aesthetic reason would seem to be arrested in Monet's series, whereas the continuous motion of the open whole of unfolding images in *Thought* immunizes the artwork against such paralysis.

Motion, of course, was not actually arrested in Monet's series, despite possible illusions to the contrary. In chapter 3 I interrupted the unbroken, continuous process of aesthetic reason by analyzing Monet's series as he had completed it so it could be imagined fully unfolded and on display before us in its entirety. By taking such a retrospective analytical approach to Monet's artworks, suspending though not arresting aesthetic reason's proliferation of his serial images, I was able to distinguish each of the moments belonging to aesthetic reason's element of aesthetic reflexivity, its corresponding type of image and democratic effect, thus each moment's unique contribution to the unfolding of the reconciliation image.

Potentially at work in Monet's series all along, then, which I suspended for purposes of retrospective analysis, the reflexive movement of aesthetic reason toward the reconciliation image opposes the illusion of reconciliation created by those artworks whose aesthetic forms paralyze the process of aesthetic reason by arresting the motion of the work of art. Where motion has been arrested by artworks and aesthetic closure imposed, to again recall my earlier examples from classicism, we would be unable to reconstruct the movement of aesthetic reason productive of the reconciliation image and the illusion of reconciliation would prevail. Nevertheless, although Monet's series is seen to offer a true image of reconciliation when we understand the reflexive movement of the work of art of his unfolding Rouen images not to have been arrested but suspended for analytical purposes, its ambiguous relation to motion and thus to reconciliation points to a limitation to how retrospective analysis of aesthetic reason in the modern artwork proceeds. Here I arrive at the final difference between my Monet and Rodin examples and its contribution to the conceptualization of aesthetic reason.

As my approach to Monet's series thus shows, an analysis of aesthetic rationality becomes problematic if it proceeds retrospectively. On the one hand, without such a retrospective analysis of the series aesthetic reason would remain elusive because aesthetic reflexivity's moments could not be neatly distinguished owing to the unbroken continuity of their motion, and its twin economies and effects and the work of art they perform to produce the image of reconciliation would be obscured. On the other hand, though, as we just learned, retrospective analysis of Monet's series also casts doubt on the truth of the artworks' image of reconciliation despite analysis of the work of art finding aesthetic reason to have been in play prior to being suspended. Retrospective analysis thus shadows Monet's artworks with the illusion of reconciliation, which by leaving his series in an ambiguous relation to motion and reconciliation creates an even deeper problem.

By adopting a retrospective analysis of Monet's series to suspend the motion of aesthetic reason in order to distinguish the moments and images and effects of aesthetic reflexivity, we are prevented from carrying out an analysis of *motion itself*, the element of aesthetic reason through which all other elements develop. Once the motion of the artwork has been suspended, the reflexive movement belonging to the moments of aesthetic reason, their corresponding images and effects, can be traced in the work of art, but the unbroken, continuous motion from one moment, image, and effect to the next cannot be reconstituted. Intervals between the movements of each image open up so that we cannot determine how one reflexive moment could seamlessly unfold to continuously produce a new and different image and effect. And missing the continuous motion for the intervals, we would fail to see what other elements or images of aesthetic reason might attach to motion to explain and be explained by its seamless quality. Without an understanding of motion itself, we cannot grasp how or if the motion of the work of art produces the reconciliation image to express the rationality of the open whole. Without an image of the image in motion, the reconciliation image cannot with certainty be seen to continuously unfold. Perhaps it is only an illusion.

With the differences between our two examples and their bearing on aesthetic reason now in mind we arrive at the following insight. If my analysis of the twin economies of aesthetic reason in Monet's artworks must fail to understand the continuous motion of the work of art, I have need of a supplementary example that illuminates unbroken motion and any new elements of aesthetic reason in addition to reflexivity it will bring to light. I need a single artwork where we can follow the *continuity* of serial images of which the artwork is composed as they actually unfold. Hence *Thought*. This new example allows me to break with the practice of retrospective analysis I adopted with Monet, so that intervals between the seamless unfolding dynamics of aesthetic reflexivity and between its images do not open up and the properties belonging to the continuous motion of the reconciliation image can appear. Adorno offers guidance here, where he alludes to the shortcomings of retrospective analysis. Analysis, to the contrary, must grasp art's "processual element," for analysis is "adequate to the work only if it grasps the relation of its elements to each other *processually*."[1]

Adorno is challenging us to explore an alternative approach making possible another way of understanding the artwork. To be able to grasp the relation of the artwork's elements to each other *processually*, to be able to grasp them *in continuous motion* so that it becomes adequate to the work of art, analysis must follow another approach that first allows us to make motion visible by making the artwork continuously move, by bringing the artwork to life. For life in its essence, as we have known since Bergson formulated it, is the continuity of motion. And art, like life, is a continuous process, one that does not start and stop. Without continuous motion, there is neither life nor the possibility for reconciliation that life, and art, offer.

RODIN: EXPERIENCING THOUGHT IN MOTION

Motion, Adorno proposes, becomes visible through an "aesthetic experience" available to each of us that accompanies a unique "gaze" we are able to direct toward the artwork, releasing its capacity for motion. Under the power of our gaze we perceive the artwork to be in motion, to be "animate," in Adorno's words. Our gaze, though "contemplative," is not the cerebral distancing ordinarily conveyed by contemplation. Here contemplation is an "immersion" in the artwork, an aesthetic experience in which we are so absorbed it becomes a "living experience." Describing aesthetic experience of the artwork in this way, Adorno means to disabuse us of our inclination to sublimate aesthetic experience through a contemplative relation to the artwork that privileges the mind by disenfranchising the body. As we gaze at the artwork's *image* of its object, our mind and our body collaborate to illuminate contradictions through which we imaginatively form a sensuous perception of the *aesthetic object itself*; it is as sensuous perception of the artwork's object that our gaze sets the artwork into continuous motion. For Adorno, variations in our aesthetic experience are less important than the way it immerses us commonly in the process of aesthetic reason, whose logic will ultimately shape our shared experience of Rodin's *Thought* in the same way it governs the movement of the work of art within the artwork.

The contradictions our aesthetic experience of the artwork makes us aware of are differences between its initial image of the object and the object apart from its image. Immersing ourselves in the artwork, our gaze identifies with differences the artwork's aesthetic identity excludes, leading our mind's eye away from this image to form a sensuous attachment to the object through which we can visualize it differently and imaginatively project new images of how it could be different from the aesthetic identity the artwork has overlaid. Repeating this process with every new image we imagine, sensuous perception sets the artwork in motion, continuing to create new images of the object that give form to the perceived differences between the artwork and the object itself.

With each revised aesthetic identity new limitations belonging to the artwork emerge, our gaze calling our attention to the representational deficiencies of the artwork's every new image of its object, all images together generating an aesthetic inertia that ensures successor images will include differences belonging to the object the artwork yet leaves out. Our aesthetic experience emancipates the object from its bondage to fixed aesthetic identities and delivers the artwork to the work of art performed by aesthetic reason. Relinquishing every representation of its object, the artwork moves through the interrelated serial elements, images, and effects of a process enabling the object to continually appear different. Modernist artworks, those in which aesthetic reason is at work, promise such an aesthetic experience that brings the movement of its object, the life of the object, back to life, to reveal in ever changing images the continuity of motion that is the essence of life itself.

I believe this is how we are to understand Adorno's concept of aesthetic experience, for which his own summary distills everything I have just tried to explain:

> Aesthetic experience becomes living experience *only by way of its object,* in that instant in which artworks themselves become animate under its gaze. . . . Through contemplative immersion the immanent processual quality of the work is set free. . . . It becomes something that moves in itself . . . the enactment of antagonisms that each work necessarily has in itself. . . . The way the beloved image is transformed in this experience, the way rigidification is unified with what is most intensely alive, effectively makes the experience the incarnate prototype of aesthetic experience. . . . Artworks' paradoxical nature, *stasis, negates itself.* The movement of artworks must be at a standstill and thereby become visible.[2]

In that instant in which artworks themselves become animate under aesthetic experience's gaze is cautionary advice. Aesthetic experience alone enables analysis to differentiate the elements of aesthetic reason by grasping, to recall Adorno's prescription, "the relation of [the artwork's] elements to each other *processually*," by grasping them as aesthetic experience sets them in motion, in other words. In expectation of arriving at such an adequate analysis of the artwork, then, by means of Rodin's *Thought* we can now graduate from a retrospective examination of aesthetic reason to the aesthetic experience of the process of aesthetic rationality. Aesthetic reason's "immanent processual quality," its capacity for *movement*, will be "set free" through our gaze and the aesthetic experience it gives birth to. If my efforts to flesh out the work of art have been correct thus far, as I now turn to Rodin everything belonging to aesthetic reason I was able to discover in Monet's series should be at work in *Thought*, along with any new elements, images, and effects my illumination of motion will make visible. All of this should come together as my subsequent analysis moves ahead toward its conclusion.

Rodin's sculpture *Thought* is of a woman's head and face sitting on a massive pedestal of rough-hewn marble, her head covered by a simple cap drawn snugly over her hair and ears and with a facial expression that is, like quietude, free of disturbance (see accompanying image). This artwork, in its visible, motionless state, is mind without body, perhaps of a mind having shorn itself of its body. An aggressive Cartesian image powerfully commanding the idea that thinking occurs uninterrupted by the body, it captures our gaze, immersing us in its point of view. As we immerse ourselves in *Thought*, its imposing unsculpted marble block gradually draws our gaze downward to the place where the dispossessed body should be, encouraging us to imaginatively form a sensuous attachment to the artwork's object by identifying with the body its mind has excluded, with sensations not brought to the fullness of thought. Our original Cartesian image begins to yield to a second image as our sensuous perception of the body brings it into focus, the body's conspicuous absence making it vividly present. Becoming a virtual presence-through-absence, the body of *Thought* incites in us a reverie revising the artwork as we imagine an image now including the body the original image left out. A third image now emerges, correcting the first. Our gaze joins the mind to its body.

With this new image subsequent and competing images can follow in turn of how a countenance that had persisted uninterrupted newly appears when disturbed by its body, by its continuous pains and pleasures and other feelings, and how thought newly appears if its composure were affected by

Auguste Rodin (1840–1917), *Thought*, c. 1895. Musée d'Orsay, Paris.

an invasion of sensations. Images now proliferate, further revising the initial Cartesian image of undisturbed solitude as well as the flow of reconstructed anti-Cartesian images that newly include the mind and body together, the limitations of each producing new images of the variations of the others. We imagine a diversity of different images of facial and bodily expressions, of thoughts with their sensations, multiplying for as long as our gaze keeps the artwork in motion performing the work of art its aesthetic rationality sustains. An important argument is being made by the plurality of images created by the processual movement of aesthetic reason our gaze ignited as we became immersed in the artwork. If thought were to think beyond thoughts that can be presented placidly, if thought were to think *different* thoughts, joyful or troubling or difficult thoughts, thoughts perhaps weighed down or lifted up or pushed forward by contradictions, criticism, and doubt or self-doubt, thought would express all this through a mind inclusive of a body opening it to the world. If we make the contemplative effort I have just described our aesthetic experience of the artwork is magical. What appears motionless is thrown into motion. What seems lifeless comes to life. With this the artwork can now be appreciated *analytically*, for through our aesthetic experience analysis becomes adequate to the artwork, as Adorno earlier explained.

ANALYSIS OF AESTHETIC EXPERIENCE

By fastening our eyes on *Thought* our gaze first immersed us in the artwork to progressively form a sensuous attachment to its object, which then moved, as though under its own power, through our imaginative serial projections of how it could appear differently. Breaking down the aesthetics of this experience, to begin with, does the aesthetic identity Rodin has overlaid its object not capture our attention, draw in our gaze, compel our immersion in the object itself? How can it not. Rodin focused our eyes on *Thought*'s sculptured head by resting it on a marble block with which it is greatly out of proportion, forcefully suggesting that the stone foundation is not there to support the far lesser physical weight of the bust but the far greater intellectual weight of the "thought" it represents. This dramatic asymmetry between the contradictory magnitudes of the bust and its base coupled with the erasure of the body accords an absolute privilege to mind over the body, as though the mind has no need for its body or relies on it only as a passive support for work in which its body does not participate. In either case the body has been excluded from *Thought* by an aesthetic identity violently imposing itself on both mind and body through its identitarian representation of its object, threatening aesthetic closure.[3] Excluding its body, an exclusion that extends to an expressionless face that seems not to be a face that is *of* a body, *Thought*, mind, thinking itself, has become rigid, having brought to a standstill any motion that animated it when it was attached to its body. With *Thought* Rodin gives us what Adorno describes as the "beloved" though "rigidified" image about to be "transformed" through an "aesthetic experience" that will enable it to become "unified with what is most intensely alive." With this rigidified image of thought or of mind or of thinking, Rodin has given us the *identity image*.

No sooner was our gaze captured by the artwork then the grotesque asymmetry created by the identity image that at first focused our eyes on Rodin's bust redirected our attention to what its rigidity depends upon. Our gaze moved gradually down the sculpture to *Thought*'s pedestal, whose massive disproportion announced itself as the placeholder for where the excluded body ought to be. Rooted in its identity image, arising from its brittleness, a contradiction has broken out releasing the artwork's capacity for movement and setting it into motion. In the location where the artwork's aesthetic identity had violently erased the body, the body's image was insinuated into its place of absence that had made Rodin's bust the exclusive center of our attention. What was actually absent became virtually present as the work of art introduced the new image of the body, awakening our sensuous perception to what *Thought*, or mind, to maintain its petrified image, necessarily excluded, namely, that which in relation to mind, in relation to its apodictic, self-subsisting Cartesian identity, is *difference*. An image of the mind excluding the body, of identity excluding difference, was replaced by the image of the mind in the presence of the body, aware of the body as identity is aware of differences on whose exclusions its truth depends. With the new image of the body Rodin has given us *the difference image*.

With the unfolding of its contradiction the identity image initiates movement to bring the difference image into view. Identifying with the body—identifying with the excluded, with difference—to return it to its rightful place, Rodin's artwork is in motion. As the body then reclaims its place, mind and body, identity and difference, are positioned to undergo further transformations, for our gaze cannot bring the body into view without our mind's eye next imagining *Thought* as a mind *reunited* with its body. A second new image is born, the first in a potentially infinite series of images through which the fixed artwork surrenders to become the changing image. *Thought*, its aesthetic identity, becomes different, the identity image having begun to relinquish its

Cartesian rigidity through its receptivity to difference. Shortly I will find this new affinity the identity image shows for difference to be an image itself, *the receptivity image*, the prelude to another image, *the imitative image*, which records the movement through which aesthetic identity actually becomes different by imitating differences it has excluded.

For the moment I will say only that identity's receptive-imitative orientation to difference, the mind's relation to difference reuniting it with its body, would also be responsible for continuing the processual motion of the work of art through which other, new mind-body images emerge. Once the new image of the mind-body reunited took shape, our imagination could begin to project images of how the artwork's resculpted persona could possibly change its expressions alive to its body's excitations, and how the body could change its expressions alive to its stimulated mind's instant messaging. Images of the artwork appearing different would proliferate, the artwork identifying with difference in multiple ways, each different from every other way the artwork newly appeared. As serial images of different mind-body relations unfolded, a third type of image would take form, which depicted the never-ending attempt of the work of art to create revised identity images of all possible ways the mind and body joined could collaborate to appear in ever-different forms. Rodin has given us *the all-inclusive image*.

With the formation of the all-inclusive image, all three types of images, the elements of reflexivity, motion, and process, and the democratic effects to which they correspond, have been the offspring of an aesthetic experience of the processual movement of aesthetic reason from which they will produce the reconciliation image. *Thought* first appeared to us through the identity image, which conferred aesthetic identity upon the artwork by recognizing only certain features belonging to its aesthetic object while excluding the rest in the naïve spirit of an Emersonian democratic individuality parading the absoluteness of its subjectivity. Features excluded by the artwork were then recognized by the difference image, a reflexive movement that worked toward the democratization of the artwork by becoming conscious of excluded differences between it and its aesthetic object. As images next proliferated of how mind-body relations could be imaginatively configured, the artwork exhibited an unending reflexive striving for a democratic all-inclusiveness of difference in new identity images of a mind and body responding to each other's thoughts and feelings, needs and wants, pains and pleasures.

So long as we remained immersed in the artwork, our gaze sustaining the processual movement of aesthetic reason, the democratization of the artwork could proceed indefinitely, with its democratic effects—its affirmations of identity, identities' alliances with difference, identities' inclusions of differences—continuously unfolding with the appearance of each new identity image inclusive of differences in mind-body relations the artwork had yet left out. Aesthetic experience, in other words, emancipated a series of elements—reflexivity, motion, and process—which together illuminated and overcame the limits of the artwork through a proliferation of images whose democratic effects, on the one hand, *envisioned* a mind and body achieving their conjugal possibilities and, on the other, *testified* to the not yet included indeterminate possibilities for new mind-body interconnections. With *Thought*, Rodin has thus given us *the reconciliation image*, which by reconciling the identity of the mind and the difference of the body expresses the aesthetic rationality of the artwork's process of continuous movement as a whole.

Between our *aesthetic experience* of the artwork, which set free the processual element of aesthetic reason, and our *analysis* of this process, which becomes adequate to the artwork when we are able to study the elements of aesthetic reason after aesthetic experience has actually set them in motion, the centrality of motion to the work of art enters into the foreground. Motion is shown to be the essence of aesthetic reason, the process of aesthetic reason itself and the element without which the reflexive relationships among the elements and images and effects of aesthetic reason could not emerge to produce the reconciliation image. Very early in *Aesthetic Theory* Adorno had alerted us to this discovery—"Art can be understood only by its laws of movement"—no doubt to guide us toward the principle of motion around which revolves everything he believes is most salient to the artwork. Our analysis of our aesthetic experience of Rodin's sculpture illustrates Adorno's claim. Once we immersed ourselves in *Thought*, the properties of aesthetic reason that we were able to distinguish retrospectively in Monet's Rouen series were then seen in Rodin's sculpture to be at work processually as aesthetic experience set them into continuous motion. Analysis then showed that as the artwork moved through the identity, difference, and all-inclusive images and their democratic effects to serially revise its aesthetic identity, it had been the forebear of the reconciliation image, an aesthetic critique of social orders founded on their exclusions of difference. As Adorno stressed, aesthetic reason's critique of "nature-dominating" reason is rooted in its power of setting "rigid determinations," the identities instrumental reason imposes on its objects, "in movement by modifying them."[4]

So Rodin's *Thought* clarifies what Monet's series of thirty artworks could only ambiguously imply after the fact of their having been completed and exhibited for purposes of retrospective analysis: motion is central to aesthetic rationality, is its essence and the essence of the reconciliation image. It becomes visible when—and only when—our aesthetic experience of the artwork sets into motion the reflexive relationships belonging to aesthetic reason's distinguishable elements, images, and democratic effects, whose movements determine the general movement of the open whole producing and expressed by the reconciliation image. By making the element of motion visible, moreover, aesthetic experience also makes visible another element of aesthetic reason we have yet to completely understand. Indeed this element—*continuity*, and its dimensions *becoming different* and *qualitative time*—become visible only when aesthetic experience throws the artwork into motion. And since, as I have tried to show, when set into motion the artwork remains in motion for as long as we remain immersed in the aesthetic experience of the artwork, this suggests aesthetic experience is of aesthetic movement that is *continuous* in two senses, as *unbroken* and *ceaseless* motion that comes to rest only for the time preceding aesthetic experience and with its end.

Experienced aesthetically, in other words, images in motion change one into another as each emerges from the one before it without temporal or perceptible intervals or gaps opening up between them. Such unbroken motion characterized the proliferation of images of mind-body relations issuing from the reconciliation of the mind and body that aesthetic experience made possible by immersing us in Rodin's *Thought*. Images in motion were themselves each authored by an image to become author of another, as the identity image authored the difference image, the difference image authored the all-inclusive image, and the all-inclusive image authored a series of ever more inclusive identity images to create the image of the reconciliation of identity and difference. By aesthetically experiencing these many images in motion seamlessly unfolding from the artwork, Adorno adds, we become "conscious of [art's] immanent process" of continuous movement when, with the conclusion of aesthetic experience, the artwork (re)appears as an image whose motion has been arrested and brought to "a standstill."[5] Without aesthetic experience's uninterrupted motion, no sooner does it cease to move than the artwork remains stalled for some interval of time in an identity opposed to reconciliation's continued striving for the all-inclusiveness of difference. And unmoving art is the illusion of reconciliation. Aesthetic experience of continuity in this unbroken sense is thus all-important. For as aesthetic experience reveals, only so long as the continuity of images in motion is maintained, gaps in time do not open up between images to convert the artwork's progress toward the reconciliation image into an illusion of reconciliation, the illusion that identity has included all differences, that it has left no difference out.

Flowing from the aesthetic experience of the artwork's continuously unfolding images in motion, then, continuity is not movement between one image that marks where motion begins and a second marking its end and the point at which motion resumes again between it and yet another image, which would be *discontinuous* movement. As the image-in-motion *itself*, continuity, it may be clearer to say, is an unbroken process of the unfolding of a single image, of an artwork continuously unfolding as an image of reconciliation, whose reflexively interrelated elements, images, and democratic effects are all seamlessly connected stages of one indivisible movement.

To say that motion is unbroken, moreover, is to invoke its continuity in its second sense as well. Unbroken motion is motion that never breaks off, thus *ceaseless motion*. Always an unceasing process through aesthetic experience, the reconciliation image, hence reconciliation itself, can never be likened to a Platonic form, to "Being," as Adorno puts it, "absolved from Becoming." As a ceaseless proliferation of images of difference the reconciliation image is a proliferation and inclusiveness of images of difference that are limitless, hence continuity as endlessly *becoming different* and the reconciliation image *becoming* an eternally unfinished image. So the artwork is not really identical to any of its perceived appearances but is rather an *"explosion* of appearance," an explosion of the many different images from the one whose "overarching form," whose aesthetic identity, that is, has been "blasted away" by aesthetic reason's continuous proliferation of images.[6] As a result of aesthetic experience, artworks should never appear to us, be perceived by us, in the same way twice.

Finally, since the essence of the modern artwork is the image in motion, aesthetic experience cannot set the artwork into motion to create the reconciliation image without altering art's relationship to time. I can make this better understood against the backdrop of the way time works in artworks that project an illusory image of reconciliation, which for the life of an artwork reproduces a selfsame, unchanging appearance of its aesthetic object. Poussin's and Lorrain's landscapes oppose any image we may have of nature departing from their classicist idealized aesthetic constructions. Supported by an aesthetic form repelling the gaze that would set these artworks into motion, they compel nature to conform to an idyllic aesthetic identity enduring in a rigidly invariant form. Rather than images in motion, each artwork reverts to the illusory condition of the still life and is valued as a likeness of the classical teleological view of nature. Reconciliation appears to be an ideal that nature achieves in the present or is an end inherent in nature realizable in time. In either case the illusion of reconciliation belongs to *chronological* time, to the achievement now or later of an ideal whose realization can be measured over the passage of time according to some quantitative scale, as though reconciliation were an aspiration only of finite and not also of infinitely open proportions.[7] If the illusory image of reconciliation is aligned with chronological time, should the reconciliation image not have a different relationship to time?

Because motion is the essence of aesthetic reason, time is *of the essence* of the artwork because it corresponds to the movement of the reconciliation image when aesthetic experience converts the artwork to the continuously changing image. As I imply by this formulation, time depends upon movement in a special way. For the motion of the reconciliation image is not only of an image continually becoming different; its motion is a continuously changing image *of* difference. By depending on continuous motion, time depends on difference, a dependency that reconstitutes time far more deeply than the obvious linear connection between motion and time. It is not simply that once in motion as a continuously changing image the artwork can no longer remain identical with itself, an appearance holding the present captive to an illusion of reconciliation eliminating any difference between the artwork's semblance and how its aesthetic object actually appears in the present or could appear in the future. Created by the motion of continuously changing images of difference, the reconciliation image is, at one and the same time, a vision of reconciliation that also recognizes the as yet unreconciled. It is an image of difference and at the same time yet another and different image, an image of the present time and yet also of a different and future time. I believe we should say the reconciliation image is a paradoxical time, at one and the same time the image of a time arrived and a time yet to come.

To speak a bit awkwardly, this "doubling of identity as difference" belonging to the reconciliation image, which is a temporal doubling whereby identity becoming different from itself is, at the same time, the future identity of a difference also and always different from the identity it is becoming at any moment, is consistent with what I have argued is the *continuous* processual rationality of the artwork as a whole. If the reconciliation image were not, *at one and the same time*, both an image of difference and an image of a difference yet to come, an image of a different present and also of a different and future time, a time arrived and a time yet to come, it would not be the ceaseless pursuit of the all-inclusiveness of difference that envisions the possibility of reconciliation while testifying to its absence. Always the doubling of identity as difference, according to its image reconciliation is not realizable in chronological time, which is the common denominator of forms of social progress calculated to be realizable in time. For differences in kind have no common denominator. Through its dependence on the movement of images of difference, time, like differences and images of difference, is *qualitative*. Thus the reconciliation image requires us to speak not of a uniform chronological time to which the progressive realization of reconciliation can be reduced, but in the plural of *qualitative times*. Each time, like each image of a qualitative difference on which the movement of time depends, is a qualitatively different and new time. And like the images to which they belong, qualitative times are not separated by discontinuous gaps and intervals, by stops and starts. They seamlessly unfold as one continuously unfolding *durational* stream of time.

Time's dependency upon movement, movement as continuously becoming images of difference, time as the movement of qualitatively different and new images, qualitative not quantitative time, times not time, in my view explain Adorno's radical proposal that art has "its own inner time." Thus, with the proliferation of images of difference in motion, that which he described as the explosion of appearance that "has blasted away the overarching form" of the artwork's aesthetic identity, also "blasts open the continuity of this inner temporality." It could not be otherwise than as such an explosive creation of qualitatively different and new images and times that the reconciliation image could envision the time when no difference is excluded while also testifying to the arrival of such a time as always yet to come. "Because art is what it has *become*," Adorno insists, "its concept refers to what it does not contain": the reconciliation image identifying difference but also identifying with difference, thus a time of difference that is always a different and new time.[8] "Democratic time," and the reconciliation image it corresponds to, is this continuously moving, changing, and becoming qualitative time. Democratic time is always, paradoxically, at one and the same time, a time arrived and a time yet to come.

Since democratic time, like the temporality of the reconciliation image it expresses, is at one and the same time both a present and a future time, a time arrived and a time yet to come, as a paradoxical time democratic time also expresses the paradoxical character of the modern artwork. And it is the artwork's paradoxical character that will return us to the artwork's capacity for motion, to the origins of its continuous motion, which as I conclude this chapter's discussion will enable me to bring to light aesthetic reason's remaining elements and images and their democratic effects. With this I will be nearer to determining if modern art and film are aesthetic analogues, if film possesses the same aesthetic form of rationality and produces the same reconciliation image as modern art. Here is how I believe Adorno understands the modern artwork's paradoxical character, which is one of the most complex as well as important problems in his aesthetic theory for its bearing on the reconciliation image.

On the one hand, the artwork's raison d'être is to endure in no form other than how it appears when it comes into being. Leonardo's *Mona Lisa* is the popular exemplar of the artwork's pursuit of immortality. But from what I have argued in this and in the previous chapter, to remain tirelessly selfsame such an artwork must *resist* its creative capacity to relinquish its aesthetic identity to continuously unfolding images of difference. It must resist the process of becoming different I traced in Rodin's *Thought*, whose reconciliation image is governed by an aesthetic form of rationality forcing the artwork to become different from itself. In classicist artworks, which would include the Leonardo, aesthetic form favored the artwork's inertia of being rather than its motion of becoming different. For if the motion of becoming different were at work to produce the reconciliation image, it would subdue an enduring appearance the selfsame artwork strives to insulate against the proliferation of images democratizing it. Inscribed in such enduring artwork is some idealized end or value or meaning it perpetuates as it works to perpetuate itself and that its aesthetic object serves instrumentally by being made to appear one way only, as though it naturally serves some preordained end by achieving a form defining it for all time. The claim to reason made by the timeless, unchanging, selfsame and self-identical, reified artwork is thus instrumental. Borrowed from a social world likewise striving to remain unchanged, its rationality produces the false, illusory image of reconciliation.

On the other hand, this artwork cannot really endure as it came into being without *also becoming implicated* in the creative process out of which its paradoxical character will arise. If it is to earn its timeless stature the artwork must necessarily express something essential or defining, unique or singular, universal or transcendental, new or unknown or beautiful belonging to its object. But here in the artwork's need to be, though also to be "eloquent," as Adorno puts it, lies its innate capacity for motion that constitutes both its instrumental claim to reason *and* its aesthetic form of rationality, its eternal selfsameness *and* the work of art able to surmount its regressive tendency toward the instrumental rationalization and reification of the aesthetic object. For no artwork can come into being and rise to an enduring level of eloquence without being *attracted* to the aesthetic object on which it imposes aesthetic identity, without first being *drawn* to its object like "a magnet to a field of iron filings." What Adorno describes with this metaphor is familiar. Like "a magnet to a field of iron filings" describes the artwork's capacity for the *movement* of its being pulled toward its aesthetic object, or the movement of pulling its object toward it, to gather the sensuous impressions from which its enduring aesthetic identity could be created in the first place. As such a creative magnetic power of attraction or "gravitational force," movement thus is, in a word, "mimesis," art's "reaction to what is not-I," to its aesthetic object, which "becomes the *imitation* of the *not-I*."[9]

An artwork's imitation of its aesthetic object, however, is not necessarily a reactive movement terminated once the artwork comes into being. Mimesis is also aesthetic reason's creative potential for setting the artwork into continuous motion. The artwork's imitation of the not-I, of the diverse "field" of qualities all belonging to its object, not only furnishes the sensory data from which its timeless selfsame aesthetic identity is constructed. Mimesis is also the artwork's potential for imitating what remains different about its object that submits the artwork's aesthetic identity to the movement of continual revision, turning the time arrived depicted by the would-be enduring artwork into a time yet to come as well, into the paradoxical qualitative, democratic time of the reconciliation image. Through mimesis movement is intrinsic to the creation of the enduring, selfsame artwork, though also to the artwork's potential for its continuously changing image. Through mimesis the artwork's paradoxical character takes shape.

In its innermost genesis, then, the artwork is a paradox of reason aligned with a paradoxical time anchored in a paradoxical orientation to motion. At its origin, its rationality governs the creation of an aesthetic identity whose timelessness depends on the *cessation* of the mimetic movement toward an aesthetic object through which artworks come into being. By reducing the object to a mere means for constructing an artwork whose enduring appearance is valued over all possible ways its object could be and become different, the rationality of such art mirrors the self-preservative instrumental reason of every society dedicated to reproducing itself in its established form. Once the artwork is created, however, its reflexive aesthetic rationality *could* re-create its aesthetic identity, whose continuously changing image of difference would depend upon *sustaining* the originating mimetic movement toward an object to which it was attracted. Such art as this values the multiplicity of the object's differences over its timeless selfsame aesthetic identity, which instead of subordinating difference to its own end of remaining the same is compelled by such art to serve the ever-mutable end of including difference to point toward the historical possibility of a democratic society able to achieve the reconciliation of identity and difference.

As all such formulations of the paradoxical character of the modern artwork would appear to clearly establish, continuous mimetic motion, which emerges as the creative force of aesthetic reason through which the artwork produces the reconciliation image, thus paradoxically originates from the same mimetic capacity for the sensuous movement toward its object through which the artwork's aesthetic identity is first formed and strives to endure as an illusion of reconciliation terminating the originating mimetic movement of aesthetic reason. Fascinated by this paradoxical character of the modern artwork, Adorno forces this question upon us: Why does the paradox play itself out in certain artworks in one way rather than another, so that continuous motion is sustained in some while arrested in others?[10] Or more to the point for our purposes, why do certain artworks produce the reconciliation image and others an illusion of reconciliation?

Adorno answers this question by going to the very core of what he has found to be paradoxical in the artwork, framing this core element as the scene of a dialectic of construction (or rationality) and mimesis taking the paradoxical forms earlier discussed—instrumental reason's construction versus aesthetic reason's revisions of aesthetic identity; identity versus difference; artwork versus image; arrested versus continuous motion; being versus becoming different; the enduring appearance of the artwork versus the work of art; chronological versus qualitative, democratic time; illusory images of reconciliation versus the reconciliation image. Adorno turns to the dialectic of rationality and mimesis as it assumes all these paradoxical forms to thus clarify the element of aesthetic "equilibrium," which, though indispensable to answering our question, is burdened by conceptual difficulties he eventually relieves by subsuming this core element of aesthetic reason under this dialectic. To answer the question of why certain artworks produce the reconciliation image and others do not, then, the element of equilibrium and its dialectic of construction (rationality) and mimesis, all elements of aesthetic reason, as well, therefore constitute my point of departure.

As Adorno explains, the motion of the modern artwork rests on both "constructive" and "mimetic" elements that are in "tension" and "divergent" by being held in "equilibrium" (which he sometimes refers to as "homeostasis").[11] At the center of the artwork, he means, there is a productive relation between its constructive and mimetic elements, or between rationality and mimesis, that is maintained as a dialectic to which the artwork owes its paradoxical orientation to motion, its paradoxical forms, and the possibility of its reconciliation image. By taking it only this far, however, the dialectical relation of equilibrium between construction and mimesis can lead to a theoretical misunderstanding of aesthetic reason I will take up shortly, which Adorno will avoid by further developing this relation's dialectical structure. When he does, he returns us to the unique role aesthetic experience plays in the formation of the reconciliation image. It is *aesthetic experience* that will account for why the paradoxical character of the artwork plays itself out in certain artworks in one way rather than in another, why motion is continuous in some rather than others, why certain artworks produce the reconciliation image and others the illusion of reconciliation. And it is aesthetic experience that will explain why there can be reconciliation images in film. Though in the case of film, I will propose, Adorno's concept of aesthetic experience must undergo a transformation, a change in form that is not, however, a change in function.

Retracing our steps in this new light, an artwork's aesthetic identity is *constructed* from the motion of sensuous mimetic impulses toward the object to which it is attracted "like a magnet to a field of iron filings." Furnishing the sensuous impressions from which aesthetic identity is constructed, *mimesis*, Adorno now adds, is also in *tension* with construction (rationality) even as it constitutes aesthetic identity, and mimesis can *diverge* from construction if aesthetic experience is present to enable it to reconstitute identity by producing the reconciliation image. We have seen dramatic evidence of this in our aesthetic experience of Rodin's *Thought*.

Adorno is arguing that after its act of construction mimetic motion responsible for the artwork's aesthetic identity becomes inhibited in service to identity's need to endure. While mimesis's work of construction is retired, its energy, however, is yet in tension with the constructed, such that an equilibrium between construction (rationality) and mimesis is achieved. Adorno's language of "divergence" suggests mimesis only waits upon aesthetic experience to set it free to submit the artwork's aesthetic identity it mimetically constructed to a continuous mimetic movement re-creating it, which returns to equilibrium the moment aesthetic experience concludes. Summarily put, at the artwork's core Adorno finds rationality (construction) and mimesis to be bound together in a productive dialectical relation of equilibrium. Rationality and mimesis each *strains* against the other to preserve both an enduring aesthetic identity to which the artwork's arrested motion has reduced the aesthetic object's heterogeneity *and* the *potential* of the work of art that, when emancipated through aesthetic experience, can reconstitute identity through a divergent continuous mimetic movement allied with and imitating the object's differences not yet identified.

Hence, it is because artworks can become objects of our aesthetic experience, as we now begin to see, that Adorno decides this dialectic of equilibrium between rationality and mimesis can be "fought out in the effort to save the fleeting, the ephemeral, the transitory in a form that is immune to reification and yet akin to it in being permanent."[12] Fought out, that is, through an aesthetic experience approaching the artwork's fixed appearance as a mere *illusion* of—hence "akin to"—permanence that it can dispel by an orientation animating the artwork to set free aesthetic reason's alliance with difference, whose multiplicity of appearances can be imitated by a continuous mimetic movement creating images converting the artwork to image. Through aesthetic experience, an aesthetic identity whose instrumental imperative to appear one way only submits to an aesthetically determined imperative is to diverge from its timeless selfsameness to continuously become different. Again, our aesthetic experience of Rodin's *Thought*.

Adorno's core element of equilibrium thus requires we imagine the artwork *prior* to our aesthetic experience of it. Equilibrium denotes a dialectic of paradoxical relations of movement held in tension between the modern artwork and its parts—between the potentially continuous mimetic motion maintaining the artwork as an open whole, as an identity becoming different and the artwork becoming image, as a time arrived and a time yet to come, as the reconciliation image, on the one hand, and on the other the arrest of motion forcing the whole to serve its parts, privileging identity over difference and artwork over image, extending the present indefinitely into the future to create the illusion of reconciliation. Because a dialectical relation of movement held in tension *between* is understood by equilibrium, arrested and continuous motion, artwork and image, identity and difference, quantitative and qualitative times are sustained as *possible* transitions from one to the other. From one *to* the other—never from one *or* the other. None of the terms belonging to this dialectical relation of tension, beginning with rationality (construction) and mimesis underlying all those discussed, should be thought of as independent of one another in the artwork, pulling it apart in polar directions. Construction must *not* be thought of as wanting, once and for all, to complete the work of identity indifferent to its exclusion of differences and the necessity for reconciliation. Mimesis, in its sensuous alliance with difference, should *not* be thought of as irreconcilably defiant of aesthetic reason's interest in creating identities envisioning the ultimate achievement of reconciliation.

Everything I have to this point stressed about the artwork and aesthetic reason rests on ensuring such a conceptual misunderstanding of equilibrium, of the dialectical relation between construction and mimesis and the multiple paradoxical forms it takes, does not arise. Here is why Adorno seeks to avoid it. For if construction and mimesis were not in equilibrium, as he explains, but rather thought of as independent forces pulling the artwork apart, aesthetic experience could not be theorized as able to set free the potential continuity of motion determining the rationality of the artwork as an open whole because the movement of mimesis and construction would be *discontinuous*, starting and stopping. Instead of proceeding serially from the identity through the difference and the all-inclusive images to the reconciliation image, the artwork could never advance beyond the creation of an original identity image. Its appearance would have been rigidly fixed by the starting and stopping motion of polar forces, which would disrupt the dialectical relation creating and sustaining the potential for the continuity of movement aesthetic reason releases by moving the artwork reflexively toward the reconciliation image. With the possibility of continuity arrested once and for all following the creation of the artwork, and without the possibility of reflection on what the artwork excludes, the identity image would appear to have completely captured its aesthetic object and the artwork will have become an illusion of reconciliation. Only with the possibility of continuous, unbroken, ceaseless movement preserved by a dialectical relation of equilibrium between construction and mimesis— where motion, its momentum held in check but pent up and in tension ready to diverge anew toward difference, in a word, *vibrant*, to borrow a term from

Jane Bennett—can the artwork be imagined to move in accordance with an aesthetic rationality harnessing instrumental reason's identity-forming power to drive it toward the reconciliation image, passing it reflexively again and again through the identity, difference, and all-inclusive images on its way there.[13] Hence our aesthetic experience of Rodin.[14]

DIALECTIC OF RATIONALITY AND MIMESIS AND AESTHETIC EXPERIENCE

Consequently, although grasping the contribution of aesthetic equilibrium to the aesthetic rationality of the artwork depends upon understanding equilibrium as a dialectical relation *between* construction and mimesis, as a relation of tension having a potential for divergence through aesthetic experience, that is, the dialectic of this relation may be insufficiently clear owing to the reduction to polar opposites with which it can be confused. Adorno's further development of the dialectic of rationality and mimesis provides the needed clarification. When he argues that the "dialectic of these elements is similar to dialectical logic, in that each pole realizes itself only in the other," he is making three interrelated claims.[15] Construction (rationality) and mimesis require each other and are mutually determining; when either pole performs its work of art, the other performs its work at the same time; and being in tension and divergent as the concept of equilibrium requires, construction (rationality) and mimesis sponsor the possibility for a continuous process of movement constitutive of the reconciliation image.

We understand Adorno's first claim in the context of one of his many discussions of aesthetic form. As the construction of the artwork's aesthetic identity, form achieves "coherence" among the heterogeneous properties of its aesthetic object. Adorno stresses, though, that "what is formed, the content . . . is mimetic impulses that are drawn into the world of images that is form."[16] Artworks are without any form whatsoever, in other words, until content, the mimetic impressions of the object having their *own* form, is conveyed sensuously, making form as much the product of sensuous impressions as of any preconceived aesthetic form. Each of the poles of the artwork—form and content, aesthetic identity and sensuous impressions, construction and mimesis—shapes the other and has no presence in the artwork outside of their interdependency and mutual determination or symbiosis whereby "each pole realizes itself only in the other."

Adorno's second claim strengthens his first by securely rooting the artwork's capacity for continuous motion in this relation of codetermination.

Aesthetic identity has a "*need* of what is nonidentical, heterogeneous, and not already formed" by the work of art, so that "mimesis receives succor" from aesthetic identity.[17] There is no construction of the artwork without aesthetic identity's sensuous motion of *reaching for* the object it needs to take form, though also without impressions then being *returned from* the object by the movement of sensuousness to meet their need for identity. Here, at an ontological level, is the idea that construction, the need for aesthetic identity, is the need to move toward its object, whose sensory impressions respond with a reciprocal movement that, in turn, meets the need of mimesis for form. Adorno judges art on the basis of this dialectic. Artworks succeed only if they result from a process of movement between the extremes of construction and mimesis. While the artwork must strike a dynamic balance between extremes to escape the polarizing pull of each, such an equilibrium must not appear to form a compromise between the contributions of construction and mimesis. Artworks must issue from a tension between construction and mimesis that can potentially yield to the mimetic motion of divergence triggered by aesthetic experience, and not from any and all resolutions of tension ending the divergent possibility for continuous movement set free by such experience.

Finally, whereas Adorno's second claim hints at the potential perpetuity of reciprocal motion that his first claim created the foundation for with the symbiotic relation between construction and mimesis, his third claim ties both together by explicitly recognizing that reciprocal motion is potentially continuous. As Adorno redescribes construction and mimesis, "their *continuity* is *demanded* teleologically by the particular elements. They are in need of continuity and capable of it by virtue of their incompleteness."[18] Against the backdrop of the two claims examined, Adorno's argument is exactly this. Responsible for constituting the artwork's aesthetic identity from mimetic impulses requiring form, *in the absence of aesthetic experience* construction and mimesis can never complete the work of art owing to their inability to bring the artwork into being except through a symbiotic relation "containing"—in the dual sense of possessing and also inhibiting—the potential for the continuous motion of both. Performing the work of art symbiotically, construction and mimesis ensure the reciprocal creation of art's capacious *potential* for motion to be the rationality to which the artwork will answer, the *possible* creation of the reconciliation image through the work of art's continuous motion of gravitating between extremes to revise the aesthetic identity of the artwork by identifying with differences the identity of the artwork has yet to include.

For Adorno, the decisive ontological point is that *the modern artwork cannot have being without the possibility of its being becoming different*. And if art cannot be without creating the *potential* for becoming different, not only motion but continuous motion emerges as the most fundamental of the essential elements of the artwork's rationality. Art is the *possibility* of reason in continuous motion toward the reconciliation image, which is the image of reason itself as the continuous motion of reconciliation. Once the *potential* for continuous motion is in these ways understood to be the ontological nature of aesthetic reason, for all intents and purposes I have fleshed out the remaining elements of aesthetic rationality: *construction and mimesis*, the possibility for the continuity of motion to which they give birth, their parent element *equilibrium* sustaining through tension the potential for a divergent continuous motion between the two.

So the question of why certain artworks produce the reconciliation image and others an illusion of reconciliation now appears answered. As Rodin's *Thought* had earlier shown us, what is decisive is that whenever aesthetic reason is present in the artwork, aesthetic experience is required to determine that one side of the paradoxical character of the artwork, its tendencies toward the reconciliation image, will prevail over—diverge from—reconciliation's illusory form. Originating in the dialectical relation of equilibrium between construction and mimesis, the artwork's potential for becoming different can unfold through our aesthetic experience as a process of continuous movement passing through a series of images—the identity, difference, all-inclusive, and reconciliation images. While this answer seems all the more recommended as I now say what remaining images and democratic effects correspond to these last elements of aesthetic reason, it must ultimately be able to stand up against Adorno's explicit declarations to the contrary that seem to render it untenable.

THE RECEPTIVITY AND IMITATIVE IMAGES AND THEIR DEMOCRATIC EFFECTS

Assuming aesthetic experience, there is even more to the continuity of motion than what I have illuminated thus far. It is not only that aesthetic reason revises the artwork's aesthetic identity through its continuous mimetic return to its aesthetic object, each return then reconstructing identity to include differences belonging to the object construction had left out. At its deepest level what continuous motion means is that the identity, difference, and all-inclusive images, like the reconciliation image as a whole, do not only record the metamorphoses of the artwork but are also themselves each passing through continuous transformations. Continuously in the process of being revised, none of these images, in other words, simply appears in one form and then in the aftermath of the work of art's movement of revision appears in a new and entirely different form. There must also be *intermediary forms* these images assume that appear in between the identity and difference and all-inclusive images, *intermediary images* that reflect the continuous changes in aesthetic identity while identity is actually *in the process* of moving sensuously toward difference and striving for its all-inclusiveness. Unlike the identity, difference, and all-inclusive images, such intermediary images, which are premised here on the idea that continuous motion means unbroken, uninterrupted change, would not only record the revisions of identity as it is in the process of being serially framed in new images. Intermediary images also would express the motion of revision itself and not just its results. The continuous motion between the images of which the reconciliation image is composed allows me to distinguish two intermediary images.

To become different, the identity image moves toward the difference image. Here I recall how Rodin's *Thought* modeled the reconciliation image, whereby his sculpture's identity image of the mind moved toward the difference image of the body, whose features a continuously revised identity image increasingly includes as aesthetic identity relinquishes its sovereignty to multiple new identity images serially more all-inclusive of bodily differences belonging to the artwork's aesthetic object. But what is missing in this scenario of revisions in the images of which the reconciliation image is composed is a not yet complete image of aesthetic identity in motion toward differences it is to include, specifically the image *between* the identity image and the difference image or between serially revised aesthetic identities of difference and difference images. Between the identity and difference images there must be an identity image *in the process of expressing openness toward difference,* just as *Thought*'s mind, an identity image, moved receptively toward its body, a difference image. Such *a receptivity image,* I now want to call it, would in Adorno's terms express an identity image's sensuous movements toward differences embodied by aesthetic objects, express the artwork's "magnetic attraction to a field of iron filings." And the democratic effect of the receptivity image would be identity's *openness* to relinquishing its sovereignty by resembling the not-I, or difference.

I want to pursue this development a step further. Since the motion of the receptivity image toward difference must precede the identity image's continuously becoming different, must there not also be, as the *follow-up* to the receptivity image expressing identity's sensuous attraction to the difference image, an image of identity's *becoming different*, an image in between the difference image and the image of striving for the all-inclusiveness of differences represented by the plurality of ever-new identity images? For example, *Thought's* reunited mind and body viewed as the image of one of the sculpture's myriad possible forms? Let me call this intermediary motion the *imitative image*, and the democratic effect of the movement of the imitative image identity's becoming different in the image of difference—or *democratic becoming*.

Theoretically, of course, there must be countless numbers of intermediary images expressing the continuous motion of the identity image in the process of becoming different. Here I theorize the receptivity and imitative images and their democratic effects not only because they express and not merely record the continuous motion of the reconciliation image's constituent images. The movement they express, attraction and imitation, is the essence of the artwork's becoming different, its uninterrupted change, the continuous motion producing the reconciliation image as an open whole. For without receptivity and imitation, without the movement of attraction and the action of continuously becoming different, the reconciliation image could never appear.

TRANSFORMATION OF AESTHETIC EXPERIENCE

No modern artwork, I believe Adorno's aesthetic theory finally allows, can come into being in the first place without his economy of elements of reflexivity, equilibrium, construction and mimesis, continuity and motion and process all driving the appearance of a parallel economy of images and effects I have discovered containing the potential for the continuous revision of an artwork's aesthetic identity. To the identity, difference, and all-inclusive images I have now added the receptivity and imitative images, all of which together, along with their democratic effects, produce the reconciliation image. If all this is correct, and I have not left anything out in my efforts to flesh out and develop a complete account of the nature of aesthetic reason and its twin economies of elements and images and effects, then there should *not* be modern artworks that create images of reconciliation and those that create illusions of reconciliation. Aesthetic reason ensures the modern artwork's paradoxical character will always be resolved in favor of the reconciliation image, which it determines to be the constant of our aesthetic experience of the artwork.

Yet although my argument seems to answer the question of which side of the modern artwork's paradoxical character prevails over the other and why, it is obviously problematic. For the necessity of reconciliation proceeding from the collaboration of aesthetic reason and aesthetic experience is seriously at odds with the opposite conclusion Adorno drew from his study of the image of reconciliation in the modern artwork, whose autonomy was shattered, as I recalled at the very outset of my discussion in chapter 3, as society became ever less human. In the history of modern art it was not the reconciliation image but the *illusory* image of reconciliation that prevailed. How, then, to explain this glaring discrepancy between, on the one hand, the unfolding of aesthetic reason responsible for the autonomy of art and the necessity of the reconciliation image that ought, *unfailingly*, to be available through aesthetic experience, and on the other the illusion of reconciliation actually dominating modern art?

Among modern artworks there are those whose historical "afterlife," as Adorno calls it, not the artworks themselves, that is, but their "interpretation, commentary, and critique," insist they appear only in certain ways and mean only certain things rather than be seen for their explosion of changing appearances and plurality of meanings their moving images entail.[19] Wherever modernity's public media shape reactions to the artwork, art can become the captive of its historical afterlife. Substituting for—by shaping our—aesthetic experience of the artwork, the artwork's afterlife arrests the motion creating the reconciliation image by putting in its place an ideological overlay manufacturing unchanging, enduring meanings of images: illusory images of reconciliation. So although modern artworks obey an aesthetic form of rationality higher than the instrumental form of reason harnessed by the work of art, the reification of the artwork through its historical afterlife prevails over aesthetic reason under modern historical conditions forcing artworks into alignment with ideological constellations arresting their movement toward images of reconciliation.

Nevertheless the artwork's afterlife through which it is reduced to uncritically reproducing the rationality of stasis belonging to social and political orders, is not necessarily its life sentence. For as the modern artwork's illusory images of reconciliation are not due to the peculiarities of aesthetic form, as with classicism, modern art remains the avatar of aesthetic reason. If our aesthetic experience of the artwork could only evade its mediation by art's afterlife, it could set aesthetic reason into motion again, penetrating the aesthetic illusions created by art's historical afterlife so the artwork again becomes the bearer of reconciliation in an otherwise reified ideological universe. As Adorno confirms, "The transformation of works is not prevented by their fixation in stone or on canvas, in literary texts or musical scores, even if the will, mythically trapped as ever, does its part in this fixation to seal the works away from time. *The fixated is a sign, a function, not something in-itself. . . . If each work is in a condition of equilibrium, each may yet once again enter into motion.*"[20]

Adorno's argument is this: As long as the artwork remains viable—in equilibrium, that is, with construction and mimesis and aesthetic reason's other elements all integral to and at work in the artwork, as they must be if the modern artwork is to be created, to come into existence in the first place— aesthetic experience *can again* set the artwork into motion, set aesthetic reason into motion with its economies of elements, images, and democratic effects productive of the reconciliation image. Since modern artworks are, at their birth, in an earlier life, let us say, in equilibrium, despite their historical afterlife—despite their "fixation," as Adorno says—they *at least remain eligible* for our gaze, our immersion, our aesthetic experience to bring them back to life and in continuous motion toward reconciliation.

Adorno's argument could not be more remarkable. By suggesting that art's historical afterlife is not a definitive barrier to setting the artwork into motion toward the reconciliation image, he qualifies his and Horkheimer's far stronger claim in *Dialectic of Enlightenment* that enlightenment is forever entangled in blind domination, a claim threatening to overwhelm *Aesthetic Theory*'s new argument. Since the reconciliation image remains viable and available to aesthetic experience, domination may indeed prevail, though as long as there is art and thus the aesthetic possibility of the reconciliation image, we would no longer be blindly entangled in domination. Adorno thus implicitly paraphrases Nietzsche: "We possess art lest we perish of instrumental reason."[21] But of course, while it is not a definitive barrier to the reconciliation image, for Adorno it is unlikely the historical afterlife of any modern artwork can be overcome. After all, the reduction of the artwork to the commodity form through the culture industry's total administration of culture de-aestheticizes the modern artwork by manufacturing its historical afterlife as a commodity distorting modern agency's perception and thus our aesthetic experience of modern art. Through its commodification becoming equivalent in some measure to anything else, the modern artwork could never be aesthetically experienced as an image of the reconciliation of identity and *difference.*

In light of my argument in this and the previous chapter, however, we must conclude Adorno's aesthetic theory is more complicated than this, for it leads beyond the de-aestheticization of the artwork to another thesis.

From what I have said we should be able to imagine the aestheticization of film by way of the modern artwork's reconciliation image having an aesthetic analogue in film. By fleshing out and developing Adorno's concept of aesthetic reason and its economy of elements I have brought into view a corresponding economy of images and its democratic effects, which all together illuminate the artwork's metamorphosis into an image in continuous motion toward the reconciliation image. When they are taken together, all of the elements and images and democratic effects in motion that Adorno's theory of the modern artwork yields could offer a model not only of reconciliation but of the way another form of images in motion—*motion pictures, film*—could replicate the movement of these elements and images and effects, their processual rationality, to create the very same reconciliation image found in the modern artwork. Benjamin would thus be wrong on two accounts when he famously alleges, "Let us compare the screen on which a film unfolds with the canvas of a painting. The painting invites the spectator to contemplation; before it the spectator can abandon himself to his associations. Before the movie frame he cannot do so. No sooner has his eye grasped a scene than it is already changed. . . . The spectator's process of association in view of these images is indeed interrupted by their constant, sudden change."[22] In the first place, painting produces the reconciliation image not because it invites spectators to the contemplation of an artwork whose canvas remains unchanging. Rather, as we have seen, *contemplation opens to an aesthetic experience throwing the artwork into motion*, so that artwork becomes image, its aesthetic identity becomes different. Thus, in the second place, painting anticipates film, whose analogical motion would then also be the defining element productive of the reconciliation image. Moreover, given film's ubiquity, the reconciliation image would appear far more often than it had in modern art. The reconciliation image will appear wherever there is film, universally, in other words, which establishes film as a form of aesthetic education superior to modern art.

Here it will again be objected that to produce the reconciliation image the modern artwork requires aesthetic experience to make art's continuous motion visible to us, precisely the aesthetic experience undone by the commodity form, and that we should expect commodification will *also* manufacture a historical afterlife ruining the possibility for such an aesthetic experience of film. But this objection is to misunderstand film, which allows us to imagine an artwork *already in motion,* its process of aesthetic reason *mechanically* set into motion without the necessity of the aesthetic experience belonging to modern art. Thus I want to imagine film's technological transformation of aesthetic experience—making both film and aesthetic experience technologically immune to the fixations produced by modern art's historical afterlife—and with it the appearance of the reconciliation image *in motion* in film.

AESTHETIC ANALOGUES: THE RECONCILIATION IMAGE IN ART AND FILM

My interest in fleshing out and developing Adorno's reconciliation image beyond the form he left it in *Aesthetic Theory* has led me to theorize the possibility of a new and unique film image that is also an aesthetic analogue of the reconciliation image he found in modern art. I propose we recognize the presence of the reconciliation image in artworks *and* in film where we observe an economy of images and their democratic effects I have argued correspond to Adorno's aesthetic form of rationality and its economy of elements. *Already in motion,* film, as does the artwork through an aesthetic experience on which its motion depends, will produce the identity, difference, all-inclusive, receptivity, and imitative images, which together create the reconciliation image. It was in my reading of Whitman's poetry where we encountered a first evolutionary form of the reconciliation image, whose rationality, composite images, and visual character all reappear in what I have conceptualized in my first bridge and this and the previous chapter as Adorno's more developed, second evolutionary form.

The reconciliation image's democratization of the artwork and film could not be more radical. Artworks and film both envision reconciliation, while also testifying to its absence by striving endlessly for the reconciliation of identity and difference. The reconciliation image proves democracy to be itself and always different from itself, a time that is also a different time, a qualitative time that is at one and the same time a time arrived and a time yet to come. Through Whitman's and Adorno's aesthetics I have found the reconciliation image, such a democratic image, in modern art, and will shortly look for it in film, our reconciliation image's third evolutionary form.

Yet despite the reconciliation image being theorized beyond the form Adorno left it in modern art, even if it does circulate ubiquitously in cinema I have thus far provided no assurance it can actually be *discovered* in film. That possibility depends on the relation of the reconciliation image to that which originally constitutes it and makes it and its politics possible, namely the narrative structure of film. Although at present they always have different and contrary meanings, the question necessarily arises of how to distinguish the reconciliation image from the film narrative to which it belongs while at the same time recognizing narrative to be the condition of the reconciliation image's existence and constitution. A variation of this question is whether there can be reconciliation images in films whose narratives are unconcerned with reconciliation or may, in fact, oppose it.

There is every reason to believe that many other kinds
of images can exist. Indeed, the plane of movement-
images is a mobile section of a Whole which changes,
that is, of a duration or of a "universal becoming."
—Gilles Deleuze, *Cinema 1*

The Reconciliation Image versus the Narrative Structure of Film

Two tasks remain before I discover the reconciliation image in film. As my discussion throughout has been devoted to theorizing the reconciliation image and tracing the evolution of its two forms, as I now prepare to turn to its third, cinematic form, I should first summarize precisely what it is I will be looking for in film. To that end I should recall the aesthetics belonging to each of its first two forms. And I should recall their politics, specifically the political project they have in common and that their aesthetics are meant to advance. For as its second form is an evolutionary development of its first, it is not only the aesthetics of the reconciliation image belonging to Whitman's poetry that meld with Adorno's work. Its politics are also attached to Adorno's second form and politically define it as much as they do Whitman's first form. To begin with, then, by summarizing the conclusions of my earlier arguments, I will distill the aesthetic properties of the two forms of the reconciliation image and the shared political project they entail. From this the reconciliation image will crystallize in the form I will discover in *The Help* and *Gentleman's Agreement*, the two films to be studied in chapters 5 and 6, each an example of how in film there are images that model, as we have come to understand it, an ideal of reconciliation between identities and differences constructed as forms of otherness.

    Prior to discovering the reconciliation image in film there will be an additional task, a final clarification that is called for. If I am to recognize the reconciliation image and the politics of its aesthetics in film, I must at the outset break with a long-standing practice of those writing about the politics of film: that of understanding the politics of films through interpretations confined to their narrative structures, the practice of either privileging narrative to the neglect of political possibilities belonging to the images of which a film's narrative consists, or interpreting the politics of images in terms of the overriding political meaning of film narrative.[1] Images, I propose, challenge meanings and politics attributed to a film's narrative structure, whereas narratology buries the politics of the image beneath the politics of film narrative.

But I also recognize that the image, including the reconciliation image, owes its existence and constitution to the narrative structure of film. So what is required is that my discovery of the reconciliation image in film account for two things: for the aesthetic and political work the reconciliation image performs independently of a film's narrative and for the work the narrative and the reconciliation image perform together. It is not simply a matter, in other words, of showing that the politics and aesthetics of the reconciliation image are at odds with the politics and aesthetics of a film's narrative. Rather, only if I show that the reconciliation image is *potentially at odds while also continuous with* the film narrative to which it generically belongs can we appreciate how the reconciliation image represents a *possible politics* emerging within though also against the politics of that selfsame narrative structure.

FIRST EVOLUTIONARY FORM OF THE RECONCILIATION IMAGE: WHITMAN

Above all Whitman wrote *Democratic Vistas* to educate America about its historical obligation to educate its citizenry in the highest values of democratic life. I have described such a political and cultural project as one of democratic enlightenment. It would be through art, or aesthetic education, that America would be taught the ideal of reconciliation, surely to heal the political and cultural divide over slavery aggravated by the Civil War between its northern and southern states, as is commonly known, but primarily to erase the deeper divisions Whitman insisted America address, the constructions of difference as otherness through the reconciliation between identity and difference. The latter achievement would realize world-historical democratic commitments implicit in two earlier political and economic stages of American development that by themselves were reconciliation's necessary though otherwise insufficient preconditions. If "a democratic enlightenment" seems too grandiose a way to describe the purpose of Whitman's great essay, we should recall the argument my introduction made for his resemblances and connections to Schiller, who may well be a mentor of Whitman's and who thought of his own political and cultural project of aesthetic education as correcting the errors of the European Enlightenment.[2]

At first Whitman appears to narrow the art of aesthetic education to poetry, to a new, archetypal American poetry composed by new, archetypal American poets, who are to break with all of literary history to become democratic enlightenment's vanguard for teaching reconciliation. Whitman cites no contemporaneous exemplars of such poetry, though in light of the aesthetic criteria for a new poetry *Democratic Vistas* recommends, against the backdrop of *Leaves of Grass* Whitman has coyly returned us to his own poetry. In *Democratic Vistas* he cuts an oblique path to his own poetry by offering us a complex though indirect set of reflections on what he argues new poets writing a new poetry must accomplish. Guided by his essay, its aesthetic-political pedagogy—"aesthetic education," in Schiller's terms—of teaching the ideal of reconciliation is what we find Whitman's own poetry accomplishing, precisely the project in *Democratic Vistas* he insists a new American poetry must embrace.

As aesthetic education Whitman's poetry teaches identity to re-create itself by imitating differences with which modern democracy potentially surrounds it. Taking difference as a model or template for reconstituting itself in the form of difference, though only "more or less" so as not to become its copy, as Whitman explains, identity becomes indebted to difference for its aesthetically re-created individuality. Difference then becomes less vulnerable to being constructed as the other, which has proven historically to be identity's practice of insulating itself from the challenges to its certainty differences threaten, challenges political interests neutralize by demonizing—marginalizing, excluding, discriminating against, and exterminating—difference.

Yet identity can imitate difference only if democracy is not first prevented from making differences available to it, only if democracy is "all-inclusive" of differences. Poetry teaches democratic all-inclusiveness by interrogating language's capacity for revealing the essence of life in its diverse forms. Finding all language inadequate to this task because poetry finds itself inadequate to this task, poetry finds essence, reality, truth to be unrepresentable because unknowable, leaving us with absences and appearances and differences. For in the absence of language knowing essences, poetry orients us to appearances. And in the absence of the essences of appearances, all appearances lack commonality and must all be different. Which is to say, in the absence of language revealing knowledge of reality, appearances in all their differences become our reality. And in the absence of language discovering truths through which majorities can deem themselves superior and differences inferior, in our reality of appearances differences are all equal. Poetry thus teaches that language, the ground of thought itself, hence of democratic thought and thought about democracy, has no grounds to exclude and every ground to be all-inclusive of appearances in all their differences, all of which are equal.

Still, a chasm may loom between democracy's all-inclusiveness of differences and identity's imitation of differences, as a reality of appearances and their differences is not in any obvious way an incentive to identity to become different in the image of difference. Whitman's poetry bridges this chasm. Its revelation of the unknown and unknowable nature of the world and of everyone and everything in all their myriad forms populating it renders the all-included mysterious, replete with wonder, hence as a whole an irresistible source of attraction stimulating every possible expression of our receptivity to difference. Making our indifference to difference impossible, indeed inconceivable for Whitman, whose own receptivity to difference is unconditional, he also pushes democratic America *beyond* the mere all-inclusive tolerance and legal-constitutional protection of difference that allows violence toward difference to proliferate in the private sphere beneath the threshold of politics and the law. Because by becoming receptive to difference, no difference excepted, identity finds democracy's all-inclusiveness of difference offering an inexhaustible aesthetic wellspring for re-creating its individuality differently through the imitation of differences. Inexhaustible because identities, of the individual, group, culture, or nation, continually striving to become different through their imitations of differences, reproduce differences in their own limitless forms. And inexhaustible because Whitman's all-inclusive democracy must continually strive to become ever more inclusive of differences, which being infinite can never all be included at once.

Whatever else Whitman meant in *Democratic Vistas* by identity as the "miracle of miracles," it must surely refer to the image he creates of America in motion, its democratic identity on all levels continuously and ceaselessly striving for the all-inclusive reception and imitation of differences allowing identities to become different in the images of difference. All-inclusiveness, receptivity, and imitation compose the three-dimensional heart of Whitman's democratic ideal of the reconciliation of identity and difference, which frees difference from the violence of being constructed as otherness and thus could not be anything else but the democratic source of his vista of a "new earth and a new man."[3]

This brings me to perhaps my most radical argument, the one to which there may be the greatest resistance (though others are surely close behind, notably my effort to *think with* Adorno *against* Adorno, whose results I will soon summarize). Only in the first instance does Whitman's poetry rely on the word to teach reconciliation. By taking the measure of language to be its failure to capture what is real, essential, or true, Whitman's aesthetic reflections on the epistemological limits of language give us not only a reality of appearances but *a poetry that serves as the natural home for appearances, for what is seen. Whitman gives us a poetry of the visual image.* Aesthetically formed on the basis of the limits of language, Whitman's visual images of appearances make appearances irreducible to essences, thus highlighting their differences while erecting a barrier to truth. Only insofar as poetry erects this barrier to truth by means of the visual image limiting us to what we can see does it also erect a barrier to the violence toward difference truth encourages by encouraging identities to secure their self-certainty through the construction of difference as otherness. Imitating visual arts, surely painting, very likely photography, Whitman creates a new art form, an art that by imitating another art, as his poetry imitates the visual arts, becomes like a visual art while not actually becoming a visual art. His poetry approximates the universal art form Schiller held was the most pedagogically advanced aesthetic form for teaching reconciliation, a thought I will return to in my final chapter.

Whitman's three dimensions of reconciliation are modeled, or taught, by three types of visual images I have named the all-inclusive, receptivity, and imitative images. Each of the visual images of reconciliation's three dimensions appear in as many as three forms that, once created from the word, convey their meaning more or less independently of language. In addition to self-standing visual images, which convey their meaning without the assistance of language, there are quasi-linguistic visual images, which either teach us how to see or simply privilege vision over the other senses. Finally, each image of reconciliation in its three visual forms is productive of a distinct democratic effect, or democratic lesson, of which there are three: the lessons of the all-inclusiveness, receptivity to, and imitation of differences. Taken together, these three types of images and their democratic effects produce one final visual image offering a cumulative democratic effect: the visual image and its lesson of reconciliation, Whitman's democratic ideal, which expresses the rationality of its antecedent all-inclusive, receptivity, and mimetic images. By expressing the rationality of a series of images in motion from which it is produced, their motion propelled by democratic identity's images of continuously striving for the all-inclusive reception and imitation of differences, Whitman's democratic ideal paradoxically envisions reconciliation as an absolute though open whole, as an ideal of reconciliation that at one and the same time *is both realized but also continuously and endlessly striven for.*

This paradox of reconciliation resembles America as Whitman idealizes it in *Democratic Vistas*—an ideal realizing itself as it travels ceaselessly through time, which records reconciliation's qualitatively new and different forms as each a continuous reaffirmation of the idealism of its earlier incarnations, real instances of a reconciliation that only fully arrives as an ideal to be continuously striven for.[4] Whether or not Whitman understood America, he understood reconciliation, which is intrinsically paradoxical precisely because every reconstitution of identity in the image of difference is yet another realization of reconciliation that with continuous revisions of identity becoming different is endlessly repeated, becoming different in the images of difference "more or less" and is thus always repetition as difference. This paradox again appears as the defining feature of Adorno's second evolutionary form of the reconciliation image.

SECOND EVOLUTIONARY FORM OF THE RECONCILIATION IMAGE: ADORNO

What makes Adorno's work on reconciliation truly profound in ways not yet appreciated, especially by those critical of his thought, becomes evident when it is summarized along with Whitman's and Schiller's, which are equally profound for the same reasons. Once we pay close attention to what has been consistently overlooked or ignored, their common preoccupation with the political question of violence toward difference, it is strikingly uncanny they respond in such dissimilar historical times with an ideal of reconciliation nearly identical in its formulation and politics. Spanning centuries, cultures, and contexts, how could such a shared response not be profound and not lend credibility to their ideal of reconciliation, its power and validity confirmed by the uncanniness of their agreement?

Just as for Whitman and Schiller before him, Adorno's ideal of reconciliation is aesthetic. It circulates in modern art, including the visual arts in which we find the ideal of reconciliation represented by the reconciliation image. Modern art's reconciliation image presupposes an alternative form of reason to which Adorno gives a name—"aesthetic rationality"—prefigured by Schiller's and Whitman's discussions of the aesthetics of artworks. And for Adorno the

reconciliation image politically reorients the historical process of enlightenment by articulating the possibility of a *"positive concept of enlightenment"*
able to achieve the ideal of the reconciliation of identity and difference, the
very same political ideal Schiller associates with aesthetic education's remediation and reform of the European Enlightenment and Whitman with art's
enlightenment of a democratic society. Art, aesthetics, aesthetic reason, aesthetic education, the reconciliation image, reconciliation, European Enlightenment, democratic enlightenment, positive enlightenment—for Schiller,
Whitman, and Adorno these are the pedagogical and political tools to overcome the construction of difference as otherness.

Of course, by providing such an advanced conceptualization of the reconciliation image and how it is produced by modern artworks, both of which I
have tried to theorize further as I fleshed out and developed his concept of
aesthetic reason, Adorno's *Aesthetic Theory* brings a higher level of theoretical sophistication to the ideal of reconciliation and its visual image than his
predecessors. Now we know, as we had not known before Adorno, more of
the complexities of reconciliation as an aesthetic and political ideal and how the
ideal is modeled by the reconciliation image. With these contributions to the
aesthetics and politics of reconciliation, Adorno prepares the groundwork
for extending the pedagogical resources of art beyond the modern artworks
to which he confined them, for finding the reconciliation image in other art
forms, in democratic media, popular culture, and ultimately in film, a project
he opposed while ironically making it possible. Such is what I have meant by
thinking with Adorno *against* Adorno.

Because the term "economy" generally refers to networks of relations of
production, I stressed the importance of the collection of interdependent and
interactive elements, the "economy of elements" in Adorno's terms, of which
he argued the modern artwork consists. Performing the "work of art" within
the artwork, Adorno's economy of elements creates the form of rationality
belonging to the modern artwork—"aesthetic reason"—*productive* of the reconciliation image. Among the elements he highlights, for example, "aesthetic
reflexivity" is fundamental for the role it plays in defining the politics of the
artwork by shaping its aesthetic rationality.

Though all artworks have a definite appearance or semblance or aesthetic
identity, certain artworks exhibit a reflexive relation to their identities, an
awareness of different aspects of its aesthetic object the artwork's aesthetic
identity has left out. Adorno thinks of reflexivity as the artwork's *consciousness
of*, though also its *alliance with* its excluded difference, making reflexivity an

eminently democratic element of the artwork orienting it toward the inclusiveness of differences belonging to its aesthetic object. Insofar as an artwork's reflexivity is sustained by our aesthetic experience of it, its orientation is toward the *all-inclusiveness* of difference. Aesthetic reason thus involves a reflexive element calling attention to the limits of an artwork's aesthetic identity, to its identity's exclusion of features of its aesthetic object, to ways the object differs from the artwork's aesthetic appearance. Reflexivity's aesthetic and political rationality is that identity ought not be exclusive but should rather be inclusive and become different in the images of the differences it omits.

Once the work of art's economy of elements begins to come to light, other core aspects of Adorno's reconciliation image begin to appear as well. A twin economy, I have proposed, can be seen emerging with the formation of his economy of elements. An "economy of images" corresponding to it, an identity, difference, and all-inclusive image, to recall the first three of the five belonging to this economy of images, suggests the reconciliation image is to be produced by an unfolding series of images the economy of elements underlies. And by way of this economy of images, artworks produce distinct "democratic effects," teach "democratic lessons." While the identity image affirms the creation and necessity of identity, by fostering awareness of differences belonging to the aesthetic object that the artwork's aesthetic identity leaves out, the difference image allies itself with difference against the presumptive certainty of identity, whose contingency and democratic character are modeled by images of difference aesthetic identity can imitate to become different itself. In addition, the all-inclusive image radicalizes the difference image's alliance with difference by continuously schooling identity about excluded differences it has yet to include despite the many times aesthetic identity might re-create itself in the image of difference. Hence the paradoxical nature of the ideal of reconciliation is pictured by the reconciliation image, which by recording continuous images of the reconciliation of identity and difference envisions reconciliation while also testifying to the unreconciled. Envisions reconciliation, in other words, as a time arrived, while testifying to the endurance of difference, to its persistent exclusions and the persistence of violence toward difference as otherness, thus to the reconciliation of identity and difference as a time yet to come.

Even with this only partial summary of aesthetic reason, which to this point appears defined by how aesthetic reflexivity continuously propels an artwork's twin economy of elements and images and their democratic effects, I believe we can already begin to see in its instruction about reconciliation that art models an alternative image of reason. Where aesthetic reason is at work in the artwork, through its allegiance to identity's inclusiveness of difference art opposes instrumental reason for enabling the construction of difference as otherness as the means to affirm identity's claims to truth. Opposes identity's false appearance of having left nothing or no one out. Opposes, in other words, art's illusion of reconciliation.

Internal to modern artworks, I find all these core aspects of the reconciliation image—an aesthetic form of rationality anchoring twin economies of elements and images and their democratic effects, which together produce the reconciliation image by engendering a reflexive awareness of differences between the artwork's aesthetic identity and its aesthetic object that revises its identity in the images of its object's excluded features—perfectly illustrated by Monet's Rouen Cathedral series. My analysis of its more than thirty canvases illuminated what I have called the work of art performed by the modern artwork. By imagining Monet's series displayed before us, we saw that by working to constitute the aesthetic identity of the Rouen Cathedral, each canvas at the same time works to reconstitute the aesthetic identity of each of the series' other paintings, thus of the series as a whole. For by representing features of the Cathedral excluded by the other artworks, each painting forms an alliance with difference, which serves as *a critical reflection* on the aesthetic identity of every other artwork, whether by "artwork" is meant each painting in the series taken individually or the series taken in its entirety. Namely, that although each painting's aesthetic identity of the Rouen Cathedral appears fixed, by including differences other artworks omit each artwork also appears to strive to overcome the exclusion of difference, thus to become different in the image of difference. Artwork becomes image; aesthetic identity is reconciled with difference.

Considering the Rouen series, then, I have tried to show it consists of identity, difference, and all-inclusive images all working together to produce an image of the reconciliation of identity and difference that, continually striving for reconciliation, paradoxically envisions reconciliation while simultaneously testifying to its absence, representing itself as a finished artwork while at the same time reflecting on itself as a moving, changing image. Viewed not as a whole but as an *open whole*, one continually striving for reconciliation, for identity *and* its reconstitution, allying *with* difference for the all-inclusiveness of difference, Monet's series offers an aesthetic education teaching three lessons for purposes of democratic enlightenment. First, the necessity of identity, to identify difference though also *with* difference, to constitute though also continually revise identity; second, the all-inclusiveness of difference, which being inexhaustible must be continually striven for; and finally, both of these democratic lessons prove for a democratic society that reconciliation is a political ideal that can be envisioned only by being endlessly pursued. Whenever, on the other hand, the continuous pursuit of reconciliation is subordinated to the achievement of its ideal, reconciliation and its image are illusory.

Monet's paintings led me directly to the element belonging to aesthetic reason still needed to complete my analysis of the aesthetics of the reconciliation image. One great value of an already completed series of artworks imagined on display before us, as was Monet's, is the clarity with which the core elements, images, and democratic effects of the modern artwork productive of the reconciliation image can begin to be distinguished as we work through the meaning of each painting's reflexive relationship to its companion artworks and to the series as an artwork itself. However, Monet's completed series in addition *presupposed the motion* of the work of art Adorno explains is the essential element responsible for the process through which an artwork's elements and images and democratic lessons must pass to culminate in the reconciliation image. Since Monet's series of paintings illustrated the aesthetics of motion after the fact of its completion, to see motion actually at work beyond what his series teaches us required a different type of artwork, a single artwork rather than the series, and an approach other than the retrospective analysis of Monet adequate only for understanding the aesthetics of the already completed series. My remaining focus on the aesthetics of motion had obvious and important implications. If I were able to illuminate the motion of the artwork actually creating the reconciliation image, in real time, as it were, I could then move to yet another medium, *film*, to determine if its motion pictures obey the same aesthetic principles creating the reconciliation image modeled by the modern artwork in motion.

Following Adorno's recommendation, I proposed we immerse ourselves in a modern artwork, Rodin's *Thought*, my choice as the aesthetic object of what Adorno calls "aesthetic experience," a "contemplative immersion" able to "animate" the artwork to make visible its movement and what yet remains to be shown of the aesthetics of the reconciliation image in addition to what I have already illuminated through Monet's series. As Adorno led us to expect, our aesthetic experience of Rodin's creation exemplified the aesthetics of motion of the reconciliation image. After our first studied contemplation of the sculpture exactly as it appeared to us, in light of which its identity seemed constructed in strict Cartesian terms as mind without body, *Thought* began to move, drawing our attention to an image of its body that identity's apodictic exclusion of it made reflexively conspicuous by its absence. With an "identity image," the mind, revised to newly include a "difference image," the body, a third, "all-inclusive image" moved reflexively into the foreground as it became possible to anticipate diverse images of mind-body relations from the image of the movement of a mind and body joined together. Our aesthetic experience of *Thought* thus allowed us to envision *instances* of the reconciliation of identity and difference, images of mind-body relations, hence also to envision an image of the final reconciliation of mind and body. Possible images of mind-body relations being endless, however, aesthetic experience allowed us to next imagine *Thought* continuously striving for revisions of its aesthetic identity through its all-inclusiveness of all possible mind-body relations. Through aesthetic experience *Thought* appears and reappears as a continuous aesthetic pursuit of the reconciliation of identity and difference, as an image not only envisioning reconciliation but one also endlessly testifying to the as yet unreconciled infinite differences of forms taken by the mind and body reunited.

Allowing us to appreciate the part played by motion in the modern artwork, *Thought* makes it evident certain artworks have a unique aesthetic reason for being. Or more accurately, they possess an aesthetic reason for *becoming*, for existing not as a finished artwork per se but as an assemblage of continuously moving images, which through imitations of the artwork's aesthetic object continuously become different in the images of difference. In continuous motion, artwork becomes image, ultimately the reconciliation image. So I believe it is correct to think of continuous motion as the essential element of aesthetic reason and as entitling aesthetic reason to be thought of as driving reconciliation. Moreover Rodin's sculpture further improves on Monet's series by newly displaying those images responsible for initiating continuous motion in the work of art to begin with, the receptivity and imitative images. We find in the receptivity image the form of the identity image that in various ways has become open to—needful of, interested in, curious about, attracted to, admiring of (and so on)—differences and their inclusiveness. And in the imitative image we find the form of the identity image that, having become receptive to difference and its inclusiveness, is mimetically oriented to becoming more or less different in the images of all that belongs to its aesthetic object the artwork has not yet represented. Here I recall Adorno's words "like a magnet to a field of iron filings," explaining what I propose are the receptivity and imitative images being drawn to and in the process of moving in the direction of difference, which the artwork then imitates to revise its identity.

For Adorno, what is at bottom responsible for a modern artwork such as Rodin's *Thought* is that its ever-present potential for the continuous motion productive of the reconciliation image is rooted in a dialectic between rationality (construction) and mimesis, or identity and difference, through which the artwork is created. Since an artwork's aesthetic identity cannot take form without imitating difference (the artwork's aesthetic object), or difference acquire form without being constructed as identity, rationality (construction) and mimesis, identity and difference require each other. And from their reciprocal need an equilibrium emerges. Construction and mimesis are held in a perpetual, irresolvable, and productive tension that maintains an artwork's aesthetic identity until our aesthetic experience of the artwork intervenes to set aesthetic identity free again and in continuous motion to imitate differences belonging to its aesthetic object. In continuous motion for the duration of our aesthetic experience of the artwork, aesthetic identity is continuously reconstructed through its continuous imitation of difference—artwork continuously becomes image. All in all the dialectic between rationality and mimesis fuels a continuous process of movement paralleling our aesthetic experience of the artwork productive of the reconciliation image.

So here is what I have argued Rodin's *Thought* shows aesthetic experience of the artwork makes fully available to us: the twin economies of elements and images and their democratic effects; the elements of motion, continuity, process, and aesthetic reflexivity, as well as equilibrium, construction (or rationality), receptivity, and mimesis, all originating and perpetuating the continuous motion of the artwork's process of aesthetic reason. All elements performing the work of art together, they convert the artwork into image—into the identity, difference, all-inclusive, receptivity, and imitative images, to which correspond the artwork's democratic effects, or lessons, those lessons I already have paired with the identity, difference, and all-inclusive images, and now the new lessons I have added to our newest images. Not only is openness to the new and different taught by the receptivity image, but the myriad forms of such openness would be pedagogically modeled by the reconciliation image as well. And there is lastly the instruction offered by the imitative image, certainly imitation itself, the act of our borrowing from those who are different to become different ourselves by means of *more or less* imitating different ways of life, different forms of thought, different beliefs and values. All these elements and images and lessons aesthetically produce the reconciliation image.

But what precisely is the democratic effect, the democratic lesson taught by the reconciliation image? Of course it is the reconciliation of identity and difference, which is fully prefigured in the series of elements and images and lessons preceding it, and that are responsible for creating the reconciliation image, which expresses the rationality of the artwork as an open, living, ever expanding democratic whole, the artwork as an image of identity overcoming its construction of difference as otherness by engaging in democratic becoming.

THIRD EVOLUTIONARY FORM OF THE RECONCILIATION IMAGE: FILM

Aesthetic experience is thus indispensable for discovering the reconciliation image in art, for it is through our aesthetic experience of the artwork that it is brought to life, thrown into continuous motion. And it is continuous motion that animates a reflexive process of movement that passes through elements, images, and democratic effects and that is secured by the complementary though also conflicting claims of rationality and mimesis, identity and difference, on its way to producing the reconciliation image. Ultimately, then, the highest value of the continuous motion of the artwork is its contribution to aesthetic education and democratic enlightenment, to enabling the work of art to teach the meaning of reconciliation through its creation of the reconciliation image. This is an argument of central importance to grasping the uniqueness of the reconciliation image in film, in *motion pictures*, that is.

Since beginning with Whitman the meaning of reconciliation takes on a paradoxical form later complicated by Adorno, perhaps we should find it unusual that the modern artwork so clearly represents such a concept. In fact, the clarity with which the reconciliation image instructs us about the paradoxical meaning of reconciliation is owed to reconciliation's aesthetic nature, specifically to the defining role played by the continuous motion illuminated by the work of art. If identity in the modern world has been rooted in the Cartesian idea of reason as cogito defining who each of us essentially is, we should find the modern artwork a paradox of reason. For while the artwork models such singular identities in its tendency to endure in the aesthetic form in which it is created, as I have shown it also models identity becoming continuously different in the images of those very differences it excludes for its purposes of self-certainty and self-definition. "Artwork becomes image," in Adorno's words, perfectly expresses the paradoxical political and aesthetic nature of reason as the rationality of self-sufficient and self-affirming identity continuously becoming different.

What is more, as such a paradox of reason the art of reconciliation is likewise a temporal paradox, which is expressed in more than one way. Seeking to endure in the form in which it is created, art continuously becoming image surrenders its claim to timelessness. Art aligns itself with *qualitative over quantitative time*, for the motion of images continuously becoming different is at the same time continuous qualitative change, a measure of change quantitative time is unable to measure. Then there are also *the present and future times* represented by the reconciliation image. Reconciliation envisioned as a time arrived by every identity image becoming different in the image of difference, and reconciliation as a time yet to come in the continuously unfolding creative process of identity becoming different. Reconciliation at one and the same time a time arrived and a time yet to come.

Yet there is a final way in which the meaning of reconciliation taught by the reconciliation image is paradoxical. Continuous motion, which drives the entire process of the work of art productive of the reconciliation image and its political and aesthetic paradoxes of reason and time, is itself paradoxical in a way rendering vulnerable its very creation of the reconciliation image. With the continuous motion of the work of art creative of the reconciliation image dependent upon aesthetic experience, Adorno questions whether in modernity we can still have the aesthetic experience of the artwork that throws it into motion to produce the reconciliation image. It is the "historical afterlife" of the modern artwork, as he described public understandings of the meaning and significance of art shaped over time by a wide range of expert and popular media, that becomes problematic. By molding public perception to view the artwork as a timeless icon having a fixed meaning, art's historical afterlife threatens the possibility of an aesthetic experience able to bring the artwork to life to contradict its iconic status by forcing it to become image. Ending the artwork's life as image, its historical afterlife turns continuous motion into the paradoxical motion of an artwork only able to appear motionless. As such an "immobile mobility," in Lyotard's terms, the artwork's motionless motion conceals its relation to difference, which becomes visible only when seen in a particular way, as aesthetic experience would allow the artwork to be seen if it were not mediated by the artwork's historical afterlife.[5] When from all appearances its motion is arrested or immobile, and the work of art is imprisoned in an iconic form by its afterlife, the artwork becomes an illusion of reconciliation, feigning its reconciliation with all possible ways an aesthetic object is different from its aesthetic identity and subjecting difference to the violence of being constructed as other than it is.

But with film it now ceases to be, as it was for Adorno, a question of whether the form of aesthetic experience he thought possible with the artwork remains possible for us. Already "motion pictures," as film is yet called, *already images in motion, already artwork become image*, in other words, prior to any other aesthetic experience we may or may not have of it, *film is already and in itself the very essence of the aesthetic experience Adorno theorized. Already in motion*, film ensures such an aesthetic experience by circumventing the threat of its being sabotaged by a historical afterlife, which brought the motion of the modern artwork to a standstill. So, rather than asking if we can have the aesthetic experience of film Adorno reserves for the artwork, we have a different kind of question. Paraphrasing my original formulation when I began this Second Bridge, can we newly theorize our aesthetic experience of the reconciliation image in film in a way showing this image to be potentially at odds while at the same time continuous with our understanding of the film narrative on which its appearance in film originally depends? If so, I believe we can then discover the reconciliation image in film representing a possible politics nesting within though also against a film's narrative, including its political narrative, which would only partly define images belonging to the reconciliation image as it in turn partly and differently defines the narrative structure of the film creating it to begin with.

MASSUMI'S BEE

This problem is more complex than I have formulated it thus far. Certainly in the age of film it agrees with viewing experience on a universal scale to acknowledge the obvious. Images of which film narratives consist regularly possess aesthetic, moral-ethical, social, or political meaning and significance not only indebted and contributing to but also *exceeding* their narrative frameworks. Who has not come away from a film struck by such transcendent effects of an image, even to the extent of remembering it long after the narrative in which it originated is forgotten, if the effect of the image had not from the beginning displaced attention to its narrative?

Since my interest in the film image is not limited to its meaning and significance in these senses, however, my discussion of the reconciliation image in film cannot rely for support on the obvious but must be raised to a theoretical level. For as my interest is in the possible politics of the aesthetics of the reconciliation image—in the political lessons its aesthetics teaches about reconciliation as a continuous process of identity overcoming its constructions of difference as otherness—the reconciliation image is connected to movement and becoming, to life, through its connections to film. Hence I require a theoretical approach placing the connections between life and image and film at its center. Bergson and Deleuze are the philosophers I should turn to. But I will do so through the more recent work of another philosopher, Brian Massumi's *Parables for the Virtual*, which as I read Bergson and Deleuze further develops arguments of theirs in a manner perfectly suited to grasping the connections the reconciliation image in film presents me with.[6]

Few would quarrel with the claim that films are produced to tell stories, and those who do justifiably argue that narrative is often the vehicle of film in the service of higher aesthetic or other ends. In different ways both camps thus privilege film narrative, which explains why the deepest interest they next share is in viewer perception: why, how, and to what extent viewers become immersed in a film. Perception will be my focus too, albeit not viewer perception "of" film narrative—rather, film narrative itself and the images of which film narrative consists, specifically the reconciliation image, "as" forms of perception. Deleuze's writings on the movement- and time-images in cinema have already improved on the illuminations of the behavior and interrelations of visual images from the standpoint of Bergson's theory of perception.[7] Equally grounded in Bergson's thought, Massumi makes theoretical advances on Deleuze's discussions of Bergson in ways extremely useful to my interest in foregrounding the politics of the aesthetics of the reconciliation image in relation to film narratives where the image appears.

By taking Massumi's work as my point of departure, I am able to think of film narratives and their images "as" forms of perception as well as "of" forms perceived. "What does the bee see and smell in the flower?" Massumi asks. "Enough to extract pollen from it. A creature's perception is exactly proportioned to its action upon the thing. The properties of the perceived thing are properties of the action, more than of the thing itself."[8] If perception is action determining the properties of the perceived, then film narrative and the images it weaves together to tell its story, all of its and its images' activity of sensing and thinking and understanding and creating that determine the properties of everything captured by images and narrated, are the *actions* of perception. No less than the bee actually seeing and smelling and extracting pollen from a flower, a series of visual images, a film, of the bee's seeing and smelling, of the flower and the extracted pollen, and the story the images tell, for example, are property-determining and thus percipient actions performed upon all the film narrates and images. No less than any "creature's perception," film is percipient action.

In light of film as percipient action, here is what is striking. As Massumi elaborates, perceptions are not only actions; they are also "actions—in their latent state. *Perceptions are possible actions.*"[9] Positioned within a continuous, durational, unbroken process of percipient activity, every perception is also an action immediately preceding other perceptions to which it is inseparably connected. And those perceptions to which a perception is seamlessly attached, the latent, possible perceptions Massumi refers to, will extend perceptions underway into the future, in different ways, depending upon which possible perception prevails. Whichever latent perception is chosen and then succeeded by another and other possibilities perception chooses in turn, will fulfill the need for which those percipient actions are performed. As I write on Massumi writing on perception, I choose from among my possible perceptions in waiting those best able to serve my need to distinguish aspects of his argument best able to flesh out the percipience of the reconciliation image in film. Or more precisely, best able to illuminate the possible percipient action of reconciliation its image performs in contrast to the action the image is presumed to actually perform according to the film narrative of percipient actions to which the image owes its existence. The possible percipient action of the reconciliation image in film I am pursuing is the *possible politics* of aesthetic education.

With the concept of perception as possible action other conceptual possibilities to which it is itself inseparably connected continue to illuminate the possible percipient actions of film images in relation to the narratives in which they originate. Following his argument that possible percipient actions extend perceptions actually underway, Massumi explains that possible actions fall into two orders simultaneously, an order of "substitution" and an order of "superposition." Possible perceptions are those whose eligibility to be *substituted* for actual perceptions earn them the *superposition* of being *conjoined* with a perception underway, which in a new form will be extended into the future by the possible percipient action it carries forward. Actual and possible perceptions form *conjunctions*, as he puts it to convey the idea that possible percipient actions eligible to be substituted for actual percipient actions are superpositioned to instantaneously replace and thus extend them into the future in new forms.

To thus extend my earlier example, as I wrote the preceding sentence, a percipient action I performed on Massumi's work, the sentence I am currently writing was a possible action that at this moment is in the process of being substituted for its predecessor with which it was conjoined and on which it was superposed. What becomes most important at this point is that substitutions, possible percipient actions, "never come in ones" but in "any number of possible next connections."[10] Every sentence I write on Massumi's discourse on perception was once one of many possible percipient actions superposed on an in-the-process-of-being-written or already-written sentence it was conjoined with and could be substituted for. And the conjunction carried forward, the possible action actually substituted for an idea on which it was superposed, was the one I thought at that moment best met my need to encourage a particular understanding of the reconciliation image in film. Namely, the understanding that the reconciliation image is possible percipient action—the possible action of aesthetic education, which by teaching the ideal of reconciliation becomes a possible politics—conjoined with and superposed on other ideas from which a theoretical argument about the reconciliation image in film is being formulated. Returning to Massumi's bee, I extend this argument further in that direction.

After explaining that substitutions "never come in ones" but in "any number of possible next connections," which implies a plurality of possible percipient conjunctions belonging to a perception underway, to illustrate that point Massumi projects possible actions of his foraging bee. "The bee may be laden and skip the flower. Or, instead of collecting, it may return to the hive to signal the source of food. Or it may be duped by a blossoming mimic into trying to mate instead. Or it may mate and eat." Let us imagine from Massumi's projection of the bee's possible percipient acts that the conjunction of the bee's perception has unfolded, and from among its "possible next connections" we *film* the one actualized to create a narrative of the action of Massumi's bee returning to the hive to signal the source of food. With this narrative a particular durational stream of perception is concluded, "a continuity," as Massumi says, "exhausts itself," and its alternative possible actions are foreclosed.[11] What is more, for anyone who has only the completed film narrative at hand and not the advantage of viewing firsthand the bee and its possible next connections Massumi's example pictures, the bee's unselected other possible actions have been erased by a narrative of sequential actions narrowly featured as a "beeline," let us say. *Or are they foreclosed and erased?*

Studying Massumi's illustration more closely, in fact, we notice that up to a point our images of the two pairings of his bee's possible actions bear a resemblance to one another. His bee skipping the flower resembles the bee that opting not to collect also skips the flower prior to reaching its hive to signal the source of food. And his bee that *may* be duped into mating resembles the bee that *may* mate prior to the first being duped or the second choosing mating and eating, while prior to either action both resemble the twin versions of his flower-skipping bee. Not one but *four* possible percipient actions are superposed on the very same foraging perception underway, making possible *four* different narratives rather than the single one that unfolds as a continuous stream of percipient activity from our single-minded, hive-returning, and flower-signaling cinematic bee.

From this we arrive at a preliminary insight whose full significance I will develop further on. As is the forager image belonging to my cinematic narrative of Massumi's bee, every image belonging to a film narrative is an action having a multiple of itself through its conjoined possible percipient actions, substitutions for it from which alternative narratives could unfold to extend it in multiple new and different forms into the future. Against the logic of narrative narrowly construed, *even if images are prescripted to serve only the narrative giving them birth for the instrumental purpose of telling a particular story, taken as percipient actions every image has other possible lives.* Every image, as does every percipient action that every image is, has other possible perceptions connected to it, other conjunctions for which it paves the way to possible other and different continuities, other and different narrative possibilities. While a film narrative forecloses or erases perceptions' possible actions by allying itself only with those possibilities instrumental to its unfolding, possible percipient actions persist as substitutions enfolded on those scripted actions on which narratives narrowly rely. *Perceptions, I am arguing, film images as perceptions, are also possible percipient actions whose narratable lives exceed their actual lived life in a particular narrative form.*

Working with Massumi's argument that "perceptions are possible actions," I have recognized that since cinematic images are perceptions and thus possible actions, actual and possible percipient images are conjoined in contrast to narratological conscriptions of visual images. Succinctly put, from film images come images as possible actions, or, put differently, from film images come "possible images," and from film images' narratives come "possible narratives." But it is not enough to create theoretical space for possible film images and their possible narratives at risk of being foreclosed or erased by a certain narrative's teleological conscription of its constitutive images. Precisely what film images are possible? More to the point, is the reconciliation image in film possible? For without the possible action of the reconciliation image neither can I have the possible politics of reconciliation its aesthetics teaches. So it is not just the possible action of the reconciliation image alone but the possible politics of reconciliation belonging to its aesthetic pedagogy I want to rescue from film narrative. Massumi can help me with both of these problems.

Unlike bees (as far as we know), our perceptions are conjoined with possible percipient actions to which we devote more or less thought. Massumi captures this idea and its implications by distributing our possible percipient actions along a continuum running between two poles. At one extreme several possible actions stored in memory, thus "already-thought," and that "overlap" or resemble one another for their earlier involvement in similar perceptual experiences, gather around a "perception pole" where they are superposed as possible substitutions for a perception underway. At the "thought-pole," the continuum's other extreme, "all possible substitutions" are collected, though unlike already-thought possible actions at the perception pole they are not intermixed with previous percipient action. "Purified" of experience, possible actions being "thought-out" are removed from action and do not resemble one another, as do possible actions coalesced around an earlier perception. For as they are objects for thought only, substitutions at the thought-pole are sharply defined *alternative* possible actions. In Massumi's words, they are "arrayed in extrinsic (either-or) relation to one another" and, removed from action, must also be either-or alternatives to possible actions superposed at the perception pole.[12]

Largely falling along the continuum *between* the two poles, however, actual and possible percipient actions typically combine perception and thought, percipient "experience of the actually under way with possibilizing extensions" taking perception "beyond itself" through actions that in new ways engage the senses with their perceived world. Being supposed here is thought's capacity to "project into a future an array of [possible] action-substitutions to choose from"—*thought's capacity to possibilize.* "To possibilize," Massumi explains, "is to stretch perception down the continuum in the direction of the only-thought."[13]

Bearing Massumi's argument in mind, it will be in the direction of the only-thought where the possible action substitution of the reconciliation image in film will be found projecting the radical possibility of reconciliation into the future. What I want to emphasize, as Massumi's argument allows, to be projected into the future, to be real rather than fanciful, and not simply real but entirely new because historically removed from earlier percipient action, possibilities must be thought-out. If reconciliation is a percipient action projected into the future as a real and radical possibility, the reconciliation image in film will thus present reconciliation in its being thought-out form—though only in the first instance.

THE RECONCILIATION IMAGE AS THE THOUGHT-OUT

Every possible percipient action, as Massumi has said, falls along a continuum between thought and perception and to varying degrees combines thought of possible action with past and present percipient actions and experience. What consequently become relevant to the possibilization of the reconciliation image are past and present perceptual experiences bound up with thought about the reconciliation of identity and difference, which together can be theorized with the assistance of Massumi's terms as follows.

On the one hand, the *possible* percipient action of reconciliation projected by its visual image in film is an either-or alternative perception to the image of the "other," to the racialized, anti-Semitic, gendered, sexualized, and class constructions of subaltern otherness in which originates the normativity of ongoing individual and collective perceptual experience of otherness and action toward the other. On the other hand, "latent" in anything perceived "are all of the differential conjunctions it may enter into," meaning that anything as it is perceived could also be perceived differently because of social relations the perceived actually is and could become implicated in.[14] Here "latency," or possibility, which Massumi calculates to be "inexhaustible," does not originally belong to the perceiver but rather to the perceived, whose latent or possible perceptible qualities possess an "energetic *potential*" stirring the perceiver to discern new images of the perceived within the complex networks of social connections to which it belongs.[15] Since latency thus entails "there is *more* in the 'thing' than in the perception of it," we should consider the either-or possible percipient action of the reconciliation image to be thought of "difference," thought of those perceived as the "other" as able to be alternatively perceived by the reconciliation image in film as *more* than other.[16]

To be precise, then, my formulation of the possible percipient action of reconciliation projected by its image in film as an either-or alternative perception to the image of the other, should now be read that the possible percipient action of the reconciliation image is its perception of *difference*. The reconciliation image's perception of difference is its *thought* of the "more" that the image selects from a vibrant reservoir of *potential* perceptions, a reservoir encouraging thought of the possibility of such new percipient experiences springing from the diverse ways difference is implicated in networks of so-cietal connections partly resisting its perception as "other," while at the same time responsible for those actual perceptions of otherness underway.

To fully grasp the significance of the reconciliation image as the percep-tion of difference, however, I want to redescribe the "more" Massumi locates within the latent, energetic potential of social connections, as the "mode of the entirely new." As this redescription enables me to better gauge the extent to which the reconciliation image is thought-out as a possible percipient ac-tion, or "possibilize[d]," as Massumi also puts it, it allows us to learn just how possible are the politics of the reconciliation image. For as would be true of all possible actions that perception selects for active service from the entirely new, whether the reconciliation image could enter the realm of possible ac-tion would be decided by what he calls "the *thought-system* of the possible."[17] We can think possibility, he argues, because we have the ability to "[connect] with a thing *as if* it somehow existed outside of any *particular* perception of it."[18] I should thus ask what that perception is outside of which the reconcilia-tion image becomes a possible percipient action. And I should ask, too, what we learn about its politics by devoting thought to the reconciliation image *as if* it were outside that particular perception, drawn from the entirely new.

First, as the perception of difference, the reconciliation image is positioned outside of the perception constructing difference as otherness. It is an alterna-tive to the particular normalized perception of the construction of difference as the other. Second, "taking it"—the reconciliation image—"as 'outside' the particular [perceptual norm] is to approach it *in general*, as if *unconnected*," which means to think through the possible *as if* it were "purified of any un-planned interference from unselected-for potentials."[19] To express this dif-ferently, possible actions that perception drafts into service from the entirely new, as I will illustrate in my following chapters by the way the reconciliation image in film perceives difference and visualizes the possible action of recon-ciling identity and difference, can be thought through *because* the image is a counterfactual, *as if* possibility *outside* existing perceptual norms.

Appearing in a counterfactual or, as Massumi puts it, "pure form," *in the first instance* the reconciliation image is thought-out independently of any social and political exigencies—of any "unplanned interference"—requiring the possible actions the reconciliation image envisions be adjusted to the per-ceptual normativity of difference as otherness. Considered *as if* it were at or very near the extreme limit of the thought pole, the reconciliation image can be thought through *precisely and only because it is disengaged* from the actions of any institutionalized, normalized politics nearer the perception pole. Selected from the mode of the entirely new outside of the particular perception of difference as otherness, the radical standpoint of the reconciliation image, of its possible perception of difference and possible actions reconstituting relations between identity and difference, is thus defined and measured. *For the ideal of reconciliation projected is positioned directly opposite the politics the reconciliation image left unselected: the already-thought, long-established liberal politics of compromise between the perceptual norm of difference as otherness and the reconciliation of identity and difference.* Since reconciliation is an ideal thought-out as a possible percipient action ending violence toward difference, *it is positioned in the private sphere where violence toward difference thrives beneath, thus outside, the threshold of politics and the law.* Not only does the thought-out reconciliation image in film thus become possible percipient action. Its possible politics are highlighted *by its opposition to its unselected, liberal legal-juridical political solutions to such violence, which leave unchanged in the private sphere conditions and perceptions of difference as otherness.*

If my attempt to theorize the possible politics of the reconciliation image is in agreement with Massumi's parable of percipient action, it is because it accurately sums up the arguments of my introduction and previous chapters on Schiller's, Whitman's, and Adorno's aesthetic theories through which I attempted to "perfect" the reconciliation image as a perceptual order of substitution for the perception of difference as otherness. Perhaps, as I earlier intimated, each of these arguments is likewise a parable in Massumi's sense. Each is a didactic lesson of the way an alternative, aesthetic form of rationality gradually though increasingly perfects an order of substitution for the rationality it lies outside of and for that reason can oppose. Each is a thought-out model of the work of art contributing to theorizing the identity, difference, all-inclusive, receptivity, and imitative images through which the reconciliation image in art would substitute its possible percipient action of reconciliation for the percipient actions of violence toward difference always underway.

Nevertheless, despite the political challenge of the reconciliation image to liberalism's legal-juridical political solution to the problem of violence toward difference, my formulation of the politics of its aesthetics also seems to highlight its political limitations. I have visualized its possible or "possibilized" politics through a "profitable disengagement" of thought from perception, as Massumi characterizes the condition of severed political connections allowing possible action in its *pure, as if* form to be thoughtfully imagined. For only under this condition of disengagement can thought complete the work of *"perfecting* . . . the order of substitution."[20] But if, as I have indicated, it is in the first instance that the possible percipient action of the reconciliation image is disengaged from action in order to be thought-out, it is only in the first instance. Now to be brought into focus by Massumi's "positive feedback loop," which traces the movement of possible action from perfection to perception, there is more to the possible politics of the reconciliation image than political disengagement for the purposes of thoughtfully perfecting an aesthetic order of percipient substitution for "perceptual actions"—the constructions of difference as otherness—underway.

FROM THE THOUGHT-OUT TO AESTHETIC EDUCATION
AND POSSIBLE POLITICS

Once possible percipient action has been thought-out, Massumi adds, it creates "anticipation" on the part of the perceiver, which makes ideas of new social and political connections "more accessible" for possible percipient action. By exciting such awareness of its imminent capacity to stimulate mental images of the possible, a thought-out order of perceptual substitution thus "shadows the [thought-out] perception with an increased charge of [percipient] possibility," which itself works to "augment the potentiality" of the perceived.[21] Possible perceptions and their possible connections, "sur-charged" and "intensified" as they become gradually intelligible to the perceiver, then form richer pools of potentials from which perception could next select possible perceptions for thought to again think through. Consequently, while at the *outset* it disengages possible percipient action from the action of perception underway, thinking's perfection of an order of substitution to "possibilize" perception is only its *initial* conceptualization of possible action chosen from a web of social and political connections its transition from perfection to perception will steadily expand. Expanding the potential of the perceived, possibilization deepens the font of connections from which new perceptions can be continuously selected and perfected and can graduate to become new perceptual lenses through which the world can be differently understood.

If my summary of this more difficult part of Massumi's argument is correct as far as I have taken it, his conclusion and its implications for my own argument become clear. "Possibilization and potentialization," he has determined, "fold into and out of each other[;] . . . perception and thought form a positive feedback loop," so that our "perception" of "things" and "thought are in a reciprocal movement into and out of each other and themselves."[22] Although possible percipient action thus begins as thought disengaged from perception underway, no sooner is it thought through then it enters into perception to enrich the potential for newer possible perceptions to be selected, thought-out, and further translated into perception, which further expands possible perception's potential, in turn. As the continuous movement between the thought of perception and the action of perception, possible perception is thus movement between thought and action. It would seem to follow from this that if the reconciliation image is a thought-out possible percipient action, as I have proposed, it would reproduce the reciprocal movement Massumi's positive feedback loop traces between thought and action. And if the movement reproduced were also political, as aesthetic education teaching reconciliation is political, the possible percipient action modeled and taught by the reconciliation image in film would be a *possible politics, the possible political action of perceiving difference differently.*

When I further consider the reconciliation image to be an avatar of possible percipient action, this is precisely what I find. The reconciliation image does travel the same circuit between thought and action Massumi maps for perception in general, with one significant difference. A unique avatar of perception, the reconciliation image does double duty. Like all other images it is in the first place a form of perception. But by modeling reconciliation in film it also becomes a special type of image, a special type of perception, one that performs a pedagogical role and whose pedagogy is political. Teaching the reconciliation of identity and difference it performs the work of aesthetic education, while the practice of reconciliation it aesthetically teaches articulates a democratic ideal. Thus I believe it is correct to argue that by serving as a vehicle of aesthetic education the reconciliation image in film is a possible percipient action whose politics are a possible politics.

So prior to discovering the reconciliation image in film, in light of my foregoing considerations of Masumi's work here is where my argument finally stands. Aesthetically "thought-out and perfected as an order of substitution" through my engagements with Schiller and especially with Whitman and Adorno, the reconciliation image as it will appear in film is initially disengaged from perception, which is the position of all possible perceptions having been or in the process of being thought-out. But when in the course of a film the images of which the reconciliation image consists unfold as they have been thought-out, they circulate through Massumi's positive feedback loop, a process I can provisionally describe in anticipation of discussing films in which the reconciliation image appears.

As the thought-out reconciliation image unfolds in each of my two films, it will move through its constituent identity, difference, all-inclusive, receptivity, and imitative images to display itself as a possible perceptual alternative to identity's perception of difference as otherness. To begin with, owing to the complex networks of social relations in which difference is implicated in each film, new perceptions of difference begin to be formed in contradistinction to its socially constructed image as otherness. As its alternative perceptions of difference then develop, the reconciliation image stimulates a sense of anticipation, on the part of viewers perhaps, though certainly on the part of each film's characters, that new social relations between identity and difference could emerge. Feelings of anticipation become connected to the reconciliation image as possible percipient action by suggesting mental images of such new relations, which produce a sense of the immanence and perhaps imminence of what the images foretell.

Through such images perception can be imagined moving and evolving beyond its alliance with identity defined in contradiction to difference, to identity becoming different through new relations to difference. Identity's image, originally frozen in institutionalized subaltern relations with its other, can be pictured undergoing qualitative change. And the increased possibilities for new identities through identity's possible new relations with difference widen and deepen the pool of potential connections between identities and differences, the possible percipient actions of reconciliation—identity's all-inclusiveness of, receptivity to, and imitation of difference—foremost among them. It will be from this pool that perception will continue to select the possible percipient actions of reconciliation it will repeatedly circulate through the positive feedback loop created by the reconciliation image, each revolution synthesizing the uninterrupted movement of the images of which the reconciliation image in each film consists.

Of course, when I shortly turn to the reconciliation image in film, it will become apparent that its revolutions through Massumi's positive feedback loop will vary between the two films I analyze. Despite its variations of form (in the sequence of its constituent images' substitutions, for example) and content, what will be constant in both films is that the reconciliation image as thought-out in my work on Whitman through Adorno and now Massumi travels the same cinematographic circuit. Circulating from perfection to perception to being thought-out again in a new form, from thought disengaged from perception to percipient action, not only is the reconciliation image as it is thought-out cinematically reproduced as a perceptual order of substitution for an existing social order's relentless perceptions and persecutions of difference as otherness. As it is so reproduced, the reconciliation image also creates an anticipatory sensibility to the possibility of overcoming the construction of difference as otherness, and through that expectation suggests images of difference different from its constructions. From these incipient images are suggested what new relations with differences can form, what new identities might be constituted in relation to and out of difference. Hence the circuit traveled by the reconciliation image in film is the possible politics of aesthetic education, which radically changes perception by teaching identity the democratic lessons of reconciliation—identity's all-inclusiveness, receptivity, and imitation of difference to become different in the image of differences surrounding it.

To be sure, it may be objected that a possible politics fostered by aesthetic education, a politics of *seeing* the world differently as a world of difference with which to be reconciled, lacks the defining element of politics—*the power to make a difference*. To reply to this objection I want to revisit Massumi's work a last time, beginning with, as I have been doing, some opening abstractions and the radical claims they underpin.

MORE THAN LIFE ITSELF

More than life itself, film presents us with unique obstacles (narratives) though also with unique opportunities (images) to reconfigure the relation between the possible and the potential in continuously unfolding streams of percipient action, of which film narrative and its visual images are types. When Massumi first takes up the relation between the possible and the potential he stresses an essential difference between them related to my own account of possible politics to which that particular difference, if taken alone, would erect a barrier. If I think of life as Bergson does in his opening chapter of *Matter and Memory*, it appears to us as the continuous unfolding of images whose "potential is unprescripted," to borrow Massumi's terms to express in another way his idea that potentiality is not of the mode of the possible. Rather, possibility can only be "back-formed from potential's unfolding," meaning we are able to retrospectively chart the order of possibilities as they had already continuously unfolded to learn that they had occupied positions that "prescript" continuity to determine the shape of its unfolding. Whereas potential refers to a thing's "still *indeterminate* variation," Massumi explains, *prescripted* possibility on the contrary is limited to what is already "implicit" in whatever position someone's or something's continuous process of development can attain, so that only "a certain set of transformations . . . can be expected of it . . . that it can therefore undergo *without qualitatively changing enough to warrant a new name.* . . . Possibility is a variation *implicit in* what a thing can be said to be *when it is on target.*"[23] According to Massumi's concept of possibility here, the "qualitatively changing" image in film I have argued for *would be excluded from possible action,* for it would "warrant a new name"—the reconciliation image—different from whatever names films themselves assign to their own images as they move, conscripted and prescriptively, toward their narrative targets.

However, Massumi is speaking here only of possibilities as they prescriptively unfold in a continuous stream of life, perhaps as the entirety of a life, and like any life cannot be lived over to a different narrative end. Art, however, especially in the case of film, does not imitate life in this respect. Images and the film narratives they make up can be replayed over and over again. Consequently another thesis on the concept of possibility belonging to Massumi's argument would then seem to apply to what I have claimed for the reconciliation image, that it is a possible percipient action having a life of its own independent of film narratives in which it originates and out of which new narratives are possible. For if I take film narrative to exemplify what he calls a "continuity [that] exhausts itself," which comes to an end, that is, then as he argues further, a "retrospective ordering enables precise operations to be *inserted along the way,* in anticipation of a repetition of the movement— the possibility that it will come again. *If the movement does reoccur, it can be captured.* . . . *It comes to a different end.* . . . A dynamic unity has been retrospectively captured and *qualitatively* converted."[24] In light of Massumi's argument here, what now becomes decisive is to think of the reconciliation image, once we have found it in a film, as a latent percipient action whose possibility I have introduced retrospectively as a precise operation along the way of the unfolding images of a film narrative. By feeding back the latent possible percipient action of the reconciliation image into the film in anticipation of its narrative's repetition, *I capture the movement of the narrative so it comes to a different end.*

So Massumi's reflections on the difference between the possible and the potential ultimately enable us to understand that if possibility were no more than prescripted variation implicit in duration when it is on target, as he initially argues, thus ineligible for any new name it could earn if it were to the contrary a qualitative form of change, then the reconciliation image could not be described as possible action. But as my earlier chapters have it thought-out, the reconciliation image is no mere prescribed variation in a film narrative only emerging as a possibility when the narrative is on target to a foregone conclusion that buries the reconciliation image beneath prescribed ends. It is also, as Massumi's formulation of possibility goes on to allow, a qualitative transformation in a cinematic narrative warranting a new name, the reconciliation image, which by enabling us to see the world differently allows us to form an image of a different world that brings a form of individual and collective life *to a different end*. For the thought-out reconciliation image is actually *feedback* from a cinematic life whose narrative has ended, feedback in the form of *the latent possible percipient action of reconciliation* the narrative concealed in its fold of continuously streaming images, and that once it crystallizes and is fed back into that narrative reconditions the conditions of the narrative's emergence. As Massumi confirms, "If feedback from the dimension of the emerged re-conditions the conditions of [its] emergence, then it also has to be recognized that conditions of emergence change."[25]

Reconditioning the conditions of an emerged form of life having deep roots in the liberal private sphere's construction of difference as otherness and its violence toward difference, by moving from perfection to perception the reconciliation image in film moves the far greater distance of "the thought-system of the possible" to reimaging the political system of the possible, moves as aesthetic education to the possible politics of reconciliation.

Part III

THE RECONCILIATION IMAGE IN FILM

This special image which persists in the midst of the others, and which I call my body, constitutes at every moment . . . a section of the universal becoming. It is then the *place of passage* of the movements received and thrown back, a hyphen, a connecting link between the things which act upon me and the things upon which I act.

—Henri Bergson, *Matter and Memory*

5
....

The Help

ENTANGLED IN A BECOMING

Now that we have a complete theoretical and political account of the reconciliation image, and in addition my Second Bridge's summaries of its aesthetics and politics along with the philosophical arguments Massumi's work provides for distinguishing the image, its meaning, significance, and possible politics from the cinematic narrative to which it belongs, I turn to discovering the reconciliation image in film.

If I have erred by insisting the reconciliation image has a life of its own independent of the narrative structures of films to which it belongs, it has been on the side of caution. Certain images of which Deleuze speaks not only possess such a life; they achieve a sovereign existence even to the extent of devouring the very characters on which depend the narratives in which they appear. "Entangling him in a becoming" is how Deleuze valorizes the fate of Mr. Klein, for example, in the film by that name whose narrative themes he estimates to be "secondary and subordinate to the impulse-image," which sweeps up Mr. Klein in "a reversal against himself, a becoming which leads him to disappearance"—that of "the becoming-Jew of a non-Jew."[1] Though my analysis of *The Help* (2011) agrees with Deleuze's assessment of the power of the image to entangle in a becoming characters scripted otherwise by a film narrative, it will support a revision of his argument that becoming entails disappearance. Becoming leads not to disappearance but rather to a different appearance, to becoming different, just as a non-Jew who becomes a Jew becomes different. This is the lesson of the reconciliation image in *The Help*, whose "work of art," as I have called the aesthetic form of rationality by which an artwork becomes image, is responsible for its characters being entangled in a becoming remaking them into new characters who write a new narrative, that of reconciliation, a narrative that becomes starkly visible against the background of the original narrative of *The Help*.[2]

THE WHITE SAVIOR TROPE

Regardless of how straightforwardly I describe *The Help*, it unfailingly reveals more complex features justifying Matthew Hughey's inclusion of it in his penetrating critical analysis of "the white savior film," whose framework for identifying such narratives fits *The Help* perfectly and must serve as my template for summarizing the film's narrative structure.[3] It is the story of Skeeter Phelan, a young white female college graduate, aspiring journalist and author, who returning home to early 1960s Jackson, Mississippi, by dint of her educated and cosmopolitan insights into their abuse by their white employers, persuades black maids to write a book illuminating their experiences with southern racism, which since the Civil War has remained unabated in many of its worst aspects and reacts with increasing violence to the developing civil rights movement. As Hughey explains, "The white savior's position in these films is a role around which the non-whites must circumambulate.... The white savior is portrayed as nearly the entire reason for black life and agency. First, black characters are portrayed as always in need of the savior and, second, without the presence of the savior, the black character simply shrivels up and dies."[4]

While from a narrative standpoint *The Help* is more nuanced than Hughey's formulation of the white savior trope would permit us to recognize, many of the film's key episodes unambiguously bear him out. Hilly Holbrook's plan to have her Home Health Sanitation Initiative published by the *Jackson Journal* is sabotaged by its fledgling reporter and would-be author, Skeeter, who opposed Hilly's "disease preventative bill" requiring all white homes to "have a separate bathroom for the colored help," whom Hilly alleges threaten the infection of whites and especially white children with race-borne illnesses. In her opposition Skeeter not only takes on Hilly, the white populist antiheroine of Jackson who disciplines the racism of all young white women of child-bearing age in the community. As the film's white advocate for black rights against the Jim Crow culture of "separate but equal," Skeeter challenges nothing less than the entire white racist establishment, which is represented by the White Citizens' Council in Jackson having endorsed Hilly's initiative along with the Mississippi governor's office eager to adopt it.

Skeeter's heroism even rises presumptuously to the level of a white parallel to the civil rights movement, as she acts to awaken blacks themselves to its political challenges to the white racist community. In one dramatic scene in the living-room of her own parents' home, her white-savior role is foregrounded as she is joined—or in Hughey's words "circumambulated"—by the family's black maid and gardener in front of the television as together they all watch Medgar Evers rallying blacks to boycott white racist businesses. Skeeter defends her actions against those of her racist mother, who interrupts the televised civil rights lesson to warn her it will only encourage black discontent and disobedience. Whereas blacks permitted to assemble in front of the media by Skeeter intimates their dependency on the agency of a white savior to wage battles with white America on their behalf, their reliance on her white-savior role is reinforced by her absence on the evening of Ever's assassination. A white bus driver about to pass through streets where racist violence has broken out insists all blacks exit his bus, after which they are shown to be virtually helpless on their own to find their way home through streets perilous to blacks indiscriminately threatened by police commissioned to preserve law and order.

Yet the most dramatic illustration of black dependency on the film's white savior is argued near its conclusion. After the publication of *The Help*, the book Skeeter and Jackson's black maids coauthor to reveal the racist conditions under which the help worked, a special Sunday black church service is convened to honor Aibileen, the first of the black maids to courageously agree to work with Skeeter on her revelatory albeit dangerous project. Despite the great poignancy of the scene, a certain irony is unavoidable. Although to express their admiration and gratitude the church pastor presents Aibileen with a copy of *The Help* signed by the members of the black church community, it is a book that would never have been conceived much less published if it were not for Skeeter, whose absence at the service ensconces the white savior as the ghost in the machine. Following the service the irony is driven home when Aibileen, in her own show of admiration and gratitude, delivers her signed copy of *The Help* to Skeeter, thus acknowledging, and also deferring to, her superordinate authorial and political role.

Other characteristics Hughey associates with the white-savior trope circulate throughout *The Help*, two of which are especially prominent. Owing to her strength of character, Skeeter's status as the outsider in relation to her own community is often dramatized, most vividly when a love interest proclaiming his admiration for her being morally independent and a talented writer subsequently rejects her for stubbornly proving to be both when the publication of *The Help* upsets Jackson by exposing its racist core. *The Help* also measures Skeeter's growth from a naïve do-gooder who earns the angry skepticism of one maid who charges, "And just what makes you think colored people need your help?," to a politically self-aware leader-in-the-making who forms a deeper understanding of her responsibility to Jackson's black community, whose members her naïveté had put at great risk, and to its white racist community, whose moral authority she strives to chasten and reeducate. So *The Help*'s uniquely agentic, alienated, and increasingly self-knowing white savior is additionally empowered by a messianic commitment to rescue her own people as she rescues those they oppress.

With the narrative structure of *The Help* illuminated by Hughey's concept of the white-savior trope, it is time to discover how the reconciliation image to which the film gives birth traces an exit out of this narrative to create a narrative that is entirely new.

THE RECONCILIATION IMAGE

Beginning with its opening scene, *The Help* exhibits the core element of aesthetic reflexivity both Whitman and Adorno found belonged to modern artworks productive of the reconciliation image. A blank notebook page is shown, at the top of which a hand we will soon learn is Skeeter Phelan's writes "The Help," the title of the book project she will coauthor with Jackson's black maids, principally Aibileen Clark and Minny Jackson. Except for the title the page remains blank, however, thus largely a visual image, which suggests two things. In its skeletal form of the title, the word authors the visual image, first as the otherwise blank visual title page itself, followed by all the moving images belonging to the film, to which the image of the title is the visual overture. Moreover the visual image of the title having served as the overture to visual images in motion, through its noticeable absence beyond the title the word yields to the visual image the story to be told with the assistance of language. From its first moments, then, we watch the film reflecting on the relationship between language and the visual image. It reflexively establishes the superiority of the visual image over the limits of the word, which as character dialogue assists in illuminating visual images it accompanies. This is made clear by the image of the title privileging the visual work of the images to follow, and by the film as it unfolds through dialogue limited to the narration of images by characters seen thinking what they say in voice-overs.

Let me recall such an aesthetic model of reflexive movement from my earlier discussion of Whitman's discovery of the visual image as the vehicle of aesthetic education and democratic enlightenment. Only in the first instance did we see Whitman rely upon the word to teach reconciliation, and then he did so primarily to stress the incapacity of language to establish what is real or essential or true, which is an epistemic move I found had multiple implications. To recall the most important, by relinquishing any claim to know reality through language Whitman confines our attention to *appearances*, to what is *seen*, for which his poetry then creates a natural home in visual images that will do much of the pedagogical and philosophical work of teaching reconciliation. My first point, then, is that through an aesthetic form of reflection highlighting the limited epistemic capacity of the word, *The Help* puts the visual image into the interpretive foreground of the film even before its narrative gets underway. Inaugurating the movement of the visual image, *The Help* sets into motion the vehicle about to perform the film's work of art. This is its reconciliation image, which, beginning with the identity image, will teach the ideal of reconciliation as it moves from one image of which it consists to another.

Once *The Help* establishes that the artwork becomes emphatically visual image, then, its reconciliation image will be produced by a flow of constituent images. When completely unfolded the reconciliation image will express what the narrative that gave birth to it cannot: the rationality of the film as an aesthetic whole *continuously becoming different from the narrative* as the artwork becomes image. As I am about to show, this flow of images punctuates the film at irregular intervals until its narrative brings *The Help* to a close. However, this does not mean the reconciliation image is composed of discontinuous images. As Deleuze's analyses of cinema show, cinematographic continuity often takes shape as a *relation* between intermittent images creating the *effect* of their uninterrupted movement.

The Help's reconciliation image is continuous in this relational way, which means the irregularly occurring episodes through which the reconciliation image unfolds show that the argument it forms need not be evident from the start, as is the narrative of the white-savior trope. To the contrary, the argumentative power of the reconciliation image is cumulative through its staggered portrayals of and responses to violence toward difference, a violence especially characteristic of the identity image, whose rigidity must be underlined for how it sets off the counterforce of the difference image it holds captive as its other. And since *The Help*'s identity image depends upon this violence for the work it performs, when I now illustrate this first image I should choose examples of it that best advance the narrative of domination and white-savior-led rebellion. By adopting this strategy I enable the reconciliation image to become visible to us at the moment its images appear in dramatic contrast to the film's narrative trope of the white savior, and I also highlight the power of the reconciliation image through its struggle with the narrative's densely layered violence.

THE IDENTITY IMAGE

Better than the film's other narrative storylines, Jackson's Home Health Sanitation Initiative reveals the unrelenting, all-pervasive racist violence through which the white community's rigid construction of its identity and of black difference as its other forms *The Help*'s identity image. Nor does it omit any violent feature of this construction explaining its self-perpetuation. Through Hilly Holbrook's white and black bathrooms initiative, which in an early scene she proudly reveals to her white bridge club friends, the white community mortifies the black body, while an even greater and more cunning violence is its consequence. Forcing the black body to be intensely self-conscious, mortification encourages self-segregation as it enforces segregation, thus doubling the violence of segregation. Segregation, of course, was to begin with the intention of the initiative, an act enabled by Jim Crow laws, which banning interaction between whites and blacks perpetuated the rule of "separate but equal" overturned by the U.S. Supreme Court. At one point, in fact, Hilly perversely justifies her initiative by citing the "separate but equal" clause confirmed by the Supreme Court's 1896 *Plessy v. Ferguson* decision but invalidated by the 1954 *Brown v. Board of Education* ruling, which became law prior to the time the film's narrative begins.

Together, this means Jackson's segregationist culture buttressed by Jim Crow laws created well-defined, discrete spaces within which whites as well as blacks were required to remain. By way of small private spaces such as separate bathrooms, no less than through geographically distinct wealthy and impoverished communities, white identity could reproduce itself in a rigid form that its spatialized segregated construction of identity and difference functioned to insulate. Frequent visual images of privileged spaces populated by numbers of the white community aggressively remind us of the confidently uncivil power of its fixed identity, as it stands out next to images loudly displaying timorous disaggregated blacks accidentally thrown together at bus stops or victimized in their powerless subservient roles as help at white social functions. Thus we watch Hilly righteously humiliating the help serving social events attended by the Jackson community's affluent young white women, whose silence implicates them in her violent disregard of the maids' feelings injured by horribly offensive things she says within their earshot.

These images additionally show that even where whites and blacks must share social spaces out of the necessity to be served and to serve, they do not really share the same space. An unfree space of the black other is designed by white identity to overlap with its free space in ways minimizing their intersection. Blacks, for example, are permitted only indirect interaction with whites through objects unavoidably occupying the same spaces at the same times. In one image Minny admonishes her daughter, who left school to support the family as a maid, "When you're serving white folks coffee, set it down in front of them, don't hand it to them, 'cause your hands can't touch." Sometimes this spatialization of white identity and its other runs to even further pathological extremes. Baby girl Mae Mobley—whose every bodily as well as psychological need is visually cared for by Aibileen, who confides this to us in voice-over images of her meeting the child's needs—is picked up but once a day by her mother, Elizabeth Leefolt. While Aibi's voice-overs offer commentary on Mae Mobley's neglect by her mother, the image they conjure further measures the obscene lengths white Elizabeth goes to maintain her separation from black Aibi by defining even her own daughter's body as a space where white-black interactions are to be limited.

As such images of whites immunizing themselves against or sanitizing their interactions with blacks vividly show, the white racist community's identity secures an absolutely static, immutable relation with the black other that white identity's construction of difference demands. So perfectly rationalized is it, the steely rigidity of *The Help*'s "identity image" denies whites as well as blacks any escape from identity's white construction. As several images show, whites even lack any of the black awareness of racism necessary for them to consider it at all problematic. Whereas, for instance, on the night of the Evers assassination a traumatized Minny painfully declares, "We living in Hell. Trapped. Our kids, trapped," with the help in another scene pictured lined up on one side of the room at Jackson's African Children's Benefit Ball, an image shows its white hostess blithely asking its white guests to express their gratitude "for all the men and women who have helped to make tonight possible." White gratitude pouring forth for the help's service at the ball shows no sign of embarrassed self-awareness of the ironic relation between white racism and the evening's charitable cause. So ironclad is the apodictic surety and repressive stability of the white identity image in which both whites and blacks are caught, we can hardly imagine how it could move beyond its steady state, unless, as it seems, we were to accept Hughey's proposal of the white-savior narrative, of a force capable of bringing about change from the outside.

Yet by showing the identity image to be so rigid as to be brittle and liable to shatter, the reconciliation image visually intervenes at the moment *The Help* seems most in need of the outside force of the white savior for the film's narrative to move beyond the adamantine racism culturally institutionalized by the identity image. As illustrated by the Home Health Sanitation Initiative, in its fully developed form the white identity image is a grotesque, motionless caricature of itself, blind even to the obvious likeness between its racist projection of the world and the world as it is. For this reason the identity image becomes vulnerable to the aesthetics of the reconciliation image, which by introducing the *difference image* in response to the portrayal of the identity image's inertness substitutes identification *with* difference for the white identity image's identification *of* black difference as otherness. Allied with difference against the immutable identity image, the difference image will disentangle difference from its white construction as otherness to catalyze the film's movement toward the reconciliation image.

THE DIFFERENCE AND ALL-INCLUSIVE IMAGES

All this begins to unfold when Skeeter asks Aibileen to contribute to a book of black maids' stories about their experiences working for Jackson's white families. Frightened by the idea and reluctant to participate, Aibi cautiously agrees to work with Skeeter but sets the terms of her contribution: she will "write [her] stories down and read them to [Skeeter]" so their book will record her experiences in her own voice. Rather than a white savior, Skeeter is Aibileen's and Minny's and the other contributing black maids' *muse*, who presides over the art she inspired to set into motion a work of art that will have two aesthetic results.

First is the publication of *The Help*, whose authorship remains anonymous to protect the newly emboldened identity of its contributing maids but that also further diminishes Skeeter's part, whose own voice is inaudible above the voices of the maids telling their own stories. In fact, when all the participating maids have contributed their stories, Skeeter's publisher reminds her to contribute her own to the finished collection, clearly indicating how far her authorial role has become second to that of the maids.

Second is the visual images of the maids themselves, who from the moment Skeeter conceives the book project are no longer pictured living their lives in ways always framed by the coordinates of the white identity image, but often as differences living apart from their construction as white identity's other. Thus after learning that to retain the respect of the white nativist organization Daughters of America, her mother fired their black maid, Constantine, Skeeter vividly recalls loving memories of being nurtured by Constantine, who once helped her through a painful adolescent experience of rejection by advising, "[You] got to ask yourself this question: 'Am I gonna believe all them bad things them fools say about me today?'" It is at this moment, when Skeeter's recollection pictures black difference rejecting white identity's construction of it as otherness, that she first imagines *The Help* and is next seen proposing the book to her publisher. Multiple times *The Help* again makes this same point, insists on it. Its work of art overcomes the inertia of the white identity image, which wants only to preserve itself in its stationary form against the ultimately more powerful black difference image, which in its alliance *with* difference sponsors difference's need for an identity resistant to its construction as otherness. That it is *art* that accomplishes this rather than a white savior is highlighted by Aibileen when she replies to Minny's panic at the prospect that the authorities will discover their collaboration with Skeeter: "We're gonna be careful. We ain't doing civil rights. We're just telling stories like they really happened."

As it multiplies images of black difference divorced from its construction as other, the difference image opens up a glaring contrast between images of difference for itself and for another enabling difference to recover what its image as the other had robbed it of: its pluripotentiality, which, through difference's conversion to otherness, was alienated from the image of black difference by the white identity image it was forced to subserve. When, for example, in violation of Jim Crow laws Skeeter visits Aibileen at her home to begin their collaboration, visibly surprised by Aibi's appearance she observes, "I've never seen you out of uniform before. You look really nice." But this rupture between black difference and its construction as other that the difference image of Aibi out of uniform makes visually explicit is in addition a transition to the all-inclusive image of difference, which unfolds seamlessly from the difference image whose higher democratic form it now appears to be. For not long after Aibi begins telling Skeeter her life story she is joined in her home by Minny and nearly a dozen other maids, all of whom confide their experiences with white employers to Skeeter. Ceasing to be invisible, each free to tell her own story in her own words, Jackson's black maids are now symbolically all-included in a visual image of difference, which through its contrast with a counterfeit image of all-inclusiveness will clarify the conditions in which difference exists as other.

When we next see the help again, on the occasion of the African Children's Benefit Ball, being thanked as a group by the white community for making its charity event possible, a second meaning of all-inclusiveness is apparent. By means of an almost confessional image unwittingly reproducing the help's actual *private role* as servants, we are afforded a brief, almost stolen sideways glance of the *public role* the help is claimed to play at the ball that reveals the fictitious terms of its citizenship. Its rights exist at the pleasure of the white racist community, whose inclusiveness of blacks as servants at its charity event is revealed to be the alienated, legal-juridical form of the help's public role cloaking its construction as otherness in the private sphere beneath the threshold of politics and the law. In contrast with this counterfeit image of all-inclusiveness, the earlier image of black all-inclusiveness (the gathering of black maids at Aibi's home) is intensified, as is its rupture with white identity's construction of difference as otherness earlier set up by the difference image. With the alienated image of the public role black difference is being denied, the thought of difference's pluripotentiality is augmented.

THE RECEPTIVITY AND IMITATIVE IMAGES

We see that by retrieving black difference from the image of otherness in which the rigid white identity image enslaved it, the difference image and the all-inclusive image of difference perceive difference differently. Together they collaborate to offer perceptions of racial difference apart from its construction as other and expressive of its pluripotentiality. Such are the perceptions of difference the movement of the reconciliation image carries forward into the film, remarkable images to which Skeeter and other characters will next become receptive and imitate.

So when Skeeter is startled by Aibileen's image in ordinary clothes, for example, her response exceeds any professional interest she could have in Aibi's personal history. While it is for Skeeter certainly a defining impression of black difference apart from its social construction, it is also her introduction to Aibi's broadband emotional life, next displayed by the image of her candid, wholehearted recollection of the first southern white child she had cared for. Skeeter is visibly, emotionally engaged by the image of how Aibi's love for the child is the enduring human element in an inhuman situation, by her spiritualized analogy of writing down this and her other stories to writing down her prayers, by the qualities of a being whose image is as mysterious as it is awe-inspiring. In a word, she is demonstrably *receptive* to Aibi, whose difference continues to evolve from Skeeter's own already partly deconstructed image of difference "out of uniform."

But Skeeter's receptivity is also prelude to *The Help*'s consummate "imitative" image of reconciliation, whose initial appearance is complex for its multiple levels of signification. As Aibi continues to describe her love for the first white child she cared for, she breaks into spontaneous laughter as she recalls her answer to being asked by him why she is black—"Because I drank too much coffee"—a response that quickly unfolds as one of the film's most subtle interactions. Undoubtedly disguising her painful awareness of the depth of such an innocently posed question, Aibi's laughter reflects knowledge of the double bind in which she is implicated, that of having to falsely explain to a child what a truthful explanation would leave incomprehensible in any event: why she is different. Aibi immediately understands she will forever be unable to avoid what at this moment she learns is her fate in white racist society: the inevitability of leaving herself inexplicable and unrecognizable despite whatever efforts she would make to the contrary. Alert to the pathos of the moment, but uncertain and respectful of what Aibileen's laughter may mean, to allow herself time to decipher it Skeeter hesitates a moment before suddenly bursting into laughter along with her. Expressing her grasp of Aibi's unavoidably absurd predicament in the very instant of her hesitation, Skeeter's sudden burst of laughter is a mimetic act of *becoming Aibileen*. It is an act of *imitation*, which educates her seeing and hearing as it does her understanding of Aibileen by surmounting the apparent impossibility of perceiving black difference beyond its image as otherness.

For its penetrating and painful subtlety this first appearance of the imitative image may be of greater importance than the second, as it arguably models how imitation regularly occurs in everyday life, suggesting reconciliation may be more common than we know. Precisely for that reason, however, when it appears a second time its lack of subtlety makes it visually and thus pedagogically more powerful. So powerful is this second image of imitation, if

I had not already thought-out the image of reconciliation it advances, it could be made sense of only by first imagining the reconciliation image.

Just as we see the reconciliation image mimetically unfold in the exchange between Aibi and Skeeter, the second appearance of the imitative image is also preceded by the continuity of the difference and receptivity images. A southern white housewife, Celia Foote, has employed Minny not only to perform the ordinary duties of black maids but to teach her the art of cooking as well as other domestic secrets she believes will strengthen a marriage at risk for her lack of mastery of such household tasks. In short order they form bonds of friendship, not least of which because Minny also enables Celia to cope with the tragedies of her miscarriages, which out of guilt she had concealed from her husband. As was Aibi's kitchen, Celia's is the milieu where the black difference image allows Minny to be seen apart from her construction as the other framed by the white identity image. Although Celia's kitchen is no more an emancipated space than Aibi's—due to Jim Crow laws' regulation of white-black domestic interactions—both kitchens put difference on display by allowing black maids to exhibit a multidimensional creativity without which white no less than black family social life would be impoverished. So when Minny seats herself in Celia's kitchen to enjoy the luncheon she prepared for them both, in violation of Jim Crow Celia ignores Minny's objections to joining her at the kitchen table by uttering words blind to her otherness. Spoken with such lilting inflection, Celia's greeting as she crosses the border from her dining room to kitchen—"There . . . you . . . are"—so highlights the visual particularity of Minny in possession of her own space ("there"), own person ("you"), and own being ("are"), it perfectly expresses Celia's unconditional receptivity to Minny's difference.

As was Skeeter's receptivity to Aibi, this second image of receptivity is followed by the appearance of the imitative image. In an image astonishing for its challenge to a narrative of unwavering racism able to be politically blunted, according to Hughey, only by the transcendent efforts of a white savior, in a stunning reversal of roles near *The Help*'s conclusion Celia and her husband seat and serve Minny at their dining-room table, which proudly overflows with dishes Minny taught Celia to prepare to secure her marriage. Imitating Minny, *becoming Minny*, Celia begins to display the range and grasp the creativity of the pluripotential senses and sensibilities depreciated by the racist white master–black servant relationship of white identity constructing black difference as otherness. As was Skeeter's earlier imitation of Aibi, by *becoming Minny* Celia's becoming is an image of *becoming black, becoming different*, thus not a *disappearance* of the identity image as we now see Deleuze wrongly alleged was entailed by the non-Jew Mr. Klein becoming a Jew. Becoming different is rather a *reappearance* of the identity image in a new and different form, an image of identity becoming different in the image of difference, an entanglement of identity and difference in the becoming different of the reconciliation image.[5]

It is possible to be still more precise. To this point *The Help*'s second imitative image, Celia's becoming Minny, becoming black, becoming different, is only the *penultimate form* of the reconciliation image, by itself an *illusory* image of reconciliation. Recalling Adorno's twofold criteria, the reconciliation image must not only envision reconciliation, as does this penultimate form; *it also must testify to its absence*, which this penultimate form does not. If the second criterion is not met, the image is illusory. For if Minny is thought to represent racial difference *as such* no longer threatened by violence as white identity's other, the false impression is created by the reconciliation image that white identity has been reconciled with racial difference in all of its possible forms. Failing to recognize the limitless abundance of difference, which is the ineliminable nonidentity of difference in excess of every instance of reconciliation, the image of reconciliation *imposes* identity on difference, further constructing unreconciled difference as otherness vulnerable to identity's violence toward difference. Hence the question to be asked is whether *The Help* not only envisions reconciliation as identity becoming different, as does the image of Celia's becoming black, but, in addition, if it testifies to the existence of differences to which identity has yet to be receptive and imitate. Put another way, is the reconciliation image belonging to *The Help* a time arrived though also a time yet to come, an image envisioning reconciliation that also testifies to its absence?

A TIME ARRIVED AND A TIME YET TO COME

In *The Help*'s closing scene Aibi's white employer has dismissed her at the insistence of Hilly Holbrook, who was outraged at discovering Minny and Aibi included an event in their book that could not only identify her as their victimizer, but by humiliating her would diminish her position in the white community. Driven from her employer's house, in a final image Aibi walks up a street that in the distance reaches a vanishing point, which as she continues to walk will continue to recede and will always lead only to a location out of frame. Aibi is thus technically, *formally* included within this final image, just as she is formally, *legally* included within white society. But at the same time the image positions her moving beyond its filmic and societal coordinates, thus on its outside, which her own voice-over helps to explain by telling us that, no longer a maid, she is now different, a writer. Presenting a new image of difference through Aibi to which no one is yet receptive and who is yet to be imitated in some way, shape, or form, *The Help* straddles two worlds as it concludes, Minny's an image of reconciliation arrived in the present and Aibi's an image testifying to a future reconciliation yet to come.

AESTHETICS OF THE RECONCILIATION IMAGE

A brief summary of the aesthetics of the reconciliation image in *The Help* shows how perfectly it mirrors its production by the work of art in modern artworks, and not only as Adorno understood its creation in modern art but as Whitman did as well. To start with, aesthetic reason made its presence known in *The Help* through an economy of elements—reflexivity, motion, continuity, equilibrium, receptivity, and mimesis, among others—Adorno had laid out in *Aesthetic Theory* as belonging to the modern artwork. But together with a twin economy of images and democratic effects (or democratic lessons) I had theorized as corresponding to Adorno's economy of elements, his work had allowed me to flesh out and further develop the rationality of the reconciliation image in modern art as the continuous parallel unfolding of the elements and images and effects of which it consists. And as my development of Adorno's aesthetic theory then led us to expect, this is what we also saw in *The Help*, with the first evidence of aesthetic reason being the core element of reflexivity, which triggered the continuous parallel unfolding of the reconciliation image appearing much like it appeared in Whitman's poetry.

So in the earliest moments of the film we were immediately reminded of Whitman's use of the word to reflexively question language's epistemic limits in order to privilege the visual image, which from that point on was the vehicle *The Help* called upon to perform the work of art that would move it toward reconciliation. By means of the element of reflexivity aesthetic reason forged an alliance between the film and the visual image, or more exactly an alliance between the film and all that the visual image is itself allied with—with the irreducibility of images of appearances to universals (essences, realities, and their truths); with images of appearances as images of difference; and with images of the equality, inclusivity, and the mystique of differences earning our receptivity. Privileging vision by orienting us to visual images of appearances in these ways, as did Whitman's poetry *The Help* taught us how to see. Either the meaning of appearances was to be seen in self-standing images, images that, largely unsupported by language, spoke for themselves, or in quasi-linguistic images paired with language for interpretive assistance, as were the film's many images accompanied by voice-overs.

Once the film's reflexive alliance with the visual image thrust the reconciliation image into motion, the element of reflexivity's parallel economy of images and democratic effects began to quickly unfold. At the outset an intransigent white identity image appeared seemingly unassailable for its construction of black difference as its other, whose powerlessness reflexively invoked images of its double, of Aibileen and Minny, who by distinguishing difference from its image as otherness challenged white identity's self-certainty. Struggling to distinguish black difference in pluripotential forms from white identity's construction of difference, these doubled images of difference then appeared alongside white identity's own double, Skeeter and Celia, both contrapuntal images to white racist identities whose receptivity to difference was preliminary to their mimetic acts of white becoming black.[6] Relinquishing its authority to remain rigidly unchanged, by way of Skeeter and Celia white identity was reconstituted in the image of black difference, while at the same time black difference acquired identity apart from white identity's no longer unassailable constructions of difference as otherness.

That entire development was the work of art performed by what Adorno referred to as the dialectic of rationality and mimesis, which holds identity and difference in a relation of equilibrium maintaining an irresolvable tension between identity's need to preserve itself and difference's quest for identity. In the reconciliation image, identity is preserved by being moved beyond its inertial state to reconstitute itself in the image of difference, which pressing for its own identity fueled the continuous movement of the artwork toward perpetual reconciliations of identity and difference. Its work of art sustained by Adorno's dialectic, *The Help* recapitulated the struggle between the rationality of identity and the mimesis of difference as the film's images of reconciliation were continuously exceeded by images of black difference still on the outside, in need of identity and in hope of reconciliation as Aibi remained on the outside in such need and such hope.

Clearly there is a complex aesthetic pedagogy at work in *The Help*'s reconciliation image that makes sense of its constituent images. The reconciliation of identity and difference is the democratic ideal taught by the reconciliation image as a whole, and not only as a realized ideal, an ideal time arrived, but also as an ideal to be continuously striven for, an ideal time yet to come. But in addition each of the images producing the reconciliation image taught its own lesson. So as the white identity image relinquishes its inertial form, it also affirms the necessity of identity through its mimetic reconstitution. The black difference image creates an awareness of difference as the excluded other seen to suffer the violence to difference invisible beneath the threshold of liberal tolerance, though it also creates an awareness of difference as the plenipotential all-inclusive image of black difference attracting white identity's receptive and mimetic interest. And there are the lessons taught by the receptivity image, which teaches white identity to find black difference in its diverse forms to be attractive in diverse ways, in other words to find in black difference its new possibilities for becoming different. Finally, there are the lessons taught by the imitative image, which teaches white identity to become different in the images of black difference to which it is receptive. Indeed, all movement toward reconciliation appears to unfold through difference—as in *The Help* through black difference—through the minoritarian, the subaltern, which as the image of the other creates the *conditions* of identity's and difference's new possibilities but as the image of difference creates identity's and difference's *new possibilities themselves.*[7]

Taken together, all these democratic effects or lessons taught by the reconciliation image form the unique pedagogy of an aesthetic education that was to have a practical purpose. For Whitman and Adorno that purpose was democratic enlightenment or a positive enlightenment, which in both cases would be modeled by modern artworks governed by an aesthetic form of reason productive of an image of an ideal of reconciliation appearing as it appears in *The Help*.

POSSIBLE POLITICS

As I prepare to turn to *Gentleman's Agreement* I must pursue the reconciliation image in *The Help* a step further. All of the reconciliation image's elements and images and democratic effects I have documented, its capacity to trace an exit out of *The Help*'s narrative to advance a new narrative, tell a different story, that of reconciliation, and its contributions to aesthetic education and a democratic enlightenment, will all guide my inquiry into *Gentleman's Agreement*, where the reconciliation image will reappear almost exactly as we have seen in *The Help*. What we will discover to be different about the reconciliation image in *Gentleman's Agreement* will not be something less than appeared in *The Help* but something more, a difference between our two films a recollection of my earlier discussion of Massumi's work will make it possible for us to see clearly from the very beginning of my next chapter. In light of our earlier discussion of Massumi, then, a final brief reflection on *The Help* will serve to highlight the addition *Gentleman's Agreement* will make to what we already have learned about the reconciliation image in film.

To recall the argument of my Second Bridge, we can see a near perfect correspondence between Massumi's terms and the unfolding of the reconciliation image in *The Help*. *The Help*'s rigid white identity image fused with white identity's construction of the image of the black other qualifies as an *already-thought* perception, a culturally ingrained racist perception long residing at the perception pole of percipient action through which black difference is viewed as otherness. As the already-thought asserts its hegemony, however, we see the reconciliation image begin to appear in the form of the image of difference. An alternative, latently active, *possible perception of difference* just beginning to be *thought-out* appears in competition with the dominant already-thought perception of difference as otherness. At its incipient stage this alternative perception, which originating with Skeeter is not yet shared by others and is disengaged from dominant percipient action at the perception pole, steadily unfolds through increasingly well thought-out forms as the all-inclusive, receptivity, and imitative images, all possible perceptions of difference.

What emerges and continuously comes to fruition in *The Help*, in other words, is in the most literal sense to be imagined in Massumi's terms a picture-perfect, thought-out perceptual *order of substitution* whereby a possible percipient action gradually superpositioned on—until it is poised to replace—entrenched perceptions of black difference as otherness ultimately does so. Beginning at the thought pole in an ideational form, the possible perception belonging to the black difference image progresses to the mimetic stage on its way to the perception pole, where members of the white community not only come to perceive black difference receptively; through imitation they begin to perceive the world as difference perceives it. But that is not all.

By Massumi's account possible percipient actions in their orders of substitution include the all-important affective dimension of *anticipation*, which *The Help* begins to generate with its first appearances of the image of black difference when it is shown in contrast with the perception of black difference as otherness. As the image of black difference evolves, becoming more affecting and complex as its pluripotentiality is displayed, the perception of difference exceeding what is known of it as the other creates an anticipation of potential new relations with black difference next portrayed in the Skeeter-Aibileen and Celia-Minny receptivity images. And, of course, Skeeter's and Celia's receptivity to Aibi's and Minny's differences creates further anticipation of new relations with black difference that will be consummated through imitation.

Yet anticipation reaches its zenith with the film's final image of Aibi, a perception of black difference moving toward a vanishing point hovering somewhere between the instances of reconciliation already shown and the open-ended possibility for reconciliation her image allows us to imagine, between a time arrived and a time yet to come. Such future-oriented anticipations of new relations between white identity and black difference, along with anticipations encouraged by the receptivity and mimetic images of their actual realizations, next foster thought of reconciliation *beyond* the racist milieu to which it is confined by *The Help*. With this, thought is prompted to recall and return to the rigid white identity image and its construction of black difference as otherness, though on this and subsequent returns it will reinaugurate the thought-out perceptual order of substitution with increasing anticipation the reconciliation image will continuously unfold as an open whole.

Hence in *The Help* there is a continuous movement between thought and action of reconciliation nourishing the possibility for the continuation of both. What Massumi's concept of perception as possible action enables us to see is this. When we consider the *images* of which the reconciliation image in *The Help* consists to be *possible perceptions*, we see they unfold according to a perfectly thought-out aesthetic order of substitution—what I have called aesthetic education—continuously projecting reconciliation into the future as a possible politics beyond the film that models it.

Tolerance, in this context, becomes
forbearance toward cultural practices
thought to be intrinsically wrong or inferior.
—William Connolly, *Identity\Difference*

6

....

Gentleman's Agreement

BEYOND TOLERANCE

With Massumi's argument still in mind, here is what *Gentleman's Agreement* (1947) adds to my account of the reconciliation image in *The Help*. Unlike *The Help*, in *Gentleman's Agreement* there is no already "thought-out" (to recall Massumi's term) order of substitution of the images the reconciliation image consists of that unfold in the course of the film from its beginning. Only as the film approaches its conclusion does an order of substitution finally and suddenly appear as a moment climaxing a delay owed to the narratively scripted dramatic events preceding it. Up to that moment of climax we watch as the film's narrative arduously thinks out the images productive of the reconciliation image.

Whereas from *The Help*'s outset its reconciliation image is well thought-out and well articulated, with each of its images in an order of substitution steadily developed and easily discernible, the narrative of *Gentleman's Agreement* struggles with developing clear images, especially of identity and difference, even of identity's violence toward difference. While *The Help* conveys and measures the power of aesthetic reason to achieve reconciliation where the violence toward difference is brutally transparent, in *Gentleman's Agreement* the aesthetic rationality of the work of art is challenged to pursue reconciliation where the violence toward difference is palpable but obscure, ubiquitous but elusive, endemic but seemingly untreatable. In *Gentleman's Agreement* the work of aesthetic education belonging to the reconciliation image is consequently more protracted and complex than in *The Help*. After being laboriously thought-out, the reconciliation image appears all at once and crescendo-like late in *Gentleman's Agreement*, rather than, as in *The Help*, early on until it becomes the rational expression of a systematically unfolded series of images. This is because of the barriers to reconciliation the narrative of *Gentleman's Agreement* mounted and the film's work of art had to overcome to produce the reconciliation image. Thus the narrative of *Gentleman's Agreement* is again our natural starting point for discovering its reconciliation image.[1]

IMAGE = MOTION

Phillip Schuyler Green, widower and well-known prolific writer, travels with his young son, Tommy, to New York to begin a new position as a journalist for *Smith's Weekly*, a successful national magazine. Together with Green's mother, they take up residence in an apartment found for them by his new editor, who at their first meeting explains that apartments can be hard to find, thus inviting speculation as to why, a question whose answer Green will discover in due course. No sooner does the collegial magazine editor, John Minify, welcome Green, than he proposes the first project he wants him to work on: a series investigating anti-Semitism, which at a social gathering at his apartment that evening he explains he has been "wanting to do for some time," to "break it wide open." There Green meets his future fiancée, Kathy Lacey, niece of his editor and a divorcée, who he learns from an exchange between Lacey and her uncle originally recommended the series topic he is assigned. To develop his series Green will at first struggle to devise a unique angle, which, at a later date after finally doing so, he will explain simply to Minify and Kathy: "I'm going to let everybody know that I'm Jewish, that's all."

A virtual stranger in New York, Green keeps his true gentile identity a secret from everyone except Kathy and his editor, so that passing for a Jew, and under certain circumstances known by the alias "Greenberg," he will experience anti-Semitism firsthand. Victimized by a range of anti-Semitic prejudices, including acts of bias from those with whom he interacts most closely, an increasingly troubled Green all too easily collects the experiences and information he needs to write his series. As news of its imminent publication circulates throughout *Smith's Weekly*, even before his series is distributed to its national audience its implications are grasped by Green's colleagues and intimates. Not only is it pervasive, but anti-Semitism may be becoming universal, as those who sincerely believe themselves not to be anti-Semitic greatly add to its numbers by tacitly supporting it. Tacit anti-Semitism is difficult to diagnose, treat, and eradicate, its offenders difficult to identify, hence its images are often at best impressionistic and question-begging, appearing in need of clearer presentation and semiotic precision. *Gentleman's Agreement* responds to such equivocal moving images with a twofold antidote. We are to become self-aware of our tacit implication in anti-Semitic practices we wrongly and naïvely believe we oppose. And on the basis of such self-clarification we must speak out against anti-Semitism by advocating legal-juridical democratic principles and rights guaranteeing universal tolerance, as we shall see the film's narrative in various ways argues.

Despite it being elementary we should take seriously the instruction the film offers when it begins, as it highlights interpretive points its narrative wants us to not miss. To begin with, we must not overlook the surname Green, symbolizing inexperience though also growth. Nor overlook Green's given middle name, Schuyler, a derivation from the Dutch meaning "scholar," which he adopted as his first name after the examples of two writers to whom he compares himself, Somerset Maugham and Sinclair Lewis, whose first names, he tells us, were also chosen by their bearers as substitutes for ordinary names. Green revealed his play of names when introduced at his editor's party, where Minify urged him to discard Schuyler as his first name in favor of Philip, a proposal to which Green willingly assented, perhaps thinking it suitably Jewish, though it also agrees with his practice of substituting a doppelganger for his identity.

These clues signal problematic developments soon in the making for the creation and unfolding of the reconciliation image. Assigned to write on anti-Semitism, Green has little personal experience with Jews, none with violence toward Jews, his one friendship with a Jew apparently having provided him no insight into Jews' lived history with anti-Semitism. His willing name changes suggests a fluid, chameleon-like relation to his identity, anticipating growth beyond it, perhaps the democratic becoming of his eventually becoming different in the image of difference, the becoming Jew of a non-Jew, though it is more tellingly also an early allusion to the ill-defined, inexact, unsettled form of his and other images in motion belonging to the reconciliation image and that assiduously unfold over the duration of the film until they at long last assume fixity. Of course his comparison to Maugham and Lewis lifts Green out of the ranks of ordinary journalists, and by situating him among great writers symbolically casts his role as that of art and thus of aesthetic rationality, which find their avatar in the image of Green performing aesthetic reason's work of art the film will accomplish. Yet as the images and process of reconciliation are not aesthetically preordained, owing to special challenges mounted by the film's narrative, and must be carefully thought-out, Schuyler, the *scholar*, returns from being thrust into the background by Philip. It is Schuyler who in the persona of his doppelganger not only must be the real avatar of art and aesthetic reason, but who increasingly shares Philip's foreground as the images forming the reconciliation image only very gradually take shape as they and their contributions to realizing the ideal of reconciliation are thought-out.

Indeed the reconciliation image as a *whole* must be thought-out—its visual form, its identity, difference, all-inclusive, receptivity, and imitative images, its dual temporalities—as an order of perceptual substitution for the scripted perceptual standpoint of the narrative. And not until it is thought-out as a whole can the reconciliation image appear. So the paradox is that if I am to discover the reconciliation image in *Gentleman's Agreement* its narrative must, for a time, dictate my analysis. For if I am to show there is a reconciliation image with a life independent of the narrative to which it also owes its birth, I must first trace the process of its being thought-out, find clarity and stability developed in the narrative where its images seem to intend only ambiguity and uncertainty. I must not only find *images in motion*, as, for example, Philip Green is constantly in motion by "let[ting] everybody know [he's] Jewish, that's all," which as we shall see frequently renders his image transient and virtually "indistinguishable from its actions and reactions."[2] I must find *motion that creates images*, specifically those belonging to the reconciliation image. Finding motion productive of its constituent images is precisely what it means to discover how our narrative thinks out the reconciliation image.

While it is at odds with our usual understanding of film to say its images appear after being thought-out in the course of a narrative structure that has, as we should expect, scripted its images to serve its own narrative ends to begin with, the narrative of *Gentleman's Agreement* itself dispels any such incongruity. As the film begins, it no sooner introduces its narrative vehicle, investigating anti-Semitism, than it places its leading character in the troubled position of questioning his approach to the assignment and even asking himself whether he is capable of writing the series. In effect the film reflexively problematizes the vehicle on which its own narrative depends and then, continuing its reflections, folds back upon itself as a thought process that works to solve the problem and ensure its narrative structure will unfold as planned.

Yet what is ultimately thought-out is not only the narrative but in addition the images belonging to the reconciliation image that, as well as contributing to it, in the course of the film will become independent of the narrative structure to which it owes its very existence.

Such a reflexive movement could be anticipated on the basis of Adorno's concept of an aesthetic form of reason driving the work of art performed by an artwork productive of the reconciliation image, as is *Gentleman's Agreement*. Reflexivity was immediately prefigured by the film's protagonist, writer Phil Green, who, assigned the role of the avatar of art, is true to the nature of aesthetic rationality by thinking reflexively. In part due to his initial reluctance to accept his editor's assignment after imagining that everything that can be said about anti-Semitism has already been said, and in part owing to the doubts he entertained about his abilities as a writer to complete his assignment, Green agonizes over his "angle" on his series topic. Distressed over his failure to arrive at a new angle and nearly resigned to defeat, he places his series in jeopardy—along with the film narrative his series on anti-Semitism would develop. After rejecting possible angles he discusses with his mother, Green makes a breakthrough. He is moved by her recent illness to admit he cannot begin to grasp her suffering without having her condition, an empathetic response through which he solves the problem of his series angle. This is the moment he decides he will put himself in the condition of the Jew, to let everyone know he is Jewish to draw the anti-Semites out. New to New York and keeping his real identity secret, he is certain no one other than his editor and his fiancée, in whom he will confide, would know he is not Jewish. No one else excepted, everyone else will treat him just as they typically treat Jews.

THINKING OUT THE IDENTITY AND DIFFERENCE IMAGES

It is remarkable that while the narrative's solution to Green's problem of inventing a new journalistic angle to anti-Semitism allows the narrative to rescue itself from possible arrested development, the narrative cannot continue to unfold without thinking out what this angle entails. To start with, knowing little to nothing about anti-Semitic violence and unacquainted with Jews despite having a close Jewish friend, Green has neither an image of Jewish difference nor one of the Jew as other on which to model himself. At this point there could be no question of Green the non-Jew becoming a Jew as the imitative image allows. At best, the image of difference he represents is only a *placeholder* for the difference image he would increasingly come to resemble if he succeeds in deepening his experience with Jews and their victimization. Having solved the problem of Green's angle, then, the narrative thus confronts a second problem. If Green has not yet had such Jewish experience, but it is precisely the goal of his feigning Jewishness, the narrative's reflexive motion shaping its work of art must respond to the need for a clarification about its choice of Green's angle. How, it must explain, can Green pass for a Jew knowing so little about Jews and the Jewish condition?

Hence, at that serendipitous empathetic moment at his mother's bedside, when he happens on his series' angle, Green goes to her mirror, *visualizes* himself as a Jew, and exclaims, "Well, it won't be the same, sure, but it ought to be close. I can just tell them [I'm Jewish] and see what happens. . . . Dark hair, dark eyes. Sure, so has Dave [Green's Jewish friend from childhood]. So have a lot of guys who aren't Jewish. No accent, no mannerisms. Neither has Dave. . . . Name—Phil Green. Skip the Schuyler. Might be anything. Phil Green." *Gentleman's Agreement* thus thinks through the problem of how all those whom Phil Green meets, non-Jews and Jews alike, will be fooled into believing he is Jewish. Just like his mirror image he will simply *appear* as a Jew, visual appearances promising immunity to public challenge. With this move the film installs the visual image as the instrument for developing the remaining narrative for which he and his journalistic series are the narrative vehicles. And the burden of proof the visual image is to bear will be underscored by being elevated over the word, which certifies the pretense only the visual image has the power to sustain. At a luncheon with his editor and staff shortly after what Green describes as a "click [that] just happened inside of [him]," as he privately recalls his decision to publicly "mirror" his difference, a Jewish colleague opposed to his series declares, "You can't *write* [anti-Semitism] out of existence." By raising and answering, thinking through, this second problem of how Green can feign being Jewish, the film's narrative makes it possible for the difference image, the Jew who Green the non-Jew is to gradually become, *to be thought-out in a visual form.*

Not only the difference image, but the identity image must be thought-out as well. What is remarkable here is that, at the time the series is proposed to Green, he accepts it, and then later invents his angle and the strategy he adopts to pursue it, *Gentleman's Agreement* names no anti-Semites themselves. This is not simply due to what the narrative leads us naturally to assume, that in addition to the smaller number of vulgar, deliberate, and well-known anti-Semitic personalities and institutions it will mention, the identities and practices of as yet unknown anti-Semites are to be disclosed by the investigation into anti-Semitism. Rather, the narrative likewise prescribes that before anti-Semites can be named there is a third problem the film must solve. Insofar as it operates at a *tacit* level of behavior and analysis, at a level not obvious to its offenders and where it is ambiguous or near certain though yet uncertain, anti-Semitism itself must first be clearly established for the identities of the anti-Semites, hence the identity image itself, to be determined. And until anti-Semitism is shown to allow its offenders' identities to be known, as with the difference image the identity image will serve as a *placeholder* for whoever they are discovered to be. How, then, does the narrative of *Gentleman's Agreement* flesh out anti-Semitism from its tacit forms to learn the identities of the anti-Semites themselves? How, in other words, is the identity image of tacit anti-Semitism, together with the difference image of the Jew, thought-out by the film's narrative?

If we agree that identity and difference are "bound together," as William Connolly puts it, whereby each is constructed in relation to the other, we can expect *images* of identity and difference to be thought-out according to the same relational logic.[3] As we shall see, this expectation is supported by Adorno's earlier discussed concepts of rationality, mimesis, and aesthetic equilibrium through which he conceptualizes a dialectic internal to the artwork. Aspiring to endure as originally created, the artwork's aesthetic identity is a construction of its aesthetic object that imposes form on the *difference* between the two. What difference there is between an artwork's aesthetic identity and its aesthetic object appears as *other* than it is. And though difference resists identity's imposition by striving for an identity of its own, it is at the same time constrained to suppress this tendency to diverge from the artwork's wish to preserve its aesthetic identity in an eternally unchanging form. This equilibrium between construction, the artwork's need for aesthetic identity, and mimesis, the artwork's alliance with difference against impositions of hypostatized form, of otherness, constitutes a dialectical relation of opposing forces and the structural precondition for the artwork to undergo transformation into a continuously moving, ever better articulated series of images belonging to the reconciliation image.

The narrative of *Gentleman's Agreement* will do precisely this. It will lock the identity and difference images into a dialectical relation of opposition and struggle through which both images are gradually developed and clarified, until each image achieves the same degree of definition and development characterizing both images in *The Help*. As we shall see, on the one hand this dialectic will steadily form the difference image through Green's many complex engagements with tacit anti-Semitism by which he is victimized while at the same time being at great pains to persuade his offenders of their acts. On the other, each engagement will further reveal the deeply hidden identity of the anti-Semite—even to itself, especially to itself—the un-self-aware habits of tacit anti-Semitic views and behavior tacit anti-Semites come to understand only at great pain to themselves. To be sure, this dialectic, through which the foundational images of the film are thought-out, is the project to which *Gentleman's Agreement* is largely devoted. For it is not only the film's identity and difference images that are developed by its dialectic. So are the images whose appearances depend on the complete articulation of the identity and difference images: the all-inclusive, receptivity, and imitative images, thus the reconciliation image as a whole produced by the aesthetic rationality governing the film's movement of the steadily gestating images of which it consists.

DIALECTICS OF THE IDENTITY AND DIFFERENCE IMAGES

Gentleman's Agreement distinguishes between "overt and tacit" forms (my terms) of anti-Semitism, and while its narrative features multiple episodes of both, its concern is with the latter, which it goes to lengths to examine. *Overt anti-Semitism*, though viewed by *Gentleman's Agreement* as odious, is portrayed as too common to earn the film's real interest in an investigation seeking evidence of anti-Semitism's complexity, ubiquity, and covertness. Such semiotic depth is absent from its straightforward, publicly familiar expressions, which in contrast to its tacit form obscure anti-Semitism's deeper meanings and significance. Green's editor thus insists he must avoid "the crackpot story [which has] been done plenty," and instead pursue "the bigger thing . . . the people who would never go near an anti-Semitic meeting or send a dime to Gerald L. K. Smith."[4] Soon Green himself agrees, his anxiety over inventing a new angle for his series having been largely caused by his discovery that "anti-Semitism in business, labor, professions . . . it's all there, but [he] can't make it give": "Every time I think I'm getting onto something good I go a little deeper, and it turns into the same old drool of statistics and protest." Believing the "crackpot" form of anti-Semitism the public sees and hears spoils the public's opportunities to know it as it really is, Green's editor at times takes an even more radical position. When his Jewish colleague insists he avoid giving anti-Semitism journalistic attention that "will only stir it up more," Minify refuses to "pretend it doesn't exist and add to the conspiracy of silence" Jews themselves participate in out of their "experience [that] the less talk there is, the better." And it is not paradoxical for the narrative to propose that this conspiracy of silence allows the notorious bigots Theodor G. Bilbo and Gerald L. K. Smith to "do all the talking."[5] Minify's point is that any talk aiding the public image of overt anti-Semitism to pass for the real thing is in actuality "silence" that only covers it up.

Yet if *Gentleman's Agreement* focuses its investigation of anti-Semitism on its tacit form where it exists insidiously beneath the threshold of politics and the law, why, despite the film's conviction that its overt form teaches us nothing about anti-Semitism we do not already know, does its narrative pay such liberal attention to overt anti-Semitic discrimination, which will become the target of political and legal-juridical sanctions on America's political horizon? An explanation is suggested by Green's attempt to persuade his editor to look into his own magazine's hiring practices after he learns of its own long history of anti-Semitic bias, which actually falls into that commonplace category of "anti-Semitism in business, labor, and professions" that admits only of the "same old drool of statistics and protest." Shocked by Green's revelation, Minify immediately revises his magazine's employment policies. Green's act was inspired by a discussion with his secretary, Elaine, who, believing him to be Jewish, confides she was hired by *Smith's Weekly* after taking a gentile name to replace her Jewish surname, which at the magazine and everywhere else had produced only failed job applications.

As this example begins to illustrate, part of the film's narrative strategy of largely limiting its study to tacit anti-Semitism is to recall the reprehensible, destructive effects of its overt form. So in addition to his secretary needing to change her name in order to find work, there is the doctor treating his mother's illness who Green takes to task for steering him away from Jewish specialists by alleging their practice of "overcharging and stringing visits out." After Green reveals he is Jewish, the flabbergasted and embarrassed doctor quickly retreats, claiming after losing his credibility, "I don't believe in prejudice." Or there is the apartment building maintenance man with whom Green has words, refusing his advice to make special arrangements to pick up his mail at the post office to obviate the need to stencil his name on his mailbox for purposes of delivery. "Greenberg" would reveal Green lives in a New York apartment—secured for him by his editor-employer—excluding Jews, making him an anathema to the building's other occupants. Finally, Green's experience at the Flume Inn deserves mention for its archetypal anti-Semitic discrimination. Knowing in advance that the Inn is "restricted," Green attempts to check in on the pretense he and his fiancée will be spending their honeymoon night there, though his real intention is to force a confrontation with the hotel management he expects will refuse to honor his reservation, which is the outcome.

These many examples of the film's episodes of overt anti-Semitism primarily appear to be offered to one end. As salient as such poignant and egregious historical examples of anti-Semitism are, the types no serious film about anti-Semitism could omit, the narrative is dedicated to treating them reflexively as ultimately inadequate to the task of analyzing the problem of anti-Semitism and its unavailing formal-legal penalties as it is historically evolving into its tacit form.

Not only do we see *Gentleman's Agreement* arguing that such examples of overt anti-Semitism fail to illuminate what I have called the identity image, that is, who the anti-Semites are and what the source and nature of their authority is beyond the already well-known anti-Semites belonging to the professions (the doctor), the corporations (the apartment building), businesses (magazines and hotels), and politics (Bilbo and Smith), those who have been the well-researched subjects of "the same old drool of statistics and protest."[6] The film's narrative also shows how examples of overt anti-Semitism have failed to develop the difference image, a deficiency the film at one point hints at powerfully. When Green tells his childhood Jewish friend about his series and explains its angle, Dave, who has found employment in New York City and is visiting in search of a home to settle his family, responds critically that he has no interest in "the poor, poor Jews." Rather, "it's the whole thing" that is of concern to him. What neither Dave nor *Gentleman's Agreement* wants to focus on predominantly, in other words, is the Jew as narrowly other, "the poor, poor Jews" about which the narrative believes it already knows too much. We are now to expand our view to "the whole thing" through which the film will form a more enlarged image of the Jew as difference than its familiar image as other provides.

Having recognized the importance while aggressively foregrounding the limitations of a narrow interest in undisguised acts of anti-Semitism, then, the narrative of *Gentleman's Agreement* delivers us to the specter of tacit anti-Semitism, which as it further develops the film's story line implicates it in the dialectic through which a second, alternative narrative of reconciliation will eventually explode into view.

Of the three episodes of tacit anti-Semitism *Gentleman's Agreement* examines, it studies one in depth, through an analysis of the interpersonal relationship between Green and Kathy, whose dialectic is fueled by an intimacy opening up everything to interrogation as it matures over the duration of the film. On the occasion of tacit anti-Semitism's first appearance in their relationship it eludes them both, no doubt owing in equal parts to their unfamiliarity with what in the longer run will nearly destroy them as their experience with it deepens, and to their not wanting to offend each other while they stand together on such untrod ground. Upon hearing Green's formulation of his series angle—"I'm going to let everybody know I'm Jewish, that's all"—Kathy's spontaneous reaction shows she believes she has just discovered something quite personal about him. "Jewish? But you're not, Phil, are you? Not that it would make any difference to me, but you said 'I'm going to let everybody know,' as if you hadn't before and would now. So I just wondered. Not that it would matter to me one way or the other."

Seeing and hearing that to Kathy it obviously does matter if he were Jewish, Phil displays thoughtful concern she interprets as annoyance, and she reacts to it in multiple ways. She cautions him "not to be so serious about it," insists he "must know where [she] stand[s]," claims she was merely "caught . . . off guard" because he always coaxed her to talk about herself while he says little about himself in return, and she excuses herself by admitting "for a minute [she] wasn't very bright on the uptake." Switching tactics to recover her dignity, if not the upper hand, she argues his angle will only cause confusion, "mix everybody up [because] people won't know what you are." Then, exasperated when learning from him that no one at *Smith's Weekly* except Minify will know he is a gentile, she exclaims, "They think you're Jewish?"

Whether Kathy is tacitly anti-Semitic will eventually turn on *why* she worries Phil will be thought to be Jewish, as we shall see. At this moment, though, an upset Phil rushes from the apartment of an equally upset Kathy, who is immediately relieved of the burden of thinking he believes her to be anti-Semitic when he as quickly rushes back to apologize. Admitting to being perplexed by her behavior—"I don't know what happened"—Phil takes responsibility for their falling out, faulting himself for being "judgmental" and "solemn," or "so serious," in her words. Yet in addition their disagreement sows the seeds of Phil's doubt from which the identity and difference images now begin to dramatically emerge. For in the course of his apology he adds, "It started the minute you spoke. I felt insulted. If I were Jewish that's the way I would have felt, and I couldn't let you off, I couldn't make it any easier for you."

So Green learns how it feels to be the victim of anti-Semitism, although at this early stage of feigning Jewishness he distrusts his feelings, for his apology indicates he is unsure if he were actually insulted and thus if his feelings were of really being Jewish. In the wake of his first encounter with anti-Semitism, then, the difference image begins to form, though, in motion, it is also unstable, as is the anti-Semitic identity image Kathy models. Both images stir *behind* Kathy's efforts to explain away her questionable behavior and *behind* Green's apologies for questioning it, though only for the moment. In the aftermath of anti-Semitism's uncertain first appearance early in their relationship, two powerfully staccato episodes intercede to clarify the tacit dimension for Green that has made anti-Semitic behavior difficult for him to discern and awkward to prove.

When Green confirms for his secretary that *Smith's Weekly* would stipulate in an advertisement for a new secretarial position that an applicant's religion will be a matter of indifference for employment, she objects that the new hiring practice amounts to "practically inviting any type at all to apply." Pressed astutely by Green to explain what she means by "any type," Elaine distinguishes between "the sort that starts trouble in a place like this" from the "sort that doesn't, like you or me," the "unobjectionable" Jews who become "the fall guy" for the "kikey ones" who are "loud and [wear] too much rouge." As Elaine then struggles to defend herself against Green's charge of anti-Semitism—that it makes him "sick" whether originating from a gentile or a Jew—she explains she "only said it for a type," it "doesn't mean a thing": "[I] even say it to myself, about me, I mean. Like if I'm about to do something and I know I shouldn't[,] I say, 'Don't be such a little Kike.' That's all."

While his accusation is technically correct, Green fails to see the truthfulness in her denials that, on the one hand, make it clear she neither intends nor recognizes in her behavior the anti-Semitism he alleges and, on the other, for good reason make his censure arguable. Elaine, we should recall, has herself been terribly damaged by anti-Semitism, having abandoned her Jewish surname to secure employment at *Smith's Weekly*. As we now see, she is the victim of anti-Semitism three times over: the first, when upon renouncing her Jewish name for employment she forsakes her very identity as a Jew to pass anonymously among her coworkers; the second, when she utters anti-Semitic slurs to rationalize her new persona; and the third, when she earnestly denies her anti-Semitism, to which she is genuinely blind. Of course, by explaining her denials and blindness the narrative's attention to the painful psychopathology of her personal history highlights the *tacit* nature of her prejudice, one she consciously loathes while at the same time is unwittingly implicated in.

With the proof of tacit anti-Semitism Elaine furnishes, moreover of how we know it to be tacit when we see it, Green's next encounter with it is uncontroversial. After his *Smith's Weekly* colleague, Bert, believing Green is Jewish, invites him to discuss his series and follows up by telling him of discussions he had in Guam with his commanding officer about anti-Semitism, he asks Green rhetorically if he were not in public relations during the war. When his colleague replies to Green's "What makes you say that?" by remarking, "I don't know, you just seem like a clever sort of guy," Green pins him down, asking, "What makes you think I wasn't a G.I.?" To which his colleague angrily retorts, "Now for goodness' sake, Green, don't get me wrong. Some of my best friends..."

Between experiencing the psychological complexity of Elaine's anti-Semitism and the transparency of Bert's, Green learns to recognize tacit anti-Semitism and confidently and stridently invests in the precarious work of persuading its offenders they are implicated. Occurring back to back, these ominous vignettes anchor the dialectic through which the difference and identity images with greater intensity steadily take shape. As a result of these two conflicts Green has begun to develop the consciousness of himself as a Jew that took root in his initial confrontation with Kathy. In the first instance Green is conscious of himself as difference constructed as otherness, as though he were to any mind's eye the assailable "unobjectionable" Jew (in Elaine's terms) or diminished as the "clever sort of guy" (in Bert's). But in his determination to expose and combat their tacit anti-Semitism, which establishes Elaine and Bert as fledgling representations of the identity image, Green's developing Jewish consciousness is also the image of difference wanting to live beyond contradiction, beyond otherness. And both of these engagements better equip him to now resume his earlier battle with Kathy, whose tacit anti-Semitism as a result will by degrees force itself to the surface of her own consciousness to become the defining characteristic of a personality that, having refused to integrate it into her self-image, integrates it into her identity image. From this point on the dialectic relentlessly reconfigures the relationship between Green and Kathy to fully produce the images from which the reconciliation image will eventually emerge.

A party to be hosted by Kathy's sister Jane and brother-in-law Harry to celebrate her engagement to Phil, though more for the purpose of introducing him to family and friends, renews the quarrel that going forward completes the thought-out formation of the identity and difference images. Knowing in advance that Jane and Harry's Darien, Connecticut, suburban friends include anti-Semites, Kathy alerts her sister to the angle Phil adopted for his series and then tells Phil of her sister's reaction: "She thought it was the cleverest way to do research [but] asked you skip the whole [feigning Jewish] thing for the party. . . . You know these suburban groups. . . . It would just start a whole mess for Jane and Harry for *nothing*."[7] When he responds assertively, "And if it were to start a mess for *something*," Kathy counters reminding him, "But Phil, you're not Jewish. It'd just ruin the party for Jane if she had problems with it." With their disagreement escalating as he proposes against her refusal that she "tell [Jane] just to call the party off," for a second time an aggravated Phil leaves her apartment and Kathy in a similar state of mind. On this second occasion of their controversy, though, Phil does not return to apologize, indicating his suspicions of her anti-Semitism have intensified. What is more, it suggests that his consciousness of what his life would be like if he were Jewish, *his identification with difference but also his condition as other*, is becoming stronger and stable.

Thus unapologetic, Phil does not this time lose ground to Kathy's rationalizations by accepting her apology for their recent strife, but is pleased to hear from her that she had visited her sister and "fixed everything up." He could attend their engagement party on his own terms and introduce himself to Jane and Harry's guests as the Jewish journalist writing a series investigating anti-Semitism. And indeed, when Phil and Kathy briefly leave the party to stroll to a nearby cottage she had built to one day share with someone she loved, he expresses pleasant surprise that all of the guests "asked about the series and thought it was fine! Not one lifted eyebrow in the bunch." Phil does not know what Kathy earlier learned from her sister and will continue to withhold from him: that Jane, as she herself put it, exercised "a little careful screening" when inviting her guests. So Kathy's anticipatory visit to Jane only "fixed everything up" by protecting Phil from the party's list of uninvited anti-Semites populating America's wealthy suburbs, and by further protecting herself from recognizing her own tacit complicity in anti-Semitism. Without a doubt her tacit complicity would have become apparent to her, would have defeated her every self-denial, if she had persuaded Phil to conceal feigning to be Jewish to avoid "a thing, a mess, an inconvenience," as she had also justified her sister's wish that his series angle remain unknown to her friends, who could not have helped revealing their anti-Semitic biases at Jane's party.

Yet Kathy could continue to postpone self-awareness of her tacit implication in anti-Semitism only by remaining entirely within her own community, whose every overt anti-Semitic act she silently disapproved of would function to assure her of her own innocence of prejudice. This, however, is precisely what she is unable to do. Being attached to Phil, who in his dual roles as the developing difference image and avatar of art and aesthetic reason advances the process of reconciliation, she cannot avoid what Todorov describes as that "plunge into otherness" through which "self-knowledge is possible."[8] Not only everything Phil represents but everyone with whom he is acquainted through his dual roles potentially enters the world he shares with Kathy as a possible alternative standpoint external to her community from which she could be forced to engage in self-reflection. And it is Kathy's inescapable vulnerability to this shared world of difference outside her own community and identity that becomes visible during two events that will clarify the identity image as they leave her defenseless against being shocked into self-awareness of being anti-Semitic.

When they learn Dave has decided to give up his job opportunity and his family's "whole future" in New York after he runs up against a wall of anti-Semitic prejudice refusing him housing, Phil suggests Kathy rent Dave the cottage she built in Darien as a solution to his friend's difficulty. Believing she is championing Dave's best interest, Kathy argues, "It wouldn't work. . . . It would just be too uncomfortable for Dave knowing he's moved into one of those neighborhoods." She insistently asks Phil, "Don't you see that? It's detestable, but that's the way it is. It's even worse in New Canaan. There nobody can sell or rent to a Jew. And even in Darien, where Jane's and my house is, there's a sort of gentleman's agreement." She struggles to refute Phil's contention that by imploring him to "face facts" that Dave would only be ostracized, denied delivery of food and even service by markets, she is "just going to give in, play along . . . not fight it." Kathy finally provokes Phil into threatening to end their relationship once and for all by declaring that she could not possibly "expect [her and Phil] to live in that cottage once [she] know[s]" how he feels about her, that she is likely anti-Semitic. In fact, that is how she interprets his disapproval of her reaction to his son, Tommy, who in tears interrupts their discussion to report having been bullied by school peers calling him a "dirty Jew and a stinking kike." Once again believing she is responding to anti-Semitism with words defining her as its opponent, Kathy comforts Tommy by repeating a version of what she often has said to Phil: "It's not true. . . . You're no more Jewish than I am. . . . It's just a horrible mistake."

If Phil's past criticisms had made Kathy even the least reflective about her possible implication in the anti-Semitism she thought she opposed, she would have known better than to palliate Tommy's victimization by con-structing his experience in a way proving Phil's suspicions true. After consol-ing his son he directly contradicts Kathy by praising him for not denying he is Jewish to those who bullied him, explaining, "There are kids just like you who are Jewish and, if you said [you weren't], it would be sort of admitting there was something bad to being Jewish and swell in not." Kathy should have known too that her construction would draw Phil's declaration that the "big-gest discovery . . . about this whole business" of anti-Semitism was that "the people who despise it and protest their own innocence help it along and then wonder why it grows . . . the good people, the nice people."

Now it is here that the narrative of *Gentleman's Agreement* and its reconcili-ation image can be argued to have each developed to the point where they can part company and move in different directions. From here my argument has two very distinct sides.

There is first *the narrative point of view*. Through the conflicts between Kathy and Phil surrounding the cottage and especially about Tommy's un-derstanding of his being bullied, the narrative point of view is entirely fleshed out and the narrative achieves closure. Neither of the two conflicts, though particularly the latter, leaves any room for confusion or doubt about the tacit anti-Semitism they prove Kathy has been guilty of through all her many rationalizations, self-deceptions, and denials accompanying her earlier dis-agreements with Phil. From the standpoint of the narrative, then, the scene that follows, a final confrontation between Kathy and Phil, is only a dramatic recapitulation of the now crystallized narrative point of view, whose explicit portrayal of tacit anti-Semitism in the image of Kathy the film's viewers can now easily determine how closely they resemble. Immediately following Phil's praise of his son for courageously identifying with the Jewish victim he willingly accepted being mistaken for, an indignant Kathy challenges her implication in anti-Semitism Phil brought to light by criticizing her construction of Tom-my's victimization. Declaring she is "pretty tired of feeling wrong," that "every-thing" she does or says "about anything Jewish is wrong," that she "know[s] what [Phil is] thinking about marrying" her because she "saw it on [his] face when [she] said *that* to Tom," she demands Phil not "treat [her] to any more lessons of tolerance," for she "is sick of it." Interrupting Kathy's tirade at one point, Phil explains that it is not just "what" she told Tommy; it was the felt affirmation her explanation of his experience with anti-Semitism had offered his son: "[That] he's the most wonderful of all creatures, a white Christian American. You instantly gave him that lovely taste of superiority, the poison that millions of parents drop into the minds of millions of children."

Thus, despite Phil's denying that he had suspected "secretly for a long time" she was an anti-Semite, their conflict about how Tommy should interpret his schoolyard encounter with hate convinced Phil of her tacit implication in anti-Semitism. Nevertheless, however unlikely their somewhat violent recapitulation of the film's narrative point of view makes it seem, Kathy and Phil must—and do—in the end find their way back to one another after Dave, in a subsequent discussion with Kathy, helps her to finally achieve self-awareness of being tacitly implicated in what she once in good faith described as "this awful thing." So the principle to which the film's narrative point of view *narrowly leads* is the lesson Kathy bitterly complained to Phil she was "sick of": *the lesson of tolerance,* which Kathy's arranging for Dave and his family to move into her cottage in anti-Semitic Darien, Phil's subsequent forgiveness, and their marriage proves she has learned at last.

But there is second *the point of view of the reconciliation image. Gentleman's Agreement* has culminated not only in a point of view narrowing the unfolding of its narrative possibilities to the political lesson of tolerance. At the climactic moment when Phil contradicts Kathy's explanation of how Tommy should have responded to his victimizers, the process of thinking out the reconciliation image also completes itself.[9] The identity and difference images have been fully formed, and with their appearance the all-inclusive, receptivity, and imitative images rapidly follow in turn. With Phil's praise of his son, the transparency of Kathy's bias reveals the tacitly anti-Semitic identity of her image, while the scene that follows affixes a name to the face, rooting the identity image's claim to superiority in her racialized Christian nationalism. What definition the difference image lacked at this stage is supplied by Tommy's courage, in light of which his father is able to articulate his and his son's identification with Jewish difference, and also by Tommy's trauma, which by subjecting Phil to the most terrifying feature of anti-Semitism—violence to family members and their possible extermination—completes his image of the Jew as the other.

It is at this same moment when Phil fills out the difference image that the three remaining images belonging to the reconciliation image come into view. Having become fully different in the image of difference, Phil's feigning Jewishness is transformed into his imitation of Jewishness. The non-Jew has become a Jew. Moreover, with the unfolding of the imitative image the all-inclusive and receptivity images retrospectively materialize. For the Jew who through imitation Phil has finally become was incipiently included all along as the developing image of Jewishness itself, as the incipient all-inclusive image of difference. It was that incipient image of difference that he feigned out of his receptivity to becoming different in the image of difference in order to investigate what Foucault called the will to truth—the will to exclude, marginalize, discriminate against, exterminate difference. If there were any doubt about this transformation Phil has undergone through the reconciliation image he represents, it is erased by Kathy's maddened recognition of his becoming different. "You've changed since I first met you. . . . Now I know why I drew back when you told me the angle [of your investigation. By changing,] you're doing an impossible thing! You are what you are for the one life you have."

THE RECONCILIATION IMAGE

At this point it appears that reconciliation rather than tolerance may be the aesthetic and political event toward which the images of *Gentleman's Agreement* are moving. Still, despite his metamorphosis, Phil's incarnation of the reconciliation image is imperfect. For though in the course of the film he becomes different in the image of difference, the non-Jew becoming a Jew, at the opening of the film his identity lacks definition. Appearing to us first in the role of a journalist and soon after in the role of journalist as a Jew, he is more a role bearer than the bearer of an identity, which remains hidden behind his roles and cannot be reliably inferred from any role he plays. We cannot deny, of course, that Phil's gradual identification with what it means to be Jewish is profound. I should rather say, then, that as the developing difference image, from the outset of the film he becomes increasingly different, though *not as an identity become different* representing his reconciliation with difference. "Identityless" according to the criteria to be met by the identity image, Phil's becoming different in the image of difference can at best offer an incomplete representation of the qualitative changes belonging to the reconciliation image, and is thus an underdeveloped model of reconciliation.

Kathy, to the contrary, however, presents an identity image whose power even exceeds that measured by her perverse resistance to the possibility implied in her encounters with Phil that she is tacitly anti-Semitic. When, in that final confrontation with Phil that all but destroyed their relationship, she reviles as an "impossible thing" his determination to evolve beyond what she naïvely defended as the one identity you inherit "for the one life you have" to live, she also allows us a glimpse of the discursive regime from which her impervious, immobile identity and its politics were born:

> You can't help it if you were born Christian instead of Jewish. It doesn't mean you're glad you were. But I am glad. There. I've said it. It'd be terrible. I'm glad I'm not [Jewish]. I could never make you understand that. You could never understand that it's a fact like being glad you're good-looking instead of ugly, rich instead of poor, young instead of old, healthy instead of sick. You could never understand that. It's just a practical fact, not a judgment that I'm superior. But I could never make you see that. You'd twist it into something horrible, a conniving, an aiding and abetting a thing that I loathe as much as you do.

As muddled as is Kathy's argument for her stunning innocence of the social construction of identity, it explains why she persists in claiming not to be anti-Semitic while being guilty of tacit anti-Semitism. Underlying her argument are crude positivist assumptions explaining both. Believing in the unassailably factual, unalterable givenness of identities at birth, for Kathy it follows that the conditions of either being or not being victimized are likewise given and immutable. While for Kathy to be Christian by birth is to be lucky to have escaped being born Jewish and the victim of anti-Semitism, it is to wrongly believe that, the conditions of birth being falsely presumed by her to dictate our fate, nothing can be done to ameliorate it, as "it's just a practical fact."

So although she is not *overtly* anti-Semitic, as the learned positivism she parrots and her sincerely expressed loathing of it explain, Kathy *tacitly* supports anti-Semitism according to that selfsame logic. She does so when she reminds Phil and Tommy that, since they "are no more Jewish than [she is]," they should not and need not be victimized, which would be "just a horrible mistake." And she does so when, to avoid the messiness of complicating her relationship with her family and her family's relationships with their friends, she refrains from introducing a Jew, her fiancé, into their presence. But since, for the positivist Kathy, these biases are grounded in the existential givens of identity and birth, she can persuade herself of her innocence of anti-Semitism while being tacitly guilty of it at the same time.[10] Hence, in view of Phil's imperfect representation of the reconciliation image, the question for us is this: Can an identity such as Kathy's, whose tacit anti-Semitic behavior rests on unreflectively learned and held positivist assumptions, which are as falsely representative of Christianity as they are of Judaism in their construction of difference as otherness, be reconciled with difference?

In the aftermath of her final confrontation with Phil, it is Kathy who initiates the discussion with Dave from which she becomes self-aware of her implication in anti-Semitism and learns the political lesson of tolerance, *both of which will now appear as narrative moments subordinate to the lessons taught by the reconciliation image.* Desperate to prove she is not anti-Semitic, Kathy looks to Dave to answer the question she is certain Phil has already answered in the affirmative: "Do you think I'm anti-Semitic?" Upon hearing Dave's assurances he does not believe her to be, Kathy declares, "You know I'm not anti-Semitic. *You're a Jew and you know it.*"

Their exchange exemplifies the receptivity image, Kathy's openness to difference resting on her conviction that a Jew could answer the question she needs definitively answered. Yet Dave's answer offers her more than assurances as he elaborates by helping her to understand the reasons for her crisis. After Kathy confides her private feelings of anger and disgust along with her silent disapproval of an anti-Semitic joke told at a dinner party, Dave's impatience with her morally superior feelings of being innocent of prejudice brings him to the point where he explains that opposing anti-Semitism requires public as well as private opposition. Then, sensing the genesis of her crisis lies within an identity whose core is constructed as rigidly positivist as we found, Dave urges her to consider an alternative image of the self that will lead her down the path of imitation. As Kathy, attentive to his arguments, turns from self-righteousness to self-recrimination as she becomes aware of her silent complicity with anti-Semitism, Dave adds, "You're not caste in bronze. . . . You're . . . *pliable*, and you can do anything you have to do or want to do with yourself."

When Dave is next seen he has returned to Phil's apartment to telephone his future employer of his decision to accept his offer, remain in New York, and live in Kathy's cottage while she takes up residence at her sister's nearby home to ensure Dave and his family are not victimized by Darien's anti-Semites. She has learned tolerance, which invites thought of the image of the all-inclusiveness of difference. But tolerance and the image of the all-inclusiveness of difference *are secondary to, indeed the effects of* the dominant imitative image that Dave's urging Kathy to see herself as pliable imagines beforehand and that leads *beyond tolerance to reconciliation*—to Kathy's becoming different in the image of difference as she sheds her tacit anti-Semitism, first through her identification with Jews whose battle for a home she makes her own, then by setting her neighborhood in motion toward becoming Jewish in part by providing Dave and his family with her cottage.

Must it at this point be added that the reconciliation image Kathy represents avoids the illusion there remain no differences with which identity has yet to be reconciled? She was but one anti-Semite; Dave's but one family of Jews. Together they represent the dual temporalities of the rationality of the whole of the reconciliation image as a time arrived and a time yet to come, as the image of reconciliation and of reconciliation as the continuous striving for an unattainable ideal.

POSSIBLE POLITICS

Visualizing the possible politics of becoming different in the image of difference, we see that *the reconciliation image projects an alternative narrative to the story line narrowly culminating in the politics of tolerance.* In a social context such as that of a white Christian anti-Semitic American suburb, tolerance of Jews, to draw upon Connolly's formulation of tolerance, "becomes forbearance toward cultural practices thought to be intrinsically wrong or inferior."[11] To the contrary, Kathy's receptive and imitative orientation to Jewish difference acknowledges as equal to her own cultural practices those on which she strives to re-create her identity. Recall her receptivity to Dave, who as a Jew she believed to be qualified to answer the question most troubling her. And recall when she understood his answer her subsequent efforts to change the complexion of her Darien neighborhood to ensure, if only in part, it becomes Jewish, in other words to ensure it too becomes in part different in the image of difference she herself has more or less become.

Of course, we are surprised to see Kathy rather than Phil, as we had expected all along, emerge rather explosively as the film's vehicle of aesthetic education, enlightenment, and reconciliation. Yet this is now easily explained. Certainly it is its rigidity, though *also* its pairing with the prevailing norms of modern democratic society, that makes Kathy's identity the better measure of the power of the reconciliation image to overcome the construction of difference as otherness. As she several times announces during the course of the film, beginning with her boast that it was she who proposed the idea of the series on anti-Semitism to her *Smith's Weekly* uncle-editor, Kathy is committed to the universal democratic principles of equality, rights, and freedoms inimical to violence toward difference. So although she held to a positivist interpretation of Christian identity immunizing her against developing a self-awareness of her tacit anti-Semitism, this "ontological closure of Christian culture," as Connolly describes it, that lay at the core of her identity was "fractured" by her secular democratic principles.[12] To be sure, once Dave persuaded Kathy it is her failure to speak out against anti-Semitism that helps perpetuate it, her desire to reconcile her identity with difference points to her having rejected her belief in her advantageous cultural position as an accident of Christian birth. Reconciliation, it appears, was Kathy's way of overcoming her tacitly lived drive of violence toward difference, which the universal democratic principles in which she also believed helped make it possible for her to reject.[13]

So as I earlier stressed, *Gentleman's Agreement*, as *The Help* also proved to be, is thus an illustration of Adorno's "dialectic of rationality and mimesis," of the elements of the modern artwork he thought to be among the most salient to its production of the reconciliation image. We watched as the relationship between Kathy and Phil developed through just such a dialectic, which unfolded in serial images of attractions and oppositions determining their relationship's evolution, its tensions, breakdowns, and renewals, its near dissolution and their final reunion. Yet it was not simply the structure of their relationship that this dialectic shaped. At the film's most fundamental level it determined *movement itself*, the very creative movement of the identity and difference, all-inclusive, receptivity, and imitative images toward the reconciliation image.

Hence in Kathy's representation of the identity image, whose rationality was rigidly defined through her construction of Jews as the other, we see exemplified what Adorno described as aesthetic identity's creative mimetic movement toward the heterogeneous, the nonidentical, difference. And while through Kathy's positivist defense of her identity its rationality threatened to terminate once and for all in an unreflective commitment to her particular construction of difference as otherness, which would have arrested mimetic movement beyond the creation of her identity image, as our film's images continued to unfold by means of their dialectic the relationship between identity and difference shaped and propelled her identity image's motion anew. Through the oppositional movement of Phil's difference image and its trope in the interpolating figure of Dave, then through the opposition of Kathy's universalistic values to her parochial allegiances, the creative mimetic movement of Kathy's identity image was reignited, leading to her identity's eventual reconstitution in the image of difference. Thus the rationality of *Gentleman's Agreement*, when understood in Adorno's terms as the dialectic of rationality and mimesis, is aesthetic, and just as it does in modern artworks aesthetic rationality issues here in the production of the reconciliation image in film.

With one decisive difference, however. For Adorno, we recall, modern artworks' movement toward reconciliation is arrested by their "historical afterlife," by interpretations, commentaries, and critiques fixing their meaning and significance as unchanging and eternal. Whatever else they may be from an aesthetic-theoretical standpoint, as such illusory images of reconciliation artworks then serve as ideological handmaidens for existing societies whose violence toward difference is ruled by instrumental reason, the offspring of the enlightenment of modern times. But we must also remember that in *Aesthetic Theory* Adorno importantly added that artworks whose motion had been paralyzed by their historical afterlife "*may* once again enter into motion" *if* they are in "equilibrium." *If*, that is, as were *The Help* and *Gentleman's Agreement*, they are animated by aesthetic reason's dialectic of rationality and mimesis, by the elements of aesthetic reason governing the relationship of equilibrium that is the aesthetic precondition for the continuous motion of modern artworks toward reconciliation.

Still, neither in *Aesthetic Theory* nor elsewhere does Adorno address the problem of *how* artworks that remain in a state of equilibrium may again enter into motion once it has been arrested by their historical afterlife, so they may again resume their movement toward the creation of images of reconciliation. What Adorno does allow us to understand, though, is that it was not the artwork per se but our *aesthetic experience* of the artwork that to begin with unlocked the artwork's movement of aesthetic reason toward reconciliation. This means it is not actually motion internal to the modern artwork that is directly arrested by its historical afterlife. Quite the contrary, it is our ability to aesthetically experience the artwork in a way that sets it into motion that its historical afterlife disables.

With regard to the creation of the reconciliation image, then, we arrive at the superiority of the aesthetics and politics of film over the modern artwork through a solution to the problem Adorno failed to address. Film is *already* in motion—it is the artwork understood as "motion pictures," as I have argued in several earlier chapters. Discovering the reconciliation image in film thus ceases to be a question of our aesthetic experience of the artwork, whose motion as it is mechanically reproduced in film is now independent of all such aesthetic experience Adorno theorized is required to set the work of art into motion to produce the reconciliation image. It is rather a question of aesthetic education, of what political lessons the artwork as pictures already in motion can teach us, thus of democratic enlightenment, the possibility of discovering the reconciliation image and its possible politics in film.

Utopia would be beyond identity and beyond contradiction, a togetherness of differences.
—Theodor W. Adorno, *Negative Dialektik*

7
....

The Reconciliation Image in Film as Universal Art Form

Taken together, *The Help* and *Gentleman's Agreement* offer us two different forms of the reconciliation image, each film modeling the image in a unique way. From its opening images *The Help* displays the reconciliation image as a well thought-out order of perceptual substitution whose constituent images fluently and lucidly emerge from the film's narrative to project a possible politics, the possibility of reconciliation, a far more radical, alternative political narrative to the politics of the film's scripted narrative driven by the white savior trope. *Gentleman's Agreement* also models the reconciliation image, though only after its scripted narrative's laboriously constructed episodes visibly strain to develop and clarify constituent images from which the alternative narrative of the reconciliation image and its possible politics will be climactically produced as the film's fixed narrative concludes.

Precisely why each reconciliation image must be narratively thought-out in its own unique way becomes apparent when *The Help* and *Gentleman's Agreement* are juxtaposed with one another to highlight the distinct form of violence peculiar to each. In contrast with *The Help*'s portrayal of racism, tacit anti-Semitism appears all the more subterranean, nebulous, and pusillanimous, and for all these reasons an unwittingly nurtured violence that is perhaps deathless. In juxtaposition with the depiction of tacit anti-Semitism in *Gentleman's Agreement*, racism appears all the more conspicuous and transparent, brazen, confident, and effortlessly brutal through its straightforward violence toward its victims. While neither film implies that either form of violence is more or less serious than the other, through their investigations of the contrasting levels of complexity of tacit anti-Semitic and manifest racist violence our films together show why the reconciliation image must be so laboriously thought-out over the course of *Gentleman's Agreement* and why it can be so efficiently and precisely thought-out in *The Help* from its opening image. As models of aesthetic education, *The Help* and *Gentleman's Agreement* are two genres of the reconciliation image in film that are thought-out and unfold in conformance with their various portrayals of identity's specific constructions of difference as otherness in which singular types of violence toward difference are rooted. Films of violence against racial and religious-ethnic differences, they join those genres concerned with discrete types of violence toward differences of gender, sexual orientation, class, intellectual capacities, physical capabilities, mental and psychological health, and so on.

According to the films I have examined, then, especially when viewed in relation to one another, what proves to be highly distinctive about the genre of a film's reconciliation image, indeed one of its defining elements, is the way its constituent images, especially its identity and difference images, must necessarily be narratively thought-out in order to illuminate the particular form of violence inflicted by one group on another. Though not only its type of violence but in addition how each film's reconciliation image models Whitman's and Adorno's dual temporalities. As a time arrived and a time yet to come, reconciliation depends on how its identity, difference, all-inclusive, receptivity, and imitative images are thought-out so that reconciliation unfolds as the alternative narrative to the dominant narrative of the film from which it was born, unfolds in its cinematic form as the "event" in Deleuze's sense, as identity's endlessly becoming different in the image of difference, a becoming different that has always just happened and is always about to happen.[1]

Variously thought-out reconciliation images appear in numerous other popular films. To name but a very few, *Pride, Tootsie, Dirty Dancing, Forest Gump, My Left Foot,* and *The Soloist* all belong to genres of the reconciliation image distinguished from one another by their studies of identity's particular constructions of difference as the other and the way their reconciliation events unfold.[2] For every genre of the reconciliation image so distinguished, moreover, there are in each genre countless varying images of identity and difference, of identity's forms of violence toward difference, of all-inclusiveness, receptivity, and imitation, of multiple and even overlapping and parallel dual temporalities, all originating in films from which narratives of reconciliation are produced by reconciliation images as differently thought-out as in *The Help* and *Gentleman's Agreement*.

Despite what we know to be its narrower narrative interests, film thus includes genres of the reconciliation image corresponding to a virtually endless diversity of differences constructed as forms of otherness and their reconciliation events. To think about the reconciliation image in film in this way is to broach the question whether it approximates a universal art form by virtue of the universality of differences and their events of reconciliation it models. This is the question I finally want to explore for how it bears on the reconciliation image in film as the vehicle of aesthetic education.

SCHILLER'S UNIVERSAL ART FORM

Throughout the early modern period that Schiller's work stands at the end of, in addition to the creation of new arts there had been an explosion of new aesthetic forms in all the arts. Schiller, I believe, must have imagined these new art forms individually and together modeled the play impulse's unlimited aesthetic capacity for mediating humanity's formal and sensuous-receptive faculties' equally boundless potential for apprehending the diversity of forms of life. For at their highest level of development, he argues in his "Twenty-Second Letter," the arts, and he focuses on music, poetry, and sculpture, *exceed* their "special [*besondren*] affinities" for particular senses and sensibilities. Music's rapport with the ear, poetry's organic framing of parts as wholes (as Aristotle thinks of epics and tragedies, he likely means), sculpture's sensuous immediacy, in other words each art's sensuously specialized creative use of form, "will disappear," he declares, as all the arts "tend to become ever more like each other in their effect upon the mind [*auf das Gemüt*]."[3] Rather than only what can be heard by the ear, like poetry (*der Antike*, Antiquity) music in addition must become oriented to the senses as a whole (*Gestalt*); sculpture (*die Plastik*, the plastic arts), which electrifies us "by the immediacy of [its] sensuous presence," must also "move us" like music; and poetry must add to its affects those of music and sculpture.[4]

But of exactly what significance is it for Schiller that as the arts evolve new and ever more sensuously receptive aesthetic forms they do so by coming to resemble each other, so that to each art's affect and its effect upon us are added the affects and effects of every other art? Or more to Schiller's point, what does it mean to think of the arts as each developing a similar effect upon the mind?

It is only in the first instance, at their earlier stages of development, it seems, that the arts are simplistically representational, each art imitating life according to its own peculiar aesthetic affinities with particular senses and sensibilities. Far more radically, we have just learned, as the arts are perfected, so that each art, by resembling every other art, imitates not life but rather art imitating life, then art, as Schiller adds, acquires a "more universal [*allgemeinen*] character."[5] With every art imitating every other art's mode of imitation, art imitating art imitating life, as I put it, hence each art eventually resembling all the arts combined, Schiller means, whether each art is taken separately or all are taken together, art's "effect upon the mind" is to model play's unlimited potential for mentoring our boundless aesthetic capacities for being receptive to and imitating *all* the world's diversity of differences. Such an "all"—as we recall Whitman imagined in *Democratic Vistas*—would be a geopolitically borderless "all" also inclusive of differences originally constructed by the European Enlightenment as its subaltern others.

With this formulation of a universal art form, in his "Twenty-Sixth Letter" Schiller proceeds to solve the problem his *Letters*' reflections on the aesthetics of reconciliation were preoccupied with, beginning with his "Twelfth Letter." His problem was to conceptualize "play" as a mediating impulse enabling reason to form the world's diversity of differences the senses apprehend, without form inflicting violence on difference by constructing it as other than it is. Simply put, Schiller's problem was to reconcile identity and difference. Schiller's solution, which artworks are to teach us, is to conceive of the play impulse as "the shaping spirit of imitation," which treats "appearance as something self-sufficient [*Selbständiges*]."[6] As the shaping *spirit* of imitation, play shapes as little as possible by sensuously perceiving appearances as having an *autonomous* form *apart* from the forms reason perceives them as having prior to play's reconciling form and sense. And what is Schiller's exemplar of such a sense able to perceive in such a shaping spirit? Once we "begin to enjoy through the eye, and seeing acquires for [us] a value of its own, [we are] already aesthetically free and the play-drive has started to develop."[7] A universal art form, an art form taking in the entirety of the world's diversity of different appearances, productive of images of reconciliation treating difference as self-sufficient in itself, as having an autonomous life and form independent of the form reason gives it, is based on the eye. Such a universal art form is visual.

Schiller's ideal of a universal visual art form thus corresponds to the idea that genres of the reconciliation image in film are potentially as diverse as forms of difference themselves. For Schiller, as we have seen, art's universal character meant that as the arts increasingly imitated one another, an art would develop whose aesthetic form and sensuous relationship to the world would enable it to reproduce all the forms and all the senses of all the arts it collectively resembled, "remov[ing]," Schiller concluded, its "specific limitations" and those limitations of the arts it imitated without "destroying" all their "specific qualities" of excellence.[8] No longer would the world's infinite diversity of differences be narrowly apprehended through the "limitations" of an art's particular form and particular sensuous relationship to the world, thus omitting or misapprehending what is different about difference. Based on art imitating the arts' imitations of life, a universal art form's synthesis of all aesthetic forms, together with their collective sensuous openness to the world, would equal the one aesthetic form able to form appearances just as appearances were sensuously received in all their self-sufficient diversity of differences. Schiller's universal art form would thus accomplish precisely what film accomplishes through its potential for accommodating the universality of differences' genres. Only such a universal art form as film is able to model Schiller's ideal of reconciling identity and difference in all its forms.

Of course, Schiller's premonition of art realizing such a universal aesthetic form through the visual arts concurs with Whitman's practice of writing poetry to create visual images. Resembling—*imitating*—a visual art without becoming a visual art, Whitman's poetry retains the "specific qualities" of verse, while its visual images overcome the "specific limitations" of the word he found was not equal to the epistemic task of conceptualizing truth, which allowed him to create a poetry oriented to appearances and their differences that found their natural home in visual images. By writing poetry to create visual images Whitman anticipates film, as I proposed at the close of my second chapter, specifically the reconciliation image in film. Finally, to draw Whitman even nearer the spirit of Schiller's idea of a universal art form created from its imitation of other arts, in our time film is considered to be a plastic art, as is the painting and sculpture and photography it resembles.

As all this now falls into place—Schiller's aesthetic theory of a universal visual art form modeling reconciliation through its imitation of all the arts' creative play of all aesthetic forms through all the senses; Whitman's verse modeling the ideal of reconciliation through poetry's capacity to imitate visual images' imitations of life; and the reconciliation image in film, heir to Schiller's universal visual art form by possibilizing reconciliation for potentially endless genres of difference—there is yet an outlier argument not to be neglected. To recall my earlier discussion, though also to add to it, Adorno not only opposes the idea of the reconciliation image in film. More fundamentally he opposes the idea of art imitating art. "All music," he insists, "purports a becoming," whereas music imitating painting—for example "the development of a spatial perspective in music is much rather a testimony of a pseudomorphism [a false form] of painting in music"—would only relinquish music's power to model reconciliation.[9]

But to Adorno's argument I countered with another. *Thinking with* Adorno *against* Adorno, I emancipated his image of reconciliation from its narrow confinement to modern art, to flesh it out and further develop it in painting to be able to then discover it in film, which means, taking what I have learned from Schiller, that film would not only be a universal art form because unlimited possible forms of difference found their genres of the reconciliation image in film. Film also becomes universal by imitating other arts, namely painting as it appears in light of my reading of Adorno's aesthetic theory. All this—the reconciliation image as a universal art form through poetry, painting, and film—is the fruit of an alliance between Whitman and Adorno whose possibility I formulated in my introduction. In a sentence, the reconciliation image in film may prove to be a universal media of aesthetic education, whose pedagogy aspires to enlightenment in Whitman's "democratic" sense and in Adorno's "positive" sense, aspires to an interchangeable democratic and positive enlightenment.

BEYOND IDENTITY, BEYOND CONTRADICTION

Supposing, in the end, that Whitman's democratic enlightenment and Adorno's positive enlightenment are interchangeable, let me finish on the note where I began in my opening chapter, knowing now that Adorno's reconciliation image must be no less present than Whitman's in this final thought.

Aesthetic education as Whitman imagined it in *Democratic Vistas*, its pedagogical work to be carried out through poetry, was no doubt intended to nurture in its highly imperfect democratic readers a democratic sensibility. Working on them within the private sphere, within the womb of civil society beneath the threshold of politics and the law, this democratic sensibility would achieve what religions and their priests and applications of morals and the law could never achieve: the reconciliation of identity and difference. Whitman's democratic sensibility assumed an aesthetic form, and its aesthetic form was mimetic, so that what its work of art created, a "myself," was owed to the imitation of everything different, human though also nonhuman, surrounding and tending inward toward this myself as this myself tended outward toward everything around it. Hence the astonishing fifteenth and sixteenth verses of "Song of Myself," Whitman's endless list of those he mentioned and strove to mention—"And you each and everywhere whom I specify not but include just the same!," as he wrote in "Salut Au Monde!"—the infinite diversity of differences he would imitate. Though only more or less.

If, like Whitman, we would seek to become reconciled with difference, to become different in the image of difference, to engage in a democratic becoming that begins with the recognition of difference having a self-sufficient meaning independent of identity and of how easily and readily identity violates difference, let us learn about imitation by following Whitman's paths. For when we do we are led from the visual image of reconciliation created by his poetry to the reconciliation image in film, and from the reconciliation image in film we are at last led to the possibility of reconciliation itself that film's reconciliation image teaches, to the once but no longer "utopian" moment to which art had led Adorno, the moment "beyond identity and beyond contradiction, to a togetherness of differences." Together, Schiller, Whitman, Adorno, and film ask us to imagine a community of differences aesthetically created through democratic becoming, thus to reimagine identity as an identity of differences.

NOTES
....

INTRODUCTION

1. Henri Bergson, *Creative Evolution* (Mineola, NY: Dover, 1998), 106.

2. Here, of course, my reference is to Tocqueville's famous critique of American individualism in the second volume of *Democracy in America II*, trans. Henry Reeve, with revisions by Francis Bowen and Phillips Bradley (New York: Knopf, 1997), 98–99.

3. See Tzvétan Todorov, *On Human Diversity: Nationalism, Racism, and Exoticism in French Thought*, trans. Catherine Porter (Cambridge, MA: Harvard University Press, 1993), 1. After a preface that Todorov concludes by saying, "And now our serious work can begin," he begins his book with the words, "Human diversity is infinite."

4. Walt Whitman, "Preface, 1872," to "A Strong Bird on Pinions Free," in *Whitman: Prose and Poetry* (New York: Library of America, 1996), 1028, Whitman's italics. Hereafter *WPP*.

5. Walt Whitman, "Song of Myself," in *Leaves of Grass*, ed. Sculley Bradley and Harold W. Blodgett (New York: Norton, 1973), 44, line 328. Hereafter *LG*. I use the Norton Critical Edition whenever I cite Whitman's poetry as it allows me to note the numbers of the lines of the verse quoted or cited.

6. Max Horkheimer and Theodor W. Adorno, *Dialectic of Enlightenment: Philosophical Fragments*, ed. Gunzelin S. Noerr, trans. Edmund Jephcott (Stanford, CA: Stanford University Press, 2002), xviii. First published in German as *Dialektik der Aufklarung* (Amsterdam, 1947); reprinted in 1969 by Fischer Verlag with a new preface by its authors.

7. Gilles Deleuze, *Cinema 1: The Movement-Image*, trans. Hugh Tomlinson and Barbara Habberjam (Minneapolis: University of Minnesota Press, 2003), 214.

8. Henri Bergson, *Matter and Memory*, trans. Nancy Margaret Paul and W. Scott Palmer (Mineola, NY: Dover, 2004), 173.

9. Voltaire, "Des Langues," in *Collection Complette des Oeuvres de Mr. de Voltaire*, book 4 (Geneva: Cramer Printing, 1756); Voltaire, *Melanges de Poesies, de Litterature, d'Histoire et de Philosophie* (n.p., 1761), 12.

10. Under the title *Dictionnaire Philosophique*, the Kehl edition combines Voltaire's *Questions about the Encyclopedia* with his *Reason by the Alphabet*, the 1769 definitive edition of his earlier *Dictionnaire philosophique portatif*, along with a number of shorter texts. I am very grateful to Gillian Pink of the Voltaire Foundation at Oxford University for clarification of bibliographical sources. The entirety of the three sections of the essay "Langues" is available from the University of Ottawa online collection of the Kehl edition, *Oeuvres Completes de Voltaire*, vol. 53 (Kehl: De l'Imprimerie de la Société Littéraire-Typographique, 1785), 152–87, which is the seventh volume of Voltaire's posthumous *Dictionnaire Philosophique*.

11. As Voltaire has been appropriately described by Karen O'Brien, *Narratives of Enlightenment: Cosmopolitan History from Voltaire to Gibbon* (Cambridge: Cambridge University Press, 1997), 21.

12. Arthur M. Wilson, *Diderot* (New York: Oxford University Press, 1972), 242.

13. Daniel Brewer, *The Discourse on Enlightenment in Eighteenth-Century France: Diderot and the Art of Philosophizing* (Cambridge: Cambridge University Press, 1993), 4. My discussion of Brewer's work summarizes major points of his introduction and first four chapters pertinent to my discussion of Diderot, enlightenment, and the visual image.

14. Brewer, *The Discourse on Enlightenment in Eighteenth-Century France*, 22, 4.

15. Brewer, *The Discourse on Enlightenment in Eighteenth-Century France*, 26.

16. Michel Foucault, *The Order of Things: An Archaeology of the Human Sciences* (New York: Vintage Books, 1973), 9–10.

17. Denis Diderot, *Letter on the Deaf and Dumb*, in *Diderot's Early Philosophical Works*, trans. and ed. Margaret Jourdain (Chicago: Open Court, 1916), 173. Original publication date of Diderot's *Letter on the Deaf and Dumb* was 1751.

18. As quoted by Brewer, "Un coup d'oeil sur l'objet ou sur sa représentation en dit plus qu'une page de discours" (*The Discourse on Enlightenment in Eighteenth-Century France*, 25).

19. Brewer, *The Discourse on Enlightenment in Eighteenth-Century France*, 148, 26, 32.

20. J. C. F. von Schiller, *On the Aesthetic Education of Humanity in a Series of Letters* (*Über die ästhetische Erziehung des Menschen in einer Reihe von Briefen*), ed. and trans. E. M. Wilkinson and L. A. Willoughby (Oxford: Oxford University Press, 2005); first published in 1795. Hereafter *Letters*. For two reasons I take the liberty of translating "Menschen" as "humanity" rather than "man" or "mankind" as has been the standard practice. By today's gender-neutral cultural standards the former is a more correct description of those whom Schiller seeks to educate. He also uses "humanity" often throughout his *Letters* as a synonym for "man," "mankind," "mankind as a whole." And as I make clear in my discussion of Schiller, humanity—its diversity, capacity to realize diverse forms of social life, and ability to achieve the reconciliation of identity and difference—is the central concern of Schiller's

Letters, which has not been fully appreciated in literature foregrounding art and aesthetics in Schiller's text.

21. Schiller, *Letters*, 7, 9 ("Second Letter"); 25 ("Fifth Letter"); 45 ("Seventh Letter"); 219 ("Twenty-Seventh Letter").
22. Schiller, *Letters*, 27 ("Fifth Letter"; trans. changed; my italics).
23. Schiller, *Letters*, 193, 195 ("Twenty-Sixth Letter"; trans. changed).
24. Schiller, *Letters*, 7 ("Second Letter").
25. Schiller, *Letters*, 25, 27, 29 ("Fifth Letter").
26. Schiller, *Letters*, 25 ("Fifth Letter"; trans. changed).
27. Schiller, *Letters*, 11 ("Third Letter"; trans. changed).
28. Schiller, *Letters*, 25 ("Fifth Letter"; trans. changed).
29. Schiller, *Letters*, 77 ("Eleventh Letter"). On Schiller's ancient Greek exceptionalism, see his "Sixth Letter," 31–43, especially paragraphs 2, 3, 5(!), 7, 11.
30. Schiller, *Letters*, 73 ("Eleventh Letter"; trans. changed); 79, 81 ("Twelfth Letter").
31. Schiller, *Letters*, 5 ("First Letter"; trans. changed).
32. Schiller, *Letters*, 5 ("First Letter"; my italics).
33. Schiller, *Letters*, 5 ("First Letter"; trans. changed; my italics).
34. Schiller, *Letters*, 37 ("Sixth Letter"; trans. changed).
35. Schiller, *Letters*, 33 ("Sixth Letter"; trans. changed).
36. Schiller, *Letters*, 75–77 ("Eleventh Letter"; my italics).
37. Schiller, *Letters*, 81 ("Twelfth Letter").
38. Schiller, *Letters*, 81 ("Twelfth Letter"; trans. changed; my italics).
39. Schiller, *Letters*, 81, 83 ("Twelfth Letter"; trans. changed; my italics).
40. Ta-Nehisi Coates, *Between the World and Me* (Melbourne: Text Publishing, 2015), 43.
41. Schiller, *Letters*, 33 ("Sixth Letter"; trans. changed).
42. Schiller, *Letters*, 87 ("Thirteenth Letter").
43. Schiller, *Letters*, 95 ("Fourteenth Letter").
44. Schiller, *Letters*, 87 ("Thirteenth Letter").
45. Schiller, *Letters*, 87 ("Thirteenth Letter"; my italics).
46. Schiller, *Letters*, 95, 97 ("Fourteenth Letter"; trans. changed; my italics).
47. Schiller, *Letters*, 9 ("Second Letter"; trans. changed).
48. Schiller, *Letters*, 155 ("Twenty-Second Letter"; trans. changed).
49. Schiller, *Letters*, 161 ("Twenty-Third Letter").
50. Schiller, *Letters*, 87, 89 ("Thirteenth Letter").
51. For example, see Schiller, *Letters*, 147 ("Twenty-First Letter"); 151 ("Twenty-Second Letter").
52. Gayatri Chakravorty Spivak, *An Aesthetic Education in the Era of Globalization* (Cambridge, MA: Harvard University Press, 2012), 1, 2.
53. Spivak, *An Aesthetic Education in the Era of Globalization*, 12.
54. Spivak, *An Aesthetic Education in the Era of Globalization*, 2.
55. Spivak, *An Aesthetic Education in the Era of Globalization*, 16, 26, 10, xiv, 34, 16. While in my view the phrase, though not Adorno's, perfectly resonates with his negative dialectic, Spivak uses it in the context of a discussion of Kant bearing on her concept of the imagination. See 16n37, 514.

56. Spivak, *An Aesthetic Education in the Era of Globalization*, 3, 26, 4, 3, 4.

57. Spivak, *An Aesthetic Education in the Era of Globalization*, xiv, 10.

58. As quoted by Spivak, *An Aesthetic Education in the Era of Globalization*, 13 (Spivak's brackets; my italics). Spivak's quote is from Immanuel Kant, "Toward a Perpetual Peace," in *Political Writings*, 2nd edition, ed. with an introduction by Hans Reiss, trans. H. B. Nisbet (Cambridge: Cambridge University Press, 1991), 114.

59. Spivak, 14 (the bracketed term "geographical" is my insertion).

60. Spivak, *An Aesthetic Education in the Era of Globalization*, 26.

61. Spivak, *An Aesthetic Education in the Era of Globalization*, 15 (quoting Kant).

62. Spivak, *An Aesthetic Education in the Era of Globalization*, 14, 17.

63. Spivak, *An Aesthetic Education in the Era of Globalization*, 16, 20, 19, is quoting (20) Schiller's *Letters*, 77 ("Eleventh Letter").

64. Spivak, *An Aesthetic Education in the Era of Globalization*, 19.

65. Schiller, *Letters*, 19 ("Fourth Letter").

66. Schiller, *Letters*, 19 ("Fourth Letter"; my italics).

67. See Betsy Erkkila, *Whitman: The Political Poet* (New York: Oxford University Press, 1989), 248; George Kateb, *The Inner Ocean: Individualism and Democratic Culture* (Ithaca, NY: Cornell University Press, 1992), 240.

68. Erkkila's criticism that I had given "insufficient attention to the fundamental *agon*" in Whitman's poetry and prose was of an earlier published and abridged version of my first chapter, which omitting material from the version published here may have invited her criticism. See Betsy Erkkila, "Review of John H. Seery, ed. *A Political Companion to Walt Whitman*," *Walt Whitman Quarterly Review* 32, no. 1 (2014): 77–83. See 81–82 for her review of my first chapter's earlier abridged version in the Seery volume.

69. Whitman, "Song of Myself," in LG, 45, line 349 (my italics); 88, lines 1324–26.

70. Jean-François Lyotard, *Discourse, Figure*, trans. Anthony Hudek and Mary Lydon, introduction by John Mowitt (Minneapolis: University of Minnesota Press, 2011), "The Bias of the Figural," 8, 3, 7 (my italics).

71. See Gilles Deleuze, *Difference and Repetition*, trans. Paul Patton (New York: Columbia University Press, 1994), 24: "However, we would be wrong to reduce it [repetition] to a difference which falls back into exteriority, because the concept [of difference] embodies the form of the Same"—as does difference for Whitman.

72. See Deleuze, *Difference and Repetition*, 127–28.

73. Krzysztof Ziarek, *The Force of Art* (Stanford, CA: Stanford University Press, 2004), 6, 7, 8, 9, 10, 11, 13 (my italics).

1. *DEMOCRATIC VISTAS*

Chapter epigraph: Walt Whitman, "Thou Mother with Thy Equal Brood," in LG, 456, lines 8–9. *Text epigraphs:* Walt Whitman, "Preface" (1855), *Leaves of Grass*, in WPP, 16; "Song of Myself," in LG, 46, lines 372–74; "Song of Myself," in LG, 42, line 281; "By Blue Ontario's Shore," in LG, 340, line 11.

1. Whitman, *Democratic Vistas*, in WPP, 953–1018.

2. Gilles Deleuze, *Essays Critical and Clinical*, trans. Daniel W. Smith and Michael A. Greco (Minneapolis: University of Minnesota Press, 1977), 56–57. Deleuze's parentheses.

3. Whitman, "Song of the Answerer," in *LG*, 168, line 33.

4. Whitman, "Reconciliation," in *LG*, 321, title of poem and line 1.

5. Whitman, *Democratic Vistas*, in *WPP*, 964.

6. Whitman, *Democratic Vistas*, in *WPP*, 953.

7. Whitman, *Democratic Vistas*, in *WPP*, 954.

8. Whitman, *Democratic Vistas*, in *WPP*, 954, 998, 955.

9. Whitman, *Democratic Vistas*, in *WPP*, 997, 955, 995, 996, 955, 1018, 955–56, 996, 997, 996, 997.

10. Whitman, *Democratic Vistas*, in *WPP*, 983, 1001, 953, 957, 995.

11. Whitman, *Democratic Vistas*, in *WPP*, 1000, 953, 956, 962.

12. Whitman, *Democratic Vistas*, in *WPP*, 1016, 954, 955, 998, 1005.

13. Whitman, *Democratic Vistas*, in *WPP*, 958, 1008, 955, 959.

14. Whitman, *Democratic Vistas*, in *WPP*, 956, 959, 979, 956.

15. Whitman, *Democratic Vistas*, in *WPP*, 998, 979.

16. Whitman, *Democratic Vistas*, in *WPP*, 965, 982, 953.

17. Whitman, *Democratic Vistas*, in *WPP*, 953, 982, 966.

18. Whitman, *Democratic Vistas*, in *WPP*, 971, 986.

19. Whitman, *Democratic Vistas*, in *WPP*, 968, 967, 968 (my italics), 998.

20. Walt Whitman, "Preface" (1855), *Leaves of Grass*, in *WPP*, 5.

21. Whitman, *Democratic Vistas*, in *WPP*, 964–965 (my italics).

22. Whitman, *Democratic Vistas*, in *WPP*, 970, 961, 1006, 1005, 993, 992.

23. Whitman, *Democratic Vistas*, in *WPP*, 981, 987.

24. Whitman, *Democratic Vistas*, in *WPP*, 959, 973, 1004.

25. Whitman, *Democratic Vistas*, in *WPP*, 972–973.

26. Whitman, *Democratic Vistas*, in *WPP*, 994 (my italics).

27. Whitman, *Democratic Vistas*, in *WPP*, 1009.

28. Whitman, *Democratic Vistas*, in *WPP*, 1012.

29. Whitman, *Democratic Vistas*, in *WPP*, 1012.

30. Whitman, "A Song of the Rolling Earth," in *LG*, 219–25.

31. Whitman, "A Song of the Rolling Earth," in *LG*, 219, lines 1–4.

32. Whitman, "A Song of the Rolling Earth," in *LG*, 220, 221, lines 15, 16, 26, 41 (my italics).

33. Whitman, "Passage to India," in *LG*, 418, 419, lines 185, 194–95; "Song of Myself," in *LG*, 86, lines 1278–79, 1283.

34. Whitman, "A Song of the Rolling Earth," in *LG*, 223, line 89.

35. Whitman, "Whoever You Are Holding Me Now in Hand," in *LG*, 115, lines 3–4; "Of the Terrible Doubt of Appearances," in *LG*, 120, line 1.

36. Whitman, "A Song of the Rolling Earth," in *LG*, 221, 220, 224, lines 38, 40, 25, 99.

37. Theodor W. Adorno, *Aesthetic Theory*, trans. and ed. with an introduction by Robert Hullot-Kentor (Minneapolis: University of Minnesota Press, 1997), 7.

38. Whitman, "Song of Myself," in *LG*, 31, 56, 51, lines 51, 609–10, 494; "Salut Au Monde!," in *LG*, 137, lines 1–2.

39. Whitman, "Song of Myself," in *LG*, 75, line 1039; 76, lines 1048–49.

40. Whitman, "A Song for Occupations," in *LG*, 214, 216, lines 61–62, 102.

41. Whitman, "Preface" (1855), *Leaves of Grass*, in *WPP*, 16, 15–16.

42. Whitman, "Song of Myself," in *LG*, 35, line 134.

43. Whitman, "Earth, My Likeness," in *LG*, 132, line 7.

44. Whitman, "Song of Myself," "Do I contradict myself? / Very well then I contradict myself, / (I am large, I contain multitudes.)," in *LG*, 88, lines 1324–26.

45. Whitman, "Song of the Open Road, in *LG*, 149, line 8; "One Hour to Madness and Joy," in *LG*, 106, line 15.

46. Tocqueville, *Democracy in America II*, 318 (my italics).

47. Tocqueville, *Democracy in America II*, 39.

48. Ralph Waldo Emerson, "Self-Reliance," in *The Essential Writings of Ralph Waldo Emerson*, ed. Brooks Atkinson (New York: Modern Library, 2000), 133.

49. Whitman, *Democratic Vistas*, in *WPP*, 984, 985, 984.

50. Whitman, *Democratic Vistas*, in *WPP*, 1016–17.

51. Whitman, "Song of Myself," in *LG*, 44, line 329.

52. Whitman, "Song of Myself," in *LG*, 43, line 302.

53. Whitman, "Song of Myself," in *LG*, 47, 77, 66, 67, 66, lines 401, 1076, 838, 845, 837 (my italics).

54. Walt Whitman, "*Preface 1872*" to "As a Strong Bird on Pinions Free" (now "Thou Mother with Thy Equal Brood"), in *WPP*, 1028 (Whitman's italics).

55. Whitman, "Song of Myself," in *LG*, 28, lines 1–3.

56. Whitman, "Song of Myself," in *LG*, 44, 45, lines 328 (my italics), 349.

57. Whitman, "Song of the Open Road," in *LG*, 150, lines 18, 24, 19 (my italics).

58. Whitman, "Song of Myself," in *LG*, 44, lines 329, 327.

59. Whitman, "Song of Myself," in *LG*, 89, line 1337 (my italics).

60. Whitman, "*Democratic Vistas*," in *WPP*, 1012.

61. Whitman, "Song of Myself," in *LG*, 35, line 130.

62. Whitman, "O Living Always, Always Dying," in *LG*, 450–51, in its entirety.

2. WHITMAN'S DISCOVERY

Chapter epigraph: Whitman, "Song at Sunset," in *LG*, 496, line 47. *Text epigraphs:* Whitman, "Faces," in *LG*, 464, lines 14–15; "All Is Truth," in *LG*, 475, lines 14–17; "By Blue Ontario's Shore," in *LG*, 340, line 11.

1. Lyotard, *Discourse, Figure*, "The Bias of the Figural," 7; "Thickness on the Margins of Discourse,"103–14; Vlad Ionescu, "Figural Aesthetics: Lyotard, Valery, Deleuze," *Cultural Politics* 9, no. 2 (2013): 146.

2. Deleuze, *Cinema 1*, 12.

3. Whitman, "Song of the Rolling Earth," in *LG*, 221–22, lines 41, 48–53.

4. Whitman, "Song of the Rolling Earth," in *LG*, 221, lines 45, 47.

5. Whitman, "Preface" (1855), *Leaves of Grass*, in *WPP*, 10 (my italics).

6. Whitman, "Song of the Rolling Earth," in *LG*, 224, lines 98, 101, 105, 107 (my italics).

7. On Schoenberg's painting in relation to his music, see Fred Wasserman and Esther da Costa Meyer, eds., *Schoenberg, Kandinsky, and the Blue Rider* (London: Scala, 2003), especially Costa Meyer, "Schoenberg's Echo: The Composer as Painter."

8. For example, Whitman's images in stanzas 8, 12, 15, 16, 31, and especially 33 of "Song of Myself," in *LG*, 28–68.

9. Whitman, "A Paumanok Picture," in *LG*, 461, in its entirety.

10. Michel Foucault, "Theatrum Philosophicum," in *Language, Counter-Memory, Practice*, trans. Donald F. Bouchard and Sherry Simon (Ithaca, NY: Cornell University Press, 1977), especially 165–69. For the entirety of Plato's texts on which Deleuze bases his reading of Plato, see *Difference and Repetition*, 319n30.

11. Deleuze, *Difference and Repetition*, 127. My discussion of Deleuze is based on my reading of his argument on 127–28, where he develops the crux of what Foucault refers to as his "reverse Platonism." All quotations are from those pages. All italics are mine except for Deleuze's italics in "provide the means . . . that of the model?"

12. Schiller, *Letters*, 192, 193 ("Twenty-Sixth Letter"; trans. changed).

13. Whitman, "Song of Myself," in *LG*, 40, lines 235–36.

14. On Roland Barthes's "hermeneutic code," see *S/Z: An Essay*, trans. Richard Miller (Oxford: Blackwell, 2002), especially 75–76, section xxxii, titled "Delay." All quotations from those pages (Barthes's italics).

15. Whitman, "Song of the Open Road," in *LG*, 149, lines 16–17 (my italics).

16. Friedrich Nietzsche, "On Truth and Lying in an Extra-Moral Sense," in *Friedrich Nietzsche on Rhetoric and Language*, ed. and trans. Sander L. Gilman, Carole Blair, and David J. Parent (New York: Oxford University Press, 1989), 248.

17. Whitman, "Song of Myself," in *LG*, 86, lines 1278–79, 1283.

18. On the aspect of Barthes's cultural code I have in mind, see *S/Z*, 100, the discussion of "stylistic transformation," where he argues, "The utterances of the cultural code are implicit proverbs: they are written in that obligative mode by which the discourse states a general will, the law of a society, making the proposition concerned ineluctable or indelible." As described here, Barthes's cultural code seems to be an apt description of the work Whitman's visual image performs by teaching the ideal of reconciliation, which has a proverbial and obligative status as a future general or societal will (a democratic vista) that is unavoidable and indelibly inscribed in a transformational style that converts words to visual images, appearances, and differences as it abandons all the traditional connections of the word to truth.

19. Antjie Krog, *Country of My Skull* (Johannesburg: Random House, 1999), 29.

20. For example, on the influence of photography and the photograph on Whitman's poetry, see Miles Orvell's excellent work *The Real Thing: Imitation and Authenticity in American Culture, 1880–1940* (Chapel Hill: University of North Carolina Press, 1989), chap. 1, "Whitman's Transformed Eye."

21. The concept of weak ontology is developed by Stephen K. White in *Sustaining Affirmation: The Strengths of Weak Ontology in Political Theory* (Princeton, NJ: Princeton University Press, 2000).

22. Whitman, "Song of Myself," in *LG*, 31, line 51.

23. Whitman, "Salut Au Monde!," in *LG*, 143, 148, lines 106, 225 (my italics).

24. Whitman, "Song of Myself," in *LG*, 49, line 441.

25. Whitman, "Song of Myself," in *LG*, 86, 41, lines 1274, 253–54.

26. Whitman, "Song of Myself," in *LG*, 75, line 1039.

27. Whitman, "Song of Myself," in *LG*, 40, lines 230 (my italics), 232–34.

28. Whitman, "Starting from Paumanok," in *LG*, 15–28, 23, lines 170–71, 175–76 (my italics).

29. Whitman, "Starting from Paumanok," in *LG*, 24, 25, lines 193, 202, 195, 197, 203, 214–15, 208, 189.

30. Whitman, "Starting from Paumanok," in *LG*, 25, line 210.

31. On many of the occasions Whitman favors the visual image he is also critical of how well we become educated through reading. One such example of his preference for the visual image over the word occurs in "Song of Myself." Immediately before he develops the visual significance of leading us "upon a knoll" (in *LG*, 83, line 1207), he offers that he would "lead no man to a . . . library" (in *LG*, 83, line 1206) to learn what he next will show is conveyed through sight. Or consider the second verse of "A Song for Occupations" (in *LG*, 211–19), where not only does he express his preference for the visual image by admiring the power of sight, but we find him evincing an animus toward "what is printed" (in *LG*, 213, line 45) and even toward what is "in this [*Leaves of Grass*] book" (in *LG*, 213, line 46) and what is offered to those who may even "read in many languages" (in *LG*, 213, line 49).

32. Whitman, "Starting from Paumanok," in *LG*, 27, lines 253–64.

33. Whitman, *Democratic Vistas*, in *WPP*, 1011.

34. The line I paraphrase is from verse 12 of "By Blue Ontario's Shore," in *LG*, 349, line 190, where Whitman asks would-be poets, "Are you done with reviews and criticisms of life? animating now to life itself?"

35. Whitman, "Eidolons," in *LG*, 5, 7, lines 1, 69, lines 4, 2, 5–8.

36. Whitman, "Eidolons," in *LG*, 7, lines 71–72.

37. Whitman, "Eidolons," in *LG*, 6, 7, lines 25–28, 49–52, 57–60.

38. Whitman, "Eidolons," in *LG*, 7, lines 46–47, 56, 55.

39. Whitman, "Eidolons," in *LG*, 7, line 65.

40. Bergson, *Creative Evolution*, 317, 369.

41. Bergson, *Matter and Memory*, 1.

42. "We have abolished the real world: what world is left? the apparent world perhaps? . . . But no! *with the real world we have also abolished the apparent world!*" Friedrich Nietzsche, *Twilight of the Idols and The Anti-Christ*, trans. with an introduction and commentary by R. J. Hollingdale (Harmondsworth, UK: Penguin Books, 1975), 41 (Nietzsche's italics). Whitman does not abolish the apparent world because he does not first abolish the real world. Rather, he argues that the real world is unknown and unknowable, a position retaining the real world on which his concept of the apparent world, if not the entirety of his work, rests.

43. Whitman, "Eidolons," in *LG*, 6, 8, lines 19, 77–79.

44. Deleuze, *Cinema 1*, 59.

45. Whitman, "Song of Myself," in *LG*, 31–32, lines 61–65. I omit Whitman's question mark at the end of his last line as he is declaring his refusal through a rhetorical self-questioning.

46. To recall Whitman, "Song of Myself," "I resist anything better than my own diversity," in LG, 45, line 349.
47. Whitman, "Song of Myself," in LG, 35, line 134.
48. Erin Manning's work has enabled us to think more deeply about the ways in which our senses actually constitute and potentially reconstitute rather than merely move in and through the political spaces we inhabit. See, for example, *Politics of Touch: Sense, Movement, Sovereignty* (Minneapolis: University of Minnesota Press, 2007).
49. Whitman, "Song of Myself," in LG, 64–65, lines 791–93, 795–96.
50. Whitman, "Song of Myself," in LG, 61, 62, 63, 65, lines 710–11, 715–17, 727, 748–49, 755, 798–99.
51. Whitman, "Salut Au Monde!," in LG, 147, line 193.
52. Whitman, "Song of Myself," in LG, 39, 37, 32, lines 221, 181, 78 (my italics).
53. Whitman, "Song of Myself," in LG, 47, 67, lines 401, 845, 847, 858; see also 71, lines 946–49.
54. Whitman, "Song of Myself," in LG, 44, lines 329, 328 (my italics).
55. Ralph Waldo Emerson, "Quotation and Originality," in *Emerson's Complete Writings* (New York: Wm. H. Wise & Co., 1929), 180, 178.
56. On the contribution of Seneca to the idea of self-transformation through imitation, see Matthew Potolsky, *Mimesis* (New York: Routledge, 2006), 57–58. And on the cultural transformation of Florence through its imitation of antiquity, see George Holmes, *The Florentine Enlightenment 1400–1450* (New York: Pegasus, 1969), especially the chapter entitled "Realist Art," 202–41.
57. Whitman, "By Blue Ontario's Shore," in LG, 340, line 11 (my italics).
58. Whitman, *Democratic Vistas*, in WPP, 1011.
59. Whitman, *Democratic Vistas*, in WPP, 964–65.
60. Walt Whitman, *Pictures: An Unpublished Poem of Walt Whitman*, ed. with an introduction and notes by Emory Holloway (New York: June House, Faber and Gwyer, 1927). Holloway initially published excerpts of Whitman's *Pictures* in the *Southwest Review* 10, no. 4 (July 1925), with his commentary on the import of the discovery. My thanks to Terri Lewers of *Southwest Review* for searching its archives and clarifying the difference between Holloway's 1925 and 1927 publications.
61. Whitman, *Pictures*, 7–9.
62. Whitman, *Pictures*, 10.
63. André Bazin, "The Ontology of the Photographic Image," *Film Quarterly* 13, no. 4 (Summer 1960): 8 (my italics).
64. Bazin, "The Ontology of the Photographic Image," 8 (Bazin's italics).

FIRST BRIDGE

Chapter epigraph: Theodor W. Adorno, "Transparencies on Film," in *The Culture Industry: Selected Essays on Mass Culture*, ed. with an introduction by J. M. Bernstein (New York: Routledge, 2002), 186.
1. As Habermas argues, in *Dialectic of Enlightenment* Horkheimer and Adorno's "totalizing critique" of reason suffers the "embarrassment of a critique that attacks the presuppositions of its own validity." Jürgen Habermas, *The Philosophical Discourse*

of *Modernity: Twelve Lectures*, trans. Frederick Lawrence (Cambridge, MA: MIT Press, 1987), 126, 127.

2. Although the term "instrumental reason" is never used by Horkheimer and Adorno in *Dialectic of Enlightenment*, this work is, as Noerr correctly points out in his "Editor's Afterword," "the most important document" for a "historical and generic critique of instrumental reason" (237). In *Dialectic of Enlightenment* the concept of instrumental reason appears synonymously as "formalistic reason" (e.g., 75), "classifying reason" (35–36), the "formalization of reason" (81), and "enlightened reason" (71), among other terms. Thus in discussions of *Dialectic of Enlightenment* it is entirely appropriate to use the term "instrumental reason" in place of any of its synonymous forms. It is difficult to identify the moment at which "instrumental reason" became the one most commonly used term in place of all the others, though it may have become commonplace after Max Horkheimer's *Zur Kritik der instrumentellen Vernunft* (Frankfurt am Main: Fisher Verlag, 1967).

3. As I will note appropriately when I turn to Adorno's *Aesthetic Theory* in the next chapter, although "aesthetic rationality" is the term Adorno used most often when referring to the rationality of the work of art, my interchangeable use of the term "aesthetic reason" is justified by his practice in *Aesthetic Theory* of speaking of "art's own reason," "reason immanent to artworks themselves," the "aesthetic *ratio*," and so on. For pagination of Adorno's many such synonymous usages for "aesthetic rationality" see chapter 3, note 7.

4. Horkheimer and Adorno, "Excursus II: Juliette or Enlightenment and Morality," in *Dialectic of Enlightenment*, 72 (trans. changed).

5. Horkheimer and Adorno, "Limits of Enlightenment: Elements of Anti-Semitism," in *Dialectic of Enlightenment*, 137, 139 (my italics).

6. Horkheimer and Adorno, "Limits of Enlightenment: Elements of Anti-Semitism," in *Dialectic of Enlightenment*, 172.

7. Horkheimer and Adorno, "Preface" (1944 and 1947), in *Dialectic of Enlightenment*, xviii (my italics).

8. Nietzsche, *Twilight of the Idols*, 51 (Nietzsche's italics).

9. Horkheimer and Adorno, "The Concept of Enlightenment," in *Dialectic of Enlightenment*, 11 (trans. changed).

10. Horkheimer and Adorno, "The Concept of Enlightenment," in *Dialectic of Enlightenment*, 7.

11. Horkheimer and Adorno, "The Concept of Enlightenment," in *Dialectic of Enlightenment*, 27.

12. Horkheimer and Adorno, "The Culture Industry: Enlightenment as Mass Deception," in *Dialectic of Enlightenment*, 94 (trans. changed).

13. Horkheimer and Adorno, "Limits of Enlightenment: Elements of Anti-Semitism," in *Dialectic of Enlightenment*, 137.

14. The authorship of "The Schema of Mass Culture," in *The Culture Industry: Selected Essays in Mass Culture*, is somewhat uncertain, though the editor of Horkheimer and Adorno's *Dialectic of Enlightenment* identifies, correctly in my view, Adorno as its author rather than Horkheimer. For the background to the question of the authorship of this essay, see "Editor's Afterword" to *Dialectic of Enlightenment*, 222.

15. Adorno, "The Schema of Mass Culture," in *The Culture Industry*, 73.

16. Adorno, "The Schema of Mass Culture," in *The Culture Industry*, 67; Horkheimer and Adorno, "The Culture Industry: Enlightenment as Mass Deception," in *Dialectic of Enlightenment*, 94.

17. Horkheimer and Adorno, "The Culture Industry: Enlightenment as Mass Deception," in *Dialectic of Enlightenment*, 106, 116, 117.

18. Adorno, "The Schema of Mass Culture" and "The Culture Industry Reconsidered," in *The Culture Industry*, 93 and 103.

19. Adorno, "The Schema of Mass Culture," in *The Culture Industry*, 65, 69; Horkheimer and Adorno, "The Culture Industry: Enlightenment as Mass Deception," in *Dialectic of Enlightenment*, 122.

20. Horkheimer and Adorno, "The Culture Industry: Enlightenment as Mass Deception," in *Dialectic of Enlightenment*, 100.

21. Adorno, "The Schema of Mass Culture," in *The Culture Industry*, 72, 69, 77, 73.

22. Adorno, "The Culture Industry Reconsidered," in *The Culture Industry*, 100 (Adorno's italics).

23. Horkheimer and Adorno, "The Culture Industry: Enlightenment as Mass Deception," in *Dialectic of Enlightenment*, 109.

24. Horkheimer and Adorno, "The Culture Industry: Enlightenment as Mass Deception," in *Dialectic of Enlightenment*, 101.

25. Adorno, "The Schema of Mass Culture," in *The Culture Industry*, 94, 63.

26. Horkheimer and Adorno, "Preface" (1944 and 1947), in *Dialectic of Enlightenment*, xiv.

27. Horkheimer and Adorno, "The Culture Industry: Enlightenment as Mass Deception," in *Dialectic of Enlightenment*, 129.

28. Here I allude to director John August's distinction between the independent film studio, which has now largely fallen under the administration of the film industry, and the independent film, which may be produced by independent studios or unintentionally by the film industry. On August's distinction, see Tambay A. Obenson, "How Do You Define Independent Film?," *Cineuropa*, February 26, 2013, https://cineuropa.org/en/newsdetail/233829/.

29. Adorno, "Transparencies on Film," in *The Culture Industry*, 179.

30. While my theoretical interest in democratic enlightenment requires I focus on discovering the reconciliation image in popular films, such as those I examine in the final chapters of *A Democratic Enlightenment*, without a doubt images of reconciliation can be found in avant-garde films, making them available to smaller, more specialized cinematic audiences. We find evidence of the reconciliation image in one such avant-garde film, "Jeanne Dielman," which Lori Jo Marso has analyzed in detail in her exceptional work *Politics with Beauvoir: Freedom in the Encounter* (Durham, NC: Duke University Press, 2017), 153–63. While Marso does not make this claim, after reading her analysis of this film it seemed clear to me an image of reconciliation is to be found there. The pleasure Jeanne experiences within patriarchal encounters sensuously transcends the limits of those encounters, and by so doing points to the possibility of reconciliation between a revised identity able to experience such pleasures in a less limited or unlimited form and the different pleasures and the pleasures of differences themselves.

31. Adorno, "Transparencies on Film," in *The Culture Industry*, 180, 182. In "The Schema of Mass Culture," and with Horkheimer in "The Culture Industry: Enlightenment as Mass Deception," Adorno is critical of later montage techniques, those he considers to be examples of "the most modern fashion" ("The Schema of Mass Culture," 66). With Horkheimer, for example, Adorno sees montage as "predispose[d] . . . to advertising" (132).

32. Adorno, "Transparencies on Film," in *The Culture Industry*, 180.

33. Miriam Bratu Hansen, "The Question of Film Aesthetics," part 3 on Adorno in *Cinema and Experience: Siegfried Kracauer, Walter Benjamin, and Theodor Adorno* (Berkeley: University of California Press, 2012), 207–50.

34. In the context of my discussion of "Transparencies" I note several of the same terms and quote several of the same passages as Hansen, allowing readers to better compare our interpretations by consulting her text to clarify differences between our readings of Adorno's essay.

35. Hansen, "The Question of Film Aesthetics," in *Cinema and Experience*, 250.

36. While Hansen and I agree Adorno's aesthetic theory contributes to film aesthetics, we stress different aspects of his aesthetic theory. Hansen focuses on Adorno's philosophy of modern music and theory of writing, while I focus on his work on visual images in modernist art.

37. Hansen, "The Question of Film Aesthetics," in *Cinema and Experience*, 228, 345n55.

38. Albrecht Wellmer, "Truth, Semblance, Reconciliation: Adorno's Aesthetic Redemption of Modernity," in *The Persistence of Modernity: Essays on Aesthetics, Ethics, and Postmodernism*, trans. David Midgley (Cambridge, MA: MIT Press, 1991), especially vii–viii, 1–35.

39. Wellmer, *The Persistence of Modernity*, viii.

40. Fredric Jameson, *Late Marxism: Adorno, or, The Persistence of the Dialectic* (London: Verso, 1990), 7.

3. AESTHETIC REASON AND REFLEXIVITY

Chapter epigraph: Adorno, *Aesthetic Theory*, 168.

1. Horkheimer and Adorno, *Dialectic of Enlightenment*, xi.

2. Adorno, *Aesthetic Theory*, 1.

3. See Jürgen Habermas, "The Entwinement of Myth and Enlightenment," in *The Philosophical Discourse of Modernity*, 111, 114, 118–19, especially 126–27 and 129. I have also examined this problem at greater length in "'Avoiding Embarrassment': Aesthetic Reason and Aporetic Critique in *Dialectic of Enlightenment*," *Polity* 37, no. 3 (2005): 1–47.

4. Adorno, *Aesthetic Theory*, 7.

5. For the elements of aesthetic reason listed here, see Adorno, *Aesthetic Theory*, for example, 7, 17, 41, 44, 60, 71, 114–15, 118, 139, 151, 176–78, 184, 190, 193, 214, 222, 246, 247, 257, 278, 280, 291, 293, 329, 331, 337, 346. Adorno's phrase "the *economy of the elements* out of which the [art]work is composed," appears on 214 (my italics).

6. For Adorno, what is aesthetically the case for visual images in the fine arts, such as painting and sculpture, is true for many other arts, such as music and literature, which fall outside the scope of this investigation.

7. For these, among other synonymous usages for aesthetic rationality, see Adorno, *Aesthetic Theory*, 6, 35, 115, 289, 306.

8. Adorno, *Aesthetic Theory*, 176.

9. Adorno, *Aesthetic Theory*, 134 (my italics).

10. Adorno, *Aesthetic Theory*, 101, 139, 186 (my italics); see 160–62 for Adorno's critique of classicism.

11. Adorno, *Aesthetic Theory*, 48, 134.

12. Adorno, *Aesthetic Theory*, 306 (my italics), 288.

13. Adorno, *Aesthetic Theory*, 35. As Robert Hullot-Kentor points out, when Adorno says "Each artwork is the mortal enemy of the other," he is quoting from his own earlier work, "Die Kunst und die Künste," in *Ohne Leitbild, Gesammelte Schriften 10*, no. 1 (Frankfurt: Suhrkamp, 1977).

14. Adorno, *Aesthetic Theory*, 35.

15. Adorno's example of the unity of the history of art is not meant to confine our attention to artworks interested only in the same or comparable aesthetic objects, which I have chosen for purposes of clarifying his argument. Determinate negation works through every artwork in relation to every other in the history of art.

16. Germaine Greer, "Artists Have Always Glamorized Prostitution: Manet Savaged All Their Delusions," *Guardian*, February 6, 2011, https://www.theguardian.com /artanddesign/2011/feb/06/manet-olympia-prostitution-courtesan.

4. AESTHETIC ANALOGUES

Chapter epigraph: Jane Bennett, *Vibrant Matter: A Political Equality of Things* (Durham, NC: Duke University Press, 2010), 14.

1. Adorno, *Aesthetic Theory*, 177, 176 (my italics).

2. Adorno, *Aesthetic Theory*, 175–176 (my italics).

3. On Adorno's concept of the "closure of artworks," see my discussions in chapter 3 in sections "Aesthetic Reason, Instrumental Reason, and Difference" and "Aesthetic Reflexivity." Adorno's thoughts in *Aesthetic Theory* on closures imposed by aesthetic form are an elaboration of his critique of identity thinking in *Negative Dialektik* (Frankfurt am Main: Suhrkamp, 1975). Consult Adorno's introduction to *Negative Dialectics*, trans. E. B. Ashton (New York: Seabury Press, 1973), 3–57, for an overview of his critique of identititarianism.

4. Adorno, *Aesthetic Theory*, 3, 139.

5. Adorno, *Aesthetic Theory*, 84.

6. Adorno, *Aesthetic Theory*, 85 (my italics), 108.

7. For a complementary discussion of the ways in which moving images model time, see Michael J. Shapiro's conceptualization of the moving image as the vehicle of multiple layers of temporality in *Cinematic Geopolitics* (London: Routledge, 2009), 130–32.

8. Adorno, *Aesthetic Theory*, 85, 108, 3 (my italics).

9. Adorno, *Aesthetic Theory*, 7, 285 (my italics).

10. For Adorno's fascination with the paradoxical character of art, see *Aesthetic Theory*, especially, 22, 23, 27, 30, 33, 68, 72–73, 78, 79, 80, 84, 107, 114, 131–32, 135–36, 138, 139,

152, 168, 171, 172, 176, 184–86, 201, 205, 212, 214, 242, 279, 347, 350, 354. As can be appreciated from just these citations, which are not exhaustive of his considerations of this issue in *Aesthetic Theory*, the paradoxical expressions of art take many forms in addition to those I develop here. It could be argued without exaggeration that this is the problem around which *Aesthetic Theory* as a whole is constructed.

11. Adorno, *Aesthetic Theory*, for example, 44, 118, 193, 244, 258, 291, 293, 331.

12. Adorno, *Aesthetic Theory*, 219.

13. I enlist Bennett's term "vibrant" to indicate my agreement with her argument that "Adorno describes nonidentity," difference, "as a presence that acts upon us: we knowers are haunted, he says, by a painful, nagging feeling that something's being forgotten or left out" (*Vibrant Matter*, 14). As I propose here, in its relation to difference the artwork is haunted by this same presence that its aesthetic rationality senses it has left out. And I also enlist "vibrant" to further illuminate what Adorno means by the artwork being attracted to its object "like a magnet to a field of iron filings."

14. Rodin once remarked, in fact, "In order to express a movement in all its character and truth, it is important that [the artwork] be at once the result of successive movements which have preceded the moment of fixity, *and that it foreshadow the sensations of the movements which follow*." For Rodin, in other words, despite how fixed its aesthetic identity appears to be, however enduring, the artwork must continue to express a movement toward its object, toward what it has yet left out. Albert Edward Elsen, *Auguste Rodin: Readings on His Life and Works* (Englewood Cliffs, NJ: Prentice-Hall, 1965), 164 (my italics). Translated by Ann McGarrell, this quotation appeared originally in H. C. E. Dujardin-Beaumetz, *Entretiens avec Rodin* (Paris: Impr. Paul Dupont, 1913).

15. Adorno, *Aesthetic Theory*, 44.

16. Adorno, *Aesthetic Theory*, 142.

17. Adorno, *Aesthetic Theory*, 176, 191 (my italics).

18. Adorno, *Aesthetic Theory*, 176 (my italics).

19. Adorno, *Aesthetic Theory*, 193–94.

20. Adorno, *Aesthetic Theory*, 193 (my italics).

21. A paraphrase of "We possess art lest we perish of the truth." Friedrich Nietzsche, *The Will to Power: A New Translation*, trans. Walter Kaufmann and R. J. Hollingdale (New York: Vintage Books, 1968), 435.

22. Walter Benjamin, "The Work of Art in the Age of Mechanical Reproduction," in *Illuminations: Essays and Reflections*, ed. with an introduction by Hannah Arendt, trans. Harry Zohn (New York: Schocken Books, 1969), 238.

SECOND BRIDGE

Chapter epigraph: Deleuze, *Cinema 1*, 68.

1. Among political theorists there are important exceptions to this practice. In *Politics with Beauvoir: Freedom in the Encounter* (Durham, NC: Duke University Press, 2017), Lori Jo Marso's remarkable study of Lars von Trier's film *Antichrist* stresses the moral and political work performed by its images independent of

and in contrast to the position of its narrative. Marso cites von Trier's statement in "Director's Confessions" that his film's "images were composed free of logic or dramatic thinking" (90). Another exception is Michael J. Shapiro's "A Philopoetic Engagement: Deleuze and *The Element of Crime*," in *Politics, Theory, and Film: Critical Encounters with Lars von Trier*, ed. Bonnie Honig and Lori J. Marso (Oxford: Oxford University Press, 2016). In this essay Shapiro continues the approach he takes to illuminate the significance of visual images in film in other of his works, such as *Cinematic Geopolitics*, where we find a complex and nuanced analytical balance between a film's narrative and the work the film's visual images perform independent of film's narrative structure. He argues this point precisely in the context of examining Vyacheslav Kristofovich's film *Friend of the Deceased*. In Shapiro's formulation, "A simple narrative account of the film's ironies does not capture how it thinks about intimate versus predatory associations and the social and global contexts within which they transpire. Much of what is thought within the film narrative involves moving images that portray complex layerings of experience and time" (130).

2. Schiller, *On the Aesthetic Education of Humanity in a Series of Letters*, 27. On my translation of Schiller's title see note 20 of my introduction.

3. Whitman, *Democratic Vistas*, in wpp, 981.

4. For one of the most demonstrative examples of this dimension of Whitman's work, see his extraordinary concluding paragraph to *Democratic Vistas*, in wpp, 1017–18.

5. Lyotard, *Discourse, Figure*, "The Bias of the Figural," 3.

6. Brian Massumi, *Parables for the Virtual: Movement, Affect, Sensation* (Durham, NC: Duke University Press, 2002), hereafter *Parables*.

7. Deleuze, *Cinema 1*; Gilles Deleuze, *Cinema 2: The Time-Image*, trans. Hugh Tomlinson and Robert Galeta (Minneapolis: University of Minnesota Press, 1989).

8. Massumi, *Parables*, 90.

9. Massumi, *Parables*, 91 (Massumi's italics).

10. Massumi, *Parables*, 91.

11. Massumi, *Parables*, 91, 10.

12. Massumi, *Parables*, 91. I am uncertain if Massumi means this too, but since substitutions at the thought-pole are sharply defined alternative possible actions, it would seem to follow that they are also sharply defined alternatives to possible actions superposed at the perception pole where perceptual action is underway.

13. Massumi, *Parables*, 92.

14. Massumi, *Parables*, 92.

15. Massumi's concept of "energetic *potential*," 92, finds a parallel in Jane Bennett's idea of a "force from the outside" acting upon our senses and sensibilities, as developed in her chapter "Circuits of Sympathy" in her forthcoming *Influx and Efflux: Writing Up with Walt Whitman* (Durham, NC: Duke University Press, 2020).

16. Massumi, *Parables*, 92 (Massumi's italics).

17. Massumi, *Parables*, 92, 93 (my italics).

18. Massumi, *Parables*, 93 (my italics).

19. Massumi, *Parables*, 93 (Massumi's italics and mine in the second instance).

20. Massumi, *Parables*, 94 (my italics).

21. Massumi, *Parables*, 94.

22. Massumi, *Parables*, 94.

23. Massumi, *Parables*, 9. (Massumi italicizes "implicit in"; all other italics are mine).

24. Massumi, *Parables*, 10 (my italics).

25. Massumi, *Parables*, 10.

5. THE HELP

Chapter epigraph: Bergson, *Matter and Memory*, 196.

1. Deleuze, *Cinema 1*, 138.

2. *The Help* (2011), DreamWorks Pictures, written and directed by Tate Taylor, based on Kathryn Stocket's 2009 Penguin Books novel by the same name.

3. Matthew W. Hughey, *The White Savior Film: Content, Critics, and Consumption* (Philadelphia, PA: Temple University Press, 2014). My analysis of *The Help*'s narrative draws upon examples from the film in addition to those chosen by Hughey, whose own analysis of its narrative is found on 7, 24, 40, 63–64, 65, 117, 123, 167. For Hughey's discussions of *The Help*'s "Constantine" and "Home Health Sanitation Initiative" episodes, which I also examine, see *The White Savior Film*, 40, 63, 167.

4. Hughey, *The White Savior Film*, 40.

5. The work of imitation performed by the reconciliation image should not be confused with "blackface," whose many racist dimensions have been examined persuasively and in depth by Michael Rogin in *Blackface, White Noise: Jewish Immigrants in the Hollywood Melting Pot* (Berkeley: University of California Press, 1998). Rogin argues, "That blackface reached the peak of its popularity in the years surrounding the Civil War points not to its affinity with abolition but to its role as a register of race relations. Blackface abolition is the exception that proves the rule: burnt cork contaminated every white American political perspective on race.... The blacked-up white body unified the body politic and purified it of black physical contamination" (43). The act of imitation modeled by the reconciliation image is, to the contrary with regard to race (or any other form of difference), a becoming different *reconstituting* white identity in the image of difference that overcomes the very construction of difference as otherness characteristic of blackface, which as Rogin correctly determines is rather *a unification and consolidation of identity around whiteness* attempting *to purify it* of black difference, and thus entails no such reconstitution of identity in the image of difference. I am grateful to Torrey Shanks and Jodi Dean for recommending I acknowledge Rogin's argument.

6. I use the term "contrapuntal" in Edward W. Said's sense of maintaining the connection between the standpoint of oppression and resistance to it. See Said's *Culture and Imperialism* (New York: Vintage, 1994), for example, chapter 1, part V; chapter 2, parts I, IV; chapter 3, parts I, IV, V.

7. While I agree with the Deleuzian position Antjie Krog cites that "all becoming is minoritarian, because you diverge from the standard or norm which defines the majority.... [There are those who] are constantly refiguring the standard through inventing in a piecemeal way new forms of life and different modes of existence," I disagree with her affirmation of Deleuze's narrow association of becoming with

"the potential for 'new earths and peoples unlike those found in existing democracies.'" Krog, *Begging to Be Black* (Cape Town: Random House Struik, 2014), 100. For an elaboration of Deleuze's argument, see Paul Patton, *Deleuzian Concepts: Philosophy, Colonization, Politics* (Stanford, CA: Stanford University Press, 2010), especially 135, 163, 173–83, 198, 202. Contra Deleuze, as I am attempting to show, the reconciliation image in film visualizes the possibility of inventing such new becomings in Western democratic societies and in non-Western societies.

6. GENTLEMAN'S AGREEMENT

Chapter epigraph: William E. Connolly, *Identity\Difference: Democratic Negotiations of Political Paradox*, expanded edition (Minneapolis: University of Minnesota Press, 2002), 43.

1. *Gentleman's Agreement* (1947), Twentieth Century Fox, screenplay by Moss Hart and Elia Kazan, based on Laura Hobson's 1947 novel by that name.

2. In a reflection on the opening chapter of Bergson's *Matter and Memory*, Deleuze distinguishes between images in motion and motion that creates images. Regarding the former, Deleuze argues, "We find ourselves in fact faced with the exposition of a world where IMAGE = MOVEMENT. . . . There is no moving body which is distinct from executed movement. There is nothing moved which is distinct from the received movement. Every thing, that is to say every image, is indistinguishable from its actions and reactions: this is universal variation" (*Cinema 1*, 58). Taking its point of departure from Deleuze's formulation "image equals movement," my argument here is that, in relation to the formation of the reconciliation image, up to the time the reconciliation image is well thought-out the narrative images of *Gentleman's Agreement* are indistinguishable from the turbulent motion (character actions) from which a well-articulated reconciliation image and its constituent images will gradually unfold and crystallize.

3. On the relational and constructed character of identity and difference, see Connolly, *Identity\Difference*, especially the preface and chapter 2, "Global Political Discourse."

4. On this notorious bigot and anti-Semite, see Glen Jeansonne, *Gerald L. K. Smith: Minister of Hate* (New Haven, CT: Yale University Press, 1988).

5. For a comprehensive introduction to the racist thought of Theodor G. Bilbo, see his *Take Your Choice: Separation or Mongrelization* (Cuttack, Odisha, India: Dream House, 2013).

6. Of course, it was the drool and protest that to an important extent led to the reforms in the film's near future through laws outlawing such overt forms of discrimination, such as the Civil Rights Act of 1964.

7. I have italicized those words in their discussions that appear to be inflected for effect.

8. Todorov, *On Human Diversity*, 356.

9. Theorists of film very often conceptualize narrative closure in ways excluding the possibility that visual images of which narratives consist do work differently than that prescribed by the narrative structure of film. Thus in a work doing much to

advance the philosophy of film in other ways, when focusing on the "nature of the moving image," the "history of the moving image," and the "philosophy of the moving image," Noël Carroll proposes that "closure transpires when all the questions that have been saliently posed by the narrative get answered. It is the point at which the audience can presume that everyone lived happily ever after and leave it at that." Carroll, *The Philosophy of Motion Pictures* (Malden, MA: Blackwell, 2008), 136. As I am arguing to the contrary, the possibility should be kept open that film images answer questions in ways the narrative structure of film does not prescribe, and moreover that images also raise new questions in addition and also in contrast to these questions raised by a film's narrative, even to the extent of projecting the possibility of alternative narratives to the scripted narrative of a film. Against arguments such as Carroll's, film images are far richer in meaning and significance than narratives capture. Other theorists of the narrative structure of film conceptualize images in such terms. Seymour Chapman's distinction between "causality" and "contingency" in narrative is one such opportunity to think of the uncertainty a visual image introduces into a film narrative, although he does not pursue this opening to argue for the independent life of the image in narrative. See his *Story and Discourse: Narrative Structure in Fiction and Film* (Ithaca, NY: Cornell University Press, 1980), 45–48.

10. When considered in light of a biographical recollection made by Hannah Arendt, who attributes her own consciousness of her Jewish identity to existential conditions, specifically to how it was shaped by her experiences with anti-Semitism, Kathy's conflation of the givenness of Jews' existential situation with anti-Semitism, which importantly helps to account for her tacit anti-Semitism, becomes more complicated, for it qualifies as an especially tragic dimension in her thinking, an erroneous belief that, all too common, influenced her thinking at its deepest levels. In a 1964 interview with Guenter Gaus for the television program *Zur Person*, Arendt, at a very moving moment early in the interview, explicitly states, "I didn't know from my family that I was Jewish. My mother was not at all religious. [My father died very young.] It all sounds very odd. My grandfather was president of the liberal Jewish community. I'm from an old Koenigsberg family. The word Jew never arose when I was a small child. I first encountered it through antisemitic remarks. They're not worth repeating—from children on the streets." "Hannah Arendt Discusses Philosophy, Politics & Eichmann in Rare 1964 TV Interview," Open Culture, posted July 16, 2013, http://www.openculture.com/2013/07/hannah -arendt-1964-tv-interview.html. My point is not that Arendt's recollection supports Kathy's confusion but, to the contrary, that Kathy's conflation arises because she fails to distinguish between Jewish identity as "difference" and as "other." Arendt is referring to her consciousness of herself as the Jewish other, whereas Kathy believes Jewish ethnic and religious identities, Jewish difference, is itself the consequence of anti-Semitism, which is to conflate the existential situation of Jewish self-identity with anti-Semitism, difference with otherness.

11. Connolly, *Identity\Difference*, 43.

12. Connolly, *Identity\Difference*, 45.

13. Here my argument is influenced by Connolly's that bearers of identities may "struggle to ambiguate or overcome this drive [to naturalize the identity given to them] because they think it is ungrounded in any truth they can prove and because they find it ethically compelling to revise their relation to difference in the absence of such a proof" (*Identity\Difference*, 46).

7. THE RECONCILIATION IMAGE IN FILM

Chapter epigraph: Adorno, *Negative Dialektik*, 153 (my translation).
1. For this sense of what Deleuze means by the "event," see Jon Roffe's translation of Alain Badiou's "The Event in Deleuze," *Parrhesia: A Journal of Critical Philosophy*, no. 2 (2007): 38, especially "Axiom 1" and "Axiom 2."
2. *Pride*, 2014, written by Stephen Beresford, BBC Films; *Tootsie*, 1982, screenplay by Larry Gelbart, Murray Shisgal, Barry Levinson, and Elaine May, Columbia Pictures; *Dirty Dancing*, 1987, written by Eleanor Bergstein, Vestron Pictures; *Forest Gump*, 1994, screenplay by Eric Roth, Paramount Pictures; *My Left Foot*, 1989, screenplay by Jim Sheridan and Shane Connaughton, Miramax Films; *The Soloist*, 2009, written by Susannah Grant, Paramount and Universal Pictures.
3. Schiller, 155, *Letters* ("Twenty-Second Letter"; trans. changed).
4. Schiller, 155, *Letters* ("Twenty-Second Letter"). Here I use "electrify" with Whitman's "I Sing the Body Electric" in mind.
5. Schiller, 155, *Letters* ("Twenty-Second Letter"; trans. changed).
6. Schiller, 195, *Letters* ("Twenty-Sixth Letter"; trans. changed).
7. Schiller, 195, *Letters* ("Twenty-Sixth Letter").
8. Schiller, 155, *Letters* ("Twenty-Second Letter").
9. Theodor W. Adorno, *Philosophy of Modern Music*, trans. Anne G. Mitchell and Wesley V. Blomster (New York: Seabury Press, 1973), 191.

BIBLIOGRAPHY

....

Adorno, Theodor W. *Aesthetic Theory*. Translated and edited with an introduction by Robert Hullot-Kentor. Minneapolis: University of Minnesota Press, 1997.

Adorno, Theodor W. *Aesthetische Theorie*. Frankfurt am Main: Suhrkamp, 1977.

Adorno, Theodor W. *The Culture Industry: Selected Essays in Mass Culture*. Edited and with an introduction by J. M. Bernstein. New York: Routledge, 2002.

Adorno, Theodor W. "Die Kunst und die Künste." In *Ohne Leitbild: Gessamelte Schriften* 10, no. 1. Frankfurt am Main: Suhrkamp, 1977.

Adorno, Theodor W. *Negative Dialectics*. Translated by E. B. Ashton. New York: Seabury Press, 1973.

Adorno, Theodor W. *Negative Dialektik*. Frankfurt am Main: Suhrkamp, 1975.

Adorno, Theodor W. *Philosophy of Modern Music*. Translated by Anne G. Mitchell and Wesley V. Blomster. New York: Seabury Press, 1973.

Adorno, Theodor W. *Problems of Moral Philosophy*. Edited by Thomas Schröder. Translated by Rodney Livingstone. Stanford, CA: Stanford University Press, 2000.

Allen, Amy. *The End of Progress: Decolonizing the Normative Foundations of Critical Theory*. New York: Columbia University Press, 2016.

Anker, Elizabeth R. *Orgies of Feeling: Melodrama and the Politics of Freedom*. Durham, NC: Duke University Press, 2014.

Aristotle. *Poetics*. In *The Basic Works of Aristotle*, edited by Richard McKeon. New York: Random House, 2009.

Auerbach, Erich. *Mimesis: The Representation of Reality in Western Thought*. Translated by Willard R. Trask. Princeton, NJ: Princeton University Press, 1971.

Badiou, Alain. "The Event in Deleuze." Translated by Jon Roffe. *Parrhesia: A Journal of Critical Philosophy*, no. 2 (2007): 37–44.

Barthes, Roland. *Image-Music-Text*. Translated by Stephen Heath. New York: Hill and Wang, 1978.

Barthes, Roland. *s/z: An Essay*. Translated by Richard Miller. Oxford: Blackwell: 2002.

Bazin, André. "The Ontology of the Photographic Image." *Film Quarterly* 13, no. 4 (Summer 1960): 4–9.

Beltrán, Cristina. *The Trouble with Unity: Latino Politics and the Creation of Identity*. New York: Oxford University Press, 2010.

Benhabib, Seyla. *Critique, Norm, and Utopia: A Study of the Foundations of Critical Theory*. New York: Columbia University Press, 1986.

Benjamin, Walter. *Illuminations: Essays and Reflections*. Edited with an introduction by Hannah Arendt. Translated by Harry Zohn. New York: Schocken Books, 1969.

Benjamin, Walter. "On the Mimetic Faculty." In *Walter Benjamin: Selected Writings. Volume 2, Part 2 (1927–1934)*, edited by Michael Jennings, Howard Eiland, and Gary Smith. Translated by Rodney Livingstone and others. Cambridge, MA: Belknap Press of Harvard University Press, 1999.

Bennett, Jane. *The Enchantment of Modern Life: Attachments, Crossings, and Ethics*. Princeton, NJ: Princeton University Press, 2001.

Bennett, Jane. *Influx and Efflux: Writing Up with Walt Whitman*. Durham, NC: Duke University Press, 2020.

Bennett, Jane. *Vibrant Matter: A Political Equality of Things*. Durham, NC: Duke University Press, 2010.

Bergson, Henri. *Creative Evolution*. Authorized and translated by Arthur Mitchell. Mineola, NY: Dover, 1998.

Bergson, Henri. *Matter and Memory*. Translated by Nancy Margaret Paul and W. Scott Palmer. Mineola, NY: Dover, 2004.

Bergson, Henri. *Time and Free Will*. Translated by F. L. Pogson. Mineola, NY: Dover, 2001.

Bernstein, J. M. *Against Voluptuous Bodies: Late Modernism and the Meaning of Painting*. Stanford, CA: Stanford University Press, 2006.

Bilbo, Theodor G. *Take Your Choice: Separation or Mongrelization*. Cuttack, Odisha, India: Dream House, 2013.

Brewer, Daniel. *The Discourse on Enlightenment in Eighteenth-Century France: Diderot and the Art of Philosophizing*. Cambridge: Cambridge University Press, 1993.

Buck-Morss, Susan. *The Dialectics of Seeing: Walter Benjamin and the Arcades Project*. Cambridge, MA: MIT Press, 1989.

Buck-Morss, Susan. *The Origin of Negative Dialectics: Theodor W. Adorno, Walter Benjamin, and the Frankfurt Institute*. New York: Free Press, 1977.

Carroll, Noël. *The Philosophy of Motion Pictures*. Malden, MA: Blackwell, 2008.

Cavell, Stanley. *The World Viewed: Reflections on the Ontology of Film*. Cambridge, MA: Harvard University Press, 1979.

Chambers, Samuel A. *The Lessons of Rancière*. Oxford: Oxford University Press, 2013.

Chapman, Seymour. *Story and Discourse: Narrative Structure in Fiction and Film*. Ithaca, NY: Cornell University Press, 1980.

Coates, Ta-Nehisi. *Between the World and Me*. Melbourne: Text Publishing, 2015.

Coles, Romand. *Rethinking Generosity: Political Theory and the Politics of Caritas*. Ithaca, NY: Cornell University Press, 1997.

Connolly, William E. *Aspirational Fascism: The Struggle for Multifaceted Democracy under Trumpism.* Minneapolis: University of Minnesota Press, 2017.

Connolly, William E. *The Ethos of Pluralization.* Minneapolis: University of Minnesota Press, 1995.

Connolly, William E. *Identity\Difference: Democratic Negotiations of Political Paradox.* Expanded edition. Minneapolis: University of Minnesota Press, 2002.

Connolly, William E. *A World of Becoming.* Durham, NC: Duke University Press, 2011.

Coole, Diana. *Politics and Negativity: Dionysus and Dialectics from Kant to Poststructuralism.* London: Routledge, 2000.

Davis, Theo. *Ornamental Aesthetics: The Poetry of Attending in Thoreau, Dickinson, and Whitman.* Oxford: Oxford University Press, 2016.

Deleuze, Gilles. *Bergsonism.* Translated by Hugh Tomlinson and Barbara Habberjam. New York: Zone Books, 1991.

Deleuze, Gilles. *Cinema 1: The Movement-Image.* Translated by Hugh Tomlinson and Barbara Habberjam. Minneapolis: University of Minnesota Press, 1986.

Deleuze, Gilles. *Cinema 2: The Time-Image.* Translated by Hugh Tomlinson and Robert Galeta. Minneapolis: University of Minnesota Press, 1989.

Deleuze, Gilles. *Difference and Repetition.* Translated by Paul Patton. New York: Columbia University Press, 1994.

Deleuze, Gilles. *Essays Critical and Clinical.* Translated by Daniel W. Smith and Michael A. Greco. Minneapolis: University of Minnesota Press, 1977.

Deleuze, Gilles, and Félix Guattari. *A Thousand Plateaus: Capitalism and Schizophrenia.* Translated by Brian Massumi. Minneapolis: University of Minnesota Press, 1987.

Deleuze, Gilles, and Félix Guattari. *What Is Philosophy?* Translated by Hugh Tomlinson and Graham Burchell. New York: Columbia University Press, 1994.

Derrida, Jacques. "White Mythology." In *Margins of Philosophy,* translated with additional notes by Alan Bass. Chicago: University of Chicago Press, 1982.

Diderot, Denis. *Diderot's Early Philosophical Works.* Translated and edited by Margaret Jourdain. Chicago: Open Court, 1916.

Dienstag, Joshua Foa. *Cinema, Democracy and Perfectionism: Joshua Foa Dienstag in Dialogue.* London: Bloomsbury Academic, 2011.

Dujardin-Beaumetz, H. C. E. *Entretiens avec Rodin.* Paris: Impr. Paul Dupont, 1913.

Duvenage, Pieter. *Habermas and Aesthetics: The Limits of Communicative Reason.* Cambridge, UK: Polity, 2003.

Eagleton, Terry. *The Ideology of the Aesthetic.* Hoboken, NJ: Wiley, 1991.

Eisenstein, Sergei. *Film Form: Essays in Film Theory.* Edited and translated by Jay Leyda. New York: Harcourt, 1969.

Elsen, Albert Edward. *Auguste Rodin: Readings on His Life and Works.* Englewood Cliffs, NJ: Prentice-Hall, 1965.

Emerson, Ralph Waldo. *Emerson's Complete Writings.* New York: Wm. H. Wise, 1929.

Emerson, Ralph Waldo. *The Essential Writings of Ralph Waldo Emerson.* Edited by Brooks Atkinson. New York: Modern Library, 2000.

Erkkila, Betsy. "Review of John E. Seery, ed. *A Political Companion to Walt Whitman.*" *Walt Whitman Quarterly Review* 32, no. 1 (2014): 77–83.

Erkkila, Betsy. *Whitman: The Political Poet.* New York: Oxford University Press, 1989.

Figal, Gunter. *Theodor W. Adorno: Das Naturschöne als spekulative Gedankenfigur*. Bonn: Bouvier Verlag Herbert Grundmann, 1977.

Foucault, Michel. *Language, Counter-Memory, Practice: Selected Essays and Interviews*. Translated by Donald F. Bouchard and Sherry Simon. Ithaca, NY: Cornell University Press, 1977.

Foucault, Michel. *The Order of Things: An Archaeology of the Human Sciences*. New York: Vintage Books, 1973.

Fried, Michael. *Art and Objecthood: Essays and Reviews*. Chicago: University of Chicago Press, 1998.

Gilman, Sander L., Carole Blair, and David J. Parent, eds. and trans. *Friedrich Nietzsche on Rhetoric and Language*. New York: Oxford University Press, 1989.

Greer, Germaine. "Artists Have Always Glamorized Prostitution: Manet Savaged All Their Delusions." *Guardian*, February 6, 2011. https://www.theguardian.com /artanddesign/2011/feb/06/manet-olympia-prostitution-courtesan.

Greiman, Jennifer. *Democracy's Spectacle: Sovereignty and Public Life in Antebellum American Writing*. New York: Fordham University Press, 2010.

Grosz, Elizabeth. *Becoming Undone: Darwinian Reflections of Life, Politics, and Art*. Durham, NC: Duke University Press, 2011.

Grosz, Elizabeth. *The Nick of Time: Politics, Evolution, and the Untimely*. Durham, NC: Duke University Press, 2004.

Habermas, Jürgen. *The Philosophical Discourse of Modernity: Twelve Lectures*. Translated by Frederick Lawrence. Cambridge, MA: MIT Press, 1987.

Habermas, Jürgen. "Theodor Adorno: The Primal History of Subjectivity." In *Philosophical-Political Profiles*, translated by Frederick G. Lawrence. Cambridge, MA: MIT Press, 1983.

Hammer, Espen. *Adorno and the Political*. New York: Routledge, 2005.

Hammer, Espen. *Adorno's Modernism: Art, Experience, and Catastrophe*. Cambridge: Cambridge University Press, 2015.

Hansen, Miriam Bratu. *Cinema and Experience: Siegfried Kracauer, Walter Benjamin, and Theodor Adorno*. Berkeley: University of California Press, 2012.

Hoffmann, Rainer. *Figuren des Scheins: Studien zum Sprachbild und der Denkform Theodor W. Adornos*. Bonn: Bouvier, 1984.

Holmes, George. *The Florentine Enlightenment 1400–1450*. New York: Pegasus, 1969.

Homer. *The Odyssey*. Translated by Robert Fagles. New York: Penguin, 1997.

Honig, Bonnie. *Antigone, Interrupted*. Cambridge: Cambridge University Press, 2013.

Honig, Bonnie. *Democracy and the Foreigner*. Princeton, NJ: Princeton University Press, 2003.

Horkheimer, Max. *Zur Kritik der instrumentellen Vernunft*. Frankfurt am Main: Fisher Verlag, 1967.

Horkheimer, Max, and Theodor W. Adorno. *Dialectic of Enlightenment: Philosophical Fragments*. Edited by Gunzelin S. Noerr. Translated by Edmund Jephcott. Stanford, CA: Stanford University Press, 2002.

Hughey, Matthew W. *The White Savior Film: Content, Critics, and Consumption*. Philadelphia, PA: Temple University Press, 2014.

Huyssen, Andreas. *After the Great Divide: Modernism, Mass Culture, Postmodernism.* Bloomington: Indiana University Press, 1986.

Ionescu, Vlad. "Figural Aesthetics: Lyotard, Valery, Deleuze." *Cultural Politics* 9, no. 2 (2013): 144–57.

Jameson, Fredric. *The Political Unconscious: Narrative as a Socially Symbolic Act.* Ithaca, NY: Cornell University Press, 1981.

Jameson, Fredric. *Late Marxism: Adorno, or, The Persistence of the Dialectic.* London: Verso, 1990.

Jay, Martin. *Adorno.* Cambridge, MA: Harvard University Press, 1984.

Jay, Martin. "'The Aesthetic Ideology' as Ideology; or, What Does It Mean to Aestheticize Politics?" *Cultural Critique,* no. 21 (Spring 1992): 41–61.

Jay, Martin. *The Dialectical Imagination: A History of the Frankfurt School and the Institute for Social Research, 1923–1950.* Boston: Little, Brown, 1973.

Jay, Martin. *Reason after Its Eclipse: On Late Critical Theory.* Madison: University of Wisconsin Press, 2016.

Jeansonne, Glen. *Gerald L. K. Smith: Minister of Hate.* New Haven, CT: Yale University Press, 1988.

Johnson, Mark. *The Meaning of the Body: Aesthetics of Human Understanding.* Chicago: University of Chicago Press, 2008.

Kant, Immanuel. "Toward a Perpetual Peace." In *Kant: Political Writings.* 2nd edition. Edited with an introduction by Hans Reiss. Translated by H. B. Nisbet. Cambridge: Cambridge University Press, 1991.

Kateb, George. *The Inner Ocean: Individualism and Democratic Culture.* Ithaca, NY: Cornell University Press, 1992.

Keller, Catherine. *The Face of the Deep: A Theology of Becoming.* London: Routledge, 2003.

Krause, Sharon R. *Freedom beyond Sovereignty: Reconstructing Liberal Individualism.* Chicago: University of Chicago Press, 2015.

Krog, Antjie. *Begging to Be Black.* Cape Town: Random House Struik, 2014.

Krog, Antjie. *Country of My Skull.* Johannesburg: Random House, 1999.

Lawtoo, Nidesh. *The Phantom of the Ego: Modernism and the Mimetic Unconscious.* East Lansing: Michigan State University Press, 2013.

Love, Nancy S. *Trendy Fascism: White Power Music and the Future of Democracy.* Albany: SUNY Press, 2016.

Lyotard, Jean-François. *Discourse, Figure.* Translated by Anthony Hudek and Mary Lydon. Introduction by John Mowitt. Minneapolis: University of Minnesota Press, 2011.

Manning, Erin. *Politics of Touch: Sense, Movement, Sovereignty.* Minneapolis: University of Minnesota Press, 2007.

Marasco, Robyn. *The Highway of Despair: Critical Theory after Hegel.* New York: Columbia University Press, 2014.

Marcuse, Herbert. *The Aesthetic Dimension: Toward a Critique of Marxist Aesthetics.* Boston: Beacon, 1978.

Marcuse, Herbert. *Eros and Civilization: A Philosophical Inquiry into Freud.* New York: Vintage Books, 1962.

Marso, Lori Jo. *Politics with Beauvoir: Freedom in the Encounter.* Durham, NC: Duke University Press, 2017.

Massumi, Brian. *Parables for the Virtual: Movement, Affect, Sensation.* Durham, NC: Duke University Press, 2002.

Menke, Christoph. *The Sovereignty of Art: Aesthetic Negativity in Adorno and Derrida.* Translated by Neil Solomon. Cambridge, MA: MIT Press, 1998.

Mill, John Stuart. *On Liberty.* Indianapolis, IN: Bobbs-Merrill, 1975.

Miller, J. Hillis. *Illustration.* Cambridge, MA: Harvard University Press, 1992.

Modleski, Tania, ed. *Studies in Entertainment: Critical Approaches to Mass Culture.* Bloomington: Indiana University Press, 1986.

Müller, Ulrich. *Erkenntniskritik und Negative Metaphysik bei Adorno: Eine Philosophie der dritten Reflektiertheit.* Frankfurt am Main: Athenäum, 1988.

Nancy, Jean-Luc. *The Ground of the Image.* Translated by Jeff Fort. New York: Fordham University Press, 2005.

Nietzsche, Friedrich. *Twilight of the Idols and The Anti-Christ.* Translated with an introduction and commentary by R. J. Hollingdale. Harmondsworth, UK: Penguin Books, 1975.

Nietzsche, Friedrich. *The Will to Power: A New Translation.* Translated by Walter Kaufmann and R. J. Hollingdale. New York: Vintage Books, 1968.

Norval, Aletta J. *Aversive Democracy: Inheritance and Originality in the Democratic Tradition.* Cambridge: Cambridge University Press, 2007.

Norval, Aletta J. "'Writing a Name in the Sky': Rancière, Cavell, and the Possibility of Egalitarian Inscription." *American Political Science Review* 106, no. 4 (2012): 810–26.

Obenson, Tambay A. "How Do You Define Independent Film?" *Cineuropa,* February 26, 2013. https://cineuropa.org/en/newsdetail/233829/.

O'Brien, Karen. *Narratives of Enlightenment: Cosmopolitan History from Voltaire to Gibbon.* Cambridge: Cambridge University Press, 1997.

Orvell, Miles. *The Real Thing: Imitation and Authenticity in American Culture, 1880–1940.* Chapel Hill: University of North Carolina Press, 1989.

Pagden, Anthony. *The Enlightenment: And Why It Still Matters.* New York: Random House, 2013.

Panagia, Davide. *The Political Life of Sensation.* Durham, NC: Duke University Press, 2010.

Panagia, Davide. *Rancière's Sentiments.* Durham, NC: Duke University Press, 2018.

Panagia, Davide. *Ten Theses for an Aesthetics of Politics.* Minneapolis: University of Minnesota Press, 2016.

Patton, Paul. *Deleuzian Concepts: Philosophy, Colonization, Politics.* Stanford, CA: Stanford University Press, 2010.

Potolsky, Matthew. *Mimesis.* New York: Routledge, 2006.

Rancière, Jacques. *Aesthetics and Its Discontents.* Translated by Steven Corcoran. Cambridge, UK: Polity, 2009.

Rancière, Jacques. *Aisthesis: Scenes from the Aesthetic Regime of Art.* Translated by Zakir Paul. London: Verso, 2013.

Rancière, Jacques. *Film Fables.* Translated by Emiliano Battista. London: Bloomsbury Academic, 2006.

Rancière, Jacques. *The Future of the Image*. Translated by Gregory Elliott. Reprint edition. London: Verso, 2009.

Rancière, Jacques. *The Intervals of Cinema*. Translated by John Howe. London: Verso, 2014.

Rancière, Jacques. *The Politics of Aesthetics*. Translated by Gabriel Rockhill. New York: Continuum, 2004.

Rodin, Auguste. *L'Art, entretiens réunis par Paul Gsell*. Paris: Bernard Grasset, 1911.

Rogin, Michael. *Blackface, White Noise: Jewish Immigrants in the Hollywood Melting Pot*. Berkeley: University of California Press, 1998.

Said, Edward W. *Culture and Imperialism*. New York: Vintage, 1994.

Schiller, J. C. F. von. *On the Aesthetic Education of Man in a Series of Letters*. Edited and translated by E. M. Wilkinson and L. A. Willoughby. Oxford: Oxford University Press, 2005.

Schoolman, Morton. "'Avoiding Embarrassment': Aesthetic Reason and Aporetic Critique in *Dialectic of Enlightenment*." *Polity* 37, no. 3 (2005): 1–47.

Schwartz, Ullrick. *Rettende kritik und antizipierte Utopie: Zum geschichtlichen Gehalt äesthetisher Erfahrung in den Theorien von Jan Mukařovský, Walter Benjamin, und Theodor W. Adorno*. Munich: W. Fink, 1981.

Shapiro, Michael J. *Cinematic Geopolitics*. London: Routledge, 2009.

Shapiro, Michael J. "A Philopoetic Engagement: Deleuze and *The Element of Crime*." In *Politics, Theory, and Film: Critical Encounters with Lars von Trier*, edited by Bonnie Honig and Lori J. Marso. Oxford: Oxford University Press, 2016.

Shapiro, Michael J. *The Political Sublime*. Durham, NC: Duke University Press, 2018.

Shaviro, Stephen. *The Universe of Things: On Speculative Realism*. Minneapolis: University of Minnesota Press, 2014.

Shaviro, Stephen. *Without Criteria: Kant, Whitehead, Deleuze, and Aesthetics*. Cambridge, MA: MIT Press, 2009.

Spivak, Gayatri Chakravorty. *An Aesthetic Education in the Era of Globalization*. Cambridge, MA: Harvard University Press, 2012.

Tocqueville, Alexis de. *Democracy in America II*. Translated by Henry Reeve, with revisions by Francis Bowen and Phillips Bradley. New York: Knopf, 1997.

Todorov, Tzvétan. *On Human Diversity: Nationalism, Racism, and Exoticism in French Thought*. Translated by Catherine Porter. Cambridge, MA: Harvard University Press, 1993.

Voltaire. "Des Langues." In *Collection Complette des Oeuvres de Mr. de Voltaire*. Book 4. Geneva: Cramer Printing, 1756.

Voltaire. *Dictionnaire Philosophique*. Kehl: De l'Imprimerie de la Société Littéraire-Typographique, 1785.

Voltaire. *Mélanges de Poésies, de Littérature, d'Histoire et de Philosophie*. N.p., 1761.

Wasserman, Fred, and Ester da Costa Meyer, eds. *Schoenberg, Kandinsky, and the Blue Rider*. London: Scala, 2003.

Wellmer, Albrecht. "Truth, Semblance, Reconciliation: Adorno's Aesthetic Redemption of Modernity." In *The Persistence of Modernity: Essays on Aesthetics, Ethics, and Postmodernism*. Translated by David Midgley. Cambridge, MA: MIT Press, 1991.

White, Stephen K. *Sustaining Affirmation: The Strengths of Weak Ontology in Political Theory*. Princeton, NJ: Princeton University Press, 2000.

Whitman, Walt. *Leaves of Grass: A Norton Critical Edition*. Edited by Sculley Bradley and Harold W. Blodgett. New York: Norton, 1973.

Whitman, Walt. *Pictures: An Unpublished Poem of Walt Whitman*. Edited with an introduction and notes by Emory Holloway. New York: June House, Faber and Gwyer, 1927.

Whitman, Walt. *Whitman: Poetry and Prose*. New York: Library of America, 1996.

Wilson, Arthur M. *Diderot*. New York: Oxford University Press, 1972.

Zenck, Martin. *Kunst als Begriffslose Erkenntnis*. Munich: W. Fink, 1977.

Ziarek, Krzysztof. *The Force of Art*. Stanford, CA: Stanford University Press, 2004.

Zuidervaart, Lambert. *Adorno's Aesthetic Theory: The Redemption of Illusion*. Cambridge, MA: MIT Press, 1991.

INDEX

....

Adorno, Theodor: on aesthetic form, 189; aesthetic theory, uniqueness of, 149–50; "The Culture Industry: Enlightenment as Mass Deception" (with Horkheimer), 132–33; "The Culture Industry Reconsidered," 132–33; Enlightenment, relationship to, vs. Whitman, 8; Hansen and Wellmer's disavowal of reconciliation ideal of, 138–40; *The Help* and, 244; on music, 278; philosophical alliance between Whitman and, 120, 122–24; "The Schema of Mass Culture," 132–33; second evolutionary form of the reconciliation image, 38–41, 204–11; thinking with, against, 124, 140, 149, 203, 205, 278; "Transparencies on Film," 119, 132, 136–39; Whitman's unknown and, 64; Ziarek on, 41. See also *Aesthetic Theory*; artworks and aesthetic reflexivity, in Adorno; artworks as images in motion, in Adorno; *Dialectic of Enlightenment*; reason (rationality), aesthetic

aesthetic education: all-inclusiveness in Whitman and, 61; *The Help* and, 245–46; imitation in Whitman and, 73, 201; poetry and, in Whitman, 59, 77–78, 81–82, 103, 201–2; reconciliation image in Whitman and, 79, 116; Schiller on, 17, 25–26, 32, 51; Whitman's aesthetic re-creation of identity, 57; Whitman's conception of, 51–52, 55, 278–79; Whitman's poetry vs. Adorno's modernist artworks, 122–23; Whitman's visual image and, 92–95. *See also* democratic effects and democratic lessons

Aesthetic Education in the Era of Globalization (Spivak), 26–32

aesthetic experience: construction-mimesis tension and, 190; dialectic of construction/rationality and mimesis, and, 186–91, 245, 255–56, 270–71; Rodin's *Thought* and analysis of, 175–78; Rodin's *Thought* and contemplative immersion, 171–75

aesthetic identity. *See* identity, aesthetic

aesthetic reason. *See* reason (rationality), aesthetic

aesthetic reflexivity. *See* reflexivity

Aesthetic Theory (Adorno): aesthetic and instrumental reason, and difference, 151–54; aesthetic identity and analysis of aesthetic experience, 175–78, 271–72; aesthetic reason, concept of, 9–10; aesthetic reason,

aesthetic experience, 175–78, 271–72; all-inclusive image, 177; contemplative immersion, 171–75; continuity element and becoming different, 179–82, 188; contrast of Monet's Rouen series and Rodin's *Thought*, 167–70; dialectic of equilibrium between construction/rationality and mimesis, 186–91, 245, 255–56, 270–71; difference image, 176–77; identity image, 176–77; mind-body reconciliation, 173–79; motion element, 167–71, 177–78; paradoxical character of artwork and, 172, 183–89; processual element, 171, 177–78; receptivity and imitative images as intermediary forms, 191–93; the reconciliation image in art and film, 196–98; reflexivity element, 177–78; Rodin's *Thought*, 166–70, 173–79, 174f, 186–87, 191–93; time, relationship to, 168, 180–83

"As a Strong Bird on Pinions Free" (Whitman), 73

August, John, 291n28

Bacon, Francis, 112, 130

Barthes, Roland, 90, 92, 287n18

Bazin, André, 117–18

becoming different: in Adorno, 167–68, 191, 193, 211–12; Deleuze and, 296n7; *Gentleman's Agreement* and, 266–67; *The Help* and, 241–43; *Mr. Klein* and, 231–32; as reappearance of identity image, 243; Whitman and, 204

Bellow, Saul, 23

Benjamin, Walter, 114, 196

Bennett, Jane, 166, 188–89, 295n15

Bergson, Henri: on duration, 106–7, 115, 118; on life, 171, 225; Massumi and, 214; *Matter and Memory*, 107, 225, 231, 297n2; on the past, 11, 16

blackface, 296n5

body: mind-body reconciliation, 173–79; as place of passage of movements, in Bergson, 231; sensuous attachment, 171–75; violence against the black body, in *The Help*, 236–38

Brewer, Daniel, 14–15

"By Blue Ontario's Shore" (Whitman), 71, 102, 113

Calamus (Whitman), 68

Carroll, Noël, 298n9

Cartesian image, 173–75

Chaplin, Charlie, 137

cinema. *See* film

class difference, Tocqueville on, 69–70

Coates, Ta-Nehisi, 23

conjuctions, 215–16

Connolly, William, 249, 255, 269–70, 299n13

contemplative immersion, 171–75

continuity: Adorno on artworks and, 157–59, 179–82, 188; *The Help* and, 235; Massumi on, 226; of motion, and dual temporality of the image, 10

copies: models vs., 88; Whitman's imitative image vs., 112–14

Creative Evolution (Bergson), 107

cultural revolution, in Whitman, 50–51

"Culture Industry: Enlightenment as Mass Deception, The" (Horkheimer and Adorno), 132–33

"Culture Industry Reconsidered, The" (Adorno), 132–33

death, Whitman on, 59, 77

Degas, Edgar, 156–58

Delacroix, Eugène, 156–57

Deleuze, Gilles: on becoming, 296n7; "birth of the new image," 11; on continuity, 235; *Difference and Repetition*, 87; on duration and film, 117–18; "image equals movement" formulation, 297n2; Massumi and, 214; on movement-image, 10, 199; on *Mr. Klein*, 231, 243; on Plato, 87–89, 287n11; on reconciliation image, 81; universe that is "cinema in itself," 108; on Whitman, 47–48

democracy, American: barrier to evil, in Whitman, 77–78; habitus of sight and democratic eye, in Whitman, 109–10; nativity of, in Whitman, 50; Tocqueville on, 69–70; the unknown and, in Whitman, 58

democratic becoming: *Gentleman's Agreement* and, 251; imitation and, 6, 26, 193; reconciliation image and, 37, 117–18, 211; Whitman and, 7, 35, 73–75, 117, 279 democratic effects and democratic lessons: in *The Help*, 244–46; in Monet's Rouen series, 160–65; of receptivity and imitative images, in Adorno, 191–93; of reconciliation image, 211; of visual images of reconciliation, in Whitman, 80–81, 117

democratic enlightenment: democratic culture of, 81; positive enlightenment and, 9, 122–24, 204–5, 246, 278–79; prior historical developments, 11–12; Schiller and, 17–26; Whitman's conception of, 51–52, 200–201. *See also* reconciliation image

Democratic Vistas (Whitman): aesthetic education in, 51–52, 278–79; the All, 72, 73–74, 76; copies vs. imitations, 113; cultural revolution, 50–51; equality, 48–49; Erkkila on, 32–33, 35; first evolutionary form of the reconciliation image, 200–204; the individual and the mass, 48–49, 114; individuality as "miracle of miracles," 71; Kateb on, 32–33; *Leaves of Grass* and, 59–61, 201; literature as artwork of the future, 49–50; nativity of American democracy, 50; overview, 33–34; poetry, privileged role of, 52–53; poetry as image-making faculty, 102; reconciliation of the individual and the mass, 53–55; shared American identity reflecting difference, 56–57; structural logic of, 47–48; the unknown and death, 57–59, 82; world-cultural hegemony, American, 51

depths, Whitman on, 67, 89–90, 94

"Des Langues" (Voltaire), 12–13

determinate negation, 155–56, 293n15

Dialectic of Enlightenment (Horkheimer and Adorno): *Aesthetic Theory* and, 145–46; on enlightenment, 8–9, 125–27; enlightenment as de-aestheticized reason, 131–32; film as de-aestheticized art, 132–35; formalistic vs. aesthetic reason, 127–30; Habermas on instrumental reason and, 120–21; history of reason (preanimistic, mythic, and demythologization stages), 127–31; on Holocaust violence, 125–26; reason, critique of, 38–39; reassessed in historical context, 135–36

Diderot, Denis, 12–18

difference: Adorno on semblance, instrumental reason, and, 151–54; appearances as irreducible and different, in Whitman, 85–91; Deleuze on, 87–89; doubling of identity as, 181–82; imitation as productive of, 114; pluripotentiality of, 239–40; as qualitative, in Whitman, 87; recognition of rationality of, 28; reconciliation image as perception of, 219–21; reflexivity as artwork's consciousness of and alliance with excluded difference, 205–6; Schiller on identity and, 19–26; the Sirens myth and, 129–30; Whitman on the People and, 54–55; Whitman's reconciliation of shared identity and, 56–57. *See also* imitation of difference; receptivity to difference; sameness

difference, violence against: about, 3; Adorno on illusory images and, 153–54; *Gentleman's Agreement* and *The Help* compared on, 274; *The Help* and, 235–38, 246; Horkheimer and Adorno on reason and, 125–32; inclusiveness vs. private sphere and, 3–4

Difference and Repetition (Deleuze), 87

difference constructed as otherness: Adorno's history of reason and, 130; aesthetic education and, 33–34; blackface, 296n5; *The Help* and, 238–39; juridical protections vs. private sphere and, 4, 65; perception and, 220–21; Whitman on, 5–6, 56, 63–64, 68–69, 78, 115, 203

difference image: in Adorno, 164; *Gentleman's Agreement* and, 253–61, 268; *The Help* and, 238–40; intermediary images, 191–93; Rodin's *Thought* and, 176–77

differences, diversity of: Adorno and, 162; film and, 275; Schiller's universal art form and, 276–77; Whitman and, 6–7, 63–64, 67–68, 73, 76, 94, 101–2, 279

Discourse, Figure (Lyotard), 36, 80

double binds, 28–32

duration, 106–7, 115, 117–18

"Earth, My Likeness" (Whitman), 68

economy of images in Adorno. *See* artworks and aesthetic reflexivity, in Adorno; artworks as images in motion, in Adorno;

democratic effects and democratic lessons

"Eidolons" (Whitman), 104–8, 115–16, 118

Emerson, Ralph Waldo, 71, 75–76, 112–13

Encyclopédie (Diderot and d'Alembert), 12–18

enlightenment: Adorno's crisis in history caused by, 145–46; de-aestheticized, in Horkheimer and Adorno, 130–31, 136; Horkheimer and Adorno's conception of reason, violence, and, 125–26; positive, in Adorno, 9, 122–24, 128–29, 146, 149–54, 204–5, 246, 278–79. See also *Dialectic of Enlightenment*

enlightenment, democratic. *See* democratic enlightenment

Enlightenment, European: Diderot's *Encyclopédie* and, 13–17; Horkheimer and Adorno's *Dialectic of Enlightenment*, 8–9; Spivak on, 28–31; Voltaire on language and, 12–13. *See also* democratic enlightenment

equality: Tocqueville on, 69–70; Whitman on, 48–49, 52–53, 99–101

equilibrium (homeostasis), Adorno on, 186–89, 245, 255–56, 270–71

equivalence, logic of, 146–47

Erkkila, Betsy, 33, 35, 284n68

Experience (Emerson), 71

eye, the. *See* vision and seeing

"Faces" (Whitman), 82

feedback loop, positive, 223–27

feudalism, Whitman on, 49, 52

film: Adorno on motionlessness and, 137–40; anticipated by Whitman, 116; avant-garde films, images of reconciliation in, 291n30; Benjamin on contemplation and, 196; characters as aesthetic details, 134; de-aestheticized, in Adorno, 132–36; Deleuze on, 108, 117–18; genres of the reconciliation image, 274–78; as images already in motion, 213, 271–72; intermittent images, 235; Massumi's *Parables for the Virtual* and bee illustration and, 214–27; as model, in Bazin, 118; narrative closure, visual images and, 297n9; narrative structure vs. reconciliation image, 42, 133–34, 197–98, 200,

213, 264–65; as percipient action, 215; possible percipient actions and, 217, 221, 226–27; third evolutionary form, 41–43, 211–13; Whitman and, 93, 108; Whitman's reconciliation image and, 117. See also *Gentleman's Agreement*; *Help, The*

formal impulse, in Schiller, 20–26

formalistic reason, 127–32

Foucault, Michel, 15–16, 87, 287n11

Friend of the Deceased (film; Kristofovich), 295n1

gaze, 171–77

genealogy, 3

Gentleman's Agreement (film; Kazan): all-inclusive image, 265–66, 268; difference image, 253–61, 268; emerging reconciliation image, 262–66; *The Help* and, 246–47, 273–74; identity image, 253–61; imitative image, 265–66; narrative and image = motion in, 250–53; overt and tacit forms of anti-Semitism, 256–61; point of view of narrative vs. reconciliation image, 264–65; possible politics, 269–72; receptivity image, 265–66, 268; reconciliation image, 266–69; thought-out reconciliation, 249–54, 265

God, 63

Greer, Germaine, 158

Habermas, Jürgen, 38, 120–21, 146, 289n1

Hansen, Miriam, 138–40, 292n34, 292n36

Hegel, Georg Wilhelm Friedrich, 7

hegemony, world-cultural, in Whitman, 51

Heidegger, Martin, 41

Help, The (film; Taylor): aesthetics of the reconciliation image, 244–46; all-inclusive image, 239–40; becoming different, 231–32; difference image, 238–40; final image and future-oriented anticipations, 243–44, 248; *Gentleman's Agreement* and, 246–47, 273–74; identity image, 236–38; imitative image, 240–43; narrative structure and the white savior trope in, 232–34; opening title page image, 234–35; possible politics, 246–48; receptivity image, 240–43; reconciliation image, 234–36

Holloway, Emory, 116–17
Holocaust, 125–26, 131
Homer, 129–30
hope, Schiller on, 18
Horkheimer, Max. *See Dialectic of Enlightenment*
Hughey, Matthew, 232–34, 242
humanity, Schiller on, 19–20, 23–25

Ideal Landscape (Poussin), 153
Ideal View of Tivoli (Lorrain), 153
identity: allegiance to, in Adorno, 161–62; imitative, in Whitman, 74; Schiller on difference and, 19–26; shared, in Whitman, 56–57; Whitman's construction of, 68, 73–74
identity, aesthetic: Adorno and, 150–52, 167–68, 172, 181, 190; artwork's mimetic movement and, 184–86; dialectic of equilibrium between construction/rationality and mimesis and, 186–91, 245, 255–56, 270–71; in Monet's Rouen series, 161–64
identity image: in Adorno, 164; becoming different as reappearance of, 243; *Gentleman's Agreement* and, 253–61; *The Help* and, 236–38; intermediary images, 191–93; Rodin's *Thought* and, 176–77
images. *See specific topics and types of image*
imagination, Spivak on, 28–31
imitation (mimesis): artwork's mimetic movement, 184–86; dialectic of equilibrium between construction/rationality and, 186–91, 245, 255–56, 270–71; play shaping spirit of, 276
imitation of difference: about, 6, 35; copies vs. imitation and Whitman's "more or less," 112–14; Emerson on, 112–13; individualization through imitation, in Whitman, 112; receptivity and, 76; Tocqueville and Emerson on imitation, 71, 75–76; Whitman and, 6, 35, 71–77
imitative image: in Adorno, 193; defined, 80; *Gentleman's Agreement* and, 265–66; *The Help* and, 240–43; in Whitman, 102–9, 203–4
immersion, contemplative, 171–75
impulses: formal and sensuous, 20–26; Schiller's play impulse, 276

individuals and individualism, Whitman on, 48–49, 53–55, 71
intermediary images, 192–93
Ionescu, Vlad, 80

Jameson, Fredric, 140
Jeanne Dielman (film; Akerman), 291n30
Jewish difference. *See* anti-Semitism, Horkheimer and Adorno on; *Gentleman's Agreement*
juridical institutions vs. private sphere, 3–4, 65

Kant, Immanuel, 17–25, 29–30
Kateb, George, 33
Kristofovich, Vyacheslav, 295n1
Krog, Antjie, 92, 296n7

language: *The Help* and, 234–35; Nietzsche and, 91–92; semiotic relation between visual image and, 15–16; Spivak on subaltern languages and linguistic diversity, 27–29; truth not borne by, in Whitman, 82–85; Voltaire's "Des Langues," 12–13; Whitman on poetry and limits of, 34–35, 61–62, 77–82, 201–2; Whitman's Nietzschean relationship to, 91–92
latency, Massumi on, 215, 219–20, 226–27
Leaves of Grass (Whitman): 1855 "Preface," 59, 67, 84; all-inclusiveness of difference in, 61–64; *Democratic Vistas* and, 59–60, 201; "Eidolons," 104–8, 115–16, 118; Erkkila on, 35; imitation of difference in, 71–77; lists in, 86–87, 99–101, 107–8, 110; receptivity to difference in, 65–70; Whitman as image of democratic becoming in, 6. *See also* Whitman, Walt, poems of
Leonardo da Vinci, 183
Letter on the Deaf and Dumb (Diderot), 15
life: art imitating art imitating life, 276, 277; Bergson on, 171, 225; as visual image, in Whitman, 104–9
literature, Whitman on, 49–50, 51, 54
Lorrain, Claude, 153, 158, 180–81
Lyotard, Jean-François, 36, 80, 212

Madam's Name Day, The (Degas), 156–57
magic lantern projectors, 137, 138

Manet, Edouard, 158
Manning, Erin, 289n48
Marso, Lori Jo, 291n30, 294n1
mass and individual, Whitman on, 48–49, 53–55, 114
Massumi, Brian, 214–27, 247, 249
Matter and Memory (Bergson), 107, 225, 231, 297n2
Mill, John Stuart, 53–54
modern art, Adorno on. See *Aesthetic Theory*; artworks and aesthetic reflexivity, in Adorno; artworks as images in motion, in Adorno
Mona Lisa (Leonardo), 183
Monet, Claude: Rouen Cathedral paintings, 160–64, 167–70, 179; *Water Lilies*, 151–52, 159
montage, 137, 292n31
moral possibility, Schiller on, 18, 23–26
motion or movement: continuous, 179–82, 212; as deep ontology of Whitman, 106–8; determined by film, 270; duration, imitation, and, 115; *The Help* and, 235; "image equals movement," 250–53, 297n2; that creates, 252; Whitman's reconciliation image and, 116. See also artworks as images in motion, in Adorno
Mr. Klein (film; Losey), 231, 243
music: Adorno on, 278; Schiller on, 275; Schoenberg's atonality, 85; Sirens myth, 129–30
mystery, Whitman on, 35, 65–68, 89–90, 96–99
mythic stage of reason, 129–30

Name Day of the Madam, Flowers and Kisses, Degas Enjoying Himself, The (Picasso), 156–57
narratology, 90
negation, determinate, 155–56, 293n15
Nietzsche, Friedrich, 91–92, 107, 127, 195, 288n42
Noerr, Gunzelin S., 290n2

Olympia (Manet), 158
"One Hour to Madness and Joy" (Whitman), 68–69

On the Aesthetic Education of Humanity in a Series of Letters (Schiller), 7, 17–26, 30–32, 89
openness to difference. See receptivity to difference

Parables for the Virtual (Massumi), 214–27
"Passage to India" (Whitman), 63, 68
"Paumanok Picture, A" (Whitman), 87
People, the, Whitman on, 53, 54–55
perception: actions of, 214; possibility, potential, and Massumi's positive feedback loop, 222–27; as possible actions, 215; possible percipient actions (substitutions) and conjunctions, 215–19, 247–48; reconciliation image as forms of, 214; reconciliation image as perception of difference, 219–21; Schiller's universal art form and, 276; thought-pole/perception-pole continuum, 218–19, 295n12
photography, 92, 93, 113–14
Picasso, Pablo, 156–58
Pictures (Whitman), 116–17
Plato, 87–89, 130
Platonism, inverted, 64, 67, 87–89
play impulse, Schiller on, 275–76
poetry: aesthetic education and, in Whitman, 59, 77–78, 81–82, 103, 201–2; appearances, primacy of, 7, 34, 80–81; democracy and poetry as image-making faculty, in Whitman, 102; epistemic limit of language and, 34–35, 61–62, 77–82, 201; nature and, in Whitman, 59; poets as joiners, in Whitman, 48; the unknown and mystery in, in Whitman, 66; Whitman's poetry vs. Adorno's modernist artworks, 122–23; Whitman's privileged role of, 52–53. See also *Leaves of Grass*; Whitman, Walt, poems of
politics, possible. See possible politics
positive enlightenment and democratic enlightenment, 9, 122–24, 204–5, 246, 278–79
positivism, 267–68, 269–70
possibility: moral, Schiller on, 18, 23–26; perception as possible actions, 215; possibility, potential, and Massumi's positive feedback loop, 222–27; possibilization, 218–22; possible percipient actions (substitutions) and conjunctions, 215–25, 247–48; prescribed, 225–27

possible politics: aesthetic domain and, 4; film and, 200, 213, 215–18, 227; *Gentleman's Agreement* and, 269–72; *The Help* and, 246–48; Massumi's percipient actions and, 215, 221–25; the reconciliation image and, 32, 38, 216; Whitman and, 7

potentialization, 222–25

Poussin, Nicolas, 153, 158, 180–81

power-free relationality, 41

preanimistic reason, 127–29

private sphere vs. juridical institutions, 3–4, 65

"Quotation and Originality" (Emerson), 112

racist violence. See *Help, The*

rationality: of difference, recognition of, 28; Schiller and, 31–32; the subaltern and, 28–29; of the whole, in Whitman, 81, 115

rationality, aesthetic. *See* reason (rationality), aesthetic

realism, Whitman on, 58, 65

reason: as cogito, 211; Diderot's *Encyclopédie* and, 16; formalistic vs. aesthetic, 127–32; Horkheimer and Adorno on violence and, 125–32; Horkheimer and Adorno's critique of, 38–39; Horkheimer and Adorno's historical stages of, 127–31; instrumental, 120–21, 145–46, 150–54, 158, 195, 290n2; Schiller on, 20–26, 31; Spivak on Kant's reterritorialization of, 29–30; of the state, in Schiller, 31–32

reason (rationality), aesthetic: Adorno's concept of, 9, 150; aesthetic experience in Adorno and, 173; aesthetic identity, aesthetic reflexivity, and, 150–51; as alternative concept of Adorno, 120–21; of art, in Adorno, 9–10; Diderot's *Encyclopédie* and, 16; *Gentleman's Agreement* and, 251–52; instrumental reason, difference, and illusion of reconciliation, 151–54; interchangeability of terms, 290n3; motion and, in Adorno, 178–79; and reconciliation as positive enlightenment, 149–50; Whitman's reconciliation image and, 115–16. *See also* artworks and aesthetic reflexivity, in Adorno; artworks as images in motion, in Adorno

receptivity image: in Adorno, 192–93; defined, 80; *Gentleman's Agreement* and, 265–66, 268; *The Help* and, 240–43; in Whitman, 93–102, 203–4

receptivity to difference: about, 6, 35; aesthetic reason and violence subdued by, 128–29; all-inclusiveness and, 65; imitation and, 76; Schiller and, 24–25; in Whitman, 6, 65–70, 76; Whitman on mystery and, 35; Whitman's unknown and, 58

reconciliation: in Adorno, Hansen's and Wellmer's disavowal of, 139–40; allegiance to the unreconciled, in Adorno, 161–62; art's illusion of, in Adorno, 152–54, 157, 169, 180–81, 193–94; defined, 33; as democratic ideal, 5; as dual allegiance, in Adorno, 161–62; of the individual and the mass, in Whitman, 53–55; metaphysical form and immanent form in Adorno, 139–40; mind-body, 173–79; motion and, in Adorno, 167–68; paradoxes of, 211–12; in private sphere, 221; Schiller's concept of, 17–26, 32; Schiller's play impulse and, 276; time, relationship to, 181–82

reconciliation image: of Adorno, 10–11, 135–40, 153, 163–64, 191, 193–96; as aesthetic ideal in three senses, 6–7; as alternative to politics of tolerance, 269–72; in art and film, 196–98; in avant-garde films, 291n30; definitions of, 81; democratic effect of, 211; film and genres of, 274–78; first evolutionary form (Whitman), 32–38, 200–204; five images of, 10–11; *The Help* and, 234–36; as legible and visible, 81; penultimate form of, 243; as perception of difference, 219–20; possibility, potential, and Massumi's positive feedback loop, 222–27; as possible percipient action, 215–19, 223; Rodin's *Thought* and, 178; Schiller on, 26; second evolutionary form (Adorno), 38–41, 204–11; third evolutionary form (film), 41–43, 211–13; as thought-out, 219–22, 247, 249–54, 265; of Whitman, 7, 114–18. *See also* all-inclusive image; difference image; identity image; imitative image; receptivity image

reflexivity: Adorno's element of, 154–60, 177–78, 244–45; as artwork's conscious-

ness of and alliance with excluded difference, 205–6; Brewer on, 14; *Gentleman's
Agreement* and, 252–53; *The Help* and, 234,
244–45; poetry and, 34–35; Whitman
and, 7, 62. *See also* artworks and aesthetic
reflexivity, in Adorno
religion, Whitman on, 49
Republic (Plato), 89
Rodin, Auguste: *Thought*, 165, 166–70,
173–79, 174f, 186–87, 191–93
Rogin, Michael, 296n5
Rouen Cathedral paintings (Monet),
160–64, 167–70, 179

Sade, Marquis de, 130
Said, Edward W., 296n6
Salons (Diderot), 15
"Salut Au Monde!" (Whitman), 66, 96, 110,
279
sameness: Adorno on film and, 132–35;
Horkheimer and Adorno on reason,
enlightenment, and, 126, 128–31; imitation
vs., 114; Schiller on, 19; Tocqueville on,
75; Whitman on, 48, 69
"Schema of Mass Culture, The" (Adorno),
132–33
Schiller, Friedrich: Adorno's aesthetic
rationality prefigured by, 204–5; *On the
Aesthetic Education of Humanity in a Series
of Letters*, 7, 17–26, 30–32, 89, 275–77;
Spivak's critique of, 26–32; universal
art form of, 275–78; Whitman's poetry
and, 203
Schoenberg, Arnold, 85
seeing. *See* vision and seeing
self-creation and self-creativity, Whitman
on, 71–76, 103–9
Self-Reliance (Emerson), 71, 112
self-standing images (Whitman), 79–80,
83–84, 98, 114–15, 245
semblance: Adorno on, 150–53; Monet's
Rouen Cathedral series and, 161–64. *See
also* appearances
Seneca, 113
sensuous impulse, in Schiller, 20–26
Shapiro, Michael J., 295n1
simulacra, 88–89
Sirens myth, 129–30

"Song at Sunset" (Whitman), 79, 93
"Song for Occupations, A" (Whitman), 67,
288n31
"Song of Myself" (Whitman), 61–68, 72–77,
86–90, 96–98, 102, 107–12, 279, 288n31
"Song of the Answerer" (Whitman), 48
"Song of the Open Road" (Whitman),
68–69, 90
"Song of the Rolling Earth, A" (Whitman),
61–64, 82–85
Sophist (Plato), 87, 89
South African Truth and Reconciliation
Commission, 7, 92
Spivak, Gayatri, 26–32
"Starting from Paumanok" (Whitman),
98–100, 102, 103
subalternity, Spivak on, 27–28
substitution, order of, 215–22, 247–48, 249,
295n12

technohumanism, 16–17
Theaetetus (Plato), 87, 88
"Theatrum Philosophicum" (Foucault), 87
Thought (Rodin), 165, 166–70, 173–79, 174f,
186–87, 191–93
thought-out reconciliation image, 219–22,
247, 249–54, 265
thought-pole/perception-pole continuum,
218–19, 295n12
"Thou Mother with Thy Equal Brood"
(Whitman), 47
Timaeus (Plato), 87, 88
time: Adorno's democratic time, 168, 182–83;
arrived and yet to come, 115, 162, 181–84,
197, 206, 212, 243–48, 269, 274; art's
relationship to, in Adorno, 180–83, 212;
future-oriented anticipations in *The Help*,
243–44, 248; literature as artwork of the
future, in Whitman, 49–50; temporal
paradox of reconciliation, 212
Tocqueville, Alexis de, 4, 69–71, 75–76
Todorov, Tzvétan, 263
tolerance, politics of: beyond, to reconciliation, 7, 70, 268–69; Connolly on, 249;
Gentleman's Agreement and, 251, 265–69;
The Help and, 246; Whitman and, 37–38,
56, 101, 202
"Toward a Perpetual Peace" (Kant), 29–30